THE GOSPEL OF GABRIEL

THE GOSPEL
OF
GABRIEL

A LIFE OF JESUS THE CHRIST

A
LIFE
OF
JESUS
THE
CHRIST

WRITTEN AND ILLUSTRATED BY

EDWARD HAYS

Forest of Peace   Notre Dame, IN

Other Books by the Author:
(Available through the publisher or your favorite bookstore)

Prayers and Rituals
Prayers for a Planetary Pilgrim
Prayers for the Domestic Church
Prayers for the Servants of God
Psalms for Zero Gravity

Parables and Stories
The Quest for the Flaming Pearl
St. George and the Dragon
The Magic Lantern
The Ethiopian Tattoo Shop
Sundancer
The Christmas Eve Storyteller
Little Orphan Angela
The Passionate Troubadour

Contemporary Spirituality
The Pilgrimage Way of the Cross
Prayer Notes to a Friend
The Great Escape Manual
The Ladder
The Old Hermit's Almanac
The Lenten Labyrinth
The Lenten Hobo Honeymoon
Holy Fools & Mad Hatters
A Pilgrim's Almanac
Pray All Ways
Secular Sanctity
In Pursuit of the Great White Rabbit
The Ascent of the Mountain of God
Feathers on the Wind
The Lenten Pharmacy
Embrace the Healing Cross
Make Straight the Crooked Ways

The Gospel of Gabriel

Forest of Peace, Ave Maria Press®, Inc. P.O. Box 428, Notre Dame, IN 46556
www.forestofpeace.com

ISBN-10 0-939516-33-0   ISBN-13 978-0-939516-33-9

cover design and art by Edward M. Hays
(The script on the front cover is an Aramaic [the language spoken by Jesus] text of the Beatitudes)

Library of Congress Cataloging-in-Publication Data
Hays, Edward M.
        The Gospel of Gabriel: a life of Jesus the Christ / written and illustrated by Edward Hays
                p. cm.
        Includes bibliographical references.
        ISBN 0-939516-33-0 (pbk.)
        1. Jesus Christ--Biography--Sources, Biblical. 2. Bible. N.T.
Gospels--Paraphrases, English. 1. Title.
BT299.2.H39   1996
232.9'01--dc20
[B]   96-43834
                                                           CIP

DEDICATION

The author of Luke's Gospel begins with a prologue and dedication; such was the style among the Greeks from the time of Alexander the Great to the first century B.C.E. (B.C.).

Noting that many had already written narratives of events about Jesus taken from eyewitnesses, Luke's author says that he decided to write them down in an orderly fashion after investigating them anew. He then dedicated his Gospel to "the most excellent Theophilus," a name which literally means "friend of God."

The author of the Gospel of Gabriel has also "investigated everything anew" and, in imitation of Luke's author:

DEDICATES THIS GOSPEL
to

Thomas Turkle

a true "friend of God"
and my publisher,
for his courage in printing this book,
for his tolerance of my madness,
for his encouragement of my creativity
and
for his many years of loyal friendship.

TO MY EDITORS, THOMAS SKORUPA AND WILLIAM CLEARY

In the publishing of no other work am I more indebted to my editor and good friend, Tom Skorupa, than in this book on the life of Jesus. I am grateful to him for his marvelous work with my manuscript, both in the polishing of its poetry and grammar and also in his insistence on certain elements. I am right-handed, and he is left-handed, which best symbolizes the creative interplay which frequently took place in our mutual editing and rewriting of the manuscript. One could find no more complex subject, so filled with deeply rooted images, theological, religious and personal, than that of the historical and mystical person of Jesus. For both of us this work was a prayer, a meditation, a rediscovery of who Jesus the Christ is for us.

I am a believer in the old proverb, "The more eyes that will see your word in print, the more that should see it before it is printed." So I am deeply grateful for the creative editorial eyes of William Cleary, who saw clearly both the weaknesses and strengths in my original manuscript. His editorial suggestions and additions made the text more readable and gifted me with a valuable lesson in the art of writing. As a perpetual student in life, I am indebted to both him and Tom for their twin gifts of new knowledge. As you read this book I wish you could see the fingerprints these two friends, my editors, left on its pages so they might be given proper acknowledgment. I also express my appreciation to my friend Johnny Johnston III, a retired newspaper editor, who proofread this book.

TO ARCHBISHOP JAMES P. KELEHER AND MY BROTHER PRIESTS

I express my deep gratitude to my archbishop, James Patrick Keleher of the Archdiocese of Kansas City in Kansas, for his gift to me of a sabbatical year. Without that gift, this book on Jesus would not have been possible. While I had been reading, making notes and drafts for it now for several years, the coming together of the manuscript would have been impossible without the extended time of my sabbatical.

I also thank my brother priests who generously encouraged me and supported my being away. The sabbatical allowed me the extended time to study the recent writings of scholars of Scripture and the freedom to write.

TO JOHN J. PILCH, SCRIPTURE SCHOLAR, AUTHOR AND TEACHER

I acknowledge my personal debt to John Pilch, a good friend who over the years has been a long-distance Scripture mentor. By our conversations and personal letters, along with the privilege of reading his pre-published manuscripts, he has inspired me and introduced me to the world of contemporary Scripture scholarship. I am deeply grateful to God for our friendship which has gifted me in so many ways.

CONTENTS

There are also many other things that Jesus did,
and said, so many that if they were to be described
individually, I think the whole world would not be
large enough to contain the books that could be written.

— The last words of John's Gospel (21: 25)

Once a word has been allowed to escape, it cannot be recalled.

— Horace, first century B.C.E.

INTRODUCTION

The Gospel of Gabriel

Not another new Gospel! No other person living or dead has had more books written about his or her life than Jesus the Galilean. In the nineteenth century alone 60,000 books were written about him.* The twentieth century has not been deficient in adding new books to the already vast collection about Jesus Christ. Regardless of your religious belief, this hunger for new insight into the person of Jesus reveals how historically significant was this one man. Yet since more books already exist than can be read, why another one?

For one thing, the time is right. Our very measurement of time begins with his birth, and there is a tangible aura of significance surrounding the beginning of the third millennium A.D. (*Anno Domini*) "The Year of the Lord" — or in the new inclusive style, C.E. (Beginning of the Christian Era).

Why another Gospel? Are not the four holy Gospels of the Bible sufficient? Do they not contain everything needed to be known about the words and life of Jesus? These and other early Gospels, such as the *Gospel of Thomas*, were written to address the unique problems with which the churches wrestled at their particular time in history, like the issue of persecution and the question of Jewish ritual laws. Today's millennium-crossing churches have their own unique struggles to be addressed.

In 1964, the Roman Catholic Pontifical Biblical Commission, when speaking of the Sacred Writings, said that the four evangelists "selected certain things out of the many which had been handed on; some they synthesized, and some they explained with an eye to the situation of the churches."* As with the writing of the Gospels of Matthew, Mark, Luke and John, the good news according to Gabriel has "selected certain things" out of the four Gospels; "synthesized" other accounts and teachings, "with an eye" or two open toward today's spiritual landscape.* It is hoped that this unique Gospel will not only challenge the reader but will inspire and stimulate further reflection on the Gospels in contemporary times.

Jesus was fond of saying, "Let those with eyes see." Opening eyes is the main purpose of this book. Problems can blur vision, and as the infant churches, forty to sixty years after the death of Jesus, needed good news with an eye to putting their struggles in perspective, so do we. Familiarity can breed contempt, and it can also blind us. *The Gospel of Gabriel* is

9

can breed contempt, and it can also blind us. *The Gospel of Gabriel* is intended to open eyes and ears closed by repetitive reading and hearing since childhood.

Senses so opened can hopefully again see and hear the challenge of the original four great Gospels with the freshness found in the fledgling churches. When the Gospels were first heard two thousand years ago, they shocked and disturbed, and need to do so again! *The Gospel of Gabriel*'s lyrical qualities reflect that the music of the Gospels was not a lullaby or pious hymn, but a revolutionary song of a new time that had arrived. We need to hear it as such again.

It would serve us well to realize how today's churches are also infant communities of disciples who are journeying into the third millennium of Christianity. Disciples of Christ thousands of years from now may well look back at this age and envy our closeness to Jesus and the events that surrounded the first appearance of the Glad Tidings a mere two thousand years ago.

Published in the year 1996 C.E. (A.D.) as part of the celebration of the third millennium of the birth of Jesus Christ.

Author's note: 1996, and not 1999, is the conclusion of the twentieth century of the Christian Era. The confusion of dates in our contemporary calendar happened because of a scribe-monk's mistake. Jesus was really born in or about 4 B.C. or B.C.E. (Before the Christian or Common Era.)[4] The error occurred in sixth century Rome, when Dionysius Exiguus, a Scythian monk, introduced a liturgical calendar that counted the years after the birth of Jesus instead of the Roman calculations established by the Emperor Diocletian. The monk determined the year of Jesus's birth by working backwards from the information of Jesus' public life beginning at age thirty, as given by Luke's author. But this was not a precise year; it was rather meant as "around thirty." Today, most scholars place Jesus' birth in or about 4 B.C.E., which was also the year that King Herod the Great died. Since both the Gospels of Luke and Matthew speak of King Herod the Great being alive at the birth of Jesus, this would seem to be the latest possible date for his birth.

A Note to the Reader

The first Gospels were not written! They were spoken and sung, handed on by means of an oral tradition. Jesus never said, "Read my words." The first spoken Gospels were poetic and lyrical, ever-fluid as are all unwritten stories. These Gospels of the lips, unlike the sentence-lined prose of our present age of print, were musical, colorful and lyrical. As such, they are delightful to the ear and captivating to the mind, and easy to remember.[5]

The Gospel of Gabriel blends a prose style with which we are familiar with the poetic, lyrical form of the first unwritten gospels. Because poetry, song and story are cousins to music and so composed for ears and heart as well as eyes and mind, consider reading this Gospel aloud.[6]

A Note on the Notes in the Reader's Companion

I suggest that you read these pages as a poetic river, letting the story flow without stopping to read the notes in the back of the book. However, if you come to a difficult bend along the river or find a jagged-rock rapids, take a detour through the nearest endnote. Its information will help you continue the flow of your reading.

A second reading of the Gospel using the endnotes will provide you with documentation on recent Scriptural scholarship. This second reading can assist you in your study of the Gospels. The Reader's Companion contains expanded notes for your prayerful reflection on the way and life of Jesus. They suggest a fresh perspective on the implications of Jesus' words and deeds for a disciple of the third millennium. Such a reflective reading of this Gospel as an exercise in prayer might promote further meditative reading!

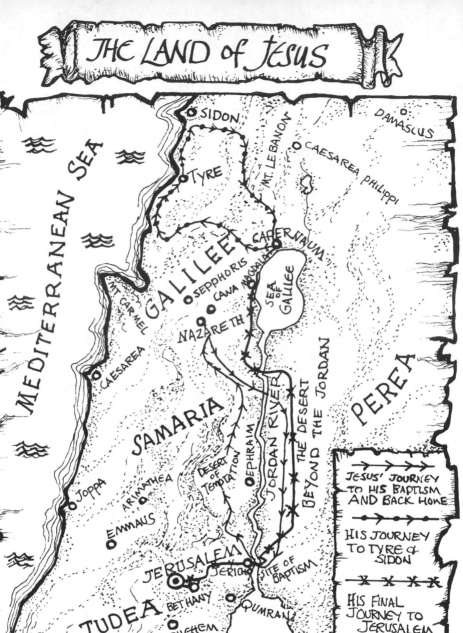

THE LAND of JESUS

MEDITERRANEAN SEA

SIDON

DAMASCUS

TYRE

MT. LEBANON

CAESAREA PHILIPPI

CAPERNAUM

GALILEE

SEPPHORIS

CANA MAGDALA

SEA OF GALILEE

MT. CARMEL

NAZARETH

CAESAREA

PEREA

SAMARIA

EPHRAIM

DESERT OF TEMPTATION

JORDAN RIVER

BEYOND THE JORDAN

JOPPA

ARIMATHEA

EMMAUS

JERUSALEM

JERICHO

SITE OF BAPTISM

BETHANY

QUMRAN

JUDEA

BETHLEHEM

DEAD SEA

JESUS' JOURNEY TO HIS BAPTISM AND BACK HOME

HIS JOURNEY TO TYRE & SIDON

HIS FINAL JOURNEY TO JERUSALEM

Preface to the Gospel of Gabriel

I am Gabriel;[1] my name means "God is Strong, *El* is Great!"
   I come like the wind when the strength of God is needed.
Enoch's book lists me as one of seven Archangels:
   It is I who visited the prophet Daniel, decoding his visions.
Though sent from God on high, I guard the gate of the soul;
   I arise from the soul's depths to flood the mind and heart.
I am the messianic messenger of the good news,
   the glad tidings, which are best read upside down
   since so often they are framed by bad news.
I am Gabriel, the guardian angel of earthbound messengers,
   sent to announce bad news to some, mad news to many,
   and always good news to the poor and outcast.

I am Gabriel, heaven's winged mystic muse,
   who carries two sacks overflowing with genius gifts,[2]
   two sacks full of ripe, creative, new seeds,
   dripping with Eden's juices of wild imagination.
Slung over my shoulder I also carry for all the sober
   an ever-elastic goatskin full of a new wine

to make earth's children drunk on impossible dreams.

I am Gabriel, heaven's compass for explorers
    who are driven from home on expeditions to the edge,
    whose only maps are star paths boldly traced
    across the ebony slates of midnight skies
    by the scarlet flaming finger of the Spirit Wind.
When these explorers stray, lose their way
    or long to retrace their steps homeward,
    I whisper in their ears like thunder claps
    and dance in their dreams the way they are to go,
    until they once again find their path, the Way.

I, Gabriel, was once sent by God to a tiny hillside Galilean village of poor uneducated peasants.[3] I was given a message for the village craftsman, part-time stonemason, carpenter and doer of odd jobs named Jesus.[4]

"Be gentle," I was told. "Unfold to him his message like a banquet tablecloth filled with delicious crumbs. Be gentle! This is a delicate process. Unfolding into fullness is not easy and takes time. Let the ripeness of his message come as slowly as does the dawn."

Chapter One

The First Visitation

It was the yellow-red hour of sunset, near the end of his day's work, when Gabriel stood at the open threshold of his shop.[1] Jesus was seated on the dirt floor, bent over, working with a chisel and hammer on a piece of wood. Even seated, he appeared taller than the average man, with strong shoulders and arms that spoke of a life of hard work. Yet he worked like an artist. He handled the chisel and wood as a musician fingers a melody upon a harp or a dancer glides gracefully across the ground.

"Hail, Jesus, full of grace. God is with you. Peace be to this house," the angel Gabriel said.

Jesus looked up from his work, troubled by the greeting he heard on the wind. The afternoon breeze rippled the knee-length Egyptian gauze tunic that Gabriel was wearing. The sun, like a giant golden melon on the hilltop, silhouetted his messenger's body, faintly revealing the chiseled form of a young Greek athlete. With a blush of modesty Jesus lowered his eyes[2] and quietly wondered aloud, "Who are you?" The fleeting vision of Gabriel's physical appearance vanished as he whispered on the wind, "Jesus, do not be afraid."

Jesus turned back distractedly to his work. Was it only a momentary mirage of the mind, he thought, a flickering trick of the shifting winds or the setting sun?

Gabriel whispered:

"Jesus, why not join the other folk of your village
who tomorrow will journey down to desert Jericho
to repent and confess their sins to Jordan John?"

He heard but did not see Gabriel, and spoke aloud, more to himself than addressing the angel:

"At age thirty, am I not too old for that?
My remaining years are now only a handful.[3]
And my mother, my aged widowed mother,
what will become of her while I'm gone?"

Like a leaf carried on the wind, Gabriel swept across the room until he was next to Jesus:

"Yes, Jesus, she is old; few are the women her age:[4]
old, gray haired, ailing, and you her only support.
Yet, do not worry or be anxious — God will provide.
Jesus, join the others who confess their sins to John!"

Facing the angel with unseeing eyes, Jesus said, "Go down to Jericho? But I've work to do!" He continued, as if conversing with the wind:

"John's a wild man dressed in animal skins,
holy but mad, a disturber of peace in our land.
My cousin, Jordan John, with his repentance water bath
wants to hurry the Coming — I take a more patient stand.
In my youth I too was anxious for the arrival of God's reign
but as a poor peasant, I've learned to be prudent.
I've learned the age-old lesson that still is true:
Forever will the rich be on top, the poor on the bottom.
Be not wild but tame, for this world will always be the same."[5]

Gabriel spoke with the power of God, "Stand up, Jesus! Your work here is finished."

Jesus slowly rose, looking nervously about, his eyes filled with fear and fascination. He looked down at the chisel in his hand. "Your work here is finished."[6] He repeated the words aloud to himself as he slowly turned the chisel over in his hand. This thought has a powerful attraction, he mused, but it also plunges me into fear as deep as a well. Nor is it a stranger: For years now I've sensed that my real work is not what has occupied my hands all these years. As a young man, I found delight in the living word of the Torah and the prophets, and in living the Way of God in our simple village life. Though a peasant's life is not easy, I've felt a joy, even sweetness, in being alone with God — something more intimate than can be found in any human friendship. But as time has passed, I've found both peace and terror in my prayer alone in the hills.[7] The sense of peace in being absorbed in God is as sweet as honey.

"But the terror!" Jesus said aloud, surprising himself by his outburst. He continued out loud but in a quieter tone, "I am increasingly haunted by the words I keep hearing in my prayer — and even when I'm working here alone, 'You are my....' I hear only those three words: 'You are my...,' and no more. I long to hear the rest of the message, yet I strangely fear hearing more."

Raising the handle of the chisel to his lips, he once again sank into deep thought: I fear God is calling me beyond the intimacy of prayer and moments of deep unity. I fear God is calling me to something more than mastering my trade and living a good life obedient to all the commandments. True, I've seen Jordan John the baptizer as being too impatient and even wild. At the same time, I am fascinated by him, and recently I've even considered myself a kind of unbaptized disciple of his. Yet, while I admire John in his strict penances, I myself am no ascetic. What am I to do? What is your will for me, O God?

"Jesus, go with the others from Nazareth's village," Gabriel said. "Confess to John and be baptized. It is what God wants!"

Jesus dropped his chisel to the floor, turned and gazed through the open door. An arched sliver of orange sun clung to the ragged rim of the hill as he turned and walked to the doorway of his single-room home and shop:

> "O God, what am I to do? What is your will?
> This day, strange voices have I heard,
> a mirage of the mind has put my sanity to the test.
> O God, hear my cry and listen to my prayer.
> Set me safely on a high rock.
> O God, you are my refuge, my fortress tower.
> Let me dwell forever in your loving arms.
> Under your wings shelter me in your power."[8]

JORDAN JOHN BAPTIZES JESUS

With expectancy and a bit of uncertainty, Jesus at last decided to join the crowd that traveled down to the Jordan. Standing in line with the others, Jesus awaited his turn to be baptized by John. A mighty wind suddenly swept down through the valley, causing the willow trees to sway like reeds along the river banks. The noisy crowd fell silent.

Out of the dense thicket of willows along the river Jordan John appeared. He raised a curved ram's horn to his lips and blew a hair-raising blast, then another, and another.[9] As the last echo rode away on the wind, John sang:

> "The bugle of the beast sounds the final battle charge;
>> the shofar of God sounds the call to atone your sins.
> Prepare God's way, make your crooked lives straight!
>> Prepare God's way, replace love for all your hate.
> Prepare God's way, eat wild on locust not on hay.
>> Prepare God's way, turn around this very day.
> Prepare God's way, repent and be skinned alive.
>> Prepare God's way, be baptized and prepare to die."

Again John raised the ram's horn to his lips and blew a piercing blast as haunting as was heard in the desert long ago when Moses called his flock.

> "Prepare for the Way, repent and be skinned alive.
>> Prepare for the Way, turn around to follow the call.
> Prepare for the Way, be baptized and get ready to die."

The long line of sinners crept slowly forward into the river's muddy, sluggish water. As each stepped in and confessed to the prophet, the sins of some were carried by the wind along the green willow trees on the banks:

> "I confess that I slept with my cousin's wife,
>> rolled in sweat and sin as he worked in the field."
> "I cheated daily at the toll booth: greed's my sin."
>> "I, a soldier, abused the fearful and weak...."

After each sinner was thrust briefly into the water by John, swallowed by the river's mouth and then belched up upon the beach, a chorus of Jordan John's favorite song would cascade along the shore:

> "Repent, be baptized and to all your sins now die;
>> cross over the Jordan as in ancient days gone by;
>> leave your sandals and your slavery on the other side.
> Repent, be skinned alive, the Coming is at hand;
>> cross over the Jordan to freedom's promised land.

> "Prepare for the Way, repent and be skinned alive
>> Prepare for the Way, follow the straight path and survive.
> Prepare for the Way, be baptized and get ready to die."

The chisel of Jesus' conscience was twisting in his heart. Palms sweating, he kept repeating to himself:

"The great ten, and hundreds of the small,
  each and every law, I have kept them all.
No lusting, no putting God to the test,
  What sins then to John shall I confess?"[10]

Gabriel then leaned close to the ear of Nazareth's repairer of sagging doors, her carver of stone, so none could hear. He whispered in rhythm with Jesus' fiercely pounding heart:

"Confess to hairy Jordan John your secret sins:
  confess your lack of lusting to take delight
  in God's rich harvest of the gifts of life,
  of feeling only shame in the flesh of your body,
  failing to rejoice in each and every part.
Confess, Jesus, your failure to be aroused
  not just by rain's sweet wetness or the sun's hot kiss,
but to taste Adam's animal succulent savor
  in good red wine or the juices of roasted lamb.

"Repent of being lukewarm in making love to God,
  not on fire in *all* your work and deeds and prayers.
Repent of your prayers dribbled from a heart
  as dry as streams of sand pouring from your hands,
  a heart empty of ecstasy, devoid of desire,
  cold as the dead ashes on your mother's morning hearth.

"Confess to John not the impatience of your youth,
  but the resignation of middle age,
  the too-comfortable patience with the kingdom's delay.
Acknowledge your tamed-dog acceptance of ugly war,
  of those sold off in slavery and bound by injustice.
Repent of your lack of a real passion for the oppressed,
  your failure to speak for the voiceless.
Confess to John the sin of your heart's true creed
  that the poor for better days will always itch.
Confess, Son of Israel, your too-meager yearning
  to see the widow and orphan released.

"Confess, carpenter! You've plugged your ears
  so as not to hear God's call.
Confess, Jesus, your sin against the Spirit Wind,

your heresy of 'You can't change this world!
The rich and strong shall always stand on top,
    the poor and weak always trampled underfoot.' "

Suddenly John paused in his baptizing and again raised the ram's horn to his lips. A long and higher-pitched call from his curved trumpet rose up from the river and echoed off the rocky hills as if there were a chorus of trumpets. The heads in the crowd jerked up in alarm like sheep hearing the howling of a pack of wolves. John sang out:

"Listen! The bugle of the beast calls us to the final battle,
    the horn of the sacrificial ram calls us to prayer.
For behold, something great is soon coming upon Israel,
    greater than a hundred Roman legions in the saddle.
See! I baptize you in Jordan's warm floodwater of spring;
    the One who's coming will submerge you in searing fire,
    will plunge you into a fiery spring-flood of the Spirit.
His winnowing fan is in his hand to sweep up the grain,
    to clean the threshing floor for the dance of death.
The Wind will harvest the good wheat into God's barn,
    and cast the evil chaff into an unquenchable fire."

John's voice rang out, "Next!" With a crooked, bony finger he beckoned Jesus to step down from among the crowd along the shore. John was as gaunt as one who had spent foodless weeks in a city under siege. Over his hairy body hung sewn scraps of camel skin:[11] where one type of hair ended and the other began was impossible to say. Appearing more beast than blessed, more a monster of the deep than Elijah returned, John stood waist deep in the river and looked out over the crowd with the fierce red eyes of a great wolf.

On the shore Jesus disrobed in dread and stepped into the river as if into his grave. As he waded in, he heard his familiar voice, now in the lapping waters of the Jordan: "You are my...." Jesus strained to hear more, but there was nothing more to hear, other than the washing of the water. As Jesus approached him, John shouted up at a group who stood watching from a distance, "You, up there, you Sadducees and Pharisees, do you not feel the Wind of God's great ax of wrath slicing through the air? The day is coming when it will find its mark and chop down your trees bent low under the weight of their wicked fruit full of worms."

Placing a bony claw-like hand on Jesus' bare shoulder, his eyes shot up higher to those standing on the cliffs above the river, "You priestly vipers, whose nest is God's temple in Jerusalem! You incense-stinking spies of the high priest! I know your thoughts: 'This wild man can't forgive sins by a river bath! His baptismal pardon mocks our temple sin offering rituals.' To you priests and scribes, who forever expand the heavy chains of the law, I say: I do not forgive! I am not the soap that cleanses away the dirt; God is the washer of these laundered lives. I only pour the water — God pardons! Be forewarned, priests! God no longer needs your sin offerings to release those in guilt and shame! The One who is coming will be both the sacred soap and the holy water that cleanses all sin."

He spun around and addressed some in the crowd, "You who only come here to spy, beware. You who come only as curious onlookers of the unusual, take heed. You whitened lilies of the valley who claim you have no need to bathe, be forewarned. The day of your disaster is coming! I am not the sunrise, I am only the cock crowing in the darkness."

As a dark ominous cloud hovered over the river, John again lowered his gaze and looked deeply into Jesus' eyes. Then, as if in bed with a lover, he whispered tenderly, "And what do you confess, cousin?"[12]

Thunder rumbled as Jesus spoke. Then John plunged Jesus under the rushing waters and held him there. When he pulled his hand away, like a cork from a jar Jesus shot out of the river in a spray of water. Again the thunder rumbled, this time at a deafening pitch, as a great cloud hovered directly over Jesus.[13] His ears filled with water, Jesus nonetheless clearly heard echoing, at last loud enough to understand, "You are my...beloved son! Upon you my favor rests!"

Then the Spirit Wind drove him dripping wet into the blazing furnace of the desert, with wild John's song still ringing in his ears:

"Prepare God's way, repent and be skinned alive,
Prepare God's way, be baptized and get ready to die."

Dripping, soaked to the skin, he was pushed onward into the desert, the haunt of wild beasts and demons, there to be skinned alive and be born again in the hot sands of a dry creek bed, the ancient bridal bed.[14] For:

Long ago, God grew sick and tired of human slavery,
   and out of order God created revolution's disorder,
     crying out to the Jews, "Escape the land of the Nile!"
Seduced into the Sinai, the Israelites were led,
   exiting Egypt's slavery into a sandy desert bed,
     under a full moon dripping with a lamb's red blood.

Like lovers longing to be under the desert moon they ran,
   God and Israel, hopelessly lovesick from the start.
So they slept together on a bed of moonlit silver sand,

promising to each other in blood that they'd never part.

But God's bride forgot that passionate desert honeymoon;
    she parted from God, taking sundry other lovers to bed!
As fickle as the ever-changing moon was her infidelity,
    but God longed to sleep again in love's great ocean bed,
    to sleep with a passion hot enough to boil away the sea,
    to awake beside the beloved on a warm bed of sand.
Seduced into the Sinai, the Israelites were led,
    exiting Egypt's slavery into a sandy desert bed,
    under a full moon dripping with the red blood of a lamb.

So the lovers could be there alone,
    the Spirit Wind drove this son of man.

CHAPTER TWO

THE DESERT FORTY DAYS

As the day wore on, the Spirit Wind drove him even deeper into the desert: "Hurry, Jesus, don't look back. No time to return for sandals or cloak; you must escape into the desert," said Gabriel, unseen beside him.

"Escape? From whom or what?" Jesus pleaded as he looked about for the source of the voice. "Why are we going further and further into the desert and not back to my village of Nazareth, to my mother and family? I have so much to do and so much to tell them."

"You heard the voice," Gabriel continued, "rumbling in the clouds at your baptism: 'You are my beloved.' "

"Yes, I heard those words as I now hear your voice. That message at the river both delighted and terrified me. I've heard those first three words for years now — yearning yet dreading to know how it would be completed. Now today in my baptism I finally heard it all. As I run deep into this desert, those words have released both my deepest dreams and wildest fears."

"You have reason to be frightened as well as delighted, Jesus of Nazareth," Gabriel went on, "for now, having heard the whole message, you can no longer go home as the same person who left! The man named Jesus drowned back there in the river; he was skinned alive! It is from this old Jesus that you must escape! Now half liberated of your old self, we hurry to the desert so you can be fully skinned of self, completely naked of the old self, to become the new Jesus."[1]

"I must stop to catch my breath," said Jesus, sinking to one knee, head hung low, gasping for air. "Before I go on, my companion, I must ask: Who are you?"

"I am Gabriel, God's messenger," the angel said, slowly taking on the human form in which he had appeared to Jesus at the door to his shop in Nazareth.

Looking up, Jesus said, "I heard you at my shop in Nazareth and back at the Jordan as I waited to be baptized, but I only once caught a glimpse of you. Now I see you plainly, and I am relieved. For I feared that I was going mad — hearing voices out of nowhere."[2]

"Do not fear, Jesus. You are not out of your mind, just temporarily out of breath." Gabriel put his hand on Jesus' sagging shoulder and said:

"Jesus, you feel you must stop and catch your breath,
    but it's the Breath of God who has caught you!
Now God and I drive you onward where you would not go,
    into the desert abode of wild beasts and demons."

"But Gabriel, I have taken no food."

"You will fast," the angel said.

JESUS' DESERT ABODE

Like Elijah, Jesus found a cave in the desert mountains to shelter himself from the searing heat. He stayed in that barren wasteland for forty days and nights, fasting from food and companionship. Jesus was all alone, and he felt the loneliness more intensely than the desert heat. Like those who live alone, he began to talk to himself, sometimes speaking aloud his wandering thoughts.

Some thirty days after he had come to the desert, Jesus cried aloud to the sun, "Why, great eye of fire in the sky, why was I driven into this desert rather than returning to my village and family? I could just as well have fasted and done penance at home as a simple disciple of John. I could have labored, as with my carpenter's plane, to smooth out the rough ways for the coming of God's kingdom." The scorching sun was as silent as the stones strewn about the mountain side.

Jesus picked up a rock and spoke to it, "God must have driven me into the desert for some reason. Was I to find something here that I could find nowhere else?" The rock gave no answer. "Perhaps," Jesus continued, "instead of fearing the desert, I am to learn to love it. For what we love we cannot fear." The silent sun and stones still refused to join in this conversation bred of loneliness. Jesus answered his own question: "Yes, that may be the reason, for I have found it to be true in that other desert, that lonely, solitary place located in my — and every — heart. Few if any are those who have learned to love that desert, which has its own kind of wild beasts and demons!" Then he sang a prayer to the rocks:

"Something's always lacking in life, always incomplete.
No love has filled me up as water risen to a cup's brim.
No synagogue service has filled the hunger of my soul;
nothing's ever perfect, something's always lacking.
No prayer I know is intimate enough with God;
no worship has ever satisfied my thirst for God.
Life's always fasting, hungry for completion;
tell me why, O God, O Holy One whom I seek."

The only sound was a hot, dry wind that swirled wildly about the entrance to the cave. A thin and skin-parched Jesus sat with his head saddled in his hands and moaned, "The loneliness in this cave is as thick as the inside of a tomb. A tomb!" he shouted so loudly it hurt his ears. "That may be the answer to my question. Only in the tomb can you taste the fullness of life. Only in death can you be full of God!"

Jesus jumped up and ran to the mouth of the cave where he shouted to the sky, "My God, I know why you drove me here! You...." His voice broke off as he reached out for the wall of the cave to keep from falling, his head swimming, dizzy from his fasting. "Jesus, take care. You're moving too quickly," he said to himself. "These days without food are taking their toll on more than your flesh."

As Jesus regained his balance, he took a deep breath and continued, "But living in this hunger has given me a new freedom. I can let go of the bottomless hunger to be filled. No longer will I be pestered by the need for perfection when I look at a chair or stone wall that I've made." Jesus stood tall in the sunlight outside the cave as an oven-hot wind laced with bits of sand whipped through the sweaty peasant's tunic that clung to his body. "I'm hungry and thirsty. I'm lonely and ache to go home, but I'm alive! While I yearn for completion, I'm sorry God, but I'm not hungry to die."

GABRIEL'S GIFT

Jesus went back inside the tomb-like silence of his cave where he continued his journey deeper into his inner desert. The following days dragged on one by one. With each day his body grew weaker from his fasting while his mind feasted on wild images and strange dreams. On the thirty-eighth day of his fast, as Jesus was sitting outside his cave absorbed in prayer, Gabriel slowly took on human form and stood in front of him.

"Jesus," he said, "to know the holy mystery of the incomplete is to be a sage. But you've been driven into this desert for more than that."

Jesus looked up, holding his hand above his eyes to shield them from the intense sunlight. "If that is you, Gabriel, I'm so happy to see you! I fear, though, that you're just another fantasy, which seems to be the fruit of my long fasting."

"Fear not, Jesus, it is I, Gabriel. I've been sent to give you this gift," he said, holding up a small brass hand mirror. "You were called into this desert for more than one profound insight. This gift will help you gain new sight." As Gabriel handed the mirror[3] to Jesus, its polished brass surface was caught by the desert sun and flashed like a bolt of lightning. "Look into the mirror, Jesus. Who do you see?"

"I see myself as in a pool of water. I see Nazareth's village craftsman, possessing my father Joseph's nose and mouth; the son of Mary, possessing her eyes."

"Look again, tell me what else you see."

"I see an honorable man who keeps the Law of Moses, a son of Abraham, a just man and one who tries to be a good neighbor."

"If that is all you see, Jesus, then you know yourself only through the eyes of others, through the eyes of your neighbors or family.[4] Look again. Look more deeply. Who do you see? Who are you? Who are you?" Gabriel's last words echoed, becoming more faint as he himself slowly vanished.

The sun, like a ball of fire, whirled wildly in the cloudless, blue desert sky as Jesus sat staring into the shiny metal mirror.

"Who am I, O God? Who am I, if not Joseph's son,
 a simple carpenter, skillful with a hammer and saw,
 whose hands can carve a stone or mend a broken wall.
I see in this mirror a just man who loves you and keeps your ways.
 Mirror in my hand, tell me — what more am I to see?

"O Holy One, you search the secret places of my heart;
 you know my thoughts and my every deed of night or day.
You see me in the darkness when I'm alone in bed;
 you know, before I speak, the words within my heart.
Hear my prayer, for you know me inside and out
 and show to me, who I am — or who — I should be."[5]

The only answer to his prayer was the silence that screamed loudly across the jagged mountains and the desert below. Clutching his mirror, Jesus climbed down from the ledge outside his cave. A few feet from the desert floor the sun caught the surface of the mirror and flashed in blazing light. Blinded, Jesus stumbled and fell, tumbling to the sand below. Unhurt but shaken, he quickly checked the metal mirror to see if it had been scratched. What he saw on its surface terrified him, for it was a pool of swirling faces, none of which was his!

JESUS IS VISITED IN THE DESERT

From the whirlpool a face covered with scabs and sores rose to the surface and filled the mirror. "I am Job," the figure said. "See yourself, Jesus, as covered with wounds and sores as I was by God." Then his horrible face faded and a bearded face with bold features took shape. It sang, "I am Isaiah, the poet-prophet. See yourself, Jesus, as one who will sing the new song." His image shifted into one of a handsome youth. "I am David, the shepherd psalmist. See yourself as a songful good shepherd who will cast down Goliath not with a small stone but a tiny mustard seed."[6]

Jesus jumped back suddenly as those three men stepped out over the flashing rim of the mirror onto the desert sand. They were followed by a tall, white-bearded elder. "I am Melchizedek, the priestly king, who sprang from the loins of no priestly tribe, nor was I ordained. Son of Joseph and Mary of Nazareth, see yourself also as a royal priest." He was followed by a gray-bearded man with powerful features. "I am Moses, your great ancestor in the faith. See yourself also as one God calls to begin a revolution, to lead your people out of slavery."

Next out of the mirror stepped a youthful man wearing only an animal-skin loincloth. "Greetings, great grandson, I am your most ancient ancestor, Adam. I am God's first chosen son made in the divine image. See yourself, whether dressed or undressed, with the same pride and joy I did before I discovered shame."[7] A woman partially clad in animal skins stepped beside Adam and said, "Grandson of grandsons, I am your ancient mother Eve, to whom God made the promise that One to come would take us back to Eden's garden. At long last you have come." Then Eve and Adam held Jesus with great affection, causing his blood to race at their primal embrace.

As Eve separated from their embrace, she pointed to the bronze mirror laying on the desert sand. "Jesus, see yourself in your ancient grandmothers."[8] Suddenly, out of the mirror danced a slim-bodied, dark-eyed woman with breasts like large melons and wearing clusters of silver ear rings. She bowed her unveiled head, giving Jesus a sly smile. "I am Tamar, an ancestor from high in the branches of your family tree. To obtain my rights as a widow, I cleverly disguised myself and fooled old horny Judah, who became the father of my twins. Jesus, see in your mirror that you possess that same cleverness."

The mirror's surface again flashed like a bolt of lightning, and out of the blinding light came a full-bodied woman dressed in red. "Greetings, grandson, I am Rahab, the harlot of Jericho. Out of compassion I hid two of Joshua's spies under one of my beds of pleasure. To those hungry for love but failing to find it in their own beds, I was a feast of warm, fleshy, delicious love. As I gave love, and myself, to strangers, see yourself as one called to love without restraint."

Jesus then heard a lovely voice singing a harvest song as a hand holding a large sheaf of wheat slowly rose up out of the mirror's surface. A striking, graceful woman now stood before him with the sheaf. "Jesus," she said, "I am Ruth the Moabite, your gentile grandmother! As a field worker, I crept under the cloak of Boaz, my wealthy landowner boss, and slept with him. Our son was Jesse, the grandfather of your forefather David. You, Jesus, are now to bring God's harvest to all people and make love to all, including the gentiles!"

Once again the mirror crackled with brilliant light as out stepped a tall, beautiful woman wrapped only in a bathing towel. "Jesus, my grandson, I am Bathsheba, wife of the officer Uriah. It was I who slept in silken sin with lusty King David your grandfather after he had sent my husband off to be abandoned and killed in war. The wise Solomon, my child with David, is an important limb on your family tree. The blood of each of us your ancestors flows richly in your blood. As crooked branches on your family tree, we're part of God's mysterious design for you who are to straighten the crooked. Look into your mirror and see within yourself the compassion to love all who are like us."

Shocked into silence, Jesus finally found the courage to speak. "You're saying that as you seduced David, I am to see myself as a seducer of others?"

"By being full of God, you will be full of an inner beauty that will seduce many to fall madly in love with God. And as David did with me, they will risk all for your love!"

Her bare shoulders bathed by the bright sun, the ravishingly beautiful Bathsheba bowed before Jesus. As she did, the other women began to clap their hands and tap their feet in a kind of vineyard harvest dance. Tamar wildly pounded a goatskin drum to a racing nomad melody as Moses, old

Melchizedek, Adam and Eve and all Jesus' elders began dancing. Rahab's bracelets and ankle rings jangled with the wild music as Bathsheba reached out and seized Jesus' arm. Then Rahab grabbed his other arm, and they whirled together in a cloud of perfumed delights and rich aromas of ancient days. Jesus' feet seemed not to touch the sand as they all danced for what seemed like hours to the wild animal beat of Tamar's goatskin drum.

Suddenly he was thrown to the ground by a violent earthquake that caused the desert floor to roll in waves as does an ocean.[9] When the clouds of dust from the ruptured earth finally cleared, he found himself lying on the sand, soaked in sweat and joy. He looked up and saw that he was all alone in the desert. He looked into his bronze mirror but this time beheld only his own face; then slowly behind it appeared the face of Gabriel.

"Gabriel," cried Jesus, "am I going mad? Who were...what was that all about?"

"Jesus, your ancient ancestors have visited you as an answer to your prayers. For now as you look into the mirror, you will see that you're more than a peasant craftsman!"

Wiping the sweat from his face, Jesus said, "If they are the answer to my prayers, then the answer requires more than I am able to be — and more that I am able to give."

"With God all things are possible," Gabriel replied, sitting down on the ground next to him. "Look deeply into your mirror, and you will see the face of one who no longer fears to be a prophet, or rejects the role of a leader or refuses to embrace the suffering of a Job. You will see a face with the strength and courage to be a hero. But you will also see one who can be as compassionate as a mother, as gentle as a tender woman, who can weep openly and be affectionate in public without shame. For you have in you the gifts of all your ancestors, and when you've balanced the opposites in yourself, you become whole. Look deeply into the mirror and you will see the new Adam."

"Gabriel, my head is still spinning from the circle dance, and I've seen so much in the mirror you've given me. But isn't it time for me to return home to Nazareth? I've been here in the desert almost forty days!"

"Soon, Jesus, but there is more you must see in your mirror. Look into it and see that God is creating something new. While you have inherited many gifts from your foremothers and forefathers, you are truly becoming a new creation. See that you are not anyone's disciple, even of a prophet as great as Jordan John." As Jesus stared into the mirror, Gabriel began to sing:

"Gaze into the mirror at what God is doing, see who you are;

see that you are not to be another's disciple.
See that you are a new Moses, that you are a new leader;
    see yourself as a new Isaiah, a poet-prophet;
    see yourself as a new Joshua, crossing the Jordan.
Look and see that you're not another's disciple,
    but are being created anew, with a new vocation, a new call."

Jesus lowered the mirror slowly. "Is not a vocation given by God for life? How can my following John be finished almost before it began?"

"Vocations in life are like Jacob's ladder which linked earth to heaven. Some climbers pause or even stop and stand on one rung the rest of their lives. God calls others, however, to always climb higher, even when it might look like they are descending. Your call to become John's disciple is a rung from which God now calls you higher."

"Gabriel, I trust that you are God's messenger. So I can accept that I'm not to be John's disciple. But that I am to be a new Moses or a priest like Melchizedek, a new Rahab or Ruth, seems impossible."[10]

"No Jesus, not impossible — for with God all things are possible! And tomorrow you will see even more. Tomorrow's dawn will begin your thirty-ninth day; for that you will need all the energy that sleep can give. Have a good and peaceful night." As the sun closed its large orange eye at the horizon, and the heat of the desert began to ebb, Jesus crawled back into his cave and quickly fell asleep.

THE THIRTY-NINTH DAY IN THE DESERT

Morning in the desert was cool and Jesus was sitting at the entrance to his cave holding his metal mirror when Gabriel appeared before him. "Peace to the new Adam," Gabriel said in greeting. "The old Adam who visited you and with whom you danced was covered by more than animal skins. His loins — and his soul — were covered with shame. You are called by God to look upon yourself and all creation as it was on the first morning — as good, very good."

"Since Adam's time," replied Jesus, "God has taught us to guard with great care how we expose our bodies. As God's people we are not to be naked, even in the darkness of night.[11] We are not like the Greeks who parade about naked."

"I'm not asking you to go naked, Jesus. I'm asking you to look upon your body in a new way. God wants you to grow the kind of new skin in which you can take pride, so the body may again be the glory of God. You are being asked to strip yourself naked not of your tunic but of shame."

"If it is God's will, I will try, but I fear it will not be easy. Since childhood I have been taught to view nakedness, and my body, as shameful."

"All conversions take time, Jesus, but they must begin. Be kind to yourself and do not rush any change. But know that God's Spirit Wind carries in the new as well as blowing away the old, that which is no longer useful. You need not cast your shame away, simply let go of it so the Spirit Wind can carry it off like a dead fig leaf."

Looking down at his body, Jesus sighed, "If it is God's will, I will try to be free of my shame."

"You must do more than try, Jesus, for it is necessary that you become a new Adam, for whom shame was unknown in the beginning. You are the new beloved son of God, and not to be shamed by your bodily nakedness is essential for the work God is giving you."

"What kind of work would require that I be naked?"

"The fullness of that answer will unfold, Jesus. Clothing gives people their identity as part of a group or class. Clothing creates boundaries; it sets you apart or it can make you one with others. Your mission is to blur all boundaries, to remove all barriers separating peoples, races, religions; barriers between rich and poor, men and women."

"This is all too much," Jesus moaned, holding his head in his hands.

"Rejoice, Jesus, do not be discouraged," Gabriel said as he slipped his arm around Jesus' shoulder. "Like your ancestors crossing the desert with Moses, this desert liberation from the slavery of shame is part of your personal exodus. The day will come when like the first Adam you will climb naked up into a tree — but another kind of tree — to gather the fruit of heaven. Once up there, however, unlike Adam, they will not let you come down! Naked before the gaze of those who have hung you there, you must recall this day. For you are to feel no shame as you hang on that tree. Your nakedness on that day will involve more than the removal of your clothing. Naked, you will belong to no moment in history, to no tribe, class or culture. Naked, you will truly be the universal one."

Creases formed across his brow as Jesus asked, "What tree am I to climb and be hung among its branches?"

"Not today, my friend. I was told that your mission was to be gradually unfolded to you, as slowly as comes the dawn. Right now, your mirror there on the ground holds more for you to ponder. Peace to you, Jesus." With that Gabriel was gone in a whirlwind of dust.

THE WILD VISITATIONS

At midday the sun stood directly over the top of the mirror that lay before Jesus on the desert earth. It suddenly flashed with light and came to life. Out of the mirror a large fish flip-flopped onto the desert floor, strangely at home out of the water. Jesus looked at the fish with eyes so hungry he could have eaten it raw. Suddenly a large, hairy goat with scarlet ribbons on its horns bounded out of the mirror in a cloud of dust. As Jesus drew back, he heard fierce growling behind him. Reeling around, he saw in the swirling dust a pack of wolves closing in, followed by a pair of desert lions and some jackals. Then he heard hissing; creeping over the rim of the mirror came several poisonous serpents coiling one upon another. Jesus drew back in dread, which was intensified by the shriek of several vultures who rose out of the mirror with a loud flapping of wings before they fluttered to the ground. The last to appear was a flock of small desert sparrows.

Jesus sat stone-still in the midst of the wild creatures, who stood and eyed him. They began circling him in a zigzag pattern. Uneasiness grew in Jesus as he spied fangs ready to strike, pointed teeth, tongues hanging out of drooling mouths, wary, stalking eyes. As the grip of fear began to tighten around Jesus, he began to pray: "O God, come to my assistance. Make haste to help me...."

The circle started closing around Jesus, the creatures' eyes more intent, the howling, hissing and flapping of wings more piercing. Then Jesus remembered the words of Job, " 'Ask the animals and they shall be your teachers; be a disciple of the birds and they shall instruct you.'[12] Yes, don't be afraid, they will teach you."

Jesus took a deep breath, trying to hold himself open to the lesson. He slowly let go, one finger at a time, of his instinctive terror. With a great sigh, he gradually began to feel a communion with the beasts and birds. Their howling and screeching triggered a primal cry from Jesus' depths that rose in concert with the creatures' own voices. Slowly they reformed in a semicircle in front of Jesus, and he dared to say to them, "Teach me, firstborn of God, each of you, what I must know."

The great fish sang out, "Jesus, like a fish out of water, be the one who shall feed the many with the food of life."

The sacrificial goat pranced and sang, "See me in yourself, for you are to bear the sins of many so the many can go free."

Then the wolves spoke out, "When you pray, howl and do not be bleating sheep, baaing, 'Blessed be God.'"

Next the lions roared, "Do not be docile as a donkey before those who rule; stand tall, your head held high."

"Jesus, do not be anxious about tomorrow," chirped the sparrows.

"Small of value are we, yet God daily cares for us."

The black vultures flapped their wings and said, "Watch and learn from us. Effortlessly we ride upon the currents of the wind, so let the Wind of God carry you with majestic ease."

Finally the vipers hissed, "Be as cunning as we serpents, for dangerous is the mission God is giving you."

Then to Jesus' astonishment, even the rocks and desert bushes began to sing in chorus with all the creatures:

"See us, son of creation, with your New Adam eyes,
    with all stars, deserts and mountains, soil and sea,
    you and we are one living body, created for holy communion,
    the fate of each is intertwined from creation's first day.
Jesus, be a new Adam, not merely Eden's caretaker;
    be not steward but spouse-lover to us and all the earth.
Be the new Adam, not a brother but One with all of us."[13]

Jesus opened his mouth to thank them, but they all had vanished in an instant; the desert again was silent. Closing his mouth, he shook his head at the mystery of this vision. Once more he was alone with his bronze mirror. Looking into it he saw only himself, but as he had never seen himself before, for his new skin was made of hide and hair, fur and scales, feathers and fins. As Jesus turned to face the setting sun, he realized that he was now one with his ancestors in creation.

THE SHADOW'S VISITATION

As his thirty-ninth day in the desert was ending, Jesus walked to the crest of a thornbush-covered sand dune. He stood watching the sun, now brilliantly seated as if upon a throne, cresting on a saddle-shaped mountain. All about him the setting sun was casting long, dark shadows of thickets, thornbushes and tall pillar-shaped rocks. As he turned away from the sun, he noticed his own elongated shadow. It slowly rose up in the air until it stood directly in front of him. The lingering light of the setting sun cast a luminous edge to the shadow.

The Shadow spoke. "Allow me to introduce myself, son of Joseph and Mary. I am your half stepbrother, or didn't they tell you about me?"[14]

Jesus stared in disbelief. Standing in front of him was a dark mirror image of himself! Then the lips of the shadow's face curled in a cynical smirk:

"You were given a mirror by which to know yourself,
    but the mirror showed you only half of who you are.

Look at me, Jesus, and see your secret side, your hidden self.
Look at me and you'll know who you really are!"

"I know who you are!" shouted Jesus, standing tall like the Lion of Judah. "And I knew you would come to visit me before I left your abode in this desert. I've feared your visit far more than that of the wild beasts who live here."

The deep voice of the Shadow replied, "The beasts to fear, dear Jesus, are not those in the desert but those inside you! As for my appearing, dear brother, how could I not come to visit you? After all, you're so thirsty to learn from everyone you meet, and I too have some wisdom to teach you — that is, if you are humble enough to be my student."

"Father of lies, primal deceiver, I desire none of your wisdom!" he cried. "Your name is Diablo, and you have no power over me."

The Shadow laughed. "Really? Even if I possess critical wisdom about yourself, about the self you fear and refuse to acknowledge, that part of yourself I mirror back with such brilliant clarity? Don't answer just yet. For now, come with me — I also have a gift for you."

Jesus' Baptism into Temptation

Then, before Jesus could answer, the Shadow swiftly carried him aloft to the top of a high mountain. With a sweep of the shadow's hand, all the kingdoms and empires of the world unfolded below, filling the desert from horizon to horizon. In the faint blue twilight of sunset the kingdoms glittered with countless tiny lights in every color as if diamonds and precious jewels as numerous as the sands had covered the desert floor.

"Jesus, you are proud to be King David's descendant,
knowing the promise of his future kingdom,
so vast as to encompass the entire earth.
You know the prophecy about the Messiah King:
all earth's kings will bow to kiss your feet.
All the power you need to rule these kingdoms is yours,
all the power you will ever need I will give.
I ask only one thing of you...but first, a gift.

"God's Chosen One, I lay at your feet this gift:
all the power to bring about the kingdom of God.
I offer the power to end all war and set the poor free,
to bring to earth an age of justice and peace.
All the power you need to rule these kingdoms shall be yours,
all the power you will ever need I will give.

I ask only one thing of you in return."

Jesus did not answer the shadowed visitor. He could feel a web of darkness being woven around him; he sighed deeply and prayed with passion:

"Please, my God, come to rescue me, your son.
O God, make haste, and come to help me;
　　you are my helper, O my God, do not delay.
Let those who love your help always say:
　　'God is great![15] God is great! God is great!
O God, make haste, and come to help me.' "

"Ah, one of David's old psalms, a favorite prayer of many whom I've visited. Like them, Jesus, I fear you will be disappointed. God will not come! Perhaps no help comes because the Old One is off in space mending some broken galaxy. Perhaps God is busy filling those ancient nostrils with the smoke of incense and burning cattle flesh ascending in stinking smoke from Jerusalem's temple."

"Diablo,[16] do not take me for a fool," Jesus said, his right hand pointed skyward. "God is Great. God alone holds the power to bring about the age of justice. God alone will I worship."

The Shadow leaned close to Jesus. "Brave talk indeed from a poor peasant stonemason who always has lowered his eyes, docile as a donkey, before a passing swaggering Roman soldier or some nose-up-in-the-air temple priest. Reject my offer, Jesus, and your mission is doomed to failure and defeat! All your efforts, toil and labor will be for nothing if you don't accept the power I have to offer. Listen to me," said the Shadow, and he began to sing:

"Be sensible, Jesus, and make a small bargain with me;
　　my clients are many and among the most famous.
I can give you the very best of references:
　　kings, rulers, high priests, Caesars of every size.
Among my well-known clients are relatives of yours,
　　like Eve and Adam, your first parents,
　　whom I helped start on the journey to adulthood,
　　free to grow and roam when they left the nest.
Or old King David, who for another's wife had eyes;
　　by a little compromise David took a lover to bed.

"If God's so great, how did I get into Eden in the first place?
　　Do you want an answer to that old puzzle, the problem of evil?

Long ago, the Old One, tired of playing with galaxies,
   invited me to a game of chance between just us two.
When day is done and milky stars fill the night sky's seas,
   God and I meet to count up who has won or lost whom.
The age-old game we play is simple tic-tac-toe.
   I'm not bad, Jesus, or even evil; I'm just a friendly foe."

Jesus held his ground though he felt the web tightening about him.
"Be gone Satan!" he cried as he lifted his arms upward to the sky in prayer:
   " 'O God, may your everlasting love be with me,
      for in you alone does my soul take refuge.
   I seek shelter in the shadow of your mighty wings;
      there I seek refuge till this storm shall pass.' "[17]

The Shadow heaved a great sigh. "Another psalm of David, that great lover of other men's wives. Please, Jesus, son of adulterous David, allow me to sing to you a few lines of that same psalm-song of your ancestor:
   " 'I shall lie down among the fierce lions,
      who devour the weak with teeth sharp as spears.
   Their tongues are as sharp as swords and arrows;
      my enemies have laid a deadly snare for my feet.'
   I'm not bad, Jesus, or even evil, I'm just a friendly foe.

"Like the Greeks, Jesus, let us enter the game of games,
   you and I wrestling as do friendly foes.
Saying no will be your biggest mistake. Think!
   Without my help you will surely fail, bringing
   shame on you — and think of your family's shame.[18]
If, alas, you say no to me, who will protect you
   when you must lie down among the lions of Rome?
I'm not bad, Jesus, or even evil, I'm just a friendly foe.

"Who will help when you're all alone in the pit
   with the ferocious lions of the temple elders?
Without my power and cunning you will surely die
   as they devour you quickly for their supper meal.
If you go home preaching justice and love,
   without my help, they'll cut you to ribbons.
With their educated teeth and sharp, learned tongues,
   you are no match for them without me on your side!
I'm not bad, Jesus, or even evil, I'm just a friendly foe.

Jesus, strike a bargain with me and I guarantee
    you'll never be shamed or made to look the fool.
Rather, you'll find on your simple peasant lips
    the cleverest of insulting replies and crafty parable stories
    to shame them and put them in their place.
I warn you, poor peasant of Galilee, reject my offer
    and they'll slice you up in a thousand little pieces.
And when they've finished, they'll hang you high
    in an old bare tree like dead meat for all to see.
I'm not bad, Jesus, or even evil, I'm just a friendly foe.
    So don't be foolish; be wise and make a little compromise."

As the Shadow's deep voice faded in the air, he disappeared as well.
Jesus stood bewildered and alone in the desert.

Night's Shadow Swallows All

The sun's orb had now vanished from view, and twilight had dimmed.
Darkness was busy sucking up all the shadows of the twisted pillar rocks
and desert brush. Satan was nowhere to be seen, not so much having
departed as becoming slowly one with the giant black shadow of night
consuming all the earth. Then out of the great dark shadow came a faint
echoing whisper:

"Jesus, I'm like a Persian merchant in a bazaar:
    I won't take no for an answer, so let's bargain.
Let's you and I strike a deal — but not tonight;
    take my offer as a pillow upon which to sleep.
You're interested, both of us know you are;
    by morning's light you'll see my deal will take you far.

O Jesus, friend, gazing into the mirror of your Shadow
    you saw in my offer your instinctive lusting for power.
You saw a hunger for others to do your will;
    with satisfaction, you saw others looking up to you.
You know as well as I your desire to be admired,
    your starving hunger to be held in great honor.
Ah, yes, I am but the mirror of your other self;
    this is not good-bye — I'll return when you decide.
Perhaps then I can be of some service to you,
    and you'll see that everything I've said is true.
I'll come back to show you more dark, sinister features
    of the kind and gentle, good and pious Jesus.

Until then, peace — or rather, unrest — be to you."[19]

Engulfed by both the darkness of the night and of what he felt within his own heart, Jesus prayed with relief:

"Indeed, O God, you are great and worthy of praise!
   I love you, O God, who have heard my cry.
You are my strength, my rock, my deliverer;
   in my great distress I called upon you, O God.
You heard my prayer and answered me."[20]

And to his prayer of gratitude at his deliverance, another voice joined his, as the angel Gabriel made himself visible and added his own prayer:

"God lowered the heavens and came down to earth,
   descended on a dark cloud, upon wings of the wind.
God was clothed in pitch-black darkness as a veil,
   wearing a garment flowing with dark ebony waters."

Placing his arm around Jesus' shoulders, Gabriel reassured him, "You did well with that visitation. You were tested and remained faithful, a loyal son of God. Now you must rest, for tomorrow after forty days you will end your fasting. Tomorrow you will go home — to become a messenger of the good news and to begin the life you are destined for."

Jesus rolled up in his cloak and proceeded to lie down. Gabriel sat watch beside him until his eyes closed in sleep.

The Way Home

The sleep of Jesus that night was crowded with frightful dreams. In one, he was a Greek athlete wrestling with his Shadow. In each contest in which they met, the Shadow won, pinning his back firmly to the ground, each time laughing with a victor's glee, saliva dripping from his twisted lips. Jesus awoke with a start, his entire body shaking with fear.

"Dreams are only night rehearsals of our fears," said Gabriel, kneeling beside him. "Don't let them disturb you. Now, since you're awake, let us begin the journey home, even though dawn is still hours away. The cool night air will invigorate you."

Jesus needed no encouragement to end his desert days. He stood up at once and accompanied Gabriel. Looking up at the stars as they walked, Jesus said, "By which route are we going home to Nazareth? By the stars, I see we are headed south, deeper into the desert. Galilee is north!"

"Yes, I know," Gabriel smiled, "but this is the only way home. The desert we are now crossing is not the one in which you spent your forty days. This desert is inside you!"

Jesus and his angel guide walked on in silence. Pondering the meaning of Gabriel's words, Jesus wondered whether this was just another dream. Fear grew into great dread as he realized that perhaps another visitation remained.

THE GREAT BAPTISM

As Jesus and his angel companion crested the top of a high sand dune, he could see, even in the darkness, that in the center of the desert was a great sea. A vast dark ocean seemed to stretch as far as the eye could see, all the way to the rim of the horizon and beyond. The drifting desert sands descended toward the sea's shore as the roar of crashing waves drew them onward. Soon the two stood ankle deep in the white-foamed, lapping waters.

Standing in the surf, Gabriel broke the long silence: "After being cooked to a crisp in the furnace of the desert, Jesus, now rejoice in the coolness of the sea."

"The sea?" asked Jesus, his voice all but lost in the roar of the crashing waves. "It's the ancient Chaos — the sea is the destroyer!"[21]

Gabriel placed his hand on Jesus' shoulder, reassuring him, "Remember the psalm prayer we prayed together last night, 'God was clothed in the pitch-black darkness as a veil, wearing a garment flowing with dark ebony waters'? The ebony sea before you is not the Chaos, it's the Creator! Your God awaits you, do not fear."

Jesus' body trembled, but without being told what to do, he stepped back onto the sand. Then he slowly removed his clothing and waded out into the turbulent swirling surf. He turned to say something, but before he could speak a great towering wave crested over him in a thunderous roar and sucked him underneath. As he cried out in both horror and ecstasy, he was dragged far out into the dark Sea.[22]

The ocean turned from blue to orange, changing into a sea of fire, flames leaping higher than the sky. As a passion flower in the moonlight blooms in minutes, so the raging red sea of flames was quickly transformed into a vast still pool of purple water that was as silent as a star. In the silence, Gabriel fell face forward on the sand, crying, "Holy, Holy, Holy God, heaven and earth are full of your glory. Blessed are those who are drowned in you so that they might be able to come in your name."

In the darkness before dawn, God gently carried the limp body of Jesus back to land and placed him on the beach. What happened in the mystery of his great baptism will forever remain a sacred secret between the two of them, as is only fitting for lovers.

When Jesus opened his eyes, he found himself lying on his back upon the sandy beach with Gabriel breathing air into his mouth. "Ah, you're alive again," Gabriel said. "Breathe deeply and fill your lungs with the freshness of this new day."

Jesus looked up and saw the night quickly escaping into the west as the sun was about to rise over the sea. The eastern sky was a soft turquoise blue, with a cluster of pink and salmon-colored clouds shaped like some vast hovering skybird. Still higher was the silver crescent of a new moon. Jesus raised his head and saw that the sea was as motionless as water in a bucket. Gabriel helped Jesus to his feet, and then began to sing:

> "A new moon, a silver sickle in the morning sky,
>   and a new day announces God's new time has begun.
> I anoint you, Jesus, with the Spirit's sacred oil
>   that you may joyfully labor for justice and peace."

With fragrant oils of the Orient, Gabriel began an angelic anointing,[23] starting with the crown of Jesus' head.

> "Dead, buried, and now risen out of the sea,
>   you're the prophet of a new song to be sung,
>   a royal, priestly prophet of God Most High.
> I anoint you, Jesus, with the Spirit's sacred oil
>   to grace your labor for justice and peace.
>
> "Oil on your head, where a crown shall rest,
>   oil rubbed over your new skin and new heart.
> Oil on your arms, as wrestling gladiators use,
>   oil on your priestly hands to offer sacrifice.
> Oil on your chest to anoint a hero blest,
>   oil on your stomach and oil on your loins."

"No!" cried Jesus, instinctively drawing back.

> "Yes, there, Jesus, the new man, and everywhere,
>   for with God there are no unholy parts.
> And you shall love the Lord your God with all
>   your mind and heart and with *all* your body!
> Oil, finally, on your legs and feet to carry the good news:
>   I anoint you with the Spirit's sacred oil
>   so you can return home as God's holy Anointed One."

By now the sun had risen in the same splendor as on the first day of creation. Jesus looked down at his anointed body. The light of the rising sun was glistening off the oil. He saw that the ravages of thirty years of aging were erased — he was new again! As Gabriel began to dress him in his brown peasant tunic, Jesus saw all of his body with new eyes. As his peasant tunic was slipped over his head, Jesus felt as if he were being vested in the elaborate robes of the high priest or a silken robe worthy of King Solomon.

"Jesus, after your baptism by John, you have now been baptized into the bottomless depths of the divine mystery and have come forth anew from the womb of God."

"I feel like a newborn babe," he said. "Are all my baptisms done? I hope so."

"Not all of them, Jesus! One final, great baptism remains a few years from now. It will mirror this one in the sea. All of these baptisms have prepared you for — and are part of — the great one that awaits you."

"Is it time to go home now?"

"Yes, after one last gift. While your new skin has been saturated with the Spirit's oil to anoint you as a prophet messenger, you also need a new tongue."

"A new tongue?" Jesus echoed in confusion.

"Yes, a tongue to replace your uneducated peasant's tongue. Open your mouth and show me your tongue."

Jesus did as he was instructed but closed his eyes, fearful of what might happen next. Gabriel kissed his own index finger and thumb, and at once they broke into flames as if they had been two dry sticks set ablaze. He reached over and took hold of Jesus' tongue. His forefinger and thumb glowing red-orange like tongs taken from a blacksmith's fire, Gabriel pinched them tightly on Jesus' tongue. Jesus' head jerked back, and he screamed in pain as his tongue turned flaming red.[24]

As the angel released his grip, he said, "Now, Jesus, as long ago in the desert the flaming bush spoke to Moses with God's voice, so your tongue will now be aflame with God's word." Quickly placing his thumb and forefinger into his mouth, Gabriel soaked them with his saliva and again took hold of Jesus' tongue, "Receive a poet-prophet's tongue, coated with God's sweet love and delicious good news. May your new tongue be ever awash with the saliva of saving power."

Jesus felt the angel's saliva upon his tongue. After the initial sensation of being seared by intense heat, his tongue now swam in sweetness, as if it had been dipped in honey. The taste in his mouth was that of the healing salve of heaven.

"Now you are ready to go home and proclaim to all who will listen that God's time and God's kingdom have come! Speak with the fire of the prophets Daniel, Isaiah, Jeremiah and Ezekiel. Speak with the sweetness of honey to attract those who have only known the taste of the bitter vinegar of religion. May your listeners be drawn to God by your words' fiery zest and the sweetness of their love. From this day hence, Jesus, may your speech be dripping with heaven's new wine to make all who have ears to hear you drunk with the intoxication of God's message."

As Jesus closed his lips, his tongue restlessly roamed around the cave of his mouth, swimming in fire, honey and wine.

"You shall return home now not the man who left it forty days ago. You shall return as the messenger of God!"

Jesus turned to Gabriel with a quizzical look. "Gabriel, I have two final questions. While my senses have been reborn in these desert baptisms, it seems that my sense of direction was excluded. I need to ask: Which way is home? And more importantly, if I am to go home as messenger, how shall I proclaim this message that God's time has come?"

"Simply be the mirror in which others can see themselves as God sees them. Do not be concerned about how you shall bear the message. You shall return home filled with the Spirit Wind[25] and oceanic love, whose force shall overwhelm you with power in word and deed. Fear nothing, only remember that you have been gifted and empowered not for your profit or your pleasure but to draw closer to God all who hear you and experience your wonderful deeds. At long last after these forty days, it is time to go home, Jesus. Go in peace and in the Spirit Wind," Gabriel said, with one hand raised in blessing over Jesus. As the angel's human form began to fade, he turned and pointed his other arm northward, saying, "That way is home — for now!"[26]

CHAPTER THREE

JESUS' RETURN TO NAZARETH

Jesus returned from the desert and gossip about him was in every ear, and so the synagogue of Nazareth was jammed the first Saturday after he came home.[1] A loud buzzing filled the little synagogue as if it had been hit by a plague of flies. Jesus had taken a place in the synagogue with the other men of the village.

"Finally he's home," one man buzzed in the ear of another. "The others who went to hear Jordan John were back over forty days ago."

"I heard, neighbor, that he became a disciple of Jordan John, and remained behind on Jordan's shore to study under him."

The man behind the two leaned over and said, "No doubt he learned how to eat locusts," and all three laughed.

In the rear of the synagogue, hidden behind a wooden screen, the women were also all murmuring to each other.

"Look how thin Jesus is," said one young woman to her friend next to her, "and darkly tanned by the sun! His widowed mother Mary surely must be glad to have him home. Poor old woman, she talks to herself a lot these days."

"Perhaps," she whispered, "he's so brown from the sun because he lost his way home after the pilgrimage to the Jordan. He was lost before,

I seem to recall, when he was a child on the road home from Jerusalem."

As Jesus stood to address them, it was if his tongue were glowing red hot. While he had felt the power of the Spirit Wind upon his tongue on occasion during his journey home, it was nothing like what he was feeling now. More than just his tongue, his entire body seemed to be seized by the great river of the Spirit.

As Jesus began to speak the words of Isaiah,[2] even the children became attentive.

THE PROPHESY IS FULFILLED IN NAZARETH

"The Spirit of the Holy One is upon me, and has anointed me to bring glad tidings to the poor..."[3]

His mother Mary mumbled from behind the screen, "To nobodies, outcasts, beggars and the destitute."

"God has sent me to proclaim liberty to all those who are held captive..."

"Yes, to those imprisoned by religion, as well as sin," she mumbled again, this time louder.

"to give recovery of sight to the blind..."

Now loud enough for others to hear, Mary added, "To those who can't see that Love is greater than the law."

"to set free the oppressed..."

She mumbled even more loudly, "The poor burdened by debt, taxes, the sinful oppression of the rich and narrow social customs."

"to proclaim a jubilee, a sabbatical year pleasing to God."[4]

"More than a year," his mother muttered loudly, "a jubilee sabbatical age, for God's time has begun."

All eyes in the synagogue were upon Jesus, and a hushed silence, almost an awe, fell upon the entire assembly.

"My neighbors and old friends," he said, as if his tongue were dripping new wine mixed with honey, "and you who are of my family clan, great has been my desire to come home with the message that Isaiah's prophecy, which we have learned by heart as children, has been fulfilled. Share my great joy that here, today in your midst, God's new time, the great jubilee so pleasing to God, has finally come!"

An uneasiness was rustling through the crowd that filled the synagogue. Jesus' tongue felt on fire, and his voice grew as full of power as the roaring of a desert lion. "I must tell you all what I learned in the desert. I, Jesus, your neighbor, have been sent by God to release all those imprisoned. For, behold, I *am* the jubilee year of pardon. I have been sent by God to bring the good news to all but especially to the poor and the least among us."

Many in the crowd restlessly began to wriggle; faces were turning sour, and some were growing angry. Jesus' face and hands were taking on a transparent glow as if he had swallowed the sun as he continued his proclamation, "Yes, I, Jesus, whom you've known since I was but a child, have returned to you to release those here who are oppressed by sin, the heaviest of all debts. I know that the eyes of many here are blind, sealed shut by fear, doubt or hate. Now is the time to be freed. Today, neighbors and family, this prophecy of Isaiah has been fulfilled, here in your hearing."

Jesus' message now perfectly clear, the crowd in the synagogue could not contain itself. Someone shouted, "The prophecy of Isaiah about the Messiah, the Awaited One, is honey to our ears, but you, Jesus, have made it an earful of stinging bees! You must be mad to think you are God's messenger and that you've come to heal us. And to imply that you are the Messiah!"

Another cried out, "We are your neighbors and you want us to believe you are the Long-awaited One? You, the carpenter's son — we have known you since you were a boy! You must be out of your mind!"

Momentarily taken aback by the intensity — the violence — of the outcry, Jesus said, "Friends, listen! The hand of God is in all of this, reaching out to you!"

The crowd's rumbling was growing into a roar as one man shouted, "Jesus, this is too much, stop before it's too late!"

The elders were all standing now, unanimous in their rejection.

"Neighbors," said Jesus, standing boldly in front of them, "your treatment of me only fulfills the old saying: A prophet is never honored in his own country. Or to say it backwards, only those of another country have faith in a prophet. Remember how a gentile leper, Naaman the Syrian, placed faith in the words of Elisha the prophet and was healed by bathing in the Jordan while the lepers of Israel were not!"

The rabbi himself now strode down to where Jesus stood and shouted in his face, "You shame us, Jesus, by comparing us to lepers! You heap shame on Israel by comparing yourself to the prophet Elisha." Many stood up and began shouting, "Shame! Shame! You shame us!"[5]

From the back came a rallying cry, "He shames us and makes us into fools. He blasphemes! Let us defend our honor and silence this madman."

From behind the women's screen, his mother screamed, "No! No! No!"

But the pot had boiled over with scalding feelings of outrage and fury. Some of the angry villagers grabbed hold of Jesus and in a moment had him on the brow of the hill on which the village was built, intent on throwing him over it.

Gabriel, guardian of God's messengers, suddenly stood unseen at the precipice, like a heron crane on one foot with its wings spread wide. Quickly he began spinning around, whipping up a whirling dust cloud, into which he drew the terrified Jesus. In the midst of the flying sand and dust that blinded and stung the eyes of Jesus' would-be murderers, Gabriel snatched him to safety. The angry crowd never really knew what happened. After these events, Jesus no longer considered Nazareth his home.

THE RETURN TO THE BEGINNING

Gabriel was familiar with Jesus' home of Nazareth. Nine months before the birth of Jesus, the angel had been sent by God to this little village of no more than a hundred people. His mission was to give a message to the fourteen-year-old daughter of Joachin and Ann, who as a child had been betrothed to the village craftsman, Joseph.

Shortly after sunrise one day, while the dew still lay upon the grass, Gabriel stood in the doorway of the one-room house of Joachin and Ann. "Peace be with you, Mary," the angel said softly, shocking her out of her prayers.

"Who are you and what do you want?" she asked, startled. "I am alone — my father is in the field and my mother has gone to the well!" Mary wrapped herself more tightly in her cloak, more from fear than from an early morning chill. Slowly she edged her way back into the corner of the room.

Gabriel stood in the doorway, with the rising sun behind him revealing his body's silhouette. "You're wearing no cloak, stranger, and your tunic is only gauze thin!" she said, lowering her head as a lily bloom droops in the breeze. "Do not be afraid, modest Mary," Gabriel said, "for you have been favored by God, who has made all things good and beautiful, beautiful like you. I have been sent to sing to you a song from the heart of your lover," and Gabriel started to sing:

"O my dove, my lily of the valley, O Mary, my rose of Sharon,
    you are so beautiful and your field so fresh and unplowed.[6]
See, the winter is past, the rains are over and gone,
    flowers appear in the fields, giving forth fragrance.
The song of the dove is heard in our land
    and the time of planting is now at hand.

"Hark, listen, here comes your lover

springing across the mountains,
    leaping like a stag over the hills.
Your lover, strong as an athlete, stands
    gazing at you with great longing through the window.
Mary, how beautiful, how pleasing you are to God,
    your slender figure is like a palm tree,
    your breasts are like clusters of the vine,
    the fragrance of your breath as sweet as apples,
    the taste of your mouth sweeter than fine wine."

Mary held her hands over her face, tinted red like the rising sun. She spoke, breathless, disbelieving. "Did Joseph send you? He is a shy man, and could never express such thoughts himself."

Gabriel moved from the doorway into the room.

"Joseph does not know that I am here; another lover has sent me, Mary — your God! The Mighty and Awesome One has chosen you to be the mother of the Messiah, to give birth to God's New Song. Yes, it's true. Your field shall be seeded with a son, and God will give him a throne greater than that of David his ancestor."

Lowering her hands from her face, she stared in disbelief. "Bear the Messiah? How can this be? Even my beloved Joseph has not come near me."

Gabriel moved closer to her and began to sing:

"The Holy Wind that overshadowed the dark waters
    which rolled in the midnight darkness of chaos,
seeding the cosmos with the earth, the heavens and all living things;
    the same Holy Wind will overshadow you, God's beautiful one.
Your young virgin's field will bloom with a child most holy,
    since the seed to be planted in your womb
    is the very seed of the Holy of Holies.
A son of God, a prophet he shall be — and more —
    a savior who will heal and whom many will shun.
    You shall name this glorious new son *Jesus*.
I sing but the invitation of your Lover,
    who longs to hear you speak your reply,
    for your voice is as sweet as you are lovely."

Mary closed her eyes in prayer and pondered but a moment before she sang out in jubilation:

"Let it be done. Yes, I give consent,
    for I am the lowly maid of my God.
I should say: Let it be tried,

since what you say seems impossible.
For God the lover is spirit, and I am only flesh."

Gabriel replied:

"O most beautiful Mary, your name is rich as perfume;
   innocent child, with God all things are possible.
Know that your aged relative, Elizabeth,
   is now six months pregnant — in her old age she's with son.

"Yes, I bear the amazing news
   that cursed, barren Elizabeth and shamed, dried-up Zechariah
   are today as fruitful as young fig trees,
   so you may know that with your God nothing is impossible.
Now, look toward your door; behold, your Lover nears.
   Behold, your Holy God approaches
   as a swirling column of smoke and sand,
   laden with myrrh and frankincense.
Prepare yourself, servant maid of God."

And as the desert whirlwind filled the small room with the fiery heat and pungent perfume of the Beloved, Gabriel turned his eyes away and departed.

INTO THE HILL COUNTRY

A few days later, Mary set out in haste and traveled into the hill country to a town of Judah to visit the home of the old priest, Zechariah, and Elizabeth, his aged wife. Was it true? Was the sign from God coming about? As Elizabeth appeared in her doorway, young Mary sang out, her voice filling the tiny house:[7]

"Blessed are you, Elizabeth, and great is God;
   I rejoice, for spring, I hear, has come to your old womb.
Your once yellowed autumn field is now fertile, I'm told,
   with God's prophetic seed,
   gifting you and Zechariah with miraculous life.[8]
I rejoice, for with God anything is possible!"

Instantly gray-haired Elizabeth was swept off her feet with enthusiasm by the Holy Spirit and began to dance and sing in reply:

"Blessed are you also Mary, among all women;
   blessed and holy is the seed in your springtime field;[9]
   I am awed that the mother of my Lord should visit me.

As soon as you sang your greeting at my door,
little John here in my womb danced with joy
to hear hidden in your song God's New Song.

"Still, how can I rejoice?
I'm too old to bear a dream,
too old to carry a prophet's penance song.
I'm too old to be a mother to the messenger
of the agelessly awaited Anointed One,
too old to nurse the prophet of this New Song."

But youthful Mary, aglow with innocence and beaming with hope,
replied:
"Yes, dearest Elizabeth, I know it's true
that God's work is always upside down.
For I'm too young to bear God's New Song;
my flesh and blood much too young
to be seeded with God's Great Dream,
and you're too old.
Upside down, dear Elizabeth, is God's plan:
you're too old, and I...I'm too young!
It can't happen but it's happening anyway."

And they dissolved in laughter and tears into each other's arms.

VISITORS AT THE DOOR

Knotted at the doorway was a crowd of the village gossip-pickers,
their sharp shrew tongues a wagging chorus: "Shameful, shameful, oh,
tisk, tisk, whatever do you make of this? Old Elizabeth, cursed for some
past sin, made barren as a stony field, is getting fat now in her old age."[10]

"Fat, my foot! Old barren Elizabeth is fat with child, can't you see?
It's shameful at her ancient age to be in such a delicate state. And our old
priest Zechariah has lost face, for another must have sown this seed."

"More shameful, my friends, I say, is this scandalous girl, no more
than fourteen; for days she traveled here alone! Yes, I saw her coming up
the road with no father, brother or chaperon. How scandalous for a young
virgin girl to have no mother or other women kin along!"[11]

"Shameful, indeed, with one foot in the grave, for Elizabeth to be
waiting with child. Shocking, to be at death's door fat with a son, with a
muted husband who can't talk. O good daughters of Israel, devout daughters

of the Law, strange times these are when ancient customs are ignored. Strange and bad times — trouble's at our door."

Elizabeth's Song at Her Doorstep

Elizabeth stomped to her door, broom in hand. She began to swing it wildly as if she were sweeping the air in front of her door. "Away with you! Off my threshold, you village wags, for these are not bad or strange times. This is a new and glorious time in our land, one fat with hope when sterile and virgin wombs are full to the brim with fertile Spirit's seeds. The world is pregnant with dream time, as angels announce what God is doing: turning the world upside down, yes, upside down.

"This is not a strange but rather a wholly new time. So away with you — go snicker at another's door."

After slamming the door, Elizabeth slowly sunk to the floor. Once inside, she and her cousin sat down together. "O little Mary, I'm too old to sing like that, too old to sing what I hear within my womb. My wrinkled womb is too old to nest a child. Oh, why did God sow a seed in this tired old wheat field?"

Mary gently wrapped her arm around Elizabeth and said, "Rest, Elizabeth, you're six moons full of life, you must be careful." Then Mary added, "Let us pray," and both women fell silent. After some time, Mary began to sing.

Mary's Song of the Messiah's Revolution

"My soul magnifies my Lover and God;
    my spirit is full of joy in the Holy One.
For God has overshadowed my springtime field,
    and filled it with the Song of Songs."

Elizabeth picked up her melody:
"Surely generations and generations to come
    will call you blessed among women,
        for God has done great things for you."

Then Mary sang again:
"The proud of heart and stiff of neck
    will have their proud thoughts scattered by God
        like frightened chickens in the yard.
God's hand shall turn all things around
    — upside down and downside up.

From their high thrones God shall tumble the mighty down;
  the lowly and those of no worth shall be given the earth.
Those now rich shall be beggars on the street,
  while the hungry shall feast at the tables of the wealthy,
  leaving the rich to fight for scraps in the ditch.
Upside down shall God turn our world."

Elizabeth continued:

"Just as God has promised from of old,
  promised to Mother Sarah and Father Abraham.
All shall be turned upside down,
  empty and desert-bare wombs turned into fertile fields,
  as full of seeds as the night sky is flooded with stars
  or the shore is filled with grains of yellow sand.
God's promise in you is impossibly fulfilled;
  yes, a virgin mother you shall become,
  bearing sons and daughters as many as the stars.
For all God's children shall be your children,
  to all you will become Mother Mary:
  Mary, Mother of God, star of the sea."[12]

Mary answered in song:

"Rejoice and be glad, faithful Elizabeth,
  for not only I, but everyone who says,
  'let all things happen according to your will'
  shall be overshadowed by the seed-sowing Spirit of God
  and shall be filled with a divine dream."

Then Elizabeth stood up and leaned against the wall, looking down fondly at Mary: "Mary, daughter of heaven, only with God's help can I bear this labor; only by God's doing can this wrinkled womb carry this gift of God inside me."

Mary stood and took her cousin by the hand. "Rest now, dear Elizabeth, for with God all things are possible, the angel told me so. Elizabeth, let us make a mother's covenant: if you'll can carry the overture, I'll carry the tune, the song of glory that follows."

Elizabeth smiled. "It is agreed. Together we'll succeed — though everything is upside down. Yet I must warn you of a vision I had in a recent dream, a dark vision I dread to share with you. One day, Mary, you will sing a song of infinite sadness. On that evil day you'll sing: I'm too old to see the New Song die, too old to watch a divine dream die, too old to bury and mourn a dead dream."

"Dearest Elizabeth, I fear that your vision's true, for those God visits are often turned upside down. Joy quickly leaps into sorrow and pleasure into pain, as disappointments rob our purses of hope and promise. Whatever lies ahead for us, we can nurse with love, for with God all things are possible! So let the two of us rejoice and be glad today, for God has done great things to you and me."

And together they walked arm in arm out to the garden behind the house where old Zechariah sat watching his melons grow and dreamt of being a prophet's father.

THE SAVIOR'S BIRTH AND THE SHEPHERD APOSTLES

Nine months later in the hills outside Bethlehem, three shepherds were keeping night watch over their flocks. Two were awake, the third slumbered, dreaming of being rich and a person of great importance. The youngest, named Samuel, played his shepherd's harp as he sang to the stars. The sheep were as calm as the night, yet the second shepherd, Isaac, was uneasy, unable to sleep, sensing something strange was adrift on the wind of this dark night.

With the suddenness of a slicing sword, a fierce wind slashed across the hills, causing the moon to be swallowed whole by dark swirling clouds. Suddenly, the angel Gabriel appeared in a luminous whirlwind and called out with an impassioned, jubilant messenger's voice:

"Glory to God and tidings of joy to all,
    glorious news to all the sheep of Israel."

Staffs in hand, Jacob, Isaac and Samuel jumped to their feet. The three shepherds stood stone-still in fright before the luminous cloud. As the cloud stopped spinning, out of dozens of whirling rainbows Gabriel stood before them:

"Isaac, Samuel and Jacob, shepherds three,
    fear not; do not be afraid but rejoice!
I am Gabriel, God's messenger angel,
    come to bring word of God's great choice.
Shepherds, you are the chosen ones of God,
    who are to announce the fullness of time:
Glory to God and tidings of joy to all,
    glorious news to all the sheep of Israel.

"Let all the people exult with great joy,

for time has grown as ripe and full as the moon.
God's time, the long-awaited age, has come this very day:
    In this year five thousand one hundred and ninety-nine
    since God with great love created heaven and earth.[13]
From the time of Noah and the great flood,
    two thousand nine hundred and fifty-seven.
From the birth of Father Abraham,
    two thousand and fifteen.
From Moses and the Exodus of the Israelites from Egypt,
    one thousand five hundred and ten.
From the time of the prophet's anointing of King David,
    one thousand and thirty-two.
In the sixty-fifth week according to Daniel's prophecy;
    in the one hundred and ninety-fourth Greek olympiad.
In the year seven hundred and fifty-two
    from the founding of the city of Rome.
The forty-second year of the empire of Octavius Augustus,
    in the sixth age of the world.
In the beginning of the age of Pisces, the fish,
    the last of the zodiac's signs, a sign of the beginning,
    when the whole world is at peace,
Nine months having elapsed since his conception,
    in Bethlehem in the land of Judah
    is born your Liberator, the Messiah.
Glory to God and tidings of joy to all,
    glorious news to all the sheep of Israel."

The oldest shepherd, Isaac, was the first to utter a reply: "Surely, whoever you are, you're mistaken! While your words are truly good news, we're only shepherds, common as dung.[14] Your long-awaited message of liberation isn't for the ears of common folk like us. It's for the Temple priests or the king or the wise scholars of our nation."

Gabriel replied with urgency:
"No, my friends! My orders were precise;
    to come to you three shepherds on this hilltop,
    proclaiming tidings of great joy
    to be shared with the whole people.
Go to Bethlehem and announce this good news."[15]

Samuel, the youngest, cried out next: "Angel of God, Bethlehem's a big town! How are we to know which child is the Chosen One?"

"This will be the sign: In a manger filled with hay you will find wrapped in swaddling clothes your infant Savior Liberator born this day."[16]

Jacob shook his head and said: "If by God you have been sent, then heaven's made a big mistake. If we dirty shepherds were to go to town, we'd be as welcome as the plague. Pray tell, angel of God, what do you take us for — fools? To go and announce that David's royal heir lies in a manger in some shabby stable? Such a message could not have come from God. You must be a demon to spin such a crazy tale."

Gabriel simply smiled and snapped his fingers, and the silent night was shattered by the sound of hundreds of silver trumpets from on high. The three shepherds looked up in shock to see the heavens ripping apart and a great gaping hole appearing in the night sky! Through it poured a wide waterfall of glistening stars that showered down upon the hilltop. Among the stars were thousands upon thousands of angels singing:

> "Glory to God in the high heavens
> and peace on earth to all those
> upon whom God's favor rests.
> Glory to God and tidings of joy to all,
> glorious news to all the sheep of Israel."

When the shepherds had collected their scattered wits, Gabriel said, "Upon you three, my good shepherds, God's favor rests. Now, go and proclaim the glad tidings to all in Bethlehem." Then, as suddenly as they had come, Gabriel and all the heavenly hosts ascended on a great updraft of wind. The great sky hole closed behind them, leaving the astonished shepherds seeing only the silent stars and a crescent moon in the night sky.

THE APOSTLES OF BETHLEHEM

A badly shaken Jacob finally found his tongue: "Surely, brothers, that was no dream! Did not all three of us see and hear it? What choice do we have? Let's go to Bethlehem to see what we can and to announce the good news to all we meet."

"And who will watch our flocks," asked Isaac, "the moon and the stars?"

"Why not? If our visitor was truly from God and we've been chosen to be the messengers," answered Samuel, "then God will watch over our flocks!"

"And, if we find the infant Messiah?" returned Isaac. "What then? What gift can we bring to the new prince of our land? You know, you dumb sheepherders, it's customary to bring gifts on such a joyous occasion!

What have we to give?"

"Music!" replied Samuel, who picked up his shepherd's harp and strummed with his fingers across the strings, "and our choicest lamb, the little pure white one we had planned to sell at Passover time when it had grown. It'll make a great gift."

Jacob placed the lamb on his shoulders, and to the sound of Samuel's harp, the three left their flocks for the stars to watch. Upon entering Bethlehem, they first came to the inn. Samuel was playing a wedding dance, while the other two sang loudly:

"This night, while you were sleeping, the Messiah has been born;
   come, join us as we go to pay him homage."

"Drunken shepherds!" shouted the innkeeper from his upstairs window. "You roughnecks, shut up! You'll awaken my guests! Be off with you before I call the guards."

Disappointed at their first response, the shepherds continued down the street shouting the glad tidings. When they came to the house of the synagogue leader, the pious Pharisee appeared in a second story window. "Be quiet, you dumb shepherds! Let decent people sleep! Why all this shouting and music in the middle of the night?"

"Sir," said Isaac with respect, "Immanuel, the Messiah, has been born this night in this very town."

"Fools, how would you know about such things. You're sinners living outside God's law! When did you three last attend worship and prayer? You foul-smelling shepherds, have you no brains? When the Messiah does come, it will not be in a flea-bitten little town like this one! And those who announce his birth will not be simpletons like you three. Unclean sheepherders, be on your way!" he shouted as he emptied his chamber pot onto the three messengers.

"I knew this would happen!" moaned Jacob. "We're just shepherds, and now we really do stink! Who's going to believe what we say?"

Samuel spoke up, "I know a woman who works a few doors from here, Mary, the town prostitute! She plays the tambourine like an angel. Perhaps, if we had more music! Yes, if our message had more music, then people would believe our story."

"A prostitute!" groaned Isaac, as Samuel knocked on her door. A beautiful woman appeared in the doorway, greeting the three shepherds like old friends.

"Mary," he said, "we're on our way to see the newly born king, the Messiah who was born this night." Then he added with pride, "We were chosen to announce his birth. Come, join us and bring your tambourine. When we've found him, you can serenade the child!"

"The Messiah? Well, I don't know any lullabies, but why not?" she replied. "Besides, business is slow tonight. But are you sure you want me to join you?"

"Yes, Mary, we're sure! The angel told us that the news was 'glad tidings of great joy to be shared by the whole people,' and that includes you! So get your tambourine and invite anyone else who wants to come with us."

"All right, I will come," and she quickly returned with tambourine in hand. With her was another woman of the house with a small handheld goatskin drum.

The Manger Parade

The three shepherds warmly welcomed the two women, and with the joyful sounds of drum, tambourine and harp, the five made their way through the dark, narrow streets of Bethlehem. To their sadness, every door remained tightly closed to them and to their message.

In a dark alley they came upon four lame beggars with whom they shared the joyful news. To the surprise of the five, the lame beggars jumped to their feet and followed them, tap-dancing and snapping their fingers to the music. Outside a tavern, they told the good news to a couple of Greek travelers and two Samaritan merchants, and all four joined their company.

After searching every street and alley and finding no baby in swaddling bands, they had come full circle back to the town gate. As they passed through the gate, a fear gnawed like a rat in the shepherds' hearts that the angels' visit had been an illusion. Still, they marched along outside the town walls, against which leaned several makeshift shelters of the homeless and the tattered tents of peasants and poor travelers.

Their joyous but simple music and the tap-dancing of the beggars awakened about a dozen children sleeping in the shacks, who, along with their parents, eagerly joined the parade. When the crowd had come to the last of the simple dwellings, Isaac cried, "Look there! An infant wrapped in swaddling clothes."

It was the smallest and most primitive of all the lean-tos, but a strange glow seemed to surround the little family inside: a caring father, a loving mother and the tiniest of infants.

Led by the three rough shepherds, the crowd of outcasts, beggars and aliens joyfully gathered before the shabby shelter of the young couple. The shepherd Isaac, acting as master of ceremonies, nodded to Jacob, who solemnly came forward with the dignity of a priest and placed a small white lamb at the lap of the infant's mother. Then he stepped back and made a deep bow. Never in all his life had Jacob the shepherd felt such dignity.

THE ADORATION OF THE POOR

Next, to the heart-pounding music of the drum and harp, the clapping hands and stomping feet of the crowd, and her own jingling tambourine, Mary the prostitute began to dance. She danced with more passion, grace and love before the infant than she had ever danced before anyone in her life.

Next, Isaac presented the two traveling Samaritans, who performed magic tricks for the child, fascinating all the children gathered around. When they were finished, the dirty, ragged children and lame beggars gathered in a circle and danced and sang.

Then, Isaac asked them all to be seated on the ground. When all were quiet, Samuel, with angel-like skill and great devotion, began to play his harp and to sing the only songs he knew: sweet songs of love and heartbreak, fascination and desire. The winter night held its breath in profound silence as all of heaven was awed by the music of the poor ascending from the little town of Bethlehem, as history itself stopped and started over again.

FROM THE ADORING SHEPHERDS TO ANGRY CROWDS

The infant's parents, Joseph and Mary, took the child and returned to their home village of Nazareth. There Jesus grew to manhood and followed his father's trade.

Now thirty years after his birth in Bethlehem, he had returned from his forty days in the desert and announced in his hometown synagogue the mission God had given him. So fiercely did his fellow villagers' reject his bold announcement that they attempted to kill him.

CHAPTER FOUR

JESUS' NEW BEGINNING AT CAPERNAUM

After Jesus' mysterious rescue from the angry mob, a familiar voice spoke to him, "Jesus, shake Nazareth's dust off your feet. No one can convert his own family or town. Their hearts are made of stone just now. It's a shame — but your destiny is elsewhere anyway."

"Gabriel, I hear your voice, but I do not see you," said Jesus, looking around. "Even if you're not here in your usual form, I want to thank you for coming to my assistance back there in Nazareth when my townsfolk wanted to throw me over the cliff. My angel,[1] you are a true guardian spirit. I've heard the ancients say that God has given each blade of grass a guardian angel. I don't know if that's really true, but I am sure that I've been given one."

"Yes, you have, and seen or not, I am God's presence abiding with you. It makes no difference how I appear. Sometimes I take on a bodily form when I have a message, but more often I'm only that small voice in your heart which guides you or challenges you."

"When I see no one, how can I know if the voice I hear is truly God's? How do I tell it from all the other voices that crowd my heart?"

"If the voice you hear calls you to go beyond the law in serving others, to love instead of hate, to pardon rather than punish, then you can trust that God is speaking. Sometimes I speak with only a fleeting, half-finished thought. But even when you are given an entire inspiration in a lightning flash, you can act with confidence, Jesus, if the voice you hear calls you to take great risks for others and for love."

"Gabriel, I took such a risk back there in Nazareth, but no one wanted to hear what I had to say. If I am not to speak to those whose blood I share, those with whom I've grown up, where shall I go? Who has ears for such news?" Jesus asked.

"The news is something new. Go to Capernaum, Jesus, cosmopolitan crossroad city by the sea.[2] Those living where trade routes crisscross may have more open ears."

So with that Jesus turned and looked back at Nazareth. He drew a deep breath and bid farewell forever to the village of his youth and childhood, feeling free of all ties to the past, with a look toward the future. He was forever now to be a gypsy ballad singer without a home.

Jesus arrived full of the Spirit at Capernaum, joining a crowd pushing through its walled gates to pass through the tollbooths of the tax collectors. To those standing in line and gathered at the gate, Jesus began to proclaim his message:

"No more waiting! For God's time, the kingdom, is at hand.
   Don't look for it tomorrow, the promised time is here.
Rejoice! Repent, and believe in my good news.[3]
   This is the moment of liberation."

As Jesus spoke, some of his listeners commented among themselves. A fisherman with his predawn catch asked, "Isn't that the message of John the Baptizer?" Next to him, a tenant farmer with a bag of wheat to sell replied, "The call to repent surely is John's, but this man says that we're not to prepare for the Messiah's coming, that it's right here at our feet!" Others laughed, "He's had too much sun. After all, has anything changed in our lives, any of the grinding oppression or backbreaking labor? Whatever it is that's coming is still to come."

The Toll Takers' Song[4]

In the tollbooth nearby sat four tax collectors, who sang:
"It's a dirty little job we've got, but someone's got to do it;
   poor Caesar's cash flow is low — poor Caesar's in a pinch.

"Step up, all of you who are waiting to pass through the gate;
   don't lag behind, and pay your tax toll:

one penny from a blind beggar's cap, a tax on charity.
Next: two pennies, pilgrim, wear and tear on Caesar's road;
   next: three pennies for peasant farmer Simon's corn;
   next: twenty pennies on the innkeeper's jug of wine.
What's this, a hidden terrorist's sword? No tax, friend,
   but grease the palm to seal the lips; forty pennies, please.
For poor Caesar's cash flow is low — poor Caesar's in a pinch."

"Next: one denarius for the fisherman's morning catch;
   next: two denarii for a night's work by the whore.
Next: three denarii for this pot of scribe's ink;
   next: five denarii on the priest's choice meat."

"It's a pleasure to welcome to our toll place
   merchants from the East riding on their camels
   with Persian rugs and sacks of fine silk.
Look at this, a jar of pure alabaster;
   for this a luxury tax of ten denarii is fair.
Tell us, merchant, whoever could afford such a priceless jar?

"Ah, the whore of Bethany, you say?
   And ten denarii is too much for her to pay?
You moan that she's a poor working woman.
   Weep not, old merchant, there's no need for pity.
Just up your price and don't fret;
   she can make it back easily in less than a day.
Then we'll tax her for giving pleasure,
   and twice we'll collect to double our pay.
Tax collecting's a thankless job, but who else will do it?

"We toll takers are willing to take on this work
   that no one else would ever do.
We're no one's friends, lepers of a sort,
   but someone's got to do this kind of work.
Caesar needs aqueducts, a coliseum or two,
   and poor Caesar's highways need repair.
There's order to keep and wars to wage,
   and crowds to feed with bread and circuses.

"Now let's tally up: one coin for Caesar,
   one coin for us; one for Caesar and two for us.
Ah, it's a dirty business, true, but a good one
   at the end of the day, once the counting's through."

Jesus smiled at the song of the toll takers. He admired their craftiness, and he also appreciated their feelings at being rejected by others. He knew most of them could find no other kind of work, having lost their land because of debts and taxes. They saw him watching them and offered him a bite to eat — which he quickly accepted, scoffing at the displeasure of the crowd.

JESUS OF CAPERNAUM PROCLAIMS THE GOOD NEWS

Jesus stood all the rest of that day in the marketplace and announced his news of liberation. Many paused to hear him say that God's time had come. Some listened with ears itchy for the new, but then found the news too good to be true. They demanded proof, some sign that life had indeed changed for the better if God's kingdom had actually come. When none was shown, they wandered off to watch a juggler or the Syrian magician's show. That night Jesus lay down in a relative's home, tired, disappointed, his heart empty of hope.

All Capernaum was still fast asleep when, before the dawn, Jesus awoke, unable to return to sleep. He tossed and turned, pricked by thorny doubts. Had it been a dream — his baptism — when he was drowned in the Sea of Love and was anointed as a prophet on the sunrise beach? Did he only dream that he heard the Voice say, "You are my Beloved," for not one person had yet believed his good news. Unable to sleep, he climbed a mountain to pray and looked directly down into an inland lake. He knelt and cried out to God a plaintive psalm:

"'O God, come to my assistance!
O God, make haste to help me. [5]
You I sought, O God, and you answered me;
   you delivered me from all my fears.
Look to God, that you may be filled with joy,
   that your face may not be covered with shame.
This poor man cried, and God heard,
   and God came to his assistance.'"

Then Gabriel appeared at his side and began to pray with him the next lines of that psalm:

"'The angel of God is encamped with those
   who are in awe of God, and rescues them.
Taste and see how good God is.'

"See, Jesus, and taste just how good God is. God hears the prayers of the just, and you are a just man."

"O Gabriel, my guardian spirit, the people here may have ears for the new, but they do not hear my new good news. If I am God's messenger, what am I to do to open their ears to the message? When I lay down last night, I felt so alone."

"Being a bringer of God's message, Jesus, can indeed often be lonely, and not everyone will have ears to hear what you have to say."

"I know, Gabriel. I've felt the frustration of not really being able to reach anyone. Like the coals on Isaiah's lips, I've felt fire in the words I've preached, but those words haven't reached deep enough to rouse the people. What more can I do?"

"Jesus, perhaps if your words are to rouse people, they should say of you what they said of Ezekiel, 'Is not this the one who is forever spinning parables?' "

"Tell parables? Jordan John never told parables. His message was short and simple, 'Repent, the kingdom of God is coming.'"

"Yes, I am aware of that, Jesus. John was an ascetic both in his diet and his preaching. But there is a difference between inviting others to the feast and actually serving them a fatted calf. You are not John, nor are you any longer a disciple of John. Be yourself. Your message may echo his, but there is a major difference: the kingdom isn't coming — it's here! It is *you*, Jesus!"

"I may not be John, but I'm not a storyteller either. I don't even know any stories. I know how to work with wood and stone, but words are something else."

"You could be like Ezekiel, who let God put parables on his tongue.[6] Trust that God will provide the stories if you provide the storyteller!"

The stirring of the wind was the only sound on the mountain. Alone again, Jesus sank deep in thought about Ezekiel. He thought about the hunger and the suffering of the people and the urgency of the message he had been given. The words about God providing the stories echoed in Jesus' heart as he sat fingering the fringe ends of his beard. Slowly he curled and uncurled the ends of the hairs of his beard as he reflected on this answer to his prayer. Then he prayed aloud again, this time with tears running down his face:

"O God, bless my lips and my tongue
　　and heighten your gift of speech in me.
Give me a tongue aflame with passion
　　so my words can set hearts afire.
Give me a tongue to speak of hope and justice,

free of bitter anger toward those who oppress others
yet honeyed with compassion for those who are oppressed."

He turned his face to the night sky and cried out like a thirsting man:
"May my lips be moist with your tenderness, Holy One,
toward all who are rejected and made outcast.
May my tongue be Spirit-torched
to inspire others to greatness.
Salt my tongue, O God, with your wisdom
and make it into a two-edged sword. Amen."

Again Jesus walked along in silence as these thoughts like seeds took root in his heart. Then as dawn lit the wick of the sun still beneath the horizon, a faint orange river of light flowed along the horizon. With a new day dawning in Capernaum, Jesus turned toward the city, still silent in the half darkness. "God will provide the stories," he said, "if you provide the storyteller." And he strode confidently back toward the city and its marketplace, full of a waiting harvest.

STORIES BY THE SEA

Jesus began preaching with parables and with renewed passion, and in a few days he gained a considerable following. The gossip of the villages was all about him now, and hearing he was speaking near Capernaum, a large group of people eventually found him near the lake and urged him to explain his message to them.

Since the crowd was great and people were pushing to get closer, he was almost forced into the water. So he climbed into the boat of one of the fishermen who had become a frequent listener of Jesus' sermons — Simon by name — and had him pull out a short distance. Seated in the fishing boat as it bobbed up and down with the waves, the crowd sat on the shore in silence waiting for him to speak. The only sound was the waves rolling in to the shore. That sound reminded Jesus of the Sea in the center of his heart, where during his desert baptism he had drowned in Love. He sat a long time in silence, awash in that divine Sea, tasting again the love of God he had experienced. Then he whispered a brief prayer:

"O God, make my peasant's tongue into your lover's tool;
play upon it with your word and your stories
and use me as your messenger and holy fool."

He began to teach them that the long-awaited kingdom was now at hand. He spoke as he always spoke from this day on. His tongue indeed became a tool in God's creative hand. To the poor who sat in the perpetual night of oppression his words signaled, like a torch in the night, the arrival of hope. As a flaming brand is used to set ablaze a bonfire, the power of his words lit bonfires in the hearts of the many who previously had only known the bitter cold of poverty and never-ending indebtedness. It is no wonder that from that day on, crowds by the hundreds came to hear him speak.

His message possessed the power to leap over the heads of the multitudes and find a home in many a heart since it was truly good news to those who lived in the midst of nothing but bad news. Unlike the others who drew large crowds of peasant people, Jesus' words never had a serpent's bite. The poor and oppressed of Galilee had recently flocked to hear the fiery rebel Zealot leaders. These moved the masses by venomous words of hate and rebellion toward the occupying Romans, the temple elite and the rich landowners. Their bitter message tasted sweet to the oppressed because it gave voice to the anger and lust for violence ready to erupt in their hearts.

Jesus, however, spoke not of hate but of love. He spoke of God's constant and unconditional love for those who had sinned or drifted from faithful religious practice, but mostly he called for "right judgment, mercy and faith." His words incarnated God's compassion and were as sweet and soothing as cool water placed on a burned hand or salve poured on a wound. With words of love he spoke enthusiastically of a whole new kingdom, a new time that belonged to God. And more importantly, he carried the message, in his own person, in his own heart and soul and spirit, of himself as a messenger of a new way of living.

"When I say that God's time has arrived," he would say, "and that we should rejoice and dance to celebrate our joy, you ask: 'What is this age of God to be like?' My answer is this. It is like the parable of Ezekiel which you've known since childhood, the story of how God lit a forest fire in Israel. God said, 'See! I am lighting a fire in you that shall devour all trees, not only the old dry tinder but the green as well. The blazing fire shall not be quenched but shall spread quickly from the south to the north. Every face shall be scorched by it, and everyone will know that God has enkindled it. None shall be able to put out such a fire.' "[7]

As Jesus spoke, each word glowed with an intense inner fire. They were ablaze as if he, not Ezekiel, had been given that primal parable. It was almost like sparks were flying in the wind over the crowd and the people were stubble in a wheat field.

"Each of us knows that a fire has a life of its own. How much more with the forest fire of God's kingdom. No human has set this blaze and so nothing human can quench its flames. Once lighted, God's fire has a divine life, and no one, neither legions of soldiers nor legions of priests, can put out such a forest fire. God has sent me to light that fire, and with great passion do I wish to see it enkindled."

To those who longed for a revolution, his words ignited a bonfire of revolutionary dreams. To those with possessions and status, they inflamed deep fears since he spoke not only of the old and dry as being consumed but also the green. No one, however, failed to see that the kingdom meant the end of what was and had been. A vision of what was to be was seeded in the imagination of each listener.

"God's fire shall be fueled by boundless love, by deeds of kindness and forgiveness. But neither shall it respect those who stand in its way — they too shall be consumed by its flames. The kingdom of God," Jesus sang out, "is like one of you who sowed seeds and from his field reaped a harvest of a hundredfold. The time of God is harvest time, when the good shall rejoice to be in God's abundant barns and the evil shall burn away like chaff, like fuel for a great fire."

Jesus' eyes, like swallows, darted from the eyes of one person to another in the crowd. Though they but briefly touched down before flying on to another pair of eyes, each fleeting look left a personal impact.

Then, as he spoke to larger and larger crowds, he saw that the scribes and Pharisees, as was their custom, had taken special places in the front, even here by the lakeside.

"To what shall I compare the time of God,
    this kingdom within that has nothing to do with space or place?
The reign of God is at hand; it's within your very sight.
    Like these waves, it's slapping up against the shores of today.
But what, you ask, can be said about this age of God?"

Jesus was quiet for just a moment, and then, with a surge of merriment, he launched into a story.

"It's like the day when God
    came a'sailing across the Sea of Galilee.
Mightier than the whale that swallowed old Jonah,
    twice again as big as old Noah's ark was God's great boat,
    with two large red sails, full to bursting with the wind.

"At such a sight, crowds gathered along the shore.
    As it drew near, folks could see the crew of God's big boat:
God's sailor crew had no angels busy at work, but big, fat rats

lowered the sails and dropped anchor by the shore.
Then ten of the rats stretched a golden gangplank to the shore.

"Down that glittering gangplank came God, the ship's captain,
    a' dancing and singing, 'All aboard, it's off to sea we go;
    no more worry, no more woe, it's off to sea we go.'
Then God spun around and danced back up the gangplank;
    whirling around again, God sang out in delight,
'Ho, ho, there's room for all, you know;
    so climb aboard, you won't be bored or want to go ashore!'

"With joy, folks eagerly pushed and shoved to get on board,
    the pious and prayerful, the good and decent, in the lead.
Standing at the gangplank collecting every fare, God sang out:
'No hurry, take your time, there's room for all;
    just have your hearts ready as you come aboard.'
One rich merchant asked, 'A round-trip ticket, if you please!'
    God only laughed and sang out, 'Sorry, it's all one-way.
You can't come back to where you were!'

"Hearing that good news, up the wide, golden gangplank
    they came: ten lepers wobbling on crutches,
    a dozen red-lipped prostitutes, five pickpockets,
    seven desperados, nine elderly village widows,
    twenty hungry, ragged orphans, six blind beggars,
    four ugly terrorists, a couple possessed by demons,
    three deaf donkeys, two stray dogs
    and a three-legged cat to lead the way,
    all happy for the chance to start life over.

"The crew of rats busily ushered the passengers to special seats:
    'Women and children, whores and lepers to the stern;
    step to the back of the boat — your seats are there!
The good and the pious, the prayerful and the Pharisees to the bow,
    to the front seats with soft cushions and a better view.'

"But God shouted, 'Oh, no! No separate seating!
    It's all first class, you know!
Now, all those in the bow, go to the stern,
    and all you in the stern, go now to the bow.'

"Chaos and confusion rocked the boat as lepers climbed over scribes,
    and beggars and the pious folk changed seats —
    all to the distress of the crew,

and the delight of God.

"Everyone finally seated, God leaped to the bow of the boat
and sang out loud and clear:
'All ashore who want to go; last call to go ashore.
 It's time to set off for new horizons.
So hoist the anchor and raise the sails,
 for it's off to sea we go!'

"Now, all those privileged passengers reseated in the stern
jumped up and scampered down the gangplank,
demanding back their hearts, to no avail.
The crew of wide-eyed rats, seeing who God had left on board,
quickly jumped ship and swam ashore.
There, they and the others shook their heads and wagged their tongues
about God's poor ship of fools.

"But old Captain God only laughed and whistled,
and from out of nowhere a great Zephyr Wind blew,
billowing the limp, red sails into a bulging bosom,
sending God's boat soaring off, like a flying fish,
to the center of the Sea of Galilee.

"Instantly a great rainbow arched from shore to shore;
and looking on it with love, God grinned like a sunrise
and reached over the side of the boat.
Down, down, down, God's long arm reached deep down,
all the way to the bottom of the sea.
Then with a mighty jerk, God pulled the plug,
and the whole Sea of Galilee became a giant whirling pool,
taking everything down the drain,
everything you could see,
even God's big boat, with all passengers on board.
All were lost with God."

Jesus laughed again and so did his listeners, more puzzled than
enlightened. He said, "This is the kingdom — and it is not coming, it is
here!"

The crowds were stunned at such an image of the kingdom. They
began to murmur, bewildered at such a teaching, their eyes filled with
questions. It was not bewilderment but anger that consumed the scribes
and priests, however, since they knew who the rats in his parable were.

As the crowds departed, Jesus said to Simon, "I've used your boat for God's message; now, Simon, let me return the favor.⁸ Put out into the lake and let's go fishing."

Simon replied, "Jesus, we've fished all night and caught nothing! But as you wish, so let it be done." Then turning to his brother and friends, he said, "Mates, push off into the deep and lower the nets." When they did, their nets so bulged that they had to call to Jonah's boat to come and help. Both boats were almost sinking, so great was the number of fish they had caught. At this, Simon fell and clutched Jesus' knees. "Leave me, Master, I am a sinner, and sinners are not graced by miracles."

"Stand up, Simon, son of Zebedee! God's miracles are bread for all, just and unjust. God hears sinners as well as saints."

Simon remained on his knees looking up at him. "Jesus, so great a catch of fish is truly a marvel, but more marvelous still are the words you speak." Then he blurted out the feelings that had grown in his heart. "I have listened to your message since you've returned from the desert, and it has turned my life upside down. As you used my fishing boat today, I saw how you lowered your net into the crowd. I was caught up in the web of your words, inspired to be a part of this new kingdom of God that has come. Never have I heard words like yours before."

"I can say the same," spoke up the fisherman John. "I felt as if I were a stack of dry straw into which a flaming torch had been thrown. As you spoke, my heart became ablaze with an overwhelming love of God. I can no longer be satisfied to be just a fisherman."

Simon's brother, Andrew, and then John's brother, James, echoed the other two. James said, "Jesus, I too was caught up by your words. I was held spellbound by the way you spoke with power and authority, by the sheer force of your words."

Jesus looked around fondly at this circle of rough working men, poor Peter now in tears, still kneeling at his feet.

Lifting Simon to his feet, Jesus looked at him with great affection, "Come, Simon, and follow me. You also, Andrew, James and John. Come and follow me, and I shall make you fishers of people! Not fish but human beings, families, cities and nations!"

They immediately set out together, leaving their boats — and everything — to become his followers.⁹

THE PARENTS' SONG OF THE CHOSEN DISCIPLES

As the four walked away with Jesus, Zebedee, the father of Simon and Andrew, and old Jonah, the father of James and John, watched them depart. Leaning against his beached boat, Zebedee shook his head and began to sing a dirge:[10]

"Woe and misery, poor Jonah, woe are we!
Our sons, our only social security for when we're old and bent —
   look, there, down the beach goes our golden years.
Alas, our welfare's been reduced to footprints in the sand.

"Look, Jonah, old partner and friend,
   we're left with only hired hands!
Here today, gone tomorrow!
   No sons to carry on the family fishing business.
What will become of us, beached by their insane mutiny?

"And recall God's law, the ancient ways sung by Sirach:[11]
'My son, take care of your father when he's old,
   grieve him not as long as he lives.
Kindness to a father will not be forgotten;
   like the sun, it will melt away your sins.'

"The village madman has led our sons
   to cast aside, 'Honor your father and mother.'
Look, Jonah, look: our golden tomorrows,
   like the setting sun, sinking into the sea,
   abandoning us — beaching us — here, high and dry."

Old gray-haired Jonah, holding his head in his hands, started to moan:
"Our sons, our bedside care in our old age,
   our crutches and canes, have run away!
Yes, woe are we, Zebedee, 'tis no enemy from afar,
   who's committed this shameful sin, this dreadful deed,
   it's a brother Israelite who's scuttled us.
As all the family's been saying, now I see: he's crazy![12]

"Yes, he's mad! His insane tale of God's big boat,
   it must have been a joke!
Blest be the Holy One, God doesn't have a boat.
   And those rats, what was that all about? I failed to see.
Joseph and Mary's son is mad — mad, I say,
   adrift in life with a leaky boat.

"And now our sons have caught the mad fever too.
   Did not God say through the prophet Sirach:
'Even if your father's mind fails,
   be considerate and gentle with him.'
It's not we fathers but our sons whose minds have failed!

Our poor boys — whatever will they do
  when they are old and bent?
Who will be their crutches and their daily bread?"

Jonah then placed an affectionate arm around Zebedee's shoulder and the two fathers tried to comfort each other.

CHAPTER FIVE

THE SPIRIT WIND

As they walked to Capernaum, Jesus led the way, followed by Simon and his brother Andrew, John and his brother James. Simon, filled with enthusiasm, said to Jesus, "Master — if I may call you that — how is it that you've acquired such powers of speech? Did you learn it from Jordan John?"

"Why, Simon," asked Jesus, "do you wish to call me *Master*? I am no priest or scribe who demands that his disciples address him with titles of honor."[1]

"What else can I call you?" answered Simon. "I feel a need to use some expression of respect, for you are unlike anyone I have ever known. You speak with more authority than do the scribes, with greater wisdom than those rabbinical teachers whom their students address as Rabbi!"

"Regardless of what you call me, Simon, I am opposed to the exaggerated respect the scribes demand of their students. What or whom does it serve to maintain those marks of honor? Those scribes who now are teachers once sat at the feet of scholar scribes who taught them and who lorded it over them. I have lived a simple life at Nazareth as a village craftsman. I have never been a student of any master, other than Jordan John — and the greatest of all teachers, the Spirit Wind. If you wish to follow me and be my companions, there can be no bowing and scraping as there is with the scribes. Each of us must use his gifts to serve the rest. We must be as a family."

"I understand. I called you Master because of your words and your ways. The parable you told in my boat about God's Big Boat was...well, it was inspired."

"True, Simon, it was inspired!" Jesus said as he placed his arm affectionately around Simon's shoulder. "You might say that the tale wagged the dog. The story was created by the Breath of God, shaped as a potter forms a bowl, by the fingers of the Wind."

"The tale wagged the dog, Master?"

"You might say I was possessed by God in telling the boat story, carried off by the Holy Wind. It was not the first time. One day in the desert, shortly after my baptism by John, I awoke upon a shore. Just as Adam came to life in the Garden of Eden, I awoke to a breath flowing into my mouth. It was God's breath, I had no doubt, for it seared my lungs and heart. It was fierce, fiery hot as the fingers of the desert sun."

"Master, I am a simple man, I do not understand."

"Comrades, it was no gentle spring breeze, this Holy Wind that filled more than my lungs. I felt its desert heat upon me again as I stood up to speak in Nazareth's synagogue. The Spirit Wind, not I, chose Isaiah's prophecy. Again today, it was the same Wind, and not I, who spun the story of God's Boat. That parable was a loaf of bread whose leaven is Isaiah's words, 'The Spirit of God has anointed me to bring glad tidings to the poor.' That parable loaf was baked by the Spirit's fire in the oven of my heart."

"The poor among the crowd," said John, "the outcasts, the sinners, peasant farmers, those without power or prestige, heard your story as good news."

"Yes, but not the Pharisees, I fear," added his brother, James.

"Master," asked Simon, "you speak great wisdom to us, and your stories are full of hope, even when they challenge us. Would you please explain the parable? It was wonderful, but what did you want us to learn from it?"

"Chew on it, Simon," said Jesus, "like a piece of hard bread.[2] I'm glad you liked the parable, and I'm grateful that you've all joined me. It's difficult to proclaim the message if you are alone; it's like an archer shooting arrows at a distant target on a moonless night. As my companions you'll help me take aim and see in many ways."

"Master, and I will call you that if you are not offended," replied

James, "your words today hit the center of the target and the center of my heart as well. It's a marvel how you've changed so since returning from the desert."

"James," said Jesus, slapping his own chest, "you've reached my heart with a direct hit just as you did when you agreed to be my companion! And, yes, I have changed. It seems as if all those past years in Nazareth I was a fruit tree covered with buds that never blossomed. My tree, green with life, ached for the buds to open. Now, blessed be God, as if overnight, the hot winds of spring finally have come, and I have begun to blossom."

"More than beginning to bloom, you are covered with beautiful blossoms," said John, "and I feel like a bee drawn by the blossom's delicious nectar. Soon, there will be more bees drawn to you, of this I am sure."[3]

"Perhaps, John, but enough talk of flowers and bees. I feel the Wind is about to blow us in a new direction."

THE HEALING OF THE LEPER

By now they had approached the outskirts of Capernaum, where they came upon a pathetic little shanty town of lepers. As they did, one of the lepers came running toward them, crying, "Jesus, I've heard of you even here in this wretched community of outcasts. They say you are full of compassion and of the healing Spirit. I know that if you wish you can make me clean."

The disciples drew back in horror as Andrew shouted, "Leper, keep your distance! You know the law. How dare you come so close?"

But the leper kept approaching. "The Wind, sir, the Wind drives me to break the law and to draw near to this stranger whom I feel sure is no stranger to God."

"Come closer, comrade," said Jesus. "The same Wind that rustled you from your shack to us, has blown us in your direction."

"Please, Jesus, if you wish it, you can make me clean."

"I do wish to make you clean," Jesus responded as he reached out to touch the leper.

"Don't break the law, Master," shouted Simon, "or you — by touching him — will also become unclean."

"I will to heal him, Simon," Jesus answered in a strong voice. "I will to break the law so as to break it open. Only when this law is broken can love escape to heal this man." Then Jesus tenderly placed his hand on the leper's scabby skinned arm and drew the leper close, embracing him with both arms. "Come, join us, friend, and live in our embrace. Leave behind being an outcast. Cast your lot with us as a new neighbor and brother. If you follow me, you will be family to us all."

"Jesus, I am a leper, I cannot join you and the others," he replied sadly, "even if I long to remain in your embrace."

"Your sickness is not the leprosy that leads to death,"[4] Jesus replied with his arm still around the man's shoulders. "The law is overly anxious. It makes any affliction of the skin a reason to make one unclean — and so a feared outcast. But, I say you are clean, and I heal your sickness of being an outcast.[5] God, who is good, will in time heal the sores that cover your face and body." And now the little family of Jesus numbered five.

THE LEPER AT THE CAPERNAUM GATE

Then as Jesus led the five disciples through Capernaum's city gates, they passed the toll booth. Jesus said abruptly to the tax men, "Nothing to declare that Caesar taxes!" To the chief collector he added, "Know that it is not you, but I, who am the real toll taker."

Matthew, the chief, looked up from his table at the customs station and laughed loudly. "Very clever, my friend, to turn the tables. Because I like you I will let you and your companions pass. But, pray tell, stranger, what tax would the likes of you collect from me?"

Jesus' eyes danced with glee. "Because I like you too I ask no toll of a mere ten percent! I ask for all your purse and more, Matthew. Hand over your whole heart and come and follow me."

Never had anyone asked Matthew for his heart. He could remember women who had asked him for love, or his fellow toll takers who had asked him for friendship, but this was different. As a moth is drawn into the dance of danger by the flame of a lamp, so Matthew knew he was being drawn into a fire so great as to consume him and all he held of value.

He looked into the face of Jesus.[6] It was as if he were gazing into a mirror. He saw himself as an adventurer instead of a coin-counting tax collector. He realized that the promise of the greatest of adventures lay in just such a dangerous dancing flight among the flames. These thoughts raced more rapidly through his mind than the quickly calculated mathematical figures he was used to.

To the surprise of the other tax collectors and the shock of the five disciples, Matthew stood up from his table. "I give you my heart — let me be one of your followers." With that he turned to his companions with a great laugh. "Come everyone," Matthew exclaimed, "we must celebrate this good fortune! Let us feast at my home tonight. You all know where I live." And he took his place next to Jesus among the companions.

As Jesus walked ahead talking with Matthew, his arm around the toll taker's shoulder, Simon spoke softly to Andrew, "Brother, another leper has joined us. First, the one with scabby skin, now this tax collector, the scum of our society, a traitor who's sunk so low as to be a scab worker for the enemy. He and his friends mingle with gentiles. Daily they rub shoulders with the impure, those who live outside the law, sinners, untouchables. Look at us, Andrew — what would our father say? And if we eat with these sinners, are we not dirty and impure as well?[7]

"Oh, I ask you, brother, why the Master breaks the law. Why doesn't he, like others, just bend the law so none can see? A tiny twist here, a tiny turn there: why so boldly for one and all to see?"

And Andrew answered, "Brother Simon, perhaps it is that Wind of which he speaks that drives him to break the laws of Moses, not fearing to tamper with the old taboos. Alas, Simon, with that same Wind at our backs, I fear we'll sail over the edge. For in his lover's embrace, we too become unclean companions of sinners! But no turning back now, for I too feel that Holy Wind upon my back."

MATTHEW'S DINNER PARTY

At Matthew's house that night, the wine flowed, Matthew's very best vintage. His table sagged under the weight of roasted lamb and fattened calf, figs, dates and fruits of all kinds and wheat bread to be dipped into rich sauces. Matthew himself reclined at the head of the table with Jesus at his right, and a long line of sinners — tax collectors and defiled people of every kind — elbow to elbow on either side, with a disciple of Jesus squeezed in here and there.

Simon and his brother and the other three disciples had never eaten such a grand feast. For them it would have been a feast fit for paradise, if it didn't feel as if they were in hell. Not only was Matthew's house filled with outcast tax collectors, but with all sorts of nonreligious people: There were several prostitutes, a couple of divorced women known for their loose morals, a number of common thieves and several uncircumcised foreigners whom Matthew had befriended in his work as a tax collector for the Romans.

What made it especially difficult for Simon to reconcile was the fact that he sensed a profound holiness in Jesus — and in himself while in Jesus' presence — and now here he was eating and drinking with sinners who didn't observe the daily religious laws, with those who had not seen the inside of a synagogue for years. Inwardly all the disciples moaned as they shared the feast with Matthew's former associates. Jesus, on the other hand, seemed not to feel a shade of shame or even a tiny pinch of guilt.

His disciples watched him laughing and joking with everyone at the table and were amazed. Again and again, his wine cup was refilled as he devoured, with obvious delight, the foods of Matthew's unholy feast.

"Simon! Andrew!" came a call. Simon turned and saw a group of men standing outside looking into Matthew's house. Among them were some pious friends, several disciples of John the Baptist and some Pharisees. They cupped their hands for privacy and asked them, "Tell us, why does your Master eat with sinners?" One Pharisee, looking with obvious disgust at those crowded about Matthew's table, whispered, "Look! He's a drunkard!"

"And tell us," pleaded the disciples of John, keeping their voices low, "why Jesus, who is a disciple of John, drinks and feasts? John's call was to fast and do penance to prepare for the Coming. Why does Jesus not fast?"[8]

Simon shrugged his shoulders and looked at Andrew for help.

Jesus Speaks on Fasting

Above the loud table talk Jesus' voice rang out, "Simon and Andrew, invite your friends to come and join the feast. I heard their questions and know they may not wish to, but at least let them come closer and listen, for I have something to say to them." Quickly the whole party grew silent, listening.

Standing up, Jesus placed his hand on Matthew's shoulder. "There is a feast this day in paradise with rejoicing more jubilant than at this table. Heaven has more joy over Matthew's joining in the dream of God's kingdom than over the hundred pious who have measured their lives inch by inch according to the rule of the law." Jesus raised his cup high and proposed a toast:

"May we all get drunk on this rich new wine:
   the love, companionship and hope
   that joyfully announce today as God's time.
Sinners, outcasts and ex-lepers who share this feast,
   in the bread of the kingdom, you will be the yeast."

Everyone at the table cheered and emptied their cups with great delight. Jesus continued, speaking as well to the crowd that hung outside the door:

"My message is one that's born of Jordan John's: Repent,
   the changing of your heart is the gateway's handle
   to open the door of paradise that's before your eyes.
God's time has already arrived;

it is not to come in some faraway future.
Rejoice, for God's kingdom is here at this table!
   The union of heaven and earth is here in this wedding tent,
   and tell me, who but real fools fast at a wedding feast?

"Repent and fast we must, but in God's chosen way;
   I sing Isaiah's song anew: This is God's fast day.
'Is this the fast I desire: your head gray with ashes,
   your stomach empty, your body in itchy sackcloth? No!
The only fasting I wish of you is to feed the hungry,
   clothe the naked, care for the widow and orphan,
   be kind to the alien, liberate the oppressed.
Do justice to the poor, then your wounds will heal.' "9

After a pause he added, "Drink up, friends, to healing justice! Drink to the kingdom, God's holy time is here."

The crowd at the table stood cheering. Matthew embraced Jesus and kissed him on both cheeks. A goatskin drum began beating and the hands of guests, dripping with grease, began clapping. Jesus threw off his outer cloak and started dancing as he began to sing an old village nuptial song that everyone knew. His feet leapt as if dancing on the wind. Then he reached out and grabbed Matthew's hands, and the two whirled around, wildly dancing to the rhythms of the music, slapping their thighs and clapping their hands.

As the room swirled around him, Matthew felt what he had only dimly perceived the moment when Jesus had invited him to join his company. He now had become Matthew the Moth flitting in and out of the flame, and the flame was Jesus! As they danced together, he cared not if, as it is for the moth, death were the end of the dance. He was drawn to the man irresistibly.

The excited Matthew felt as if he were dancing a village wedding dance. At first it seemed to him that he was the bride and Jesus the groom. Then with the next turn Jesus danced with all the grace and seduction of a bride. As Matthew wrestled with this dual experience, Jesus shouted, "The flame is God, Matthew, have no fear. It's glory to die dancing!"

Soon all the guests had joined in. Even Simon, to his surprise, found himself dancing with sinners, and feeling no shame.

"I fear, Andrew," he said later, "that I've felt more than the Spirit at my back. I fear I've been gripped by the Spirit Wind as if by some madness. As I danced, I felt not a flicker of guilt nor shadow of shame."

A Frightened Jesus Retreats to Pray

Simon felt no guilt at all about the evening, but not so Jesus himself. As he left Matthew's feasting table that night, by the glow of a flickering lamp he saw his shadow loom large across the wall. Jesus realized how much he had enjoyed the crowd's applause, the acclaim of those once exiled but now welcomed home. He had taken pleasure in the admiration, the hero worship and love he had seen in the eyes of his disciples, especially the youthful John.

That night he slipped away from his small sleeping group and went up the mountain to pray. [10] As he climbed, he said to himself, "He has kept his promise, the one he made to me in the desert. He has returned again to barter for my soul."

The Sick Come to Jesus

It was not long before people were coming to Jesus for more than just to hear him speak of God's kingdom. The sick and lame, the infirm and blind, those possessed of evil spirits, all came to him. [11]

When those in need first gathered at his door, he told them, "I am not a physician. Look at these hands! They're a workman's hands, the hands of a stone mason, a carpenter who works with wood. These are not hands of a folk healer."

But young, bright John reminded him, "The people believe you are a prophet sent by God. And God gives prophets like Elijah more than visions; they're also given healing powers!"

"John, you know I have never claimed to be a prophet, but my heart does go out to those who suffer. I wish I had the power to lift from them the burden of their pain, but I am a messenger, not a physician."

But that did not satisfy John. "Did you not say in Nazareth when you proclaimed the words of Isaiah that you had come to give sight to the blind? Were you not sent to restore sight to the eyes as well as the heart and the soul?"

Realizing the truth in John's words, but puzzled at this emerging call to heal, Jesus again slipped away one night and went up the mountain where he loved to pray.

> "O God, come to my assistance,
>   O Lord, make haste to help me.
> My heart grows hot within me,
>   as embers glowing orange-red,

ready to leap upward in flame.
There is a burning desire within my soul,
    a longing to help those who suffer,
    but I am no healer!"

"Beloved of God," Gabriel said, appearing beside him, "your heart has ears, and they are divine ears when you feel the people's cries of pain. That is part of being one with God. When you are one with God, you suffer God's pain in seeing those you love suffer. You feel the pain of a sick society suffering injustice, as well as personal sicknesses. The depth of your compassion and prayer not only opens the ears of your heart but opens you to the power to heal.

"Hold out to me your laborer's hands,
    so stained by many years of hard toil.
I will consecrate them anew for you
    as holy hands to heal by heaven's own medicine."

Jesus held out his hand to Gabriel, who began covering his hands with kisses as moist as oil. Jesus felt a strange heat in his hands as Gabriel raised his face, full of affection, to sing a blessing:

"At birth, God gave to you but one mouth,
    one tongue as a gift with which to speak.
By this anointing, may each hand become a mouth
    to speak boldly with five-fingered tongues.
Three mouths in all with eleven fiery tongues
    has God now given you to heal a deaf world
    so it may better hear your good news.

"Jesus, speak now with more than lips,
    speak also with all your holy fingers.
Speak to them with both voice and hand,
    and cure all the sickness of the people.
The healing of body and mind will become
    the kingdom's sign for all to see.
Now you must let God's healing power
    flow freely from your newly anointed hands."

Jesus stood amazed as Gabriel lifted his hand toward the sun. His index finger glowed orange-red and burst into a flaming dagger. Holding open Jesus's hands, Gabriel lowered his raised hand and plunged his flaming finger through Jesus' palms. Jesus cried out, feeling all the agony of a red-hot spike being driven through both of his hands. In mystic agony he all but fainted, but within minutes the pain ebbed, and soon he sat on his heels and watched the now-faint holes in his palms slowly disappearing.

> "These pierced hands, Jesus, can now heal,
>   yet each time they touch the sick
> you will feel the pain of God's power
>   racing through them to heal the wounds.
> You will feel the sting of disease
>   stabbing back through these holy palms
> as you consume, like some starving beggar,
>   their sufferings as your very own.[12]

> "Healer Jesus, no sickness you cure
>   will simply vanish like the morning dew.
> As God's healer you're now a holy thief;
>   their purse of pain will always be yours to take.
> Know, Jesus, what's required on your part
>   when those sick of body and of heart
>   come to seek your holy healing powers.
> Let God's power move through your hands and heart."

And from that day onward Jesus went about, empowered to heal. Those upon whom he laid his hands were healed of their sicknesses, the lame, the blind, the deaf and those possessed by evil and impure spirits.

Jesus did not fear the pain of their illnesses, which was always sucked mysteriously into his soul. He was more afraid of the power of his own dark shadow to lead him astray. Keeping his heart firm and meek, he would send home all those he healed of various afflictions in peace and also with the stern warning: "Tell no one of this."

CHAPTER SIX

THE MYSTERY OF JESUS' IDENTITY

From that time on, Jesus took the sick and lame away from the crowds to heal them.

To those he healed of blindness, he would say, "See to it that you tell no one.[1] Go and give thanks to God." He also firmly told those whose sins were forgiven, and the lame or diseased he healed, that they were to speak of it to no one. As his reputation grew and the crowds who came to hear and see this wondrous person multiplied, so did his desire *not* to draw attention to himself.

Jesus told his little band of disciples that even they were not to speak of his miracles, which astonished them. "Master," asked John one day, "are these marvels not the signs to be worked by the Messiah? The prophet foretold that the Anointed One would give sight to the blind, make the lame walk and the deaf hear." The others voiced their agreement. Then a certain Simon from the city of Cyrene, a farmer who had recently begun to travel along with his disciples, asked Jesus bluntly, "If we are to help you spread the message, is not your being the Messiah at the heart of that good news?"

"Simon, you are a welcome addition to our family, but you are both right and wrong. I am the anointed one — it was a sunrise anointing I shall never forget. Yet that title *Messiah* is a mirage like we see in the desert. It's an illusion created not by the heat of the sun upon the sand but by the zealous needs of the crowds."

"The Messiah an illusion?"

"Yes, the people dream of a hero savior who will single-handedly drive the Romans into the sea and throw Herod from his luxurious throne. They lust for a god-hero who will turn the rich into beggars while they, the poor, can be like spectators in the coliseum cheering their champion on to victory.

"The kingdom, God's time, will never be completed by the coming of a single man, even a God man. Only when each and every one of you, each woman, man, widow and child, each poor tenant farmer and common laborer, does the work of God, will the kingdom come. Only when each of you takes responsibility not only for yourself but also takes constant care for the welfare of all, and so becomes a Messiah too, will the kingdom come.

"God's Messiah is not some lone savior, or a royal champion coming on the clouds, but a royal people appearing everywhere. Only a great priestly nation of anointed ones will change these times to God's time.

"Thus, I use with great care that dry-as-tinder term 'the kingdom of God,' for it is no kingdom composed of subjects and cities. Rather, it is a special quality of time that breaks in like a thief upon ordinary time. Wherever it appears, it fills any place with justice and peace, with nonviolence and joy — and most of all with love. God's time is above all a lover's time. For these reasons and for a personal one, I choose to stand in the shade, out of the glare of fame."

Then the Cyrenean asked, "Why, Master, do you prefer the shade? Only because it's cooler there?"

"No, Simon, because in the shade I have no shadow!"

None of the disciples understood this, but they were afraid to ask what he meant.

The Disciples Discuss Jesus

One day when Jesus was not with them, the disciples sat together and talked about why they had followed him.

"He is like a healing mirror for me," said Judas Iscariot, another newcomer to the band of disciples. "By the way he treats me, I see myself not as I or others are accustomed to, but as I long to be seen, as someone deeply loved and of great value."

"I know the feeling, Judas," replied Simon, brother of Andrew. "It's as if he sees me through God's eyes — without my failings and faults. And you all know I have a lot of faults! But how I love that man. I would follow him to the end of the sea."

"No more than I love him," added John. "I've never known anyone like him."

"I became his follower after hearing him speak one day," said Simon the Zealot. "His words reached out and seized me like a prisoner in chains, yet his passionate words have liberating power too. After he finished speaking that day, something stronger than me drove me to beg to become a disciple."

"What were those words, Simon, that had such power over you?" asked Andrew.

"I shall never forget them. He said, 'From the days of John the Baptist until now, the kingdom of God has suffered violence, and the violent are taking it by force. Whoever has ears should hear.' Brothers, my ears heard! Yes, they heard what they had longed to hear for years. Here at last was one who could lead the revolution to restore Israel. Each time the master speaks of the kingdom or God's time, I recall his words about the violent taking it by force. Any day now, I know he will announce an uprising in Israel."

"Simon, I'm not so sure about that," replied John. "Perhaps he meant violence not to others, but to what's evil in oneself. One thing we all know is that his words are as full of life as he is, and that he promises us an abundance of life."

Andrew now jumped into the discussion about the meaning of Jesus' words. "Truly, John, his words are full of *life*. That's the reason I became one of his disciples. Jesus has the power to take ordinary words that are thin as air and make them into flesh and blood!"[2]

The others looked puzzled as Andrew continued, "His parables, and his sayings like 'Do not be anxious about tomorrow' are transformed as if into living beings, who accompany you, continuing to speak to you for days, even weeks, after the Master has spoken them. Who knows, perhaps his words may outlive all of us! And it's true not just for us disciples but for many in the crowds who come to hear him. Many have told me how his words have gone home with them!"

Then one by one, they each talked about the fateful day they had first encountered Jesus and his almost magical power to attract them. A disciple named Nathaniel spoke of Jesus' mystic power to see beneath the surface, to see into the heart of things and people, as when Jesus had supposedly seen him "under the fig tree." "I'll never know how he managed that," said Nathaniel, "I felt sure I was alone." Again and again they mentioned his personal love for them and how he was for each a reflection of their true selves. A couple of them who had been disciples of Jordan John the Baptizer saw in him the Long-Awaited One of whom their former master had spoken.

The reasons they followed him seemed as many as there were disciples: the strength of his love which liberated them to love freely, the power of his presence, which seemed able to transform all he met; his sense of daring, which challenged their timid fears, and the sense of authority with which he spoke of his oneness with God. The discussion ended with the question that frequently arose among them: *Just who was Jesus?*

Jesus Sings of His Identity

So some time later, the disciples took Jesus aside from the crowds and asked him, "Tell us, Master, here in private where no one but we will hear, who are you?"

Jesus replied, "Listen to the crowds, they will say who I am. I am Jesus, son of Joseph, child of Mary. I am Jesus of Nazareth and now Jesus of Capernaum." Looking down at his calloused hands, he added, "Jesus the village craftsman, worker with stone and wood."

Simon quickly spoke up, "Master, we know all that. Please tell us who you really are."

Jesus sat down and gathered all his disciples about him. Then he began to sing to them:

"I am the vine, you are the branches.
　　I am the gate, you enter only through me.
I am the good shepherd, who abandons no one.
　　I am the way, come follow me.

"I am the vine press, you are the grapes.
　　I am the shofar, the new Israel's call to prayer.[3]
I am the serpent, whose bite heals the sick.
　　I am the doctor, a bitter medicine that cures.

"I am the cry of a lover's great ecstasy.
　　I am the bridegroom, large is my passion.
I am the bride: come quickly to my bed.
　　I am the honeymoon, never to end.

"I am the leaven, a small pinch will do.
　　I am the oven, you are the dough.

I am the bread, your daily manna.
I am the fish that enriches your meal.

"I am the wine that makes you drunk with dancing.
I am the goat, bearing the sins of all.[4]
I am the vinegar, to all who rule others.
I am the cup, the bread and the meal of the feast.

"I am lightning that splits the mighty cedar.
I am the raging flood, laundering the world.
I am the sea, far too deep to fathom.
I am the dark forest: enter and lose your way.

"I am the beginning of the way to God, the alpha.
I am the tip of the dog's tail, an omega end.
I am the sunrise and the sunset.
I am painful birthing and painful dying.

"I am blind Samson, pulling down the temple.
I am hobbling Jacob, hiding his limp.
I am Adam, naked in innocent delight.
I am Eve, fascinated by the serpent smile.

"I am the rapture on whose wings you can fly.
I am the eunuch who guards God's bed.[5]
I am the king who has no throne.
I am the slave who wears no chains.

"I am love and I am in love.
I am free and I am held bound.
I am mad,
for I AM."

As Jesus pronounced the Sacred Name, Judas Iscariot quickly covered his ears. Simon the fisherman, mindful of the law binding those who heard blasphemy, almost instinctively ritually ripped his tunic.[6] With enlarged eyes the others sat tongue-tied, stunned.

Jesus then asked, "And you, Simon, who do you think I am?"

Regaining his composure, the former fisherman boldly responded, "You are no murdered prophet of old raised from the dead, as the common folk say. You are the Long-Awaited One, the Messiah, the bridegroom at the feast of God's kingdom come."

Jesus raised his finger to his lips, "Blessed are you, Simon. But tell no one this secret of secrets. I solemnly order you to tell no one who I am! But let me tell you, Simon the fisherman of Galilee, who *you* are. You are

Simon the Rock. From this day forward you shall be Simon Peter, and on you my house will stand or stumble."

Simon blustered a moment, then blurted out, "Master, I am a sinner. I am not worthy."

Jesus answered him solemnly. "Simon the Rock, remember that fact and you'll never stumble. Now, let me ask you all: Who are you? Don't tell me you are the son of so and so, or from this tribe or that village. Who are you?"

JESUS CHALLENGES THE DISCIPLES

"We are sons of Abraham and Sarah, heirs to God's promise. We are God's chosen people," replied Simon Peter proudly.

"No! We are slaves of Caesar," shouted Simon the Zealot, "prisoners of our religion, ageless victims of oppression, permanent refugees, exiles and aliens even in our homeland! As members of a sinful race we were branded by God with an unredeemable curse when we were thrown out of paradise."

Squabbling broke out within their little group. Some sided with Simon the Zealot, others with Simon Peter.

"Silence, little ones," said Jesus. "Both Simons are correct. But you are more than any of those things, more than chosen or cursed, since to be chosen is also to be cursed. Consider well my question about who you really are. Do not answer me now.

"Take 'Who are you?' to bed with you tonight,
    sleep with her as with a forbidden lover.
Take her to work, soak her in your sweat;
    take her to your meals — make her your diet.
But most of all, elope with her into the desert,
    that solitary secret place within your hearts.

"Strip her naked of all your neediness and illusion
    to find the only answer that's true.
Be patient. Be gentle and fall in love
    with that haunting question: Who am I?"

Jesus paused to let them digest what he had said. Then he added, "The one with the right answer will not only be praised by me but gifted by God. But look at the sun, it's late. Come, it is time for us to be on the road again. Let us depart in peace — yet restless with that holy, haunting question."

THE CALL TO THE NEW DISCIPLES

Long before sunrise, Jesus felt God's Breath upon him as he laid curled in sleep. At first it was gentle, and so he drifted in and out of slumber. Then it came with greater force until he rose from his sleeping mat and left the house. The Wind drove him out of the town and up the mountain to pray. There he said his morning prayer:

"Hear, O Israel, the LORD is our God, the LORD alone.
You shall love the LORD your God with all your heart,
with all your soul, and with all your might. "[7]

Alone in his deserted place, he sought the same intimacy he had felt at the end of his forty days when he had been washed out to sea. Absorbed in prayer, he was startled when Gabriel appeared: "Jesus, tell me, are you praying because you have doubts about being the Anointed One?"

"Though you startled me, Gabriel, I'm glad you're here. And, yes, at times I doubt if what I say to them is truly the message of God inspired by the Wind-Spirit, or only the longings of my heart."

Gabriel began to sing to him:

"Inspired by the Wind, it was Isaiah's words you spoke,
in your village synagogue, fresh from the desert.
No need to await for the Anointed One, you said:
Good news to the poor, the nobodies, I will bring.
To prisoners, I've come to show the way to liberty,
to open wide the eyes of the blind to the light of day.

"Jesus, don't you see, for your mission to be fulfilled,
you must start with that last divine call.
In order to let the oppressed go free,
and proclaim liberty to all those held captive,
first you must give sight to those who are blind.
Your call is to open blind eyes of more than a few,
to open the eyes of all, both near and far,
as far as Jerusalem or even Rome, and beyond,
as near as the eyes of your family of disciples,
nearer still, Jesus: *to open your own eyes.*"

Jesus shook his head and groaned, "Gabriel, I feel as confused as Simon. How am I to open my eyes?"

"Peel off the scabs that have grown there since you were a little boy." Reaching over, Gabriel gently touched Jesus' eyes. "These are scabs of tradition left by family and neighbors. You call your little group of disciples your family. But if it's a family, there's something missing. Where are the women?"

Jesus reached up and touched his newly opened eyes and then began to stroke his beard as he plunged into deep thought. It was still the half darkness of early morning and the wind was the only sound on that deserted mountaintop as he prayed in silence.

"My scabs are the traditions, the customs of how we — and I — have seen women," Jesus spoke to the wind, his heart now pounding in excitement. He rose and continued. "I begin to see how blind I have been to their imprisonment. We treat women as inferior to men; they have no legal rights. We see them as dangerous to our piety, seducers to sin, and potential threats to a family's honor — and they are guarded as closely as prisoners until they're married."[8]

"The scabs are falling off, Jesus, and you see more now."

"I've been blind, Gabriel. Only now does this predawn prayer heal my eyes to see how the customs of our nation's tribal days have become prison walls that year by year grow taller and thicker."

"Does the vision," asked Gabriel, "apply to the message you've carried?"

"If I am to throw open the dungeon doors and release those held bound, then I must do what I can to liberate women. A family without women is merely a brotherhood. Yet, how can women join me and not be shamed in the process? As for my men companions, custom would expose them to shame if they traveled with women who were not their wives or daughters."

"There it is, Jesus," Gabriel shouted to him, "*shame*! But rejoice in your concerns about shame. For in shame is the answer to your doubts over whether you are truly the long-awaited Anointed One."

"I see," Jesus said slowly and painfully, "or I think I see. Is God asking me to wear shame and to be a shameful savior? A shameful savior...." This last phrase he swallowed with difficulty, as if it were a large, unchewed piece of goat meat. His face was twisted in pain.

The sun now had risen over the Sea of Galilee, amber laced with gray storm clouds billowing in the morning sky. The damp smell of rain was in the air. In the sea below Jesus could see fishermen dragging their boats to shore after their night of toil. Seeing them, he thought of his disciples and prayed:

> "Whatever can I say to them so they will see
> what I myself have found so difficult to see.
> No angel adviser do they have as do I
> to help them be true to God's new word."

Gabriel placed his arm around Jesus' shoulder as he picked up Jesus' simple prayer and raised it to a jubilant song:

"They have *you*, Jesus, who are much more than an angel;
   in your madness they trust, why else would they follow you?
In your good words they've found their hope renewed,
   this new teaching, in time, they'll also see as true,
   and their wives and daughters will agree with you.
Those loyal friends who follow you in this, as before, will be few.

"Now, Jesus, to help them see; tell an old story,
   a story you and they listened to but did not hear.
Tell how in Eden God made man and woman,
   created Adam and Eve as equal companions,
of the same flesh and same bone, with souls alike,
   saying, 'Now become one flesh, one body be.
First I made you one, then I made you two;
   now, by love, you two must become one again.' "

Jesus held up his hand in protest: "Was not God speaking of the *marriage* rather than the *equality* of men and women?" But Gabriel responded:

"Son of Mary, are you not the long-awaited Bridegroom?
   Is not God's time the time of the wedding feast?
In your new family, there will always be differences,
   but there should never be boundaries of inequality.
Male or female, slave or free, all one in you;
   gentile or Jew, all are to be one in you."9

"Gentile," gulped Jesus, "did you say *gentile*? My soul has already been stretched wider than the sea. Whatever do you mean, *gentile or Jew*?

"Perhaps I am rushing, Jesus, but the time is shorter than you think. For now, I agree, this time of morning prayer has pulled your soul beyond its seams. As you wrestle with this new message from God, recall your visitation in the desert by Adam and Eve. Today, new-Adam Jesus, you must look at women as equals, look at them as Adam looked at Eve. Recall as well those women who came to you in the desert, your ancient grandmothers, who came with gifts you now need to use."

Jesus walked back to his Family's encampment. But it was an altogether new day for the little circle of companions. That day Jesus did something new that caused dismay among his chosen disciples. He began to invite women as fully equal members, to become his disciples and to join his Family.

THE WOMEN DISCIPLES OF JESUS

Jesus went from town to town proclaiming the good news of the kingdom of God. Among his disciples were the twelve men who first accepted his invitation to become his companions, and also some men and women whom Jesus had cured of various infirmities and evil spirits. Among these were Mary Magdalene, whom he had cured of seven demons, Joanna, the wife of Chuza, who was the great King Herod's steward, Susanna, and other women. These provided for the disciples' needs out of their resources.[10]

One day, after leaving a town where Jesus had spoken, the disciples rested by the roadside. On this occasion the women were sitting apart from the men. "Susanna," Joanna said, "we know the Master healed many of us of our various infirmities. Of what affliction did he heal you?"

"I was a cripple before Jesus cured me," she responded, eyes full of gratitude. Then she began to sing:

"Crippled as a child, I limped about,
    forever lame, yet it was God's will.
Too weak to stand without a crutch,
    and as a poor peasant girl I had none.
My mother promised me one some day:
    a crutch, she'd said, 'if God sees fit.'

"I hobbled about the house till the day
    my parents arranged for me to stand,
    and I met the man who would be my crutch.[11]
As cook, servant, lover, soon a mother,
    I hobbled, but at least I'd left home.
Crippled as a child, I limped about,
    forever lame, yet it was God's will.

"But death came to my crutch as well as to my son;
    I dearly grieved, for he was kind to me.
Now I hobbled with no hope of support,
    I was widowed, alone in bed, alone in life.[12]

Then one day Jesus passed our way;
    he looked with love and said to me,
'You have limped in life, crippled,
    but no longer, for this *isn't* God's will.
Stand up, my dear sister!' he said to me —
    mind you, he called the likes of me 'sister' —
'Stand, for you need no crutch or cane;

come, sister, come and dance with me.'
Crippled since birth, I now limped no more
for Jesus came and *did* God's will."

Salome, another disciple, cried, "A healing miracle! How blest you are — as are all of us." Then each of the women disciples added to the tales of how they once had been held captive but were released from their prisons. They sang in gratitude for how Jesus had freed them from dungeons of desert dogmas demeaning women as property, how he had treated them as persons of honor.

MARY MAGDALENE'S SONG OF GOD'S GIFT

Then Mary, a shapely woman from the village of Magdala on the Sea of Galilee, began to speak. "The Master healed me as he did Susanna. I was crippled not because I lacked a man, but because I had too many of them! Jesus cured me, and some other women of my ancient profession, of leprosy."

At the mere mention of that dreaded disease, several of the women drew back in fear. "Don't be afraid, sisters, to touch my skin," Magdalene said, "for my leprosy was of the spirit, not of the body. My malady was being an outcast. Yes, I was 'unclean,' more untouchable than the tax collectors. Indeed, my sister prostitutes and I could sing with them: 'It's a dirty little job, but someone's got to do it.'"

Mary paused and sighed deeply. "Jesus liberated me from all that when he drove out of me seven — yes, sisters, seven — demons. The worst of them was named self-hate, whose seven tongues all sang the same song, day and night:

"'Your skin may be fair and your breasts full,
    but you are fully covered with evil and ugly sin.
All of your body, Mary of Magdala, is soiled;
    unclean, unclean are you.'"

"Oh, Mary," cried Susanna in compassion, for she had loved Mary like a sister from the moment she had joined the Family. The other women shook their heads in solidarity.

"Yes, possessed by that demon of self-loathing, it was not for pleasure that I gave my body to men. I saw myself as Magdala's privy. I sold myself to young boys who were curious to know what sex was all about. I gave myself to men who came covered with sweat, whose breath was heavy with garlic or with wine. I was the donkey of Magdala by the sea, a beast of burden and brief pleasure, mounted for a fleeting ride. And worst of all were the men who came not for pleasure, but to play out the cruelty of their anger toward all women. It was not just self-hatred but their hatred that I had to bear.

"Then one night, Jesus came to my door and handed me a simple bronze mirror, saying, 'Look, beautiful daughter of God, and see yourself as your God sees you. For you are not the privy but the prize of Magdala. Come now and follow me, and your great love will set you free.' "

The other women had never heard Mary's story before, and they began to weep at the sadness of the tale and the beauty of her liberation. Jesus' mother walked over, placing her arm around Mary. Her silent mother's embrace sealed the women disciples' shared moment of affirmation and grace.

"So that's how Jesus healed me of my possession and how I came to be favored as one of his disciples," Mary continued. "But I fear, sisters, that my tale has cast too somber a tone for us, and that it has painted too dark a picture of God's gift of sex. As one who knows more about sex than most, permit me to sing a brief song." And Mary began to dance as she sang:

"Sisters, aware of woman's poor and sad state,
    let us thank God and praise the Lord for creating sex.
For men are always ready for more of their favorite sport,
    hot blooded, never grown-stale-like-bread sex.
Yes, my sisters, thank God for creating sex.

"Aware, my friends, of our sad state as women,
    to be donkeys of burden would be our fate,
    if old God the ever wise had not created sex.
Thank God for not making men like other creatures,
    who only want to make love in mating season.
Think of our fate if sex were only once or twice a year.

"So, able to mate every day, men must keep us around;
    or else I fear they'd make us live in the barn.
For good reason God made every day mating season,
    or we'd be with the other beasts of burden who chomp on hay.
Believe me, sisters, I know what I'm talking about.

"But as great a gift as sex is, it's God's sex that's here to stay,
    for God's sex is more than to increase and multiply;
God's sex is a lusty pinch of paradise before we die.
    Yes, my sisters, thank God for creating sex."

The women laughed heartily at Mary's song, all but Mary the mother of James and Joseph. She curled her lip to her nose in disgust. Susanna asked, "Mary, we all know that sex is one of men's favorite pastimes, but what's this *God's sex* that you sang about?"

"It's a marriage not of husband and wife but of love and sex," replied Mary Magdalene. "Fortunate and blessed are those wives whose husbands truly love them, especially since parents select who it is we shall marry and not we ourselves! Families' choices, sad to say, are more about counting sheep and goats, cows and plots of land than counting how much love is in the heart. Blessed by God are those wives lucky enough to be loved, for whenever sex is wed with love it is the doorway to heaven here on earth."

Mary then spoke with great feeling of her love for Jesus: "He has the power to heal you just by the way he looks at you. I would follow him to the grave. When he healed me, he taught me to see myself as he sees me, through what he calls Eden eyes. He sees only wonder and beauty, with eyes empty of greed."

"I know of what you speak, Mary," Joanna added, "but he healed me of a different possession."

"Joanna, you are not a poor peasant like most of us," said Susanna. "You are a noble woman, your husband a steward in King Herod's court. You know firsthand the good life, the finer things in life. Tell us why you became a disciple of the Master."

JOANNA'S SONG OF LIBERATION

Joanna, plump from the good life, smiled and said, "Royal courts hold no treasures to satisfy the heart which cannot be found in the poorest peasant hut. The Master is correct, the richer you are, the harder it is to be happy. True are his words that God's kingdom of joy is closer to you peasant women than to those of Herod's court, if you but love. Like Mary Magdalene, I too had an exorcism. The Master drove out of me, a good Jewish girl, not seven demons but seven angels!

"First, he drove out of me the holy angel of *belief*
    that in Scripture each and every word is literally true,
    like the stories of creation, Jonah and Noah, to name a few.
Next, he exorcised my old angel named *perfection*,
    who tormented me endlessly to make everything just so.
Then Jesus drove out the angel of God's holy name, *He*,
    to whom I had prayed with devotion every day and night.
Next, he banished my unholy angel named *blind faith*;

now I freely question — even doubt — without guilt.
Then he liberated me from the pious angel *holy gloom*,
      who said that with God nothing is funny, silly or mad,
      who made my poor prayers desert dry and forever sad.
He freed me from the angel of *being a good girl*,
      from the need for a pious compliance with the powers that be.
He finally drove out the angel of a *politely narrow vision*,
      and liberated me to see the possibilities of his holy Way.
Freed of my angelic possessions I sought more life,
      more that I could find in Herod's court.
And so I asked to follow him and live his way of love."

Joanna looked at the others with mock seriousness. "Sisters, while the Master treats us like equals, the men disciples fear the thought of us as peers. If you really want them to treat you as an equal, let me share this royal device. In place of a veil, you must wear one of these!"

From her bag, Joanna removed a long black, beautifully curled man's beard. To the wonder of the women, she tied the fake beard around her ears with a cord.[13] Their amazement turned to laughter as she said in a deep bass voice: "Pay attention, my dear ladies: If you want men to treat you with respect, then never leave home without one of these. Leave aside your linen veils when you dress, and wear one of these hairy black veils if you want to have influence in this world.

"There are marvels of every kind, strange and wondrous sights to be seen at Herod's court. As the spouse of King Herod's faithful steward, I have seen many bearded women, noble women from the fabled East and those concerned with Babylon's business. Yet few who came to juggle affairs of state at Herod's palace would appear as ordinary women. With their faces adorned with long hairy beards, however, men truly treat them as equals!

"So put no veil over your baby smooth face. Rather, wear a curly, black fake beard and your dealings with men will gain manly power. If you want to stand eye to eye with any man, then take my advice. Drape your face with a beard like mine."

Jesus Speaks of Power to His Women Disciples

As the women clapped and laughed, their fun was interrupted by a string of uncontrolled guffaws. Jesus had finished his rest and was standing behind them, roaring with laughter.[14] "Never in all my life have I seen such a funny sight," he said as he continued to chuckle. "How did you...?"

"It's only a fake, Master," Joanna replied, embarrassed, as she quickly removed the beard and sheepishly stuck it in her bag. "I was just having a bit of fun with the other women. I was showing them how women in the royal court earn the respect of men."

"Respect?" replied Jesus as his smile quickly transformed itself into a raised eyebrow. "Do you mean respect as the kind of fear people have for those who hold power over them?"

The women were silent and Joanna blushed, but Jesus smiled again and said, "Friends, do not be ashamed. I know our efforts to establish your rightful place among us are not welcomed by all, but in my Family you must be women, not men. Be careful, sisters, for those who are oppressed dream of having power over those who are their oppressors. This must not be the case for you. No, never return oppression for oppression. Beware of all aggression even in the name of justice."

"You respect us, Master," Susanna said, "but the men disciples still treat us as they did before."

"Conversion takes time. You and the other women disciples must show patience, even as you hold to your sense of urgency at their slowness to open their eyes and see. But be women with all the gifts God has given you, for only then can you awaken in my male disciples compassion and care. And they, as men, are to awaken in you independence, a vision wider than your home and hearth. I know how the pagan women — with or without beards — who are in authority, lord their power over men. It is not to be like that with you. Those who wish to be treated with respect must become servants to the others."

"Master," moaned Salome, "all our lives we've been servants to others; to our men, to our children, our mothers-in-law. I thought you released us from our captivity!"

"Salome, I have! Before you followed me, you had no choice other than to be a slave, for such were the codes of conduct the village customs forced upon you. Now that you are liberated, you can freely and passionately choose to serve all in love. All in my Family, women and men, are called to this way. This life of service, especially to the nobodies of this world, to the sick and lonely, can be the source of the greatest honor shown within our new Family. Humble service when performed with great love can be truly liberating, can even be ecstasy! And, Salome, God made each of us, man and woman, for ecstasy."

CHAPTER SEVEN

JESUS DIVIDES THE DISCIPLES

Jesus went apart to pray. After some time he cried aloud, "Far too large! My Family has grown far too large. So many disciples now, both men and women. While a blessing, it's also a curse. Lost is the intimacy of earlier days, gone too the close feelings of family. A pleasant problem, but one I need to resolve. O God, help me!"

Gabriel appeared to Jesus as he was lost in prayer. "Jesus, once you lamented that few listened and none believed, and now it feels like too many. As always my advice to you is to bed your problem in your prayers. Then you'll be told what to do." Jesus nodded his gratitude and prayed. "Come, Spirit Wind, find me up here where you love to roam, and sing me your wisdom."

After a night of praying alone on the mountain, a solution slowly formed in the heart of Jesus. Like Moses, he would divide his many followers. The first group would be composed of twelve men and several women. They would live as a household, eating and traveling together, becoming loyal and intimate friends. They would be mirrors to one another; each one's behavior would be reflected in the eyes of the others. That would help them to live what they believed, and their life commitment to his Way would further be revealed through them to those outside their small group. This first group would be called the Family.

A larger group, some seventy-two men and women, would form the next circle of disciples that would come to be known as the Village. Jesus envisioned each of these disciples becoming a neighbor to the other, even if their dwellings were miles apart. They would care for each other's needs — and the needs of the families of the disciples in the Family — as if they lived next door.

The large crowd of followers in the outer ring beyond the Village and the Family were referred to as the Children of God. The Family and the Village, being fewer in number, would act like leaven buried in the loaf of the Children of God. The Children of God had simpler needs: They hungered only after bread for the day — and, if lucky, perhaps some left over for tomorrow — and to have some of their many debts canceled. Of this outer ring of those who listened, Jesus asked only that they be good, kind and love one another. He would speak to them in parables or in general terms, as when he said, "Treat others as you want to be treated yourself."

From those disciples who belonged to his Family and Village he called for sacrifice, faith and loyalty to himself and his message, and a self-sacrificing love. They were to love God with all their heart, soul, body and mind, and to love each other as they loved their very selves. In living out these minimum requirements as close disciples, he would call them to increasing degrees of perfection in mercy, dedication and the ways of love.

While grateful for this inspiration during his night of prayer about how to organize the large group of followers, Jesus found difficult the choice of which of his many disciples would belong to the intimate Family. Sighing deeply, Jesus prayed:

"O God, come to my assistance,
    O God, make haste to help me,
    as I now choose the twelve. It shall be:
Simon, the Rock, and Andrew, his brother;
    James, hot blooded but loyal, and his brother, John,
    the youthful, who brings an idealism they all will need —
    and I am fond of him.

"Next, Philip and Bartholomew, Matthew, the tax collector;
    Thomas, the bold and passionate,
    James, son of old Alphaeus.
And then Thaddeus, nicknamed Jude;
    for the eleventh, a rebel spirit,

I choose another Simon, called the Zealot.

"This zealous Simon is a difficult choice; he is so angry with the Romans, so hungry for revolution, that he will easily hear another message when I speak of the kingdom being at hand. Yet, the heart of this Zealot is truly filled with zeal. It needs only to be redirected. Would that my other Simon, the Rock, was as single-minded in his zeal and not so compromising.

"One more will make the holy number twelve,[1]
 but which one out of so many should I choose?
Perhaps, another Simon, the one from Cyrene?
 While he hasn't been with us long enough, I feel,
 he sees the secrets I've hidden like seeds
 in what I say and do.

"Or perhaps it's Judas Iscariot I should choose;
 he's a practical man and good with money.
At times a bit rude, but also very shrewd.
 O God, which of these two shall I choose?"

No wind blew and no voice spoke that night on the mountain to give a clue for Jesus' choice. Perhaps the dark silence, however, had its own message. As the moon moved across the night sky to the west and dawn began to open her bright orange fan, Jesus had decided. "It is done: Judas Iscariot I will choose."

Then, with a deep sigh, he set his eyes like flint. "And just to turn the world upside down for a moment, women shall belong to our innermost circle on the same footing as men — but only six of them." Jesus added with a smile, "Did not my mother tell me since childhood: 'One good woman is worth two men.'

"In my Family, along with the twelve men, I want these women disciples to belong: my mother, Mary; Salome, who is the mother of James and John; Susanna, the widow; the humorous Joanna; Mary, the mother of James and Joseph; and Mary Magdalene of whom I'm so very fond."

Coming down the mountain, Jesus called his people together and told them of his decision. As the names of the twelve and six were announced, some disciples rejoiced, and some naturally were saddened. Jesus reassured those not named. "I am yours, all of me, and you are all my Family, even if you are not among the twelve and six I've named, I was guided by God's Wind."

Simon of Cyrene saw his not being named among the members of the Family with unique eyes, saying to himself, "God's holy design, I know, is written in this plan. Yet I shall count myself among the hidden members of his Family. The Master knows of my great love for him, and I'm ready to follow wherever his way shall lead."

THE BEATITUDES

With all the followers finally organized into groups and units, Jesus seemed more relaxed — and so did his disciples. People kept coming to listen to his words, and often would listen for hours in rapt attention. On one particularly beautiful day, as bright sunlight glistened off the Lake of Galilee, a great crowd of his disciples and a multitude of people gathered. They came from Jerusalem to the south and Tyre and Sidon to the north. First Jesus healed those tormented by unclean spirits and those with various diseases. Almost everyone sought to touch him, since power seemed to go forth from him.

As the main body of the crowd sat on a hillside in eager anticipation, Jesus began to speak, this time not as a candle or lamp glowing in the darkness, but with the terrifying power of a bolt of lightning crashing through a forest of dead wood. Sparks leaped from his words as he sang of God's time having arrived. The crowd was swept away by his fiery words as if they were hundreds of little boats floating on a sea of fire. Time and again as they listened, Jesus would suddenly stop, point to someone who seemed in pain, and scream, "Depart, unclean spirit from that person."[2] Each time, the woman or man would leap up, cleansed of the evil spirit, and shout in joy. Without pausing, Jesus would again plunge into the fiery sea of his message: "Look not toward the horizon to find God's kingdom — for it is here! Look at one another, whether farmer from the north or citizen of Jerusalem, Jew from Jerico or Greek from Sidon, and see God's presence in each other's faces. You are the very kingdom of God!"

Then, in the midst of the crowd's amazement, his voice leapt toward a woman in the crowd: "You over there, yes, you the woman with the painful leg, stand up!" The woman stood and threw down her crutch as her family joyously cried out, "Blest be God!"

With the raw energy of a lion, Jesus began to stride through the crowd seated on the grass, continuing to speak. As he passed by, eager hands would reach out to touch him or his clothing. Healing power flowed freely from him. Reaching the center of the massive crowd, he suddenly stood still, and with outstretched arms and possessed by a great inspiration, he sang out:

"Blessed are you poor, you destitute and beggars,
      the nobodies of this world,

for yours is the kingdom of God.
Blessed are you who are hungry,
    for you shall be satisfied, filled to contentment.
Blessed are you, the sad, for you will laugh and dance;
    great joy will be among your rewards from God."[3]

Then he dropped his left arm to his side and swung his right arm outward above the crowd like a reaper's harvest scythe. His words, sharper than any reaper's blade, sliced through the air over the heads in the crowd:

"Woe to you rich: look not to tomorrow's reward,
    for you've been given your reward today!
Woe to you who are fat and feel no hunger,
    for you will know a hunger beyond that of beggars.
Woe to you who rejoice in these times of soul-grinding oppression,
    for I promise you that you will know
    a sorrow greater than any alive today."

Jesus stopped and lowered his head. After a long pause, he slowly lifted his gaze. Those nearby later spoke of seeing tears in his eyes. Then, as the sun appears after gray days of rain, he smiled. He looked directly at all his disciples and sang out:

"Blessed are you who are elastic and ever-flexible,[4]
    for you will not be broken by change.
Your new wine skins shall bulge but not burst
    when filled with God's intoxicating new wine.
Blessed are you who are content, for you shall be richer
    than all the kings and queens of this earth.
Blessed are you who are discontent with the justice of this age,
    or discontent with your prayers and holiness,
    for you shall be fueled with a prophet's fire.

"Blessed are you who are ambivalent,
    who can embrace the inconsistencies of life
    in love and hate, the good and bad, indeed, all,
    for you shall not become religious fanatics.[5]
Blessed are you celibates, who are not married to success,
    for you will not be defeated by failure
    but shall live and work full of hope.[6]
Blessed are you who are generous,
    for you shall grow in the likeness of God.
For stinginess tightly squeezes more than your purse;[7]

it chokes to death your loves, your heart and soul.
Blessed too are you who are humorous,
who can laugh at yourselves, religion and all of life,
for you shall escape from the demon *pride*.

"Brothers and sisters, look around now at all this holy nation. When you live among those who are blessed — the elastic, the content and discontented, the inclusive, those not enslaved to success, the generous and humorous — know that you live in the kingdom and that God's day has dawned."

THE NEW COMMANDMENTS

With that Jesus bid farewell to the crowds and took his disciples apart by themselves. He said, "Remember how Moses led the chosen people into the promised land long before they crossed the Jordan. After his encounter with God on Sinai, Moses gave them the signs of those who had crossed over into God's promise when he gave them the ten great laws. Those who lived according to God's commandments — You shall love God and your fellow Israelites; You shall only take an eye for an eye and not the entire head or the other's life; You shall not abandon your aged parents; You shall not kill; You shall not lust after another's spouse; these and the others — were already in the promised land.

"Now I likewise give you signs of those who live not in Caesar's — or even Moses' — time, but in God's time and kingdom.

"Those living in a land flowing with milk and honey
are those who return kindness and love for injury or insult.
They offer the other cheek when someone slaps them.
They love rather than hate their enemies.
When someone steals their cloak,
they eagerly give them their tunic as well.
They are generous to all who beg alms of any kind from them.
When they loan to others, they do not expect any return.
They only observe the behavior of others and do not judge them,
nor do they judge themselves, nor even the rich and powerful!
They bless and forgive all
who offend them or cause them pain.
When you live among such people,
you live in the middle of God's time."

"Master," replied Simon Peter, beside himself with excitement, "to live among such people would be living in heaven and not here on earth!"

"Well said, faithful companion! God's kingdom is heaven come to earth."

"But," Peter questioned, "how can we possibly remember — and keep — all these new commandments?"

"They are not commandments, Simon, but rather a map for the kingdom. And they are signs on the map. When you see them about you, you are in the reign of God. They are easily remembered and also kept by remembering only one: just love. Love God, yourself and others with all your heart. Be compassionate as God is compassionate.[8] There, it's simple, don't you see?"

THE DISCIPLES RESPOND TO THE NEW WINE

The silence of a closed door filled most of the disciples, and Jesus looked them in the eye: "Do any of you wish to leave? I need not be a visionary to see that for some these new ways to live and love are not easy." No one spoke a word. They needed time to mull over all he had said, so they drifted away in twos and threes, all of them wondering where this prophet was leading them, but thrilled to be part of his Way.

In the morning, they all set out for the next town, with a few going on ahead to prepare the town for Jesus' arrival. Simon the Zealot, Simon Peter, John and Judas, along with Simon of Cyrene, who had been invited to travel with them, walked a distance behind the others as they discussed the Master's words.

"This new teaching of the Master," said Simon the Zealot, "about how we are to love and to act is clearly only for women and children! Do good to those who hate you! Bless those who maltreat you! When someone strikes you, do not defend yourself! Only weaklings do not stand up for their own or their family's honor when they are attacked. This is all too much to bear! These are words for the ears of cowards and cripples, those afraid or unable to defend their honor and family name."

Judas, who carried the Family's purse, exclaimed, "I agree. 'If someone takes your coat, give them your shirt as well'! That's pure madness! 'Give to all who ask of you, all who beg from you'! Have you counted the number of beggars at the city gate? We'd be broke before noon if we gave to every one of them!"

Simon Peter said, "I don't know. I admit that these words seem to present an impossible way to live in the real world. But even if I don't understand it, I trust in the Master's wisdom. Don't you men?"

Judas' reply was firm. "The Master is wise in holy things, but a fool when it comes to finances. Did he not say to 'lend without expecting repayment'?"

"That's not what I heard," Simon of Cyrene responded. "I heard the Master saying that as his disciples we are to treat all whom we meet as members of our personal family. We are to love them as our parents loved us. They provided for us without expecting any investment on their love. And, Judas, think of our parents and how greatly we are in debt to them! Yet they kept no account ledgers of all they spent on us in coins, in hours and in energy as they cared for us. What I heard the Master say was, 'Give to others in the spirit of how you were given love: give to them as if they're family.'"

Simon Peter responded, "What you say is true, Simon. 'Do to others as you would have them do to you': as a child I learned such a rule from my parents and from the village rabbi. Jesus has echoed our ancient wisdom of the golden rule."[9]

At this point young John got up sufficient courage to speak. "Indeed, to treat others as you wish to be treated is a golden rule, but Jesus has given to us greater than a golden rule. His is a diamond rule! Even when others do not treat you well, you are to love them as you love yourself!"

Judas objected. "Not all parents, Simon, love without expecting a return. Even as a child, mine demanded much of me. Yet you, John, agree with the Master that we need to freely love others even when their rule of life is far from golden and as cold as a bronze coin."

"Yes," replied John, "because his diamond rule calls us to be a reflection of God who lets the rains fall on the wicked and the just, who gives a good harvest to sinners and to saints. We are to be compassionate to one another as God is compassionate. Like loving parents, God doesn't keep a ledger account of every gift given away, like one who is expecting repayment. So we are to love others, not simply our family and friends — but even strangers, whom we are to see as our new neighbors!"

JESUS SPEAKS OF THE KINGDOM TIME

By this time the group had reached their evening resting place. The ancient tradition of hospitality reached out to welcome any traveling group such as theirs, and there were many such groups on the move in those days. The Family lived and slept in an encampment with food donated by their listeners. Often friends or relatives along the way were able to give them a meal in exchange for entertaining stories and information about politics and religion — and, of course, the thrilling sermons by the mysterious man everyone said was a prophet. After the group had gathered that night, Jesus asked, "What were you discussing on the road as we walked here?" They all remained silent. So Jesus, in folk song melody, sang of God's time, dramatizing each line to their delight:

"Sit down, my friends, for you're tired and weary of heart,
and listen as I speak of God's time, the kingdom on earth.[10]
If God's time is to break in upon brutal Caesar's time,
then each of us must try to live ahead of our time.
Some love to live in yesterday, the good old days,
but those who love God must choose a better way.

"We live today in ugly war time, in deadly revenge time;
we must strive to live beyond our present ways.
We're trapped in old dead time, when love's returned
only for love given, and kindness exchanged for kindness.
But I tell you: love your enemies, even those who harm you;
be generous and kind, and share your gifts with all.

"For God's time, my companions, is turnaround time,
when you turn your enemies into dear friends.
For only good friends give away cloak and tunic,
making themselves naked for another's sake.
When charity is weighed in the scales of justice,
it's tainted by the tin, and cold to the touch.
So be generous beyond justice with your love:
Love those who hate you and love your enemies as well.
Some love to live in yesterday, the good old days,
but those who love God must live in this new day."

When the song was ended, the Family applauded. But not all were happy. "Master," moaned Simon the Zealot, "truly it would be turnaround time for me to love like brothers the Roman dogs who rule us. How can I love those I hate, those whose army occupies our beloved homeland? How can I bless those who abuse me, and not stand up and fight? Only the weak and the fearful bend down like lambs to injustice and oppression."

Jesus nodded and smiled at his well-meaning companion. "Simon the zealous, how else can we break the endless cycle of hatred and violent revenge? As summer follows spring, revenge is an endless cycle in which winter leads only to winter — one long season of death and destruction! How else can we break into a new season unless we refuse to give back the evil that was given to us? Look around, the entire world is enslaved in that cycle of hate, and it is only broken when you bless those who curse you and do good to those who do evil to you. And when you are unable to bless them, at least you can ask God to bless them. They will need that blessing since by their violence they will become reapers of the evil deeds they sow."

Jesus paused. In a soft voice Simon of Cyrene added, "You only harvest what you plant." Jesus smiled at the farmer Simon and nodded in approval.

Simon the Zealot lowered his head, looking solemnly at his feet. Jesus rose and came over, and, placing his hand on Simon's shoulder, said:

> "So you hear this teaching in disbelief,
> and you say to yourself it is only for the weak,
> those unable to strike back, or women!
> Well, Simon, you're right and you're wrong,
> for only the brave and strong can return love for hate.
> Only men strong enough to be as women
> can love in such a new and brave way!"

All jaws dropped open as if lightning had struck just a step ahead of them.

"No!" shouted Judas.

"No!" shouted Simon Peter.

Jesus had nearly had the dissatisfied disciples in the palm of his hand, but this last statement had struck a nerve with every single hearer. Even some of the women disciples were confused.

"You want us to become weak and womanly and call it strong?" the Zealot asked. "Master, this is beyond us." Even John was astonished.

Jesus answered, "Allow me to explain. We men can respond in moments of great danger or emergencies with heroic acts of bravery, but women often must endure pain beyond some fleeting crisis! Remember your mothers and your wives when they carried their children within their wombs for so many months. God has so made women as to be able to tolerate the pain which nature asks of them! Whether gifted by God or learned in the hours — and sometimes days — of childbirth, they often find strength to endure pain and suffering for long periods of time."

The disciples sat in silence as the women nodded their heads in agreement. Then Jesus continued, "Those who are to be my disciples are called not just to respond to emergencies but to the heroic pain of living a new way of life for the rest of their lives. To follow my way requires a heroine's strength."

"Master," replied Simon Peter, "your words are difficult. What you ask seems impossible! If these new commandments are *the* new wine, *then* please give us the old!"

"Simon the Rock," said Jesus with an earnest grin. "Remember, I said that upon you my house would stand or stumble. Don't stumble over these words. Don't try to compromise them so as to make them easier for people to live out. If you do, my followers will stumble on you, Simon Peter, as one would over a rock! You say you find my words too difficult; I'm sorry, but these words about the new way we are to live are not mine!"

"Master, if they are not yours, then which rabbis teach them? To my knowledge they are not found in our Scriptures," replied James.

"All I speak to you has been given to me by God. James, you must believe me. My friends, at times, like you, I hear these words for the first time as I speak them. And often I also find them difficult to embrace! I do not find it easy to practice what I say! I fear a day is soon coming when I shall be tested to see if I myself can love my enemies, if I can forgive those who betray me and inflict pain on me."

Judas spoke up. "Master, while your words are difficult, they do contain great wisdom. Once you said, 'Give and it shall be given to you in good measure, pressed down and shaken together and in great fullness shall it be poured into your lap, for the measure you give will be measured back to you.' So if we give as you say, we will get so much more back. It's only good business sense then to follow these new laws — if we trust that a rich harvest will be our return."

"Yes, Judas," Jesus replied, "but remember, I also said lend and give without expecting repayment. That even includes giving to God! Give to God without expecting anything in return! Your generosity must always mirror God's, who gives freely, without any desire to be repaid. Truly, this is the greatest test of your loyalty, your faith, in God."

By this time night had lowered her purple star-speckled curtain, which shone like lamps peeking through a thousand tiny holes. The Family of Jesus shared their simple evening meal and prepared to retire, the women on one side of the fire, the men and Jesus on the other. When all were still, Jesus said aloud his night prayer:

"Hear, O Israel, the LORD is our God, the LORD alone.
  'You shall love the LORD your God with all your heart,
  with all your soul, and with all your might,'
  and you shall love your neighbor as you love yourself."[11]

With that he lay his head down but was full of thought. He had surprised himself with the last line of that prayer. Without thinking, he had added it to the ancient prayer he had said ever since he was a child. He smiled, saying softly to himself, "Those two loves *should* be linked as one." From that night onward, each morning and evening when he prayed the *Shema*, he always added that line about loving neighbor as self.

JESUS AND JUDAS TALK ABOUT MONEY

Jesus was already rolled up in his cloak, prepared to sleep, when Judas Iscariot crouched beside him. "Master, I know it is late," said Judas "and it's been a long day, but I need to speak with you. It is important."

Raising himself up on an elbow, Jesus said, "Speak, Judas, it's never too late to talk to a brother."

"Master, I think we should speak confidentially, apart from the others."

Jesus rose and followed Judas some distance from their camp where they sat together on a large rock under a half moon. Even its faint light was enough for Jesus to see that Judas had taken his customary pose, his left hand resting on his forehead. He was thus able to hide the purple-red birthmark that ran from his left eyebrow past his eye and then halfway down his cheek. Jesus had wondered if this birthmark was the reason Judas was often bitter and cynical.

Then Judas suddenly removed his hand. "I know, it's a habit of mine," replied Judas, as if reading Jesus' thoughts. He added with a strained laugh, "It's my mark of Cain!"[12]

Jesus reached over and touched the birthmark gently with his fingers. "Judas, you have not killed a brother. This is not the mark of Cain, not an evil birthright. God creates nothing but good; still, your mark must be terribly hard to bear.

"Yet whatever is given at birth must be somehow for our good or the good of God's plan. The mystery of life is discovering the good we must work out of whatever appears to be a defect." Judas did not answer.

Jesus then asked, "Now, Judas, what is this urgent matter that you must share with me?"

"Master," he said with feeling, "we are almost to the end of this tour of the towns, and our Family's purse is almost empty. The disciples have been away from their work and farms, and plan not to return home until we have completed this tour.[13] They cannot offer any more resources. I have gone to the wealthy women all I can for additional funds, and even they are strapped for silver. I am anxious and worried: How are we to pay the taxes and buy our bread and wine?"

"Be not anxious, Judas." Then, remembering his visit by the beasts and birds in the desert, Jesus added, "The sparrows and the wild beasts are not anxious about tomorrow's meal. They know God cares for them. We are to do the same."

"Excuse me, Jesus, but that sounds like pious nonsense!" Judas replied, neglecting the term "Master," the title of respect which the disciples usually used. "I feared you would respond in just this impractical way. That is why I wanted us to come apart from the others. If we are brothers, then let us speak as equals. And let us talk practically, not poetically. I'm no dreamy eyed, fuzz-faced John who fondles your every word. I'm Judas, the realist. Soon, Jesus, we'll be penniless! Do you next intend to teach us lessons in humility, asking us to go about begging for our bread?"

"No, Judas! We travel among the poor; we are never to beg our food from those who hardly have enough for themselves! Even among the rich, we are never to beg! I do not want my disciples to beg, other than...." Here Jesus paused as if in prayer, "...other than from God! If we have daily needs, then let us pray. Those who sit as beggars at God's gate will never go in need!"

Judas sat silently a moment before he spoke. "Be reasonable, Jesus. We need to be more prudent when it comes to finding the money we need. I have thought about this and have some proposals. For example, when you speak to the multitudes, the disciples could take up a collection so that those who are delighted to hear the good news can express their joy.

"Then there are your miracles. You never ask anything from those you cure, even though some have paid a fortune to healers without finding relief. The families of cripples or those possessed by impure spirits should be approached to make, let us say, a suggested donation."

Jesus smiled at first, then grew serious. "No, Brother Judas, only magicians charge for their marvels! I'm no magician or sorcerer. Recall David's psalm song:

> " 'Hear these things, all you peoples;
>   high and low, rich and poor alike.
> Those who trust in their wealth —
>   who boast in their abundant riches — are fools.
> For who can redeem oneself?
>   Who can pay God the price of redemption?
> Too costly is the ransom of one's life;
>   when one dies and departs this short life,
>   nothing, not a coin, can be taken along.
> No matter the riches, they're left behind.' "[14]

"Amen to that!" replied Judas with a smirk. "However, I was not speaking about amassing some great fortune. I'm only anxious about how we shall eat in a couple of days."

"You are correct to be concerned, Judas, for that is your duty among us as the keeper of our purse, but do not be anxious. Being concerned is different from being a prisoner of anxiety and worry. When I stand next to the campfire, I am concerned that my cloak does not catch fire. If I were anxious, I would be too fearful to stand close to fire, even to keep warm. I'd be awakened at night, fretting about catching on fire."

Judas' face turned bitter. "Jesus, please, no poetry for me. Don't you see that refusing to deal with the issue of our need for money is playing with fire. It's dangerous."

"Perhaps, Judas, but not as dangerous as playing with money! Money is the root of all evil. As for charging for our ministry:

"I did not barter with God over the price of the good news,
     or pay for parable stories, or new eyes for the blind.
No cost for new legs for the lame, or to free those bound by sin,
     or for keys to prison cell doors — freely these were given.
And freely they'll be given by us to all, without charge."[15]

Judas moaned and threw his arms in the air. "I'm afraid, Jesus, that this visit is a waste of time, yours and mine. Jesus, I'm surprised that a sage like you believes that anything in this life can be free."

Jesus' face now showed his anger.

"Judas, the good news is not free!
     Redemption is a ransom, far from free.
     Someone will always pay a price for it.
I agree that nothing, even love, is absolutely free;
     it binds you to someone forever.
Freedom, most of all, is never free,
     nor are healing or the good news without cost."

"Well, Jesus," said Judas, his tone sour with sarcasm, "all of those who have heard the good news so far must be deaf, for they've made no response that fits in my purse. And those whom you've healed must still be afflicted, for our purse holds no silver singing songs of gratitude! This is a waste of time, asking a dreamer to consider the cost of the dream. No disrespect intended, Jesus. I know that our ancestor Joseph, Jacob's son, was just such a dreamer."

"I recall, Judas, that along with being a dreamer he was also an excellent manager: Joseph was Pharaoh's royal officer who resourcefully provided for Egypt's lean years of drought! Perhaps like Simon Peter, I should give you a new name. I should call you 'Judas Joseph the Provider.' Yes! I ask you, Judas, to be a Joseph in Egypt for us; prudent with our resources as you plan for the future — and while doing so, abiding with great confidence in God's care for us. Trust that if you and the rest of us seek God's way of justice and peace with all our hearts, all we need will be given to us. I come proclaiming God's good news. If it cannot be lived out in the raw realities of daily life, then how can it be *good* news?"

Judas sat silently, staring at the moon. He was moved by Jesus' gesture of giving him a noble new name, but Jesus could feel the cold resistance still present in his silence.

"Tomorrow, Judas, when the Family gathers for morning prayer, we shall be beggars knocking loudly at God's door. We shall knock not to make God aware of our needs, but to make us aware of God's great loving care for us when tomorrow, or the day after, our daily needs for money will be supplied as was the manna in the desert."

Judas said nothing. But his shoulders spoke, twitching as he wrestled with doubt. Slowly he stood up, the half moon behind his head forming a luminous halo, half of which was black. He spoke with great feeling:

"O Jesus, Master, if you only knew,
    how I've longed to believe in you.
How I've hungered for your love,
    not in the dark, hiding,
but out in the sunlight,
    even with this evil mark branded on my face.

"I, like a beggar, come crawling to you,
    for I too have lusted after a miracle.
I've dreamed of being graced by you,
    not given a cleansed soul but a new face.

"But fate, or God, has dealt me a curse
    to be scarred for life and looked on as a leper.
While those who are beautiful are looked on as good,
    the ugly are routinely seen as evil.
Women shun me, men look the other way.

"O Jesus, how I've longed to believe in your dream,
    yearned for faith in the things that you say,
    longed to believe in your liberating new love.
How I've hoped it was a dream that's made out of brick,

not a web made of moonbeams and soft morning mist.
O, Jesus, how I have longed to be loved by you,
to be first among your many lovers."

Judas hung his head, ashamed that in a moment of weakness he had exposed himself and his deepest yearnings. Jesus slipped his arm around Judas' shoulder and said softly, "Come, it's late. Let us leave this night to the moon to stand guard while we sleep."

Jesus kissed Judas on his birthmark, and the two walked back to the camp in silence.

Chapter Eight

Gossip about the Good Shepherd

Jesus' reputation quickly spread from village well to village well, and was the topic of gossip for the men who sat daily at the town gate:

"I hear he heals the sick, forgives sins;
    he's a holy prophet full of God's Spirit," said one.
Another replied, "The gossip I hear going around
    says he's a glutton, drinks wine like a fish,
    eats at every feast and cleans his dish."

The oldest in the crowd said, "If he's a prophet of God, then I'm a clown!"

When he was told about this gossip, Jesus moaned, "Alas! To what shall I compare this generation? They're like fickle children sitting in the marketplace.

"I played a flute, but none would dance,
    John sang a dirge, but none would weep.
Jordan's prophet took neither food nor drink;
    they said, 'he's mad and has a demon.'

"I enjoy meals and wine, and they sling mud;

'Loves his wine too much — he's a drunk,
and he eats with sinners,' they whine.
These opinions are of no concern to me,
for wisdom will say who's right or wrong;
she will pass judgment in God's good time."

Now, a certain rich Pharisee named Simon invited Jesus to dine with him, curious to see this famous peasant preacher.[1] News of Simon's dinner guest leaped like fire among the stubble along the gossip lanes until it reached a lady of the night, a known prostitute of the town. The flutes played wildly that night, the wine flowed and platters of choice food filled the table as the guests reclined, feasting.

The woman infamous for her sexual sins appeared carrying an alabaster jar of fine ointment. She came up and knelt beside Jesus, bathing his dusty feet with her tears. She wiped them dry with her long, black silken hair, covering his bare feet and shaggy legs with her kisses. Then with great extravagance, she emptied all of the alabaster jar of precious oil upon his feet, rubbing it over his feet and legs.

If by chance someone had not noticed her before, no one could now ignore the aroma that filled Simon's house. As a cloud covers a mountaintop, his house and table were engulfed in a great sensual cloud of exotic perfumes. Simon the Pharisee noticed, of course, and said to himself, "If this peasant preacher were truly a prophet, then surely he would have known at once what sort of woman this is who is touching him. It's clear to me that if he's a prophet, he's one without feeling in his legs and feet and whose nose is dead as stone!"

All eyes were on Jesus and this woman clinging to his feet, as she surely must have done to some of her late-night visitors in whom she found more to love than a few coins.

Moved by her expressions of affection, yet filled with other feelings, at first Jesus did not know how to respond. He drew in a deep breath with his eyes closed, and in so simple an act he heard Gabriel whisper in his ear, "Moses was a good shepherd, and so was your ancestor David. Why not tell a shepherd parable to Simon the stiff-necked. Don't worry about what you're to say; let God's Breath inspire your parable."

So Jesus said to his host, "Simon, would you and your friends like to hear a story?"

"Wonderful, my honored guest. I've heard tell you're a good storyteller. By all means entertain us with a tale." Simon asked for silence among his guests. Jesus took a drink of wine, wiped his lips and began.

The Parable of the Good Shepherd and the Lost Sheep[2]

A great orange sun hung above the horizon of a brown and purple painted desert as a certain shepherd searched for one lost sheep, though his ninety-nine others were safe. The dry creekbeds and thorny thickets he had combed for hours. Now he climbed along a stone cliff where he suddenly spotted his lost sheep high above on a rocky ledge.

"Ah, there you are," he shouted joyfully. "I see you up there! I've been looking for you for hours. I was afraid I wouldn't find you."

The sheep shouted back to him, "Go away! I'm fine. It's great out here, and I feel so free. Look at how beautiful the desert is, and there's more than enough grass to eat. Go away. I want to be alone, so go back to the others."

"Please," said the shepherd, "come down from up there. It's getting late; it's almost sunset. It'll be dark by the time we get back to the rest of the flock. They'll be so glad to see you, they'll want to throw a party!"

"They will not! I'd bet not even one of them has missed me. Am I right? Who among that self-centered bunch would want to throw a party because a stray is back? Name one!"

"Perhaps," replied the shepherd, "but I missed you! At the end of the day, as I carefully counted my sheep, I found that you were not among them. I just had to leave at once to come and find you. I like you — you've got spirit and spunk. I love that in you. But even if none of the others missed you, they're a good bunch."

"A good bunch of what?" moaned the stray sheep. "They're a bunch of petty, narrow-minded, self-serving wimps. Whenever I'd talk about striking out from the flock for an adventure, they'd all groan or shriek with horror at the idea of anything so risky. They'd preach that there's no security outside the flock!"

"Don't be so judgmental, little one, though what you say is true. They're not the most adventuresome flock, I know, but I love them just the same. But look, the sun is beginning to set. I'm concerned about them, being so far away at nightfall."

"You know as well as I what they're up to while you're away," replied the sheep. "Every other time you've left, even briefly, they'd be busy at it!"

"You mean having meetings or fighting over who's in charge

while I'm gone?"

The lost sheep nodded, adding, "That too, but I was thinking of their other addiction."

"You mean, making laws? Yes, I'm afraid they have a real appetite for making laws, big ones and little ones. You're right, even though I've only been gone for a couple of hours, I'd wager that by now they've made up a big batch of new laws. Sheep love laws; I think it gives them a sense of security. But come, my little one, the sun has now disappeared beneath the horizon; it's time to go home."

"No thanks," said the lost one, "hanging around with that sterile flock has never been home for me. Oh, I've loved you, shepherd, enjoyed being close to you, but I don't want to go back to being one of them. They're mean-spirited, judgmental, selfish and self-righteous!" Starting to climb up to an even higher ledge, the sheep continued, "Thanks anyway, I'd rather go it alone than travel with that bunch!"

"Well, no matter where you roam," said the shepherd, "know I love you, and that you will always have a place in my heart."

The little stray sheep was touched by the shepherd's great affection, and was tempted to return to the flock. Humming, the shepherd began climbing up toward her: "Come down, let's go home. The others need you. I need you; life won't be any fun without you. You're the kind of spunky sheep that makes sheepherding a delight. There is no fun when I'm left with only timid, law-abiding sheep. Come on, let's go home."

"No thanks, friend. I've got a better idea. Let's you and me strike out together! Yeah, just the two of us. Wouldn't that be wonderful? Leave that bunch to themselves. Don't worry about the wolves getting them; those sheep can take care of themselves. We both know they can be more vicious than wolves!"

"Well, maybe, but I love them, all ninety-nine, docile and petty as they are. And I also love you! But I'm sorry; as much fun as it would be, I can't go off alone with you to explore the world. I must go back, and I want you to come back with me. I'll tell you what: I'll make you a deal. And I promise you, come hell or high water, I'll never go back on my promise."

"What's the deal?"

"You'll have to trust me, but you'll like it."

As the first stars of night winked in the soft blue evening

sky, the stray sheep agreed to the shepherd's offer and came joyfully skipping down the rocky ledges. Hours later, as a big round moon stood a pale watch over the sheepfold, the shepherd returned to the flock, carrying the lost sheep on his shoulders. The ninety-nine were all fast asleep, and not a single one of them stirred from their dreams of green pastures and still waters. There was no welcome home party.

But the good shepherd, being also the honest shepherd, was faithful to his promise. Once again the flock was back at an even one hundred sheep. However, the fallen away, spunky, runaway sheep wasn't with the flock! No, it spent the rest of its days, true to the promise, wrapped around the shepherd's neck, riding affectionately on his shoulders.[3]

Simon and his guests remained silent, *not* showing the customary courtesy of applause.

THE SHAMED JESUS SHAMES

Then Jesus raised himself on an elbow and turned toward the woman who lay at his feet with her arms wrapped around his legs.

"Simon, are we not to be compassionate as our God is compassionate? Do you see this woman? I was your invited guest, yet you did not give me water to wash my dusty feet.[4] Indeed I am only a peasant, but even in the poorest of homes we treat our guests with dignity! Yet this woman, whom you scorn, has cleansed my feet with her warm tears of repentance. She shames your discourtesy. You, my host, neglected to greet me with a kiss, yet she has not ceased kissing my feet and legs. You did grant me the usual courtesy of anointing my head with oil, yet she has broken open an expensive alabaster jar, lavishly anointing me, pouring oil over my feet and legs.[5] And more than the alabaster jar, she has broken open her heart and poured out upon me her lavish love in great extravagance. I say to you, Simon, and to all of the rest of you at this table, her many sins are forgiven! For behold how much she has loved, and the more you love, the more you are forgiven."

The table of guests suddenly broke apart, not as a jar of sweet perfume, but as one filled with rage. One man shouted to all the others, "Who does this man think he is that he can forgive sins? Only with a temple ritual and sin offerings are sins forgiven. This is outrageous!"

Standing up before them with the greatest of dignity, Jesus lifted the woman to her feet, "Come, my sister, let us leave this house. Your sins are forgiven, for indeed your great love has saved you. Now you may go in peace, but not alone. Allow me to escort you home, for it is not proper for a lady to be out alone on the streets at night."[6] Together they went out the door and disappeared down the dark street.

His disciples, deeply embarrassed by the sinful woman's fondling of Jesus in front of the Pharisees, scribes and other guests, stood up and in short order also left the house. They, however, did not follow Jesus but departed for their encampment in the opposite direction.

Simon the Pharisee clapped his hands and said, "Let the flutes play and the music begin again. Stay, friends, I pray, there are ripe fruits, baskets of juicy figs and grapes for your delight. How rude of this Jesus! Your pardon I beg, my honored guests. I had no idea he is such a crude peasant — and a sinner too."

Among the guests that night was a certain temple scribe from Jerusalem who was visiting his family in the town. He had obviously attended the dinner to see Jesus and to affirm the reports he had heard about him. He made careful notes of everything he had heard around town concerning this Jesus of Galilee, as well as the shocking events of this night at Simon's house. He especially observed one of the disciples of Jesus who seemed extremely distressed over the events of the dinner, a certain Judas Iscariot. It was not clear if the disciple's anxiety had been caused by his master's behavior with the whore, or by the actions of the woman herself, at whom he would hardly look. None of these things he had seen or heard would the temple scribe forget when he returned to the holy city.

That scribe left the next morning for Jerusalem. Upon arriving at the temple, he was told that the high priest had requested to see him. At once the scribe rushed to the high priest's private chambers where he found a small group gathered. The high priest was seated at the head of a table illuminated by many hanging lamps. He was just beginning to address the group.

The High Priest's Secret Meeting

"Priests, scribes and scholars, devoted disciples of Moses, I welcome you. Tonight, I have invited you here for an unofficial — you might even say a *secret* — meeting. You are, shall we say, a select council of the Sanhedrin as well as my trusted elders.[7] I have called you because I am in need of your wise counsel. The issue is one Jesus of Nazareth, or Jesus of Capernaum — or it seems one could give any number of towns as his home, since he wanders with no fixed dwelling. For our records, let us refer to him then simply as Jesus the Galilean."

Holding up a scroll, Caiaphas, the high priest, continued, "I have received this message from King Herod. It seems his peace is disturbed by what he hears of this man, Jesus, a wandering preacher in King Herod's domains. Herod fears he is an incarnation of John the Baptizer, whom he had beheaded. Herod seems to believe the folk-talk that John has arisen from the tomb. Poor Herod, we know he always suspects others are plotting to be on his throne — or in his bed!"

A ripple of faintly audible laughter flowed through the group.

"I would have handed over this silly matter of a dead prophet rumored to be risen from the grave to one of you to investigate, but for this," he said, lifting up a second scroll. "It's a message from our illustrious Roman Governor, Pontius Pilate. He too has written, asking me what I know about this Jesus of Galilee and his small gang of followers. Pilate's spies have reported to him that certain members of his followers speak openly about a new kingdom that is appearing, of a rebellion against Rome. Pilate's spies quote these words of a certain Simon, a Zealot Party follower of Jesus."[8] Caiaphas read from the parchment scroll:

"I sing of you, my holy sword of God's wrath,
    my weapon of the will of the All Holy One,
    for not peace, but justice, is God's will.
Take up your sword and we shall overcome;
    take up your manhood and we shall overcome.
Be no virgin who has never drawn a sword;
    be no eunuch who has no sword to draw.
Be not castrated by fear or a need for security,
    like one whose dagger hangs limp and useless.
Take up your sword and we shall overcome;
    take up your manhood and we shall overcome."

Handing Pilate's scroll to a scribe, Caiaphas continued, "Granted, this is typical crude, if not lewd, peasant speech, yet it is filled with a rebellious fire. Pilate's spies have also reported that this Jesus denounces violence and the sword. Furthermore, and this I find of great interest, Pilate's reports state that this man's message seems directed more against us, the religious authorities, and our temple sacrifices than against Rome. Pilate wants my opinion. Is this Jesus a political threat to Rome and the Emperor, or merely a threat to our religious authority? He awaits my reply; so tell me, what have you heard about this man Jesus?"

"High priest," spoke up a scribe, "he's a simple, uneducated peasant craftsman who worked with wood and stone. His home village is an insignificant town in Galilee named Nazareth. For a short period of time he was reported to be a disciple of John who baptized along the Jordan. Now this man is no one's disciple but has gathered a small band about him, though he shuns the title of teacher. This will shock you: Among his disciples and companions with whom he travels are half a dozen or so women! As for his views on rebellion, he is reported to have said, 'The kingdom of God will only be taken by violence.' But we do not have witnesses; it is only hearsay."

"Very interesting, my friend, but hearsay and gossip at the village well are of little value," sighed the high priest. "Two witnesses are required by law. Have any of you actually heard the man speak?"

"I have, Caiaphas," answered another scribe. "He never uses the term *the kingdom of God* without tacking on other vague expressions, like *God's time*, *the age of God* or *the reign of justice*. He calls the poor 'blessed' and says they will inherit the earth."

"Ah, he's clever not to use inflammatory terms like *kingdom* loosely. However, for the poor to inherit the wealth of the world, or anything else, then someone or something has to die!" said Caiaphas. "But tell me, what are these reported attacks against the temple?"

The scribe went on. "High priest, to begin with, this Jesus forgives sins! Like John, he deals directly with sinners, but unlike John he does not ask them to confess their sins. He just forgives them without sending them here to make sin offerings to our priests."[9]

"He forgives sin? Only God can forgiven sin! You actually heard him forgive someone's sins?" asked Caiaphas.

"Well, he does not say, 'I forgive you.' Rather, he simply states it as an accomplished fact, saying, 'Your sins are forgiven.'"

"My, my, it sounds like we are not dealing with some simple peasant prophet with dirty fingernails! We may have more on our hands than some passing little dust storm stirring up the poor in the back country. He's smart enough not to say that he forgives their sins. Perhaps ever-anxious Herod is correct; tell me more about this Jesus," the high priest said, leaning back into his chair with a finger raised to his lips.

"High priest," said the scribe who had been at Simon's feast, "he's known to consort with prostitutes, tax collectors and sinners. He and his disciples disregard the requirements of religious washing purifications and are casual in how they keep the Sabbath rest. And...and he...."

"Yes, yes, go on, what else does he do?"

"High priest, he works wonders; he heals the blind, cures the lame, drives out demons and heals lepers, usually concluding these cures by saying, 'Your sins are forgiven.' The lepers he has cleansed, however, he directs here to the temple to show themselves to the priests as is required by the law of Moses."

"Ah, this peasant preacher captures my curiosity. First, he forgives sin, showing no need for our usual rituals. Then after curing lepers, he sends them to our priests to add injury to insult, to shame them by demonstrating his powers over sickness and sin."

The scribe went on, "He also makes a paste of mud and his spittle and uses it to open the eyes of the blind or to untie the tongues of mutes. It's also said that he walks on water, and has stopped a violent storm dead in its tracks in the midst of the Sea of Galilee. Then there are reports that at a wedding in the small village of Cana he changed over a hundred gallons of water present for religious purifications into wine! And no ordinary wine — the guests at the wedding said that it was the best of vintage wine."[10]

When the scribe paused in the litany of wonders, Caiaphas asked, "Did you leave out that he's also a rainmaker, or hasn't he yet attempted that? [11] So, our Jesus is a magician, or is he a miracle-maker?"

"He has to be a magician and a sorcerer!" answered another scribe.

"Tell me then," asked the high priest, leaning forward with a glint in his eye, "as a magician, does he charge money for these cures? No, don't say anything, for I can guess the answer. He doesn't, correct? How then, learned doctors of the law, shall we discern whether this Jesus of Galilee makes magic or miracles? The answer to that question is critical, for if he is a miracle worker, then God is on his side."

"High priest," said one of the priests, "he must be a sorcerer for he mocks the temple and our holy priesthood. In my opinion he's a magician who is possessed by Beelzebub, the Lord of Flies."[12]

"You're probably correct," replied Caiaphas, "but that only begs more questions. For example, when our priests here at the temple remove sins by means of a sin offering through the sacrifice of doves or lambs, does the sin disappear because of magic or by divine power? The definition of magic or miracles is determined partly by how you view them. So, speaking of flies, was Moses a magician or a miracle worker? Was it a miracle or magic when he turned his staff into a serpent? Was he in league with Beelzebub or with God when he rained down plagues of frogs and flies to terrify the Pharaoh and all of Egypt? To those priests of Egypt his power, without doubt, was an act of magic!"[13] Then, forming a pyramid by placing the tips of his fingers together with his palms spread apart, he said softly, "Which of the two, then, is Jesus — a magician or miracle worker?"

The discussion continued as various reports were given about what Jesus may have said or done. In the middle of a long exchange, the high priest, growing tired, held up his hand and said, "Elders, doctors of the law and members of this secret council, tell no one what has been discussed here this night. It is late now, time for us to retire. I shall report back to King Herod and to Governor Pilate that we are investigating this man and his small band. What we need is someone inside that group of followers whom we can count on for reliable information about Jesus' movements. Does anyone know of someone whom can perform this service for us?"

After a silence, broken only by the sputtering of the oil lamps, the scribe who had attended Simon the Pharisee's dinner spoke up. "I believe, high priest, I might know just such a man."

WEEDS IN THE FIELD OF THE FAMILY OF DISCIPLES

Meanwhile in Galilee to the north, Jesus and his disciples traveled from town to town, announcing the arrival of God's kingdom. From what eyes could see of the cloak of their community, it was a loving family. Many hungry for such intimacy wished that they might have been chosen to live so close to the Master and share in the love of the Family. But all cloaks, even peasant ones, have linings; they have both outsides and insides. One day Jesus came upon Susanna who was sitting apart from the others, sobbing. "Susanna," he inquired, "why are you crying? Has something happened?"

"It's old Mary, she's at it again! Like an old hen, she's pecking at us younger women."

"You don't mean Mary, my mother?" asked Jesus.

"No, I'm talking about the other Mary, the mother of James and Joseph, from your home village. She never lets the rest of us forget that you and she are related as family and insists on being treated in a special way."

"Susanna, you know as well as I, that in my Family we all are to treat one another as brothers and sisters, as equals. I'm afraid that Mary was like that when James and Joseph and I all lived in Nazareth."

"She treats us as if we were her daughters-in-law, ordering us around: 'Go get supper ready,' or 'Go wash my dear sons' clothing.' Surely, Jesus, it's not as if we women disciples were married to the men and had wifely obligations!"

"No, of course not."

"And Jesus, Mary is such a busybody; her daily bread is gossip. She's always murmuring against you to the other women disciples outside our little group. Perfect strangers come to know everything that happens here among us and then they tell others. She constantly finds fault with what you say or do. Like an old door swinging on a rusty hinge, she's been groaning away about how you let that woman fondle you so sinfully at the Pharisee's dinner."

"Hmm...."

"Never to your face, mind you, Jesus, but behind your back! She even says you don't follow God's ways and that you twist Scripture to fit your purposes. She complains that you talk too much about enjoying life, and that while you talk about equality, you don't show it. She complains constantly that you don't show the same favor to Joseph and James that you shower on young John."

"A mother tends to favor her own flesh."

"Master, she's such a pest. We women have given her a name, as you did Simon. We call her Mary the Murmurer. She's always murmuring about what you say or do, about your decisions or how we live together as a family. She refused to let her son James even sit next to Mary Magdalene, convinced she's trying to seduce him."

All this obviously troubled Jesus very much. "Susanna," he said, "even in the midst of your pain with Mary, God's call is still to be compassionate — with an encompassing compassion. That means that you must include her, faults and all, within your heart. I will join you in praying for her, even as I'm painfully aware that nothing does more harm to family or community life than those who murmur. Murmurers are like moths; they destroy a good garment from the inside. As they grumble and complain, they're eating holes in the fabric of community." Jesus groaned deeply as if he were carrying a heavy load up a steep hill.

Then he added, "Like any of the others in or outside our little group, Mary is free to disagree with my decisions or what I say. But how I wish she and they would complain to me, and not behind my back, sowing seeds of discontent among us!"

"Mary the Murmurer has several who agree with her," added Susanna, who — now that she had spoken of her problem and her pain — was not about to stop until she had completely emptied her troubled heart. "She's gotten some women along with some of the men disciples to support her when she denounces your way of making women equal to men. She says the old ways of our people are best when it comes to women! 'They're to serve their men — it's God's law. From birth in God's eternal design women are meant to wait upon the needs of men.' "

Jesus' face clouded over. "Oh, how this angers me, Susanna. I'm also angry at myself for failing in leadership. While I go about saying that God's kingdom is here among us, we have a long way to go before even we in our little group are able to embrace such a new kingdom. But I'm not surprised that some of the men are eager to hear Mary's old fashioned views on women and eager to be waited upon by them."

"I'm sorry, Master," said Susanna, "for bringing you such problems."

"Don't feel bad, Susanna. I appreciate your honesty. You've helped me see that while I say God's time is upon us, in truth it's only partially dawned. It's not even daybreak."

"Master, I'll try to practice compassion with Mary."

"Thank you, Susanna, and I hope you can go in peace."

Susanna did leave in peace, feeling so much better for having emptied her heavy bag of anger and anxiety. Jesus, however, now carried some extra burdens, weighted down by the news of the hidden bickering, murmuring and lack of harmony among his small group. Walking alone away from the group, he began praying as he cried aloud, "Look at me, O God. I'm both angry and sad. If these my specially chosen disciples are unable to live in the peace and love of your kingdom, how can the whole world?"

"Only slowly will they and the world learn how to live in heaven's harmony," said Gabriel, appearing beside Jesus as he walked the lonely hills.

"Thank you for coming," Jesus said with a smile, "for I am more depressed by this infighting among my little group than by the opposition of the scribes and Pharisees. I knew that some of the men disciples have found my words difficult and have murmured. Now I must add Mary, and who knows who else, to the ranks of the murmurers."

"Congratulations, Jesus, you're doing a good job," Gabriel said.

"Congratulations? What do you mean, I'm doing a good job?"

"As a new Moses, how can you expect to be freed of the thorny problems he encountered with the Exodus community as they crossed the desert? He also had to deal with complainers and those who criticized him. Among any group or community are those who murmur, who would find something to complain about. So, Jesus, can you do what you told your disciples to do — bless those who injure you instead of confronting them?"

"You mean, do nothing?"

"Blessing them, loving them as you hold up to them the mirror of God's love — even in the face of irritating murmuring — is hardly what I would call doing nothing. Besides, how else can God's day come unless it dawns out of such real daily life experiences? This will be good practice."

"Practice?"

"Yes, practice, for when the day comes when you will have to forgive those who really cause you pain, who truly injure you and not simply irritate you. Murmurers are the itchy sackcloth penance that must be worn by anyone who strives to usher in a new way. Moses wore just such an itchy garment of grumblers under his tunic for forty years. Surely you, Jesus, can wear one for two or three."

Jesus looked profoundly shocked. "Two or three! Gabriel, have I so little time?"

No answer came. When Jesus looked about, he saw he was alone.

Jesus and his group of close followers worked their way from village to town, gradually affecting the whole of Galilee with the good news. Jesus seemed to have an endless store of parables that explained his prophetic vision and he seemed more than ready to look for meaning in every event.

JESUS SPEAKS OF PAIN AND SUFFERING

One day Jesus seemed more quiet and distant than usual. Judas asked if someone in the Family had in any way displeased him.

"No, Judas, neither you nor any of the others are to blame. If anyone, it was caused by Adam and Eve, or even God!"

"What do you mean, Master?"

He pointed to his mouth, saying, "It's just another toothache, Judas.[14] Just another in a long line, but soon I'll not have to suffer that pain any longer — at my age I don't have many teeth left in my mouth. Decaying teeth, gray hairs, aging and death are all part of our family inheritance from Adam and Eve. Or perhaps they're part of the up and down path of life God designed from the beginning."

"You should have told us about your tooth. Perhaps we could have helped somehow."

"Since I was a boy, like you Judas and the other men, I've learned to suffer pain in silence, not moaning and weeping for pity, not drawing attention to myself. A true man suffers in silence."[15]

"I could get a willow tree branch for you to chew on; they say it steals the pain.[16] Or I could go to town to get some pincers to pull it when it loosens. The Greeks say not to use the pincers if the tooth isn't loose."

"Thank you, Judas, no willow twig or pincers. This pain is a prophet and a mentor from whom I have some lesson to learn. Like any good student, I must be silent so that my teacher, pain, can speak to me."

"You speak as the wise ones of old," said Judas. "They said, 'Let him sit alone in silence when suffering is laid upon him. Let him put his mouth to the dust; and perhaps there may yet be hope.' "

"Not just *perhaps*, Judas, there *is* hope, for hope is the flower of love. We are called twice daily in our prayers to love God with all of ourselves, and loving God means loving all that God sends us. I am struggling with the lesson of how to learn to do more than just endure pain — how to do more than just live with pain but to love it as part of Life — which is but another name for God.

"Right now, though, Judas, I don't feel, as the ancients say, like putting my mouth to the dust; it's more like wanting to put my mouth to a hard rock so I can knock out this tooth. But teacher pain must be as much a part of life as joy. Perhaps God designed pain as part of life, just as night and day are part of time. But, forgive me, Judas. I'm beginning to sound like the philosophers, splitting hairs over the meaning of words."

"Master, escaping pain sounds more sensible than learning to love it. It's hard to see pain as coming from God."

"Judas, pain seems essential if any change is to come in one's life or in the world. All change and reform causes pain to some as it brings joy to others. And denying yourself for the reign of God is always painful, but it's a good and redeeming pain. For anyone to change an old belief, a cherished prejudice clutched for generations, is not possible without pain. Those who flee from pain will still suffer and also will find that little has changed in their lives or in the world."

"Personally, Jesus, I try my best to avoid pain when I see it coming; I've had enough pain already in my life. An infected, aching tooth, however, isn't something you can flee."

"The pain of a toothache will pass, but the pain of a heartache sometimes can remain for a lifetime. As it is said in Proverbs, 'Like an infected tooth or an unsteady foot is a faithless man in time of trouble. Like a moth in clothing, or a maggot in wood, sorrow gnaws at the heart.' "[17] Jesus held his hand to the side of his face in a moment of obvious jabbing pain.

Then he went on. "Judas, this pain of my infected tooth will pass when I get it out. What I dread more is the deeper pain caused by unfaithfulness, by a failure of loyalty. That will be no small moth nibbling on my cloak, as the wise ones said in Proverbs, nor even a toothache. It will be a piercing pain like a spear driven into my heart!"

And the two embraced like brothers, both determined to be faithful.

Chapter Nine

The Disciples Return Home

The tour of the Galilean towns having been completed, Jesus dismissed the disciples who had traveled with him so they could go home to their families. Some returned to their farms to plant their crops, the fishermen went back to their boats. Jesus, however, disappeared from the public scene. Some said he had returned to the desert, others said he had gone to Capernaum, but no one knew for sure. Still, no one was alarmed. They all knew him as a private person and often even a recluse when they were not together on the road.

When Simon Peter arrived back home, his wife, Ruth, greeted him with great delight, overjoyed to have him back. At the dinner table his first night back, the simple feast was enriched by loving conversation about everything that had happened while he was away, all the excitement of Simon's travels, and all the home adventures of Ruth and their three daughters. And when the oil lamp was nearly out, they all retired to their common family bed. As they snuggled down, Ruth and the children eagerly begged to hear his traveling tales.

"Oh, my, what I've seen traveling with Jesus! Scabby lepers' skin cleansed; the blind given new eyes. The hobbling lame have thrown away their canes; those possessed by fierce demons freed, and those hungry for good news given their fill. I've heard ten thousand holy puzzles and riddles; parables that are so filled with wisdom as to be fit for Solomon the king.

"Little ones, this may be too deep for you to appreciate just now, but, oh, Ruth, traveling with the Master is truly the greatest of all joys. It's to be alive in God's holy time, a new age, almost a dream world. It gives to life a meaning full of hope and promise. And Jesus has given me a new name, dear; he calls me Peter now, or sometimes Simon Peter, the *Rock*."

"Oh, Simon, it's so good to have you back. I was afraid when I heard Jesus say that his disciples must leave father and mother, wife, son, daughter and all they own for him, that we'd never see you again."

Peter began to whisper, for their daughters were falling asleep. "My dear, Jesus speaks in black and white. When he says things like, 'You must *hate* father and mother,' what he means is we must love both God and him much more than any other — and that if choose you must, choose God. Unlike Jordan John, Jesus' way is love and good cheer. He calls us not to fast from drink or food — or from wife — the very best of good news." And with that he stroked Ruth's arm with great tenderness.

Ruth whispered back into Simon's ear, "Simon Peter, you are my rock too, upon whom I've built my love and life. This news you speak is truly good, for I feared you'd never be back in bed with us, with me.

"Then I heard at our village well, the unbelievable story that he'd invited women to join his group, but, unlike me, women 'beautiful and slim,' they said." Then Ruth whispered in his ear again. "Simon, dear, now listen, our little dears are fast asleep."

"Ah, yes, my dear Ruth," he said, touching her face, "the kingdom, the Master often repeats, in God's time is like a wedding feast. I'd love a taste of God's great wedding wine."

"And I the joy of waves upon a great rock. Come, my fisherman, let us two plunge far out into the deep, and make sweet love before we sleep."

So Simon, like the other disciples who returned to their homes, returned to his work and enjoyed being with his family again. But after some weeks, the message came to him that Jesus was again gathering together his Family. When the morning arrived to leave home to return to Jesus, Ruth expressed what they both felt.

"Simon, it is torture to see you leave. It's been so good having you home again with us. The children and I, even my mother, will miss you."

"And dear, I will miss all of you, even your mother."

"I know, Simon, that you need to do this. It's hard to let you go, but I also know that you will be a better husband and father when you next return. Each time you are with the Master, he works his magic on you."

Then she began to giggle. Holding her hand to her face, she added, "You're even a better lover."

Simon chuckled, his face pink like the dawn. "I think my Master would be happy to hear that! And I am truly blest to have a wife as understanding as you."

They walked together a little way down the road, and Ruth said, "I wish I could accompany you as do those other women, but I have the children and mother for whom I must care, and the house and garden."

"Dear, you do accompany me even when you remain here — and you are more than simply in my thoughts. You and I, as husband and wife, share the same mission of announcing the arrival of God's kingdom. By your fidelity to our home and children, you make possible my ministry. We are two in one body, as we celebrated so wonderfully last night. And, as one, you also are a disciple of his."

"Truly I feel that too, Simon, but I shall still miss you not lying next to me in bed. Yet I know the day is coming when we shall go forth together to announce the kingdom."[1]

"You know that I will miss you too," he said, kissing her. "May that day you speak of race to us. And now it's time for me to say good-bye. Peace, my dear, and may God bless you and our home until I return again."

JESUS AND THE TWELVE GO TO BETHANY

After his time in solitude, Jesus decided to make a trip to Bethany in the outskirts of Jerusalem to prepare for a future tour to the holy city. He sent word ahead to the homes of his small band of traveling disciples that only the original twelve were to accompany him while the women disciples would meet him when they returned to Galilee. So Jesus and the twelve men went to stay with his friends, Mary, Martha and their ailing brother, Lazarus.

The day they arrived was hot as an oven, and they were as unexpected as the three angels who visited old Sarah and Abraham. Martha was surprised and delighted by Jesus' visit. She immediately busied herself preparing a meal and caring for the guests, while her sister Mary chose to sit at the feet of Jesus in the middle of the circle of his disciples. Following gossip about the fox King Herod and local political problems, the subject turned to the struggles and concerns of family life. After some spirited discussion, Jesus said to his friends:

"Do not worry about your daily needs,

about what you are to eat, drink or wear.
Is not the life God fills us with
more important than these?

"Learn a lesson from your teachers,
the beautiful lilies of the field.
They do not toil or spin their robes,
yet old King Solomon in all his glory
was never dressed in such splendor."

The disciples smiled, and Simon Peter spoke up with glee: "Master, not to toil or labor is truly good news. The kingdom of God is like one long Sabbath day with no work."

James also was overjoyed. "Yes, may God's time, an age of no toil, come quickly, for this kingdom sounds like heaven!"

Meanwhile, out in the kitchen, Martha was sending a message to her sister, as she angrily banged her pots and pans, slamming cupboard doors. The message to her sister Mary was clear in the din:

Bang, crash, bang; come and help me.
This is not a day of Sabbath rest.
You and I have work to do, don't you see?

As she was busy preparing the meal, Martha overheard Jesus and muttered to herself: "Jesus, why don't you learn a lesson from the lilies on the hill. If, like them, I didn't work, you'd get no meal! And if everyone did what you propose, how would we survive? These pious sayings of yours are too unreal."

Jesus looked at each of his disciples, then continued speaking:

"Seek first the kingdom, live in God's holy time,
and all things you seek will be yours.
Enough worrying about poor tomorrow's fate;
for today has enough problems of its own."

Martha's mutterings became more audible. "I'll say it does. Today, I've got all the kitchen work to do by myself. Who's got time to worry about tomorrow?"

"Learn a lesson from the lilies of the field," Jesus went on, "and sometimes do *not* be like them!" Mary at his feet, nodded her head in agreement.

"Master," said Simon Peter with a wrinkled brow, glancing at his friends, "now you really confuse us. First you say we should be like the lilies of the field; then you say we should not be like them. Which one is it? Or is this another riddle to solve?"

Jesus smiled, "Blessed are the ambiguous, for life is full of paradox, Peter."

"Master," said Mary, "when you say we are not to be like the lilies, don't you mean we are not to be like the daylilies that bloom only when the sun is full, and at night close up tightly?"

"Exactly, Mary," said Jesus. "While you, my friends, are to be like lilies in their beauty and simplicity, in their lack of anxiety about what to wear, do not be like those lilies that only bloom in the light of day. But the daylilies teach yet another lesson, for they grow hardy in stony ground and the poorest of soils."

"Master," moaned Simon Peter, "once again, we've cast our nets into the deep and caught nothing with all this talk of flowers. Unlike Mary and the other women, we men who are providers can't be concerned with such things, and so your meaning is lost on us."

"Listen well, Simon, for hard lessons
     can be learned from delicate flowers.
Indeed, my disciples must usually survive without the light,
     must spring up and flourish in the worst of times.

"It's easy to be a disciple when the sun is bright,
     when all the cheering crowds are on your side,
     when neighbors and authorities smile on all you do.
Blessed are those who can bloom in the darkest night,
     and blessed are those who still can bloom
     when overshadowed by angry conflicts and rejection.

"Blessed also are those who do not fail to bloom
     when they're planted among stony hearts and ears,
     planted in the midst of rocks of ridicule and jeers.
Blessed, comrades, are those disciples who are not lily-livered,
     who are not fearful cowards fleeing the evil's darkness,
     with no hope of being delivered from dark forces."

"Lord," cried Simon Peter, "never will we be cowards who flee. Never will we be lily-livered and forget or forsake you."

As Jesus began to respond, Martha stomped into the circle of disciples, pointing an accusing finger like a weapon at her sister Mary. "Master, are you not concerned that my sister has left me all alone to prepare the meal? Tell her to get up and help me!"

Jesus sighed, "Martha, you are right. Forgive me for failing to see. It's not right for you to labor alone preparing a meal for us. It is not you but I who should be serving this meal, for I have come not to be waited upon, but rather to be a slave to others."

Martha was stunned. "You, Master, prepare the meal and serve the table? Never in my house," she replied, "that's woman's work!" Shaken, the men disciples nodded in agreement.

"In my Family, Martha, there is no such unjust division of labor. Come here and sit beside me." He made room and the flustered Martha sat down. "Brothers and sisters, know that Martha has been busy with the first of all sacred rituals, hospitality. It is holy work and priestly work to show loving care for guests." Jesus placed his arm around her, adding, "Let her caring be sung wherever the memory of this day is repeated."

The disciples nodded in agreement.

"Master," asked Andrew, "which one, Mary or Martha, in your eyes, chose the better part?"

"They are, in a way, twin sisters, and both have chosen the better part. Nor should either choice be taken away. Like opposite sides of the same coin, loving service and loving listening are sisters. So too, prayer and ministry — reflecting on God and feeding God's hungry — are twin sisters. Martha, since childhood all of us have had to work hard, so it comes more naturally as a way to serve God than does sitting quietly and listening as Mary did. Most find it easier to make their labor their prayer than to labor to pray. Yet when you see yourself in the mirror as both a Martha and a Mary, then you will be whole and full of God's life. For work and prayer are two holy twins. Use both to enter God's time so you will not end up as lily-livered disciples!"

Young John spoke up, "Lily-livered? You've used that term twice now, Master. Just what does it mean?"

Jesus smiled. "You are brave, John, to admit not knowing something rather than pretending to understand. Here's what it means to be lily-livered. It's been the custom among Greeks and Romans to sacrifice an animal before entering battle to look for a sign from the gods. If the animal's liver is rich red, it's an omen of victory. If the liver is pale white as a lily, it foretells defeat. Such a lily-livered omen calls for retreat. So, a coward's heart is as white as is a lily blossom."[2]

"Master," said John, "may my heart be red as wine. May I never disappoint you and seek never to be separated from you."

"We shall pray that is true for you, John, and all of you," replied Jesus. "And may I never disappoint you as well. Now it is time to enjoy this meal Martha has poured her soul into, even if it's been warmed over the fire of her anger."

At their dinner that followed Jesus insisted on waiting upon the table. After they had eaten, he also went into the kitchen and helped the two women clean the dishes, much to the dismay of the men disciples.

Later the men were resting under the shade of a great sycamore tree outside the home of Martha, Mary and sickly Lazarus, when Jesus and the women joined them. Jesus said, "The question arose at dinner as to the nature of God's kingdom. This time of God of which I speak is like a mustard seed that a farmer took and sowed in a field. That seed, as you all know, is the smallest of seeds. Yet when full grown it becomes the largest of plants. The birds of the air come and nest in the branches of this large bush."

The disciples, except Matthew, looked up in silent wonder into the branches of the mighty sycamore. The only sound was the wind rustling its leaves, except for a strange scratching sound. Suddenly, Jesus said in a stern voice:

Jesus' Song to Matthew

"Scratch, scratch, Matthew, put down your tollbooth pen;
    each deed and each word I say you drown in ink.
Stop your constant scribbling and open your heart.
My words are *living*, don't imprison them with your pen;
    words of life must be alive, not mummified manuscripts.

"Matthew, put down your pen; be not my scribe
    but my disciple, my comrade and friend!
Moses' scourge was scribes with pens and embalmer's ink,
    enclosing God's fiery word in scrolled mausoleums,
rolling up God's love embalmed in aged yellow scroll-shrouds.

"Tell me, where's our beloved Moses, God's passionate lover?
    Entombed along with the pillar of fire and manna from the sky.
Dead are his holy words, put into graves scratched by pens,
    buried by the priests, they now lie in long straight rows.
So Matthew, stop scribbling as a scribe,
    writing down all my parables and my clever asides,
    carefully tallying up my miracles, the wonders you've seen.

"Put down your pen, my friend, and see
    that you and the others are my words.
Live loudly my words when you're under the whip;
    be living words under the deadly rain of insults and sharp stones.
When you're my living memory, my words will be ever free

to sing and dance at home and in lands we'll never see.

"Matthew, tax not my patience, collect no toll upon my talk.
 Matthew, put down your pen and take up your...cross."

Here, Jesus stumbled in his speech, tripping over his careless word. He paused; then, with a cough, he said, "Take up the harder work: to tell others of me by your deeds."

Suddenly, Jesus stood and said, "The afternoon is gone. Excuse me, I must go." He left the circle of disciples sitting under the sycamore tree and began to walk westward toward Jerusalem.

"Where is he going?" asked Matthew, his pen dangling in his hand.

"To his favorite retreat place, his secret prayer place among the olive trees," replied Judas, "on the slopes above the Kidron Valley, a garden called Gethsemani."

"Did you notice," asked Simon the Zealot, "how the Master stumbled when he told Matthew to not carry a pen. But, did I hear him say, 'Take up your *cross*?' "

"Yes, he did say cross," replied Simon Peter, "but the word caught like a fishbone in his throat. He seemed to find it by surprise upon his tongue. How strange to say to us, 'Take up your cross.' Only bandits and rebels against Rome carry crosses — upon which they must die!"

No one said another word about what he had said. Simon the Zealot, however, smiled, saying to himself, "Perhaps, just perhaps, it is a hint of what's to come. Perhaps at last, an uprising to liberate our land. No longer shall we be impotent eunuchs of once-proud Israel."

JESUS IN GETHSEMANI

As Jesus walked along the road, in the distance the golden orange halo of the setting sun crowned the great temple dome. Jesus fell to his knees in the olive garden grove.

"O God, come to my assistance, make haste to help me.
 Cross: I fail to see where that ugly word came from.
 Poor rebel bandits caught by the Romans
    are nailed up to die on those two-limbed trees.
 I fear that it was you, my beloved God,
    who upon my tongue did plant that seed."

"Jesus, it was no slip of tongue," Gabriel said,
    suddenly becoming visible and kneeling beside him.
"Yes, the Spirit implanted the word on your tongue

and may make you spit it out again some day.
Jordan John's dead, beheaded as you well know;
   and you must soon choose which road you'll take.[3]
I'm to warn you, Jesus, that time is short."

"Jordan John," said Jesus, "was a lamp aflame for all to see;
   a prophet of fire, a great messenger of God."

"A great light was John, indeed," the angel replied,
   "a spark that grew into a holy flame.
Jesus, you kneel tonight, praying at a crossroads
   in a garden where olives are pressed into oil,
   but time now presses in on you.
You must choose: You may return home, a peasant worker in wood,
   docile, tamed, in speech discrete, causing no trouble —
   then you can die old and quietly upon a bed of straw.
Or keep your present course as John stayed true to his.
   Unlike him you will not lose your head in the stroke of a sword,
   but worse, you will hang, crucified, nailed to a Roman cross!"

The words seemed to fall like a giant limb of a wind-crippled tree, crushing Jesus. "No!" he cried out to the darkening sky, covering his face with his hands. "My God, my God, must your terrible will be done?" Then he realized he had no choice, so linked to God and God's dream did he feel. Over the Holy City the evening star appeared large and clear in the pink-salmon-colored evening sky as he stood and walked back slowly toward Bethany.

The Road North to Galilee

The next day Jesus and the disciples left to return to Galilee. On the road north, not far from the holy city, they came upon an execution place, a row of trees of the dead, Rome's favorite cure for rebellion. The air was heavy with the stench of death. Roman soldiers stood guard over the most recently condemned criminals who hung dying on their crosses. The pain-filled screams of those still living filled the air as the group of Galileans hurried by.

Simon the Zealot muttered to himself, being careful not to be heard by the soldiers. "Zealots, their only crime was being guilty of refusing to be eunuchs. I dream of the day when we can nail the Romans to their own crosses."

At the end of the line of crosses was an empty one, a single upright shaft awaiting its crossbeam and the poor victim who would hang on it.

"Simon," said Judas as they passed by, "do you also have nightmares of being the dead decaying fruit hanging on that last tree that's empty?"

Jesus shuddered.

Jesus Speaks of Holy Greed

Later, passing through a village on the way north, James came to Jesus and said, "Master, we saw someone in this village who was driving out demons by using your name. Several of us tried to stop him since he does not belong to our Family or your other disciples!"

"How shameful," said Simon Peter, "to steal your name so filled with healing power, a name from which demons flee."

Jesus, however, replied, "Do not prevent him from using my name. For those who are not against us, even if they do not belong to our group, are for us! Let us not hoard holy things. Let us not limit God's power to do good in the world by falling into holy greed. God's ways often appear to us as crooked, while our straight ways often look crooked to God."

Then, moving off the road into a grove of trees, Jesus had the disciples sit down to rest. Out of the threadlike thoughts that were tangled in their hearts, he began spinning a yarn:

The Parable of the Trees

One day, God regretted exiling Eve and Adam from Eden's grove and retired the angel of the flaming sword at the front gate. Throwing away the padlock, God swung open Eden's garden gate, saying, "All of Eve's children are welcome to come home again." By droves they came into God's grove of every kind of tree — apple, olive, pear, oak, fig, sycamore — every tree God had created. A big sign in a hundred tongues read, "Choose for a home any tree you like. In its branches find peace and rest."

Satan saw God's paradise gates open and slyly slipped inside. Sly Satan came not as a snake but as the wisest bird, a wise old owl perched in a tree near the entry gate. As the children came in, the wise old owl hooted, "Tell me, clever children, what is 2 plus 2?"

"That's easy," they replied, "2 plus 2 is 4."

With a mother's proud grin, the owl replied, "That's correct! My, my, you are clever indeed. For 2 plus 2 can never ever be 7 or 5 or 3; 2 plus 2 can only be 4, since truth is always one.

Now, my dears, the same is true for trees; only one of these trees can be the true tree."

The confused children replied, "But didn't God say, on tree creation day, that all trees were created good?"

With a grandmother's toothy grin, old wise owl hooted in response, "God lied! So be very careful, for some trees are evil, some fake with wax fruit and all the rest are poison!"

Cautioned by the wise old owl, some children chose to live in the oak, some in the sycamore, others in the pear. They lived happily after, each in his or her chosen tree, till one day when old owl visited each tree, speaking the same message to each group: "Hoot, hoot, clever children, you remembered that 2 plus 2 is 4. How wise of you to choose your tree for it alone is true. See the others in that tree over there? It's an evil tree. Rejoice and thank God, for only yours is the true tree."

From tree to tree sly Satan flew, singing loudly to each his devilish song of one truth and only one truth. The children threw angry words at those in other trees and argued over which was the oldest and tallest tree. They began to throw rocks and even to kill each other. In the name of truth they chopped down each other's trees.

In the midst of that holy war of truth a rooster came, crowing loudly to announce the dawning of God's new time. Into the grove of trees there came a band of children of the kingdom. The old wise owl hooted, "Children, what is 2 plus 2?"

They replied, "2 plus 2 can be 4, or it can be 22!"

"Impossible!" screeched owl. "2 plus 2 can only be 4. Since ancient ages truth is, and must be, only one."

The children only laughed, which was acid in the ears of the proud old owl, who flapped his wings angrily and flew away. So the new children chose not to make their home in any of the trees, but lived happily in a weed — yes, a weedy bush named the mustard bush.

THE SONG OF SIMON OF CYRENE

Simon Peter scratched his head, confused, while some of the disciples laughed. Simon of Cyrene, who had joined the family on the way from Bethany, laughed loudest. "Master," he said, "may I sing a tail to your song?" Smiling, Jesus nodded agreement.

"This is a little tail I tag onto the Master's tale: No great tree but only a weed springs from a mustard seed. What dumb birds would build a nest in a weed with no permanence? Who but God's birds would find a home in a weedy bush?

"As a farmer, I know that mustard bushes, once seeded in a field, quickly grow into legions, taking over all the land. How foolish to plant them where they can't be contained.[4] But kingdom folk are like mustard, spicy hot to season the pot. The kingdom's a tiny mustard seed — once sown in the land, it becomes a creeping sea of weeds choking out the neat rows of the holy temple's field, shortly thereafter to take over Ceasar's farm."

THE LITTLE CHILDREN COME TO JESUS

Finally back in Galilee, Jesus and the disciples who had accompanied him to Bethany were joined by the rest of the disciples in his Family and some who belonged to his Village. As they stopped at a small town to rest by the road one day, little children came up to them and Jesus blessed them. Some of the men rebuked the children and tried to chase them off. When Jesus saw this he was indignant: "Let the little children come to me and play among us. We have nothing to hide; all I have to say I speak in the open. So let them come, even if they spy." The women disciples were especially quick to understand. Mary Magdalene, who knew a thing or two about village gossip, sang to the delight of all:

"Free to come and go, bless the little children dears;
    with big ears and eyes, in and out of homes they pass.
Then with their little ears full, back to mommy they run,
    for she, like her neighbors, bored, is eager for juicy news.
Blessed be village life, where good news is another's woes,
    like the gossip of who's sleeping with another's spouse.
And blessed be the children, the cute little spies of village life."[5]

"But, Master," asked a confused Simon Peter, "have you not told us before that unless we become like children we cannot enter the kingdom? Did you not also say that anyone who receives a child in your name is being a host to you?"

"Simon, Stone of the Sea, that's true. God's age is for those who become like children. Yet we all know that childhood is not all sweet and innocent, free from work, sweat or threat. And while the kingdom is a time of pure openness, God's time is not play time. The real reason it's blessed to be like a child is that these little ones are nobodies, the lowest of all, on the bottom rung. Children are the poorest of the poor; to such as these belongs the kingdom!

"Yes, children are the cutest beggars, and though that makes them graced in God's sight, they're still *forced* to be beggars. It's that way as well with our Family: we've only God to rely on to defend our rights. It's true that the kingdom is at our door, and it's for chosen outcasts. The kingdom belongs to nobodies, yes, the poorest among us. When you welcome such a nobody, a beggar or stranger, at your door, truly, I say, it's I you greet."

The disciples sat stunned at his words about becoming not simply poor, but nobodies! For most of them had joined Jesus thinking they would become somebody important. His words this day were ripping gaping holes in those dreams.

Not seeking to soothe their shattered illusions, Jesus stood up. "Come, my friends," he said, "we've rested enough. It's time for us to be on the road again." As they left the town, a couple of ragged children ran along, taunting them, "Nobodies, nobodies, you're just a bunch of nobodies!"

CHAPTER TEN

THE MISSION OF THE DISCIPLES

Jesus desired his disciples to experience directly God's providence and taste the manna of daily miracles. So he sent them out to proclaim the good news and heal the sick, giving these instructions:

"Go forth: I give you power over unclean spirits;
　heal the sick, and proclaim that God's time is here.
　Go with nothing, no bag or money and only one tunic."

Judas complained immediately, "Master, do you intend for us to live in such dire poverty, not even to have a spare tunic?"

Jesus replied, "These instructions are for your growth, that you may be transformed, not as a way of life to last forever."

Judas was still not satisfied. "Master, as your students, what is it that you want us to learn by departing with nothing but the tunics on our backs?"

"Judas, you are not my students, you are my followers.[1] I have called you to follow me, to be swallowed up by God and to be made new by the Spirit, just as I was transformed in the desert. If you travel with nothing but God's presence, you will find that you have everything! Then you will know firsthand the fiery taste and feel of God in your life and not believe something only because I have spoken about it. As with fire, those who have felt searing flames truly know the feel of fire, unlike those who have only been told about fire!" Then he sighed and said,

> "The harvest is great, but the harvesters are few,
> Let us pray to the master of the harvest
> to give us more harvest hands."

So he gathered the disciples to pray for awhile in silence. There was a confident waiting in the silent prayer, for as Jesus had said to them many times before, "Knock and it shall be opened. Seek and you shall find."

Following their time of prayer, the women had a brief conference among themselves, after which Susanna spoke up. "Master, Mary Magdalene, Joanna and I, along with some of the other women in your Family, wish to be sent into the harvest field too. We know we're women, but like Ruth of old, who labored in the fields of Boaz, we are willing and able to labor at the hard work of the harvest."

"God is Great!" exclaimed Jesus. "Our prayer has been answered. But before I send you into the harvest, there's the issue of your honor. I could send each of the twelve out alone, as I myself first went. However, even for you women to travel together in pairs is not possible without shame being cast upon you. So I will send you on the mission two by two, one woman and one man, traveling as brother and sister, but appearing to the casual eye as husband and wife."[2]

This creative solution to the problem, allowing the women to also proclaim the kingdom, disturbed some of the men disciples. Simon Peter moaned to himself, "Oh my, what will my dear wife think?"

There were other objections to the mission. "Master," asked Judas, worrying again, "if we are not allowed to carry a purse and take money with us, several of us are concerned about how we shall buy our bread."

"Judas, and you others, how else can you taste the manna of daily miracles if you are not at risk or in need? Only when you are needy are you ripe for the touch of God in your life. I assure you that God will provide all you need if you are totally dedicated to making this time of history into God's holy time."[3]

Unwilling to let go of his concerns about their daily needs, Judas asked, "Can we then ask money of those we heal of impure spirits for the service of liberating them? I am not alone in feeling that we should be repaid for our service."

"No, my friends, freely I was given the power to heal and freely I give it to you. You must likewise give it away to those who are in need. Do you know what age it is? It is God's time and the kingdom is here.

Whenever we live in that holy hour and place, it is the time of unconditional love. In my Family it should always be thus. Here's what I want you to remember:

"Do not peddle the kingdom of love
    from door to door to those with no ears.[4]
Never force your medicine on the sick,
        not pestering people to take your gift,
        nor making them sick with pains of guilt.

"When hearts are freely opened to you,
        then generously pour in the gift of good news.
Heal the sick, lift the burdens of pain,
        and do not be anxious about your pay.
A favor for a favor, a gift for a gift:
        as you heal them, you in turn will be healed;
        give miracles, and you'll be given miracles.

"Healed of their pain from impure spirits,
        with a spirit of pure gratitude and thanks,
        they'll tend to your body's needs in return,
        healing your homesickness by opening their homes,
        giving you a meal and a place to rest.

"Beware, my friends, of the god of money,
        for every slave has but one heart.
You can never serve two masters:
        you'll love the one and hate the other.
So choose you must as to whom you'll serve:
        Will you be a loving slave of the God of heaven
        or a loving slave of the god of wealth?
        Remember — do not peddle the kingdom of God
        from door to door to those with no ears."

His summary was troubling to many. "Master, are you saying that we're to be like slaves?"[5] asked James, the son of Mary, amidst the murmuring of some of the other disciples. They were made deaf to the rest of his message by his use of the word slave, which pierced their ears like a nail. "Moses freed us from Egyptian slavery. Each Sabbath day of rest is to remind us that we are no longer, nor shall we ever again be, slaves! Surely you do not intend us to return to slavery here in the promised land?"

Jesus pressed his point. "Yes, my brothers and sisters, you are to be slaves to Love! You are not to be like hired servants who are free to come and go, but slaves who belong body, soul and heart to their master or mistress, who is Love, who is God. Only in such slavery is there security! You know as well as I that no master or mistress who has a totally devoted personal slave will fail to feed, clothe and care for so beloved a slave — and will even make that slave an intimate member of the household! So it shall be with God's care of you."

Jesus continued, "James, Judas and the rest of you, learn a lesson from the women disciples here. Some were healed of evil spirits, cured of various afflictions, and how did they respond? Yes, with great generosity. Learn from the women."[6]

"What lesson, Master, would you like us to learn from Mary the Murmurer, the mother of James and Joseph?" asked Simon the Zealot with mischievous delight. Mary, in response, curled her lip, about to speak, but instead only spoke with her eyes. It was not a peaceful message.

"Simon," said Jesus, "it seems you still have much to learn about family and generous love. Open your heart, Simon. Like the women disciples, you must first have great openness to receive a gift, whose real source is God. Once you have an open heart, the greater the gift received, the greater will be the gift given in response. The women have not ceased to be generous; they have supported us, some from their meager means, others from their wealth."

Simon became silent. Judas was likewise silent in speech, but his heart was filled with voices. Simon Peter spoke out loud what some of the others felt, "Master, we men have left everything to follow you."

"Yes, Simon Peter, I know you have. And I promise you and all the others who have chosen to place service to me and God's reign before that of work or families, you will be given a hundredfold in this life and life eternal in the next."

"Some do not believe, Master," said Judas, finally expressing some of what was brewing in his heart, "in a next life! Scholars like the Sadducees, who know God's Law inside and out, teach that there are no angels and no life after death. Will you explain what you mean by 'life eternal'?"[7]

"You are right, Judas, some believe in life after death and some believe only in this life. When you return from your mission, we will talk more about this. Now it is time for all of you to prepare to depart. But I cannot send you out to work for the kingdom without a feast to strengthen you. We shall have a special celebration tonight, and tomorrow you will depart at sunrise."[8]

THE LAST SUPPER BEFORE THE MISSION

That night, by the Sea of Galilee, they shared a meal of roasted fish and not the usual daily barley loaves but rich wheat bread.[9] Judas, concerned as always about the cost of such a meal, objected, but Jesus insisted that it must be special. At the meal Jesus himself served the roasted fish and bread to all, even to the women disciples, again causing a kind of scandal among the men. Jesus, as host and hostess, steward and slave, waited upon them with great delight.[10] When the extravagant supper was over, Jesus rose and took a cup of wine, saying:

"Bread and fish shared has made us all one;
> now let this cup of new wine overflowing
> sing of the new days in God's new time,
> sweet to the tongue, sweeter still to the heart.
It is my love I give in this wine as a living sign
> to you, my disciples, as you depart in peace."[11]

Then Jesus passed the cup of wine to his disciples, each of whom drank from it. Moving among the circle of men and women disciples, he placed his hands on their heads, each in turn, and prayed:

"Receive the Spirit of the holy
> to make those who are broken whole,
> to help the unholy see their unseen holiness.
Receive God's Spirit of the pure
> to heal those with impure spirits.
Receive the Spirit, holy and pure,
> so you, the holy and pure of heart,
> can see God in all."

Then as the leaping orange flames of the fire danced up toward the dome of night's great dark feasting hall, Jesus began to dance around the fire, singing and gradually drawing each of them into his zestful dancing...until all of them were whirling and spinning in twos and threes, and listening to the irresistible folk melody of his song:

"Come, dance with me in Eden time
> as God danced with Adam and Eve,
> bare feet pounding on the holy soil.
Come, dance with me in endless time
> as God has danced wildly with the stars
> each night since time first began.

"Come, dance with me as Adam did with Eve.

Come, dance with me as archangels dance.
Come, dance the good news until the dawn,
   so your bare feet dancing on the road
   will sing that God's wedding feast is here.
As near as I now do dance with you,
   say, 'So close has God's kingdom come,'
   say, 'It's in your hands, at your feet,'
   proclaim it with the joy of this dance."[12]

Late into the night they danced and sang, celebrating the wonder of the Spirit of God coming upon them. As Jesus had been, they were now blessed to bring glad tidings to the poor. The Spirit of the Master was theirs as well. Later, when the events of that night were remembered, some spoke of hearing drum music. Others said it was only the waves pounding upon Galilee's shore. It was, however, not the beat of waves, but of the angel Gabriel playing the goatskin drum of that Spirit's wedding feast! It was God's drummer, to whose desert drum beat all the prophets of old have danced.

Joyfully the disciples joined Jesus; circling around the fire, they danced to the angel's drum, stomping in delight. Wild, crazy, drunk with friendship and love, they all danced and danced, with one exception: Judas. He fled in silent protest into the night.

THE DISCIPLES RETURN FROM THEIR MISSION

When the disciples of the Family returned from their mission, they were full of stories about how God had worked through them and cared for them, how they had been protected and never lacked for bread or a place to stay at night. Jesus marveled at the little miracles they had experienced firsthand. He rejoiced that they no longer believed just because of his word and example. They now knew from their experience that as long as they sought the kingdom with zeal, all their needs would be met.

Jesus found no joy in the fact that before they departed Mary had forbidden her sons James and Joseph to travel with a woman disciple but insisted that they go together. Upon the disciples' return, Mary grumbled loud enough for all to hear: "Women should bear babies, not the Gospel — that's a man's work." Jesus prayed to himself, "O God, come to my assistance, and give me patience. O God, hasten to silken my ever-itching sackcloth of those who resist change."

All this happened in Galilee by the sea.

THE ROAD TO TYRE AND SIDON

From there, Jesus and his disciples went off to the district of Tyre and Sidon along the Mediterranean. [13] As they set out on the unfamiliar road, Simon Peter asked, "Master, why have we left the familiar territory of Galilee and set out for the northern frontier? Where are you taking us?"

"To the edge, Simon, and once we've fallen off the edge, perhaps we shall find the truth." The men disciples dropped back, gathering in small murmuring clusters as Jesus walked alone up ahead.

"Nervous?" Gabriel asked, as he appeared beside Jesus but unseen by the others. [14] "Like Simon, does it worry you to be leaving the known for the unknown?"

Jesus said, "I feel drawn up this road to pagan Tyre by some strange power...."

"Ah yes, Jesus, we know what or, I should say, *who* drags you and your little family of followers along this seacoast road."

"Gabriel, I have learned from you that God's ways are not ours, and they often confuse me. I thought my mission was to gather to God the lost of Israel, my own people, not to announce the good news to these pagan foreigners, these gentile Greeks and Phoenicians. They were born blind to the word of God."

"Jesus, were you not called, in Isaiah's words, to heal the blind? What better place to feel the excitement of being an opener of eyes, even of those born blind, than on the road to the fabled twin cities of Tyre and Sidon? But as you walk along the road, consider this: You feel my presence and even see me, yet are your disciples not blind to who walks beside you?"

"Well, yes, yet at times I wonder if Simon of Cyrene or young John can see you. They have eyes of mystics, who see more than others see."

"What about you, Jesus, who have eyes that see more than others? What do you see?" As he pondered, Gabriel began to sing:

"Many are the scabs that cover the eyes of those who see,
　　and many are those with a longing for God who live along this sea.
To see God's rich design of life, look with eyes that are scale-free,
　　and read God's first word boldly scribed in every plant and seed.
God loves variety: Look in the sea and up in the sky as well;
　　the earth is richly blessed with many kinds of fish and birds,
　　of plants and flowers and countless different trees. [15]
Open wider your kosher eyes, Jesus, stumbling son of Joseph,
　　for God has not just a chosen bride; God's a lover with a harem."

"Gabriel, you're pushing me over the edge. To open my eyes as you propose would make me a blind fool to the wisdom in the book of Moses. Yet what I see written in this holy book of land and sea, in the green gospel of Genesis' trees, only affirms your wisdom to me."

Just then Simon Peter cried out. "Master, we're treading toward danger on this road along the sea."

"I'm afraid!" Simon the Zealot joined in. "Remember the angry words of the prophet Jeremiah, 'A cup of wrath I shall pour down their throats, throwing them into vomiting fits, driving mad the kings of Tyre and Sidon and those who live along the pagan shores of the sea.' "[16]

Jesus stopped along the path and said, "Thank you, my two loyal Simons, for the honesty of your feelings. Do any of the rest of you wish to speak your concerns about being in this gentile land?"

From the circle of his disciples not a sound was heard, though many wanted to echo what the two Simons had said. Finally, like a jar being broken, James the Orthodox shattered the silence as he uttered words dripping with discrimination: "These pagans are mad and evil dogs. Their religion's like a cursed leprosy; it's best that we go no further. Let's turn back to the holy land before it's too late. This heathen land along the sea is evil, full of demon, pagan temples, dens of gentile dogs and swine. Let us flee these mad and evil dogs and their religion's leprosy."

James' lament was cut short by a certain Greek Phoenician woman who ran up the road to Jesus, crying, "Wandering holy man from the Lake of Galilee, gossip of your healing power has traveled here ahead of you. In the name of your God and our god Aesculapius, god of healing,[17] cure my poor daughter of the demon who holds her bound 'round with chains of iron."

Jesus stopped and spoke sternly, "Woman, should I take the bread from the children's mouths and throw it to the dogs?"

"Sir," she replied without hesitation, "even the dogs under the feasting table are thrown scraps on which to chew. Throw this dog a small scrap, and heal my poor daughter." Then clasping the hem of his cloak, she pleaded, "I beg you, sir, please give my daughter but a crumb from your large loaf."

"Woman," said Jesus, pausing as he looked out at the sea teeming with many kinds of fish. He watched the various birds along the shore seeking food in the tide waters. Then he continued, "In the name of your Aesculapius with his serpent staff, in the name of Moses with his healing bronze serpent staff,[18] in the name of the God and Source of all, my sister, go home, for your daughter is freed of her demon." The woman burst into tears and ran away toward her home, crying out with exultation.

But Simon Peter disapproved. "Master, you let a woman cling to you, a gentile unbeliever who'd made a fuss. You break not only the holy law of our land, you even break your own command to us not to carry the good news to pagans! Master, tell us, what's going on?"[19]

Jesus replied with an understanding smile, "Remember, dear Simon, how God favored Ruth, a Moabite and no Jew, and Tamar, who was a Canaanite, for their great cleverness. This, then, is the meaning of my healing gift: First, wrap yourself around God's holy knees, in prayer refuse to rise until you're fed. However hopeless your beggar's pleas, God will hear you. Then, open your ears to hear when old rules and laws need to be broken open. For love — compassion — is the one law you need to obey. Finally, open your eyes so you will not be blind to our God who is blind to all frontiers."

Once again Jesus had shocked his disciples into silence, not by his words about prayer, but about a God whose love knows no religious frontiers. As they continued down the road to Tyre and Sidon, some of the group followed him, not understanding his words, but only with the hope they would, some day. Others were tormented by fears that their Master was, as many said, crazy. Jesus walked alone and well ahead of the others, anxious about what lay ahead for him and for his disciples.

CHAPTER ELEVEN

THE TRAVELING THEATER OF APOLLO

The next day Jesus and his group of traveling disciples entered a small town south of Tyre. They saw a crowd was gathering in the marketplace in the center of town, but it was not to welcome them. The people had their backs to Jesus and the disciples and were looking toward the opposite end of town. Then Jesus saw the object of their interest. Lumbering into the town was a great wooden cart carrying a rainbow-colored, striped tent. In front of the wagon walked two men making music with a drum and pipes.

The town was being visited by two traveling groups at once. Jesus with his small band of disciples and the troupe of wandering Greek minstrels, acrobats and actors reached the marketplace at the same time from opposite directions. The crowd of townsfolk and the Family of Jesus flowed together into one, as out of the striped tent atop the cart stepped a man in a magnificent many-colored robe.

"Look, friends," Joanna said, "the actor's cloak is as splendorous as Joseph's many-colored coat."

The actor bowed gracefully to the crowd and said, "I am Gamos, your host and servant of the gods. Your attention, if you please, fair citizens of this noble town along the sea, as well as you wandering Greeks, traveling merchants from Persia, you Phoenician traders and also, it appears, some Jewish visitors from Galilee. Welcome all! Now, one and all, draw close and hear good news."

Pushing forward lest they miss something, the crowd encircled Jesus and his disciples, some of whom were horrified at even being near the heathen spectacle of a theater.

"This day," Gamos continued, "Zeus and the gods of fortune have smiled on you by sending to you the Traveling Theater of the Actors of Apollo. Bless the gods who have directed our feet to your doors. With Olympian pride and the blessing of the gods, we shall provide for you tonight grand entertainment fresh from the stellar stages of Athens, Corinth, Crete and Tyre. Tonight, we will present something old and something new to stir your souls, for we are no mere actors wearing masks, but are priestly performers as in the old and golden days of Greek theater. We are wandering artists of sacred comedy and tragedy to entertain and enlighten you."

"Master," Simon Peter said as he tugged at Jesus' arm, "let us quickly be out of here. Theater is for unclean pagans! Their plays are immoral and indecent, sowing sin in eyes and ears." Joseph and James' mother Mary voiced loudly her agreement with Simon Peter. While some disciples were fascinated and wanted to stay, others cried, "Yes, lest God strike us dead, let us all leave this place."

Jesus simply replied, "Let us at least listen with open ears and eyes to the announcement this Greek actor is making."[1]

"Distinguished guests," cried Gamos, "after sunset as the Vesper Star dances in the early evening sky, we shall perform for you as in the ancient days when the drama was in an *orchestra*. For our foreign guests, that word means 'the dancing place.' Tonight there will be dancing and song in the orchestra, where, as in olden days, there are no spectators except for the gods![2] Everyone here will be a participant in the drama liturgy, unlike modern theater. Again, for our foreign friends, that word *theater* comes from *theatron* which means 'the seeing place.' So tonight we will have a drama not to be watched but to be entered into and celebrated by all."

"Master!" muttered James, the brother of Joseph, but Jesus put a finger to his lips, signaling silence.

"Tonight in place of a show," Gamos continued, "my companions and I shall grant you immortality. The gift of the gods through the sacred art of drama is to live in another time, to relive earlier times with a pulse in the present so as to foreshadow future times. As in the time of the great playwright, Thespis,[3] we have more than thirty different masks to help us enact the timeless realities. But now, good citizens and travelers, we must prepare the stage-altar and the ritual objects of the sacred drama. Please return this evening after the evening star has appeared and be our guests for a divine feast, the play." Gamos bowed deeply and stepped inside the tent as the crowd of townsfolk began to drift away.

JESUS SPEAKS TO THE CONFLICT IN THE FAMILY

"Come," said Jesus, addressing the whole family, "let's find some food and drink here in the marketplace." As they ate their evening meal, none spoke openly of the Greek troupe of actors. When they were finished with their meal, all eyes were upon Jesus.

"Tonight I will go to see this play the Greeks will perform. Those who wish may accompany me.[4] Those who do not may wait at our camp."

It was James — nicknamed "the Orthodox" — who challenged Jesus' decision. "Master, we know God speaks to us through you, but surely God would not permit attending anything so sinful, so vile and diabolic as what will take place this night in the marketplace."[5]

Jesus answered gently. "James, I understand your feelings, which are shared by others among us, for such is the moral teaching of our religion. However, I have a question for you. Is our Passover Seder meal sinful? Or is the eating of an Exodus meal under tents, which we build with palm branches on our rooftops on the feast of Tabernacles, vile and diabolic?"

"Of course they're not!" replied James as several others nodded agreement. "They are holy feasts of our faith which God and Moses have commanded us to observe."

"Recall, then, what the actor Gamos said tonight about reliving earlier times as a lamp to cast a shadow on future times. Is not God's commandment to celebrate for all generations the Passover meal but a reliving of an earlier time in which all at the table, even the youngest, became actors in a holy drama of our liberation — with God as the only spectator? Friends, with open minds look again at our solemn feast days, each one holy and from God. Are they not holy plays enacted by us in the theaters of our homes? And as Gamos said, they are not theaters for onlookers, for who comes to the Passover meal to look or listen? No, at these feasts all are celebrants, all sacred priestly actors! As he said, such liturgical drama-actions make us immortal for we live in the past and in the future — and in eternity! If our Passover as a domestic drama is not a work of the devil, then tonight's Greek play will not be either!"

There was a shaking of heads among the disciples, some up and down, some sideways. Jesus continued, "Friends, because the Holy Wind at our backs has brought us here, have no doubts. Besides, this has been a long day. I feel we are in need of entertainment, surely also in need of enlightenment. In God's design, as one is entertained one can achieve inner-attainment and so be given light for the mind. I know that some of you feel that the actor's masks are graven images and so are forbidden by the second commandment. By wearing masks, however, these Greeks are but good hypocrites!"

"Good hypocrites, Master?" replied Andrew. "You have condemned the Pharisees and scribes on numerous occasions for playacting, for being hypocrites. Now you speak of good ones?"

"Yes, let me tell you some of the things I learned as a young man, when I worked with my father in building a theatre near Nazareth. The masks the priest-actors shall wear tonight are not worn to disguise some hidden evil, but to play the roles of various characters and to symbolize the struggles of daily life, sometimes lighthearted and joyful, sometimes horrible and tragic. Good hypocrites are those who do not hide their evil under a pious mask, but like actors in the theater they act kindly or with patience toward others, even when they don't naturally feel so inclined. Such actors often become holy, becoming the mask they wear as they act in a way they *should* feel rather than how they actually feel. But enough talking, or we'll miss the play! So, let us go tonight not just as part of the audience, not only to listen or be spectators. Let us go as priestly celebrants of the drama. Look, the evening star has appeared; it's time to go."

The disciples, some with little heart for what they were doing, joined Jesus and the villagers as they took their places in the half circle in front of the great wagon in the marketplace.

The Greek Passion Play of Dionysius

Two acrobats appeared, flip-flopping with flaming torches, then setting ablaze several pole torches and lamps in front of the stage which had been unfolded from the wagon. By means of ropes and pulleys, a backdrop curtain of a forest scene was unrolled behind a tall barren tree trunk in the center of the stage. After a roll of the drums and wild music from the pipes, the actor Gamos stepped forward and said:

"I Gamos, your priestly servant, welcome you
    our distinguished guests in this city along the sea.
Tonight, this traveling theater of the gods presents,

for your entertainment, not a comedy or sexual farce.
We celebrate no play by Sophocles or Euripides
but rather a great tragedy by the Greek poet Nonnus,
his play about the god of the vine, Dionysius the divine."[6]

Onto the stage, now aglow in yellow torchlight, stepped an actor wearing the gold face mask of a handsome youth.

"Away with him," shouted someone in the crowd. "We want no sad tragedy tonight! Give us a comedy to lightened our spirits, for our lives are full of tragedy!"

"Then, sad folk," shouted Gamos, "all the greater the need for this drama of Dionysius. Yes, *Dios-nysos*, the young god. Behold Dionysius, the son of the great god Zeus. Let the play begin."

The gold-masked actor danced into the center, his half-naked body draped in a dark goatskin.

"Tonight, the tale of Dionysius, the divine son,
the only god whose mother was a mortal,
whose father was the father of all gods, Zeus.
Tonight, the bittersweet tale, 'Dionysius in the Tree.' "

With a courtly bow toward Jesus' group, Gamos continued: "Let me give some background for the strangers here: Dionysius is the divine patron of apple, fig and all fruit-bearing trees, the god of the vine and of wine. He is the god of ecstasy and great goat god of fertility, patron of the divine dance that steals away the soul and the most handsome of all the youths of Attica. You farmers among us will recognize his symbol: behold his holy winnowing fan."

The actor removed his golden mask. Beneath it was another mask of a human hero. From under his goatskin tunic he brought out a round shovel-shaped basket as he began to sing:

"I am Dionysius, the divine winnowing fan,
who throws the harvest grain into the air
so the holy wind can separate the dusty chaff.
The good, ripe grain falls into my basket
through heaven's sacred winnowing fan.

"At birth I was placed in a crib of winnowed grain,
thus defining my task in this life:[7]
To separate the good from the bad,
I am the separating savior and judge.
I am Dionysius, the divine winnowing fan,

who throws the harvest grain into the air
    so the holy wind can separate the dusty chaff."

Then in the center of the altar-stage, Gamos appeared again, joined by a chorus of six men in costume, singing:

"Dionysius left home to roam far over the seas,
    a holy wanderer, gifting all those who love him.
The Olympian dancing hero, half man and half goat,
    with twin holy gifts of inspiration and imagination.
Even the kingly lion and great eagle lack imagination,
    the wondrous godly gift to see what is not yet,
    to create, like a god, from images in the mind,
    to be inspired, enthusiastic, possessed by the divine.
Dionysius, the hopping goat-god with shaggy legs,
    half man, half goat dancing in hills and glens,
    in him the divine and the animal are wed as one.

"All were possessed by love for the divine dancer
    who drove them to the edge of insanity,
    filling them with holy inspiration and dreams divine.
But the dancer must pay the piper, and the traveler the toll,
    as hot Summer collects a fee from virgin Spring
    and senior Autumn coolly robs old Summer's purse
    to pay in full aged greedy Winter's deadly toll of tolls.
So, Dionysius the Divine, in being the patron god of dance,
    paid for the dance of life with his own flesh and blood;
    great was his ecstasy — even greater this hero's agony."

The actor wearing the goatskin, having danced about during the song, now ended his dance with his back against the large bare tree stump. Onto the stage appeared several actors wearing sinister black masks. They rushed to the tree trunk where they fastened the defenseless Dionysius to the tree with ropes, ripping off his golden hero's mask to reveal a pale white mask beneath it.

The drum pounded like rolling thunder and the pipes screamed wildly as the black-masked figures drew long knives from within their robes and savagely stabbed at the hanging figure of Dionysius till he fell to the ground.

Then, hidden from view, the chorus wailed:

"Dionysius, son of the great god Zeus,
    as the fruitful vine, you've been pruned,
    your life-vine brutally trimmed back.

Now you are a gnarled dead stump, cruelly cut down,
butchered like the fat goat of the feast."

The stage became empty. There was a long silence. Then the drum and pipes again played wildly as the actors who had slain Dionysius now reappeared, dressed in the costumes and masks of women. They screamed in great anguish, flinging themselves over the dead body of Dionysius. Then a figure of majestic beauty, wearing an old woman's all-white mask and costumed in black as a mourning queen, gravely processed onto the stage. The chorus announced her.

"Behold, worshipers of our traveling temple theater:
holy Demeter, earth mother, mourning her dead son.[8]
See! With a needle and thread she sews him together again,
reknitting her son's mangled dead arms and legs
so as to bring him to life again, to birth him anew."

The ashen, white-faced figure of Mother Demeter saddled with sadness the dead body of her son Dionysius in her lap. Wails of grief broke from her mouth. Then in the midst of her lament, invisible wires raised the divine son onto his feet. He stood alive with both arms outstretched, once again wearing the golden mask of one resurrected from the dead. The crowd roared its approval as he was raised by the wires toward the heavens, vanishing into the top of the tent on the wagon.

Then, to clashing cymbals and the frantic music of the flutes, golden masked Dionysius once again stepped onto the stage, wearing clusters of grapes around his head and carrying in his arms a small white lamb. Gamos, the narrator, sang out an explanation: "Worshipers here at our holy, traveling temple, tonight you've entered into the divine mysteries. Together with us you've celebrated as holy priests the sacred drama of life turning to death and death unfolding unto new immortal life. You and we are not separated by the stage; as one body we all have suffered, died and rose.[9]

"Tonight through the good poet Nonnus' ritual play the gods have united us in the holy mysteries. We are together in earth's greatest drama: Life to death, suffering to glory, then to endless life! As one we have lived the undoubted truth that our souls are immortal, incorruptible. As the dead pruned vine lives again, so do we, for the dead pass across the sea of suffering to settle forever in a better, happier place. While we live, let us strive to order our lives, without and within, so as to be purer, wiser and kinder."[10]

Then to the crowd's applause, all the actors came to the front of the stage and bowed. Gamos stepped to the front and, with a majestic bow, said: "On behalf of my companions, priestly actors and servants of the gods, I bid you all a blest good night. Tonight, regardless of nation or religion, we have all been family in the reenactment and pre-enactment of what makes us all one: death and life. As the great Greek playwright, Euripides, said, 'Time will reveal everything; it is a babbler and speaks even when not asked.'[11] May time babble to each of you the truth of tonight's play, and may the road and highway on which the gods escort you take you safely home. If you've enjoyed this play of worship, share whatever wealth you can with us poor hypocrites of the highway who have entertained you this night."

It was clear to all the disciples how deeply the play had captivated Jesus. "Judas," Jesus said, wiping tears from his eyes and beard, "be generous to these artists who have raised the curtain on life for us."

Judas was bewildered. "Master, I fail to see what moves you to tears, and I further fail to see why we must waste our limited funds on these pagan pretenders. If we have not sinned against Moses and the tradition of our elders by attending this play, we have at least wasted our time! Now, are we to waste our money as well?"

"Judas, be generous, be generous," Jesus replied. "A great gift they've given, and so a great gift is the only response." Jesus then stood up, his beard and face still moist with tears, and walked from the crowded marketplace into the darkness of the night.

Jesus Retreats to Pray by the Sea

Standing alone on the shore by the sea, Jesus continued to sob, having been deeply touched by the powerful message of the Greek drama. Wiping the tears from his eyes, he said aloud to the night sky:

"Tonight, tonight, the curtain rose;
    by torchlight, I saw beyond the veils
    we all weave to curtain God's call.
Tonight as the curtain slowly rose, I saw
    that it was I who stood at center stage,
    I who stood with my back to the barren tree.
Tonight the mask was ripped from my face,
    from Jesus, the hypocrite of Nazareth,
    masked actor playing obedient son of God.

"Tonight, the crowd wanted a comedy,
    a lighthearted play to lower the curtain
    and hide all their sorrows and pain.

As Gamos said, no comedy or farce,
    no merry medicine can heal the deepest pain.
Instead, to cure the wound, they enacted a tale
    of the brutal killing of the divine son.

"But he rose from his mother's arms
    to stand full of life, yes, eternal life!
I saw my life played out in this Greek play,
    for the curtain rose up on my destiny
    and revealed the heart of my identity.
God is Great! Tonight my own curtain rose,
    and I know the drama God expects of me."

Like a wave washing upon the shore, the angel Gabriel joined Jesus. Placing an arm firmly around his shoulder, with his other hand he wiped away the tears as he sang a lullaby:

"Weep, Jesus, and let your grief flow,
    for God makes use of strange prophets.[12]
Tonight, it was not Isaiah but Dionysius
    who raised the curtain for you to see.
You saw yourself as the vine of ecstasy,
    as the new wine and the scapegoat divine.[13]

"Weep and grieve, but do not fear,
    for God will truly raise you up;
    God will raise you from the grave.
Then all the human children of God,
    and birds, beasts and all life shall follow
    your rising out of death's ditch.
For now, weep and release your grief."

"Gabriel," Jesus answered, regaining his composure, "messenger of God, I am afraid of the truth I saw this evening as my curtain raised. I saw in this Greek tragedy played out on the road to Tyre and Sidon what will soon be played out for me on the road to Jerusalem." He spoke with intense earnestness, "I wish to embrace the message from God that was performed tonight; if for no one else it was surely performed for me. Yet I'm terrified to take up my cross and die.[14] Tell me, dear companion, what will come of all my work to bring about the kingdom? Will all my labors be lost like waves washing out into the sea of time? Gabriel, my eyes long to see beyond today, to see if I am really to die, as it seems, upon a Roman cross. If so, how can the death of a wandering peasant preacher make any difference? How can a brutal death on a cross bring about the fullness of God's time, the end time?"

JESUS STRUGGLES WITH THE FUTURE

As they stood watching the waves crashing in upon the shore, Gabriel stood beside Jesus. After a long silence, Gabriel began to sing:

"Come, Jesus, let's look to the future of the choice you may make.
   You who often speak of not being anxious about tomorrow.
You asked what will happen to your family of disciples
   and your labors for the kingdom if you choose to die?
Know that your death, though one among many thousands,
   will not be forgotten, will never be lost!

"Your cross will not be buried in a forest of crosses;
   it shall become a cosmic pole of hope, a standard of victory.[15]
Like Moses' healing serpent staff so will your own cross be,
   to heal the pain and fear of death that each heart knows.
Your peasant's death in this small corner of the world
   shall become for the whole world the roadmap to eternal life.

"If you die, will your dream and your work also die?
   Will your message of love be carried out to sea and lost?
See the waves beating upon this stony shore;
   one wave cannot beat a stone into pebbled sand,
   so your work alone cannot break all hearts of stone.
But trust that after you're gone will come countless other waves,
   pounding with your passion upon hearts' stony graves.
Waves for centuries, yes, millenniums yet to come
   will grind into sand, earth's hard rocky shore,
   to form an earth pliable to new shapes and dreams.
Childless Jesus, your descendants will be like stars
   as numerous as in the sky above or the grains of sand below,
   till all the earth shall know what time it is:
   everywhere and for all, it will become God's time."

They began walking and listened to the primal music of the dark sea's pounding surf. Jesus reached down and took up a handful of sand, then let it flow like dried water through his fingers. "Such a long time, Gabriel; it took so long for the waves to grind hard rocks into this soft sand. It makes me weary to think it will take that long for the kingdom of God to be a reality. I'm already tired of beating against the rocks, and I'm afraid it is

I who will be ground to dust by those rocks." With a sigh deep enough to sear his soul, Jesus said, "It is late, time to go back. Time to go up to Jerusalem, there to face down the powers of evil, whatever they may be."

"Yes, go to Jerusalem to die for all peoples, to die as well for all creation, from the sand at our feet to all those millions of stars up there in the night sky. It's time also for you and all who follow you to see with God's eyes that there are no frontiers, no solo saviors."

"You mean, not even me, Gabriel?"

"Indeed, Jesus, remember these waves and be free as a wave[16]
to lead the many to be the few willing to die in love for all,
to sacrifice the gift of life for all races, tongues and ages.
It's time to go home for your rising in the east;
you are the light of the world
and must first become its sacrifice.
You are to be the golden dawn of the Sabbath of justice;[17]
you are the sunrise of the world's Sabbath of peace."

Jesus struggled to understand this mystery of millenniums of labor so soaked with hope. "Gabriel, you did not answer my question. Before we leave here tonight, can you tell me, if I die upon a Roman cross, what will become of my Family, who are like a flock of sheep? Is it God's will that they also be crucified with their shepherd, all of us together dying in a family forest of Roman trees?"

Gabriel was silent. When Jesus turned to repeat his question, he saw he was alone on the beach. As Jesus turned to go back to the Family's camp, he could hear the far-off howling of wolves, and it filled his heart with dread.

Chapter Twelve

The Road to Jerusalem
Jesus' New Requirement of Discipleship

Jesus and his Family, after traveling through gentile territory, returned again to Galilee. Jesus now began to say, often to his closest disciples, "If you wish to be my disciple, you must deny your very self, take up your cross and follow me."

Some of the disciples recalled the Greek play about the death of Dionysius and said to one another, "Why is the Master speaking so much about carrying a cross? The Master is no rebel bandit. Does he see himself as another Dionysius, who will die upon a Roman tree?"

Overhearing them, Jesus turned and said, "Brothers and sisters, it's time to pause awhile, not because we are tired, but because we have come to a crossroads in our journey."

Sitting down, and gathering them into a semicircle in front of him, he continued:

> "All I asked when you first came to follow me
> 	was to put my mission and God's kingdom first,
> 	ahead of father, mother, child or spouse,
> 	and to leave all to follow me.

"Brave were each one of you to follow me,
    for many others counted the cost far too great.
Now, God is asking far more of me and you;
    do you feel it at our backs, the Spirit Wind?
It pushes us down this pilgrim's road to the holy city
    and the final crossroad, the final choice?"

His jaw set and his eyes as determined as flint, he continued,
"For myself, my friends,
    I have chosen to go up to Jerusalem
    there to be arrested and handed over,
    in shame and defeat, to be crucified.
Greater is the cost to follow me now,
    so you're free to go back home, if you wish.
Or take up your cross and come, follow me!"

"Master," Thomas replied instantly, "you will not go alone to whatever awaits you. We shall go with you to Jerusalem to protect you or, if necessary, to die with you!"

"Thomas, the bold and brave," Jesus said as he reached over and placed his arm on Thomas' shoulder. "Pray that you, and the others, can be so loyal. But it's time to be setting out. Any who wish to, take up your cross and follow me."

This was a decisive event in the life of the whole community of disciples. While all the members of his inner circle, the Family, decided to take up the road to Jerusalem along with him, many other disciples, for dozens of reasons, chose at that moment to part ways with him and his mission.[1] It was a time for saying good-bye, which brought more than a few tears, especially to those who came personally to bid Jesus farewell. When it was all over, and the small group that remained started together down the Jerusalem road, they were as sad as a family preparing for a funeral. And in a sense they were.

The Rich Young Man

As that solemn band traveled down the road that day, a rich young man came and fell at the feet of Jesus, saying, "Good Master, I wish to be your disciple."

Jesus recognized him as the son of a wealthy farmer who had recently died and left everything to his son. Jesus said, "Friend, why do you call me *good*? Only God is good." Then, looking fondly at the young man, he added, "I'm pleased you wish to be a disciple, as I would love to have you as a member of our Family."

"Thank you, Master. I am so pleased."

"Go home now and sell everything you own and give it to the poor; then come and become one of us."

The man looked stunned, then lowered his head in disappointment. He stood silently weighing the cost of Jesus' very difficult conditions for following him.[2]

"Strip!" said Jesus, to the shock of all. "Unless you become as naked as Adam, you and I cannot be friends." Jesus paused and observed the effect of his words on the young man and his disciples.

"Strip, Master?"

"Remove everything you use to clothe your nakedness: your power and wealth, the land deeds to your many farms, all those debts owed to you, gathering interest. Make yourself as naked as Adam to all that you foolishly feel protects you from a cold night or a dismal future — take that clothing off! Remove your armor, the soldier's iron breastplate you wear to protect yourself from others who may hurt your heart or soul by words or deeds. Throw away your sword of significance, the honor of your state in life that protects you from being weak or vulnerable. If you wish to follow me, my friend, do so nude!"

With sadness, the young man turned slowly and walked away, for he was very wealthy and had many possessions and much power and prestige. Jesus sadly watched him depart, for he had thought highly of him. Then, turning to his disciples, he said: "How sad but true: It's easier for a camel to pass through the eye of a needle, than for the rich to enter God's kingdom."

"Master," gasped the amazed disciples, "if one must be as naked as you demanded of that young man to enter the kingdom, then who can enter?"

With irony in his voice, Jesus said:

"Friends, the rich have no time or need to love God;
they're too busy worshiping a golden god,
too busy with holy wealth's daily rituals.
They're always praying to the fickle lord of riches,
protecting and increasing their many possessions,
yet what they possess they don't own, it owns them!
Woe to the rich, for their future is sad,
all their rewards they've already had.
The kingdom of God is the time of full justice,

and living God's justice requires seeking a holy balance,
a sharing and equality of the good things of life,
a free flow of all the gifts God has given."

"You speak," said Judas, with everyone listening closely, "as if to have riches is a sin. Is not wealth a sign of God's blessing? Do not the Scriptures promise that those who are faithful to the Law will have their barns overflowing with good things?"[3]

Jesus shook his head. "Judas, you must rethink how you understand wealth. In God's eyes, it is the poor who are blessed rather than the rich! The world and the golden god of wealth bless well the rich, but God blesses the poor."

The Poor Young Woman

Soon after that they entered a village where they came upon a young peasant woman baking bread in an outdoor oven. Seeing Jesus passing by, she called to him, "Jesus of Nazareth, please allow me to join you and your disciples."

"Sister, leave your oven and come and follow me." He looked fondly upon the beautiful young woman with deep, dark eyes.

"Sir, let me first remove my loaf of bread from the oven. If I can take it with me, I will not go hungry today. Then let me go to get my goat, and I will be ready to follow you."

"No, take nothing with you at all. Strip yourself naked, sister! I want you to be completely naked before you follow me!"

She looked at him in shock, as did all of the disciples and some of the townswomen who were gathering at the oven.

"Sister," Jesus went on, "now, at this moment, be as naked as Eve, then come and follow me. Leave your bread in the oven and your goat tied to the post, or you will not be worthy to follow me."[4]

The young woman stared at him in disbelief, "Others have said you are mad, now I see it's true! I know I'm poor, but I'm not so destitute as to shamefully go about stark naked for you or anyone else."

"I'll compromise with you," replied Jesus with a laugh. "You don't have to be stark naked, you may wear a cross." He turned to his disciples and said, "Come, sisters and brothers, it is growing late and we must be on the road again."

Looking back at the young woman with love in his eyes, Jesus said, "How sad, the gate is so narrow and so few can enter. It's easier to put a needle through a camel's eye, than for the poor to enter the kingdom of

God! It is not an easy thing for anyone."

Overwhelmed at the image of trying to pierce a camel's eye, the disciples cried, "Master, who then can be saved if both the rich and poor will find it next to impossible to enter the kingdom?"

"With God," he replied, "all things are possible."

"Master," asked Salome, who had the courage to ask what the others were thinking, "did you not teach us, 'Blessed are the poor, for theirs is the kingdom; they will live in God's time'? Now this poor young girl, who owns only one goat and wished to bring only enough bread for the day, is refused entrance to our Family, and thus to God's kingdom. Are we also to go about as naked as Adam and Eve?"

"Salome, and all the rest of you, yes, I did say that, but please, keep your clothes on! I did say that it's blessed to be poor, but possessing a goat as well as gold makes you far too fat for the kingdom's narrow entryway.

"And far too fat for the needle's eye is that one thin word whose name is *my*. *My* bread crust, *my* gold chest, *my* ivory palace, *my* clay hut. Two little letters, yet it's the biggest word we say. Yes, it's old fat *my* that blocks heaven's gate. So, clothed or not, be naked of *my* or *me*; be as naked as Adam, as nude as Eve. Then you'll discover to your great delight that the Way is easy and the gate is wide.

"Our naked first parents in Eden's garden didn't own a single thing in sight. Yet daily they took such great delight in all the creatures and birds in flight, in all the land and in every tree. Alive in paradise, they were truly free. But on this side of Eden's garden gate, we feel we must first own something before we can enjoy it. So blinded, we're unable to employ the gifts of life that are ours in paradise.

"So I say, travel as lightly as did our primal parents, even on this side of the garden's gates. Enjoy the sunrise, the sea or a flower, and all the trees as your great treasure. Enjoy your riches in the mountains and rivers and all the sparkling diamonds in the star-filled sky. Travel lightly as did Eve and Adam, and you'll awaken naked each day inside new Eden. Delight in smelling, seeing and hearing, and wherever you are, you'll taste of Paradise.

"Yet few are those who can truly strip, and be naked enough to enter into God's time, which is Eden's time, through the needle-eye gate of paradise."

DINNER ON THE ROAD

As Jesus and his Family continued to travel the road to Jerusalem, the disciples pondered these new requirements of the way of discipleship.

When news spread that Jesus was leaving Galilee, many were eager to hear him speak again about God's kingdom. One day, even though they were in an area far from the villages, a vast crowd gathered. Jesus took pity on them, saying, "These poor people need to have some food, or else they will faint."

Philip replied, "Master, where can we go to obtain enough food to feed them? There are thousands gathered here."

"We would need a king's treasury," added Judas, "to feed such a crowd."

Jesus asked his disciples, "What have we brought along for ourselves to eat?"

"Seven loaves of bread and a few fish from yesterday," they answered.

Jesus astonished his disciples by asking the crowd to be seated in small groups. He took the bread, blessed it, broke it and distributed it, and then did the same with the fish.

As Jesus stood up and himself began to serve the bread and fish to the hungry crowd, Simon Peter asked him, "Lord, sharing a meal is a sacred time for our family. Are we even to eat with nonbelievers? This crowd contains Greeks, Phoenicians and many Samaritans!"

"Simon, Simon, whenever I feed the hungry, everyone is welcome! Recall that in the reign of God there are no frontiers! If the kingdom is here, then nothing should separate any of us who are open to God!"

That day over four thousand were fed by the disciples sharing their few loaves of bread and a couple of fish.[5] When all had eaten their fill, Jesus told the disciples to gather up all the food that was left over; twelve full baskets were collected.

"Sisters and brothers, see the sign," said Jesus. "This is how it is in the kingdom. God's time is a harvest time with more than enough good, if common, things like bread and fish. It is also a sign that:

"I am the new Manna; come and eat all that you wish;
   get your fill of me, in this humble bread and fish.
I've fed the many hungry, for I am the bread of life;
   I'm the fish of the feast and God's great delight.

"All hungry for life, feast on my bread-and-fish flesh;
   be filled with life eternal, never again to hunger or thirst.
If you feed on me, you'll never meet death in this vale of tears."

Many of the remaining disciples complained, "He calls himself bread and fish! These recent sayings are impossible. First, he demands equality between the men and the women in our group. Then he asks us to learn lessons from gentiles. Now he says we are to eat *him*, that he's to be our food and drink! We are not cannibals, what does he mean calling his flesh fish and bread? Madness, this is madness!"

That day even more of the disciples of his Village group refused to follow him any longer and departed for their homes. Jesus watched them heading north and said to the Family, "Do not some of you also wish to leave?"

"Where would we go?" Simon Peter replied. "You have the words of life, even when your words are puzzles beyond our understanding."

Jesus looked gratified. "Recall the Greek play about Dionysius, the winnowing fan," he said. "I remember Jordan John saying that the Awaited One would have a winnowing fan in his hand.[6] He would come to separate the good wheat from the chaff. You, my friends, are being separated from old comrades by the Wind, as I toss all of you, and myself, up in God's winnowing-fan basket. Do all of you find my words strange to your ears?"

A Mother's Song of the Eucharist

Then Salome, the mother of James and John, sang:

"Master, your words are no puzzle to women like me,
     for every mother takes the child of her womb
     to feed without limit on her rich, full breasts.
Breasts that once in beautiful love lured her man to her
     now feed their child with another source of love,
     with the flesh of her milk, with her white lifeblood.

"It's a mother's mystery of which you speak
     when to us you say, 'Come, eat and drink of me.'
You are the bread of heaven, the food and drink of life;
     in woman's words, you're God's round full breasts,
     bread full of love's sweet milk, red wine milk for all to suck."

Such talk made even a few more of Jesus' followers depart. The idea of Jesus as God's Manna and, more shocking, as God's breasts, was unthinkable to many. A much smaller group of disciples followed him down the road. Only the twelve and the six and a handful more remained loyal, for now.

The Pharisees Demand a Sign

Along the road leading south they also met a group of Galilean Pharisees, who were known for their zeal in prayer and fasting, and living the Law of God as precisely as possible. These men approached Jesus and pretended to bid him a safe journey, for they knew he was on his way to Jerusalem.

"Peace, Rabbi," said their leader. "You are one known for your compassion and your zeal for the coming of the kingdom of God. Like the crowds, we are eager to believe you may be the one whose arrival Jordan John proclaimed was now at hand. If you are the one whom all Israel awaits, show us some sign that God has sent you. Surely that is not too much to ask so that we might also believe in you."

"A sign, some great wonder, you ask of me:
shall I, like Moses, part wide the Red Sea?
Or, like Elijah, rain down fire from the sky,
make rain or the sun spin or the moon die?
You ask for a sign to show I'm from God?
No sign will I give you but the sign of Jonah."

In confusion and disappointment one of the Pharisees replied, "The sign of Jonah, what kind of sign is that? Are you saying you're another reluctant prophet, a prophet who's swallowed alive and after three days is spewed up from the belly of the beast?"

"Only the feeble of faith," said Jesus, "are hungry for signs and wonders. I have not come to rouse those with closed hearts by working signs in the skies. The sign I gave you, your closed minds cannot understand." Beckoning his disciples to follow him, Jesus said, "Come, my friends, it's time to go."

As the group moved off down the road, Jesus began to laugh. At first it was only a chuckle, then it grew like a tremor that begins to shake the earth before an earthquake. Soon his whole body was rumbling with great mirth. Laughing loudly, he shouted back to the departing Pharisees, "I am not another Jonah! I am the great Fish!"

SONGS OF THE HOLY TEMPLE

The Pharisees departed, lamenting, "He says he's a 'fish.' Whatever does than mean? He must be mad!"

As they drew closer to Jerusalem, some of the women disciples began singing the great jubilation psalm:

" 'All you peoples, clap your hands,
shout to God with joyful cries;
God is great, highly to be praised.
Mount Zion, city of the King,

God dwells within your temple;
we ponder your everlasting love.

" 'Lift up your ancient gates, O Jerusalem,
God's holy city, Zion, home of our God.
One day within your courts, O God,
is better than a thousand elsewhere.' "[7]

To their surprise, Jesus began to sing a different song:

"Jerusalem, O Jerusalem, God doesn't live there any more!
From that cold, gold and stone house, God walked out the door!
God's at home in homes with opened doors and open hearts.
John lived on Jordan's bank; there the crowds came from afar,
but I have no home where you can visit, so it's not you
who come to me, but I and God who come to you.

"O Jerusalem, sad Jerusalem, God doesn't live there any more!
God feels trapped inside, closeted within the temple's holy doors.
Ours is a gypsy God, at home in every home and even inns of sin;
ours is a God with wanderlust that rests only in an open heart.

"O Jerusalem, empty holy city, Jerusalem, doomed city,
we go to you not to dwell in God's holy house,
but only to pay our loving last respects."

"Master," asked James the Orthodox, son of Mary the Murmurer, "if the temple is no longer God's house, now where will we offer sacrifice?"

"James, daily you are to offer sacrifice on the altar in the temple of your heart."

Andrew asked, "Master, then who will be our priests?"

"Sisters, brothers, it would be better if there were no priesthood if what you mean by 'priest' is what we now endure! If you mean priests who hold spiritual power over you, then I say get rid of them. But if you mean a new kind of priest, who's willing to be both the one who offers sacrifice and also the bloody victim, willing to be a slave to others, constantly at their beck and call, then let each one of you be a priest! Indeed, God calls for such a priestly people!"[8]

"Master," Simon Peter cried out, almost in alarm, "with no temple, does that mean we would have no high priest?"

"Simon the Stone, in the kingdom there is no high priest, because to have a high priest would mean there must be lower priests. In my Family you all are equal. If there is one who is higher, it's the one who serves the rest. But enough! Stop trying to compare the new kingdom's time to old temple time! For behold, I make all things new, even time!"

Disappointment lingered among the disciples. Simon Peter was sad that there would be no high priest in the new age. James was disturbed not so much about the new priests, but because the sisters in the Family, especially Mary Magdalene, would be included among the new priesthood. It seemed their master was getting more bizarre.

THE VISITOR IN JESUS' BED

That night Jesus did not sleep well. He tossed and turned, awoke and then fell back into sleep again. Toward morning, he was awakened by the sensation of someone lying next to him. He rolled over and found that inside his cloak was his Shadow![9]

"O, Jesus," said the Shadow, " just think of it: you, the goat of God! What a privilege — painful, I agree — but to be *the* scapegoat and bear the sins of all the people. What a noble calling! Not only to bear the sins of your nation but, I heard, those of all people who have lived and will ever live on this earth."

"Be gone, Evil One," Jesus moaned, half-awake.

"O, Jesus, I'm just your other half, your shadow brother, far more intimate and close to you than any lover could be. How can you drive me off like a pestering flea? Now, as you slumber lightly, half awake, consider this thought. I give it to you as a fraternal gift and ask nothing in return."

Jesus tightly closed his eyes, trying not to listen to the voice whose hot breath massaged his body.

"Beloved of God," the Shadow continued, "if you wish for all the people to embrace your good news that God's kingdom is already here, you need some great sign to awaken them. The sign of a single death upon a cross could easily be missed. A lone crucifixion on some foreign road in a remote part of the world is but a fly speck in history! Consider, instead, the thunderous impact of thousands of crosses! Yes, as many crosses as the number in the crowd you fed in the desert, or even more! Jesus, how could the world ever forget such a massive sacred slaughter of your devoted disciples eager to die beside you to announce the early arrival of God's time?"

Jesus wrestled with the validity of this idea of so great a sign as thousands of crosses. It danced wildly in vivid images in the night of his sleep. Could this be the way it should be?

"Think, Jesus," the Shadow went on, "about how the eyes of scribes and priests, even the Greeks and Romans, will be opened to the truth of your message when they are knee-deep in a mighty river of blood flowing out across the land from Jerusalem. Can you see it, a broad sacrificial red river, fed by thousands of streams flowing out of you and your disciples? You can lead them to glory; your words hold great power and can move the multitudes to anything.[10] You are not the lamb of God, you are the goat of God! Lead your sheep-disciples to greatness and glory as they take up their crosses and follow you to the sacred slaughter, one great final sacrifice for the greater honor and glory of God."

Jesus felt the clinging-hot presence of his Shadow coiled tightly around his body and shuttered, "O God, come to my assistance, O Lord, make haste to help me!"

THE SHADOW'S SONG OF SUCCESS

"Rather, Jesus, it's God who needs your help!
  God needs your assistance to hasten
  the awakening of all earth's peoples.
I solemnly assure you, Jesus,
  if you can lead your disciples in one act
  of communal immolation and sacrifice,
  it shall be a sign sung about for ages.
This group sacrifice, not your death alone,
  will be the great sign to change hearts.
A thousand other crosses next to yours
  will cleanse this whole world of sin.

"A sacrifice of thousands of God's lambs,
  not a marvel of rain from blue skies,
  nor giving to a bunch of blind beggars
  the miracle of bright shining eyes,
  will be the sacred sign of signs.
A thousand other crosses next to yours
  will cleanse this whole world of sin.

"Not bread for the many from a couple of loaves,
  nor walking on water in a storm-tossed sea,
  but only the loyalty of those who love you,
  faithful, loyal to the bitter end,
  will be the sacred sign of signs.
A thousand other crosses next to yours
  will cleanse this whole world of sin."

In the darkness before dawn, before any cock had crowed, Jesus rose from his sleeping mat and prayed:

> "Hear, O Israel, the LORD is our God, the LORD alone.
> You shall love the LORD your God with all your heart,
> with all your soul, and with all your might,
> and you shall love your neighbor
> as you love yourself."

Then he gathered his cloak about him and went off alone to plunge deeper into prayer.

MOTHER MARY'S AUTUMN SONG

The next day as they continued their journey southward, the women asked Mary, the mother of Jesus, if she thought they should take up a cross.

> "Sisters: Do as he says, do whatever he says,
> for pain, like joy, is part of life.
> Do not flee from the pain you face
> lest you lose joy in a flight from life.
> Do as he says; take up your cross.
>
> "On in years, older than most women,
> I've been blessed with an autumn life.
> Wrinkled as parchment, my widow's skin,
> my eyes see less, but my heart sees more.
> In my old age as I did in my youth,
> even more, my soul magnifies my God.
>
> "My soul's still full of hope in the promise,
> only now I see it will take more time
> to cast all the rich off their thrones,
> to feed all the hungry with good things.
> The dream of which I sang so long ago
> needs time to unfold as God foretold.
> Today, the hungry are as many as then,
> the oppressed are still as many too,
> but I have not aborted the beautiful dream.
>
> "My old autumn soul magnifies my God,
> my old tired soul still rejoices in God,
> even if all the rich are still in power,
> and all the powerful still rule the day.
> The seed of my womb has now grown tall;

he isn't high noon or the holy sunset
of judgment's last and fiery day.
He is the dawn, the sunrise of God's great day."

THE WOMEN'S SONG

"O Mary," the women sang, "blessed are you:
  though you say little, your spirit overflows with quiet confidence.
While we frequently grumble and often complain,
  you simply say to us, 'Do what he tells you.'
Mary, be our intercessor, for if Jesus is the new Adam, then you
  are the new mother Eve, earthen mother of creation.
You are the new earth mother, holy Demeter,
  you are the mother of all living beings.[11]
Even though old, your spirit remains tender as a green sprout
  and ever beautiful as the flowers of spring.
Holy Mary, mother of God, pray for us saints,
  now and at the hour of our birth."

MOTHER MARY'S SORROWFUL SONG

"Sisters of the way," Mary sang in reply, "I am no goddess,
  but if I'm the harvest's patron, I fear I shall bear the harvest pain.
Like Demeter, I'll also be the holy sorrowful mother,
  knowing heart rending pain as well as harvest plenty.
If the goddess Demeter is my mirror, I ask you to recall
  how she made holy every small and common household act.
The house and garden were her holy shrines;
  her temples were the vineyards and the fields.
The fields in olden days belonged to those women who
  plowed the earth, scattered the seed and reaped the harvest.
My son has made each house holy, a domestic temple shrine
  for prayer and sacrifice — all work in fields and gardens, holy.
He has also sent you women, and your sisters to follow,
  into the fields as reapers for God's great harvest.

"Sisters, I'm no youthful new Eve but an old hag in widow's black,
  no mother goddess dressed in earthen browns and greens.[12]
Look and see me as another sorrowful mother Demeter,
  who soon, I fear, will saddle my son in this old lap.
On that fateful tragic day to come, I'll be forced as was she
  to attempt to sew together my dead and mangled son.

I rejoice in God the gambler, who gambled on more
    than my teenager's 'yes' to enter into my virgin womb.
I praise God who gambled that I would not lose heart,
    that I'd keep saying 'let it be done' to the bitter end.
Rejoice, sisters of God's time: as I have been, so each of you
    has been called by God to a holy motherhood.

"Sisters of the kingdom, rejoice in your women's work that shares
    in God's creative work; whether birthing a child or baking bread.
Be creative with your crosses, making them into birthing beds
    by which you can bring forth the soul of the new and glorious age.[13]
I say, 'Do as he says,' and 'take up your cross';
    each of you must be a mother Eve to one and all.
Married or not, be mothers with big fat laps that can saddle
    the hungry and sad, and mend their mangled limbs and hearts.
Live each day crowded with hope, and to conflict's angry shouts
    answer only with quiet confidence, saying little, but filled with hope.
Raise not your voices in anger; respond with the velvet violence
    of sweet, gentle peace, green and tender as an olive branch.
My son, the dawn, has come; high noon can't be far behind,
    so live in quiet confidence — and, yes, 'do whatever he says.'"

JESUS AND THE DISCIPLES IN LONELY EXILE

Late one afternoon about sunset, at the encampment halfway to Jerusalem, the disciples began searching for Jesus, as they had not seen him all day. Usually when he slipped away to spend the day in prayer, he was back with them for the evening meal. After several hours, Matthew heard a voice singing in distress, "O come, O come, Immanuel, and ransom captive Israel."

"I've found him, shouted Matthew to the others, or at least I've found his voice; I still can't see where the Master is." The other disciples came running to Matthew as the sad voice sang even louder, "O come, O come, Immanuel, and ransom captive Israel that moans in lonely exile here until the son of God appears."

"Where is the Master?" asked Simon Peter. "That is surely his voice, but he's nowhere to be seen!"

"The voice is coming from over there," cried John, "from that old well by the stone wall." The disciples ran to the abandoned well and in the fleeting light of the day's end looked down inside. As they circled the flat stones that rimmed the old well's opening, they could barely make out

Jesus looking up at them from the dry, dusty bottom some twenty feet below.

Raising his arms toward them like a beggar, he wailed, "O come, O come, Immanuel, and ransom captive Israel, who moans here in lonely exile."

"Master," shouted Simon Peter into the well, his voice echoing down its hollow shaft, "what are you doing in this abandoned well? Did you fall in? Are you all right?"

"O Simon, how can I be all right when I'm in exile?"

"Master, what do you mean? You're in your homeland in Galilee! How can you be in exile in your own home?"

"I did not fall into this dungeon," groaned Jesus. "I was cast into exile like our ancient ancestors in Babylon over five hundred years ago.[14] O come, O come, Immanuel, and ransom me, ransom all of Israel."

"Get a rope," Simon Peter ordered. "We must get him out of there; for see, the evening star has already appeared in the west. It's growing dark."

One of the disciples ran to the nearby village and quickly returned with a long rope which they lowered down the old well. As they proceeded to pull Jesus up to the surface, he was still singing loudly:

" 'Go up on the high mountain, herald of glad tidings;
    cry out at the top of your voice, herald of good news!
Here is my servant whom I raise up,
    my chosen one in whom I take great delight.' "

Simon Peter reached his hand out to Jesus as he was drawn near the top of the well. As he did, Jesus' voice again filled the growing darkness:

"God calls us, each of us, like laboring women
    to give birth to justice's victory.
God has called us to open the eyes of the blind
    to bring exiles trapped in darkness out of the dungeon.
Say to the prisoners, you and I, and all:
    'O come, O come! Come out, O Israel!
Even in the gloomy darkness, show yourselves,
    for God will cut a road through the mountains,
    will make the rough roads smooth and level.' "[15]

The disciples gathered around Jesus in silent wonder as he finished singing, "I was in exile, as was Israel long ago. Are we not all exiles, even here in our homeland?" Seeing the confusion on their faces, he continued, "Have you never felt like exiles here in the promised land from which the promise has been stolen?"

"I for one have, Master, as have many others," replied Simon the Zealot. "I feel like an exile, a refugee in chains — or like a eunuch, who is powerless." Just as the stars in the night sky were coming into focus, the voices of the others soon grew into a chorus of agreement.

"Come," said Jesus, "gather all the disciples; we must be on the road."

"Master," groaned Simon Peter as he went off for the others, "it's night! How can we travel in the darkness?" When Simon Peter returned with all the other disciples of the Family, Jesus raised his staff in the air and swung it forward, pointing south down the road, leading them off in the darkness as he sang:

"Sing a new song to our God, all you faithful;
   you who are blind, look and see.
Walk in the darkness without any light,
   trusting only in God who guides us."[16]

Thick, dark clouds spread across the night sky and ate up the stars and the rising full moon. The disciples stumbled along through the gloomy darkness. Walking in the dark night like those who are blind, for the first time they truly felt the meaning of the poetic passage of the prophet Isaiah, whose words had formed Jesus' song.

"Master," Simon Peter lamented, "we trust that you know what you are doing, for we are indeed walking in the darkness. We would follow no one other than you on this road."

"Simon Peter, and all of you," Jesus said cheerfully as he stopped and faced them, "look at your feet." They did so, not knowing why, as Jesus began to sing again:

"How beautiful upon the mountaintops
   are your feet that bring glad tidings,
announcing peace and carrying the good news
   that our exile is over; for see, we are going home."[17]

As Jesus stopped singing, the disciples gathered in a group around him in the darkness, struggling to understand the purpose of this night journey.

Then John spoke. "Master, this is a parable, your being in the well and this walking in darkness, isn't it? I don't mean some story, but a prophetic action meant to be a parable. The Babylonian captivity was a terrible time for our people; they were taken away from their homes and land. Yet along with the story of the Exodus, its memory remains vivid even today." Then John began to sing David's psalm:

" 'By the rivers of Babylon we sat mournful, weeping,
  in exile remembering our beloved homeland, Zion.
We hung up our harps on the willows of that foreign land,
  and sat songless in our sorrow, our tongues sewed silent.
'Sing a song of Zion,' our tormenting captors taunted us,
  but how could we sing a new song to our God in exile?' "[18]

Placing his hand on John's shoulder, Jesus replied, "You have understood the parable of our night journey, John. Yes, the reason we are traveling in the darkness of night is to awaken us to see that the kingdom, God's time, is also the time of liberation from exile. The Spirit of God is upon me to proclaim liberty to the captives. Only the liberated can sing a new song! There can be no zest and joy in life for those in exile."

"Master, you have named for me a feeling that I only thought I knew," said Mary Magdalene softly.

"Yes, Mary, we have each been made exiles by the empire and the temple, by those who have stolen from us God's promise of freedom. Adam and Eve were the first exiles and, as their children, each of us longs to go back home. Tonight we are homeward bound! So let us stop singing the old songs and sing a new song that is filled with real joy."

"Master, what old songs?" asked a puzzled Thomas.

"Stop singing those old songs that keep you tamed and satisfied in your chains of captivity. Stop singing those old songs filled with words that keep you in your place, and that keep *them* in their high places.[19] The songs, Thomas, of your prayer and worship can call you to liberation or entrench you more deeply in your slavery.

" 'Sing to God, and to all peoples, a new song;
  sing of a new day, Liberation Day.
We have been released from captivity, my friends,
  so let night's darkness and the depths of the sea rejoice,
  let all the trees of the forest rejoice.'
Rejoice, for God is busy making a new creation,
  and has promised to plant anew in the desert
  the cedar, olive, pine, myrtle and the plane tree.
Then the forests will again, like green clouds,
  cover all the eastern slopes of Judea."[20]

"Master," said James, the brother of Joseph, "the eastern slopes of Judea that descend to the Dead Sea are the ancient desert wilderness, the ground is covered with rocks. God has willed it to be so. How can forests bloom there?"

"God did not will it!" replied Jesus. "Those hilltops were not always a stony dry desert but very long ago were covered with great forests. It was not God, but greed and men, that cut down the trees, stripping the soil of its protection.[21] Then came year after year of violent winter rainstorms that washed away the soil, leaving only desert rocks. Just as Israel is in captivity, so is the earth! The coming of God's time, in Isaiah's prophecy, also means the redemption and liberation of all the earth from its slavery to our greed and its exile from the human family. All creation groans in agony and also cries out, 'O come, O come, Immanuel, and ransom us along with Israel.'

"But come now, friends; we have rested long enough. It is time to take to the road."

"Master, why must we always be on the road? I'm glad to be on this pilgrimage to the holy city of Jerusalem," said Simon Peter, "but why must we always be traveling?"

"Because, dear Simon, the kingdom of God's time comes only for those who are on the road, on the way. The road we travel is always a way in the wilderness because the fullness of God's time has not yet come. But we do not travel as pilgrims. Pilgrims visit a holy place and then return home. We are not pilgrims; we are refugees returning from exile. Freed from bondage, we are on the road as the new exodus. We are always on the road to remind us that we are immigrants who have left our homes and lands to seek a new land.[22] This new promised land is truly the one promised by God, a land of justice, equality, peace and compassion for all."

Sometime after midnight Jesus ended their journey so they could camp for the night. The weary disciples rejoiced in this decision and quickly fell asleep after their long hours on the road. Jesus, however, was still awake when the dark clouds parted to reveal the full moon directly overhead. A peaceful white light flooded the dark earth, making it almost as light as day. As Jesus drank in the beauty of the hill country bathed in soft light, he faintly heard an echo on the night wind: "O come, O come, Immanuel, and ransom captive Israel." He listened in silence for some time as those words lingered at the edge of his ears. Then he slowly sang to the moon and the heavens, "Rejoice, rejoice, O Israel, to you *shall* come Immanuel."[23]

CHAPTER THIRTEEN

TO JUDEA BEYOND THE JORDAN

Jesus and his companions finally crossed the border out of Galilee and continued on their way toward Jerusalem. One spring morning they crossed over to the west side of the Jordan River and continued southward through the district of Judea beyond the Jordan.[1] When they came to the area in the desert near Jerico where John had once baptized, the crowds flocked to hear him. Along the river with its thick groves of willow trees, Jesus spoke to them.

"What did you come out here to see when Jordan John was here?" Jesus asked. "A reed or willow branch swaying in the wind? What did you come to see, someone dressed in royal purple like King Herod? Such as these are found in royal palaces. You saw someone more regal than a king when you saw John. A new Elijah dressed in camel skin was he, yet even more than the prophet messenger of whom Isaiah sang. Executed by the forces of evil, John became a new Passover lamb whose blood announces the new Exodus. I assure you, of all those born of women, none has been greater than Jordan John. Yet the very least in the new kingdom of God is greater than he!"

"The least of our company is greater than John?" asked Mary Magdalene, who often felt she was the least of those whom Jesus had invited into his Family.

"Yes, for those who can embrace more truth than John knew — those of you who know that the radically new time of God is here among you at this moment — are greater than he. I also assure you that to fully embrace not just a part but all of the kingdom's radical message can be as costly as it was for John. Like John, I too call all to repent and be baptized. Come, follow me and live in God's time." Mary thanked Jesus for his answer, but — like so many of the disciples — remained bewildered.

SOME PRIESTS INQUIRE ABOUT BEING A DISCIPLE

Then one day some priests and scribes from Jerusalem appeared in the large crowd. A priest named Eleazar began the confrontation: "You speak words of truth about how we are to love God. If you invite everyone to follow you, then why did you not call any of the priests to join your intimate group of disciples?"

"Go home," answered Jesus, "and learn the meaning of the prophet Hosea's words, 'It is love I desire, not sacrifice; intimate knowledge of God, not holocausts.'² Then come, priest, and you yourself may ask to be my disciple. Go home and change your clothes; learn the meaning of the prophet Joel's words, 'Lament like a virgin adorned in sackcloth, mourning her young lover. Wail, you vine dressers, for the vine has dried up and the fig tree is withered.' " Anger seemed to be rising in his voice. " 'O priests and ministers of the altar, wail and dress in sackcloth day and night. Proclaim a fast for yourselves.'³ Then come and ask to be my disciple, for I have come to call sinners, not those who see themselves as righteous."

His words stung like wasps in their ears. They left immediately to return to Jerusalem and report what they had heard and seen.

"Master," asked James, Joseph's brother, speaking softly to his angry leader, "they are priests of God's altar, chosen and holy. Why were you so harsh with them?"

"Good James, and all of you, my Family," he said, "my words are like distant thunder, they announce the coming storm. True, not all priests and scribes are self-righteous, yet their very life at the altar hinders their conversion. While they carefully keep every detail of the laws of ritual worship, they ignore the law of love. Since they are seen by the poor to be holy, they need to truly become holy. Instead, they are like locusts feasting on the harvest field, no more than holy tax collectors. Just as they themselves exclude tax collectors from the community, considering them as impure as sinners, so I consider the priests and scribes too impure to be among my intimate disciples. Yet, the kingdom is closed to none! The rich, the powerful, the scribes and priests, however, by their attitudes exclude themselves. They find the gate to the kingdom too small to get through and the cost too great."

JESUS SPEAKS OF LOVE

"The commandments of Moses and all the other laws are like limbs by the hundreds growing outward from the tree of the Law of God.[4] They are not difficult to keep. All of them are kept easily just by keeping the one great Married Law."

"Married Law?" asked a sympathetic Pharisee in the crowd. "Do you speak of the law that forbids divorce between husbands and wives?"

"No, I speak of God's marriage between the two great laws of Moses. It is the wedding between the groom law, 'You shall love your God with all your heart, mind, soul and body,' and the bride law, 'You shall love your neighbor as you love yourself.' The two shall be one, and what God has put together, let no one divide. In that one law of love, all laws have reached perfection. Keep it and you keep the hundreds of others."

The good Pharisee smiled. "You have spoken well, Jesus. Indeed, love of God and neighbor is at the heart of all the laws of our religion. However, we are concerned that as a teacher you have said almost nothing about sexual behavior, while it is central to our religion."

"First of all, friend," said Jesus, "I am not a teacher! Call neither me nor anyone else teacher, father or mother; only God is that holy trinity to us."

"If you are not a teacher, what are you?" asked the Pharisee.

Jesus grinned and smiled gently, pointing to his chest. "I am the lesson! Learn me, learn me by heart."

He laughed, but the crowd, including the disciples, at once began talking among themselves, asking if this was a new parable. Jesus allowed them to debate awhile the meaning of what he had said; then he spoke again, "Teachers only teach, but lessons lived are difficult to forget! My disciples are not to be students who memorize my every word. I call you as disciples to be lovers, not parrots.[5] I am the map, you could say. If you are not on a journey, then you don't need the map![6] I am a seamless robe. Wear me only if you are seamless yourselves, naked of all divisions."

Just then a less than friendly Pharisee spoke. "*Map* or lesson, you, Jesus of Galilee, seem to have too many identities. When we asked you for a sign, you gave us the sign of Jonah, and you said that you are the great fish. Do you mean you are cold-blooded like a fish, and therefore not governed by the heat of passion?" Jesus was seated on a rock, and now the crowd pressed in, sitting in a great cluster at his feet.

"At times I wish I weren't."

The now scornful Pharisee continued his questioning. "Some of us thought you were referring to yourself as blessed by God, to be without curse, since in Noah's flood the fish were the only ones not afflicted by God's curse. Is that what you mean?"

"No," he answered, "for being blessed by God is also to be cursed."

Now another Pharisee joined in the questioning, pretending to be simply seeking information. "Others said that since the word for fish in Greek is *Ichthys*, the name of the son of the sea-goddess Atargatis, whose name means womb, you are calling yourself a god!"[7]

Again Jesus laughed. "I am simply the great fish and my disciples the little fish."

Now the man became openly belligerent. "Fish are also viewed by our pagan neighbors as bringing good luck, and as an aphrodisiac, a food arousing sexual feelings, since fish are associated with their love goddess.[8] Also, fish are sacrificial creatures and so are considered by the pagans as fitting for sacred feasts. Is that what you mean?" He spat out the words with consummate scorn. Jesus seemed unmoved, unthreatened.

"What you say is all true," he replied, "and you will soon see the way of the fish come to pass."

Like leeches sucking blood, the questioners clung on tightly. "Tell us then, Jesus," asked the first questioner again, "lesson, fish, or whatever you are, your ideas on the subject of a marriage that has become painful, as dry as an empty well. We've heard tell how you've said that any man who divorces his wife and marries another commits adultery against her. That is contrary to the teaching of Moses!"

Jesus drew his feet up under him and made himself comfortable. "Be at ease, my friends," he said, "and do not take offense at this new wine I'm offering you. It may not fit well into old wine skins, nor satisfy every taste, but a Spirit Wind from heaven fills my lungs, and I cannot but speak of it.

"Before Moses, God spoke in the garden. I speak of the kingdom, a return to that garden, to Eden's time. In the beginning, as you know, all things were made in God's design. In Eden's vineyard, a man and woman in love were like squeezing two grapes into new wine. Once the two were turned into wine, how could they become two grapes again? The same is true of friends who have become one, or companions drunk on some great cause. Marriage is a mirror of all loyalty."

"But Moses said otherwise!" responded the man.

Jesus grew ardent. "In the desert poor Moses led people with hearts harder than stones. So then as now: because of the hardness of their hearts, he permitted a man to divorce a woman. However, that law does not allow a wife the same right! But I say a woman has honor as does a man; a woman can be shamed as well. Thus, a woman's honor must be equally guarded. And like leprosy, the rot of an abused law spreads.

"Divorce is a knife that cuts up families, flocks and herds; it's not just a separation of husband and wife. It is an illness full of pain and anguish, and not every illness can be healed. A family's disgrace calls for bloodshed to clean the slate, which leads to more bloodshed in a vicious cycle. When a man throws out his wife to stand on her own feet, she may be forced to sell her body and her soul.

"I am no fool. I know well that a marriage can go as dry as a desert pool in summer, can become empty of love and even full of hate. Painfully, the new wine of love can become vinegar! Sad as it is, then, let unloving spouses part. It is not so much divorce I denounce as an unjust system of abuse and disgrace that breeds violence, especially against women."

He raised his hands in a kind of blessing and looked for the faces of his Family in the crowd.

"I call my disciples to be like God, to never return
    anger for anger, violence for violence, hate for hate,
    for both war and adultery do I abhor.
I am the lesson, learn me; I am meek and of humble heart,
    and only such shall pass with me through kingdom's gate.

"Violence for violence I heartily condemn,
    adultery in marriage I disdain as well,
    in heaven's scales they weigh the same.[9]
Like my call to naked poverty, my ways
    are like rungs on heaven's ladder.
They're not commandments, for I give none,
    other than to love God, self and neighbor.
No more laws do I make to burden the poor;
    I only give a way, the way of love."

THE QUESTION OF MORALITY

"By whatever strange name you called yourself," snarled a scribe in the crowd, "you are still a teacher, God knows! People come to learn from you. You say you give no laws, but only rungs on a ladder. Does this new religion you teach have no laws controlling sex? God's laws carefully fence in how and what we eat and with whom; so too with sex. Like every human activity, sex must be fenced in on all sides or else disaster, not God, becomes king. Good fences make a good religion."

"Well spoken!" smiled Jesus at these hostile words. "You are right when you say that good fences make good religion. But it is precisely religion, and not God, that builds fences and then makes her priests and scribes their zealous guards. But hear me well, friend, and all my disciples as well. I do not bring a new religion, so I do not build fences regarding sex — or what foods to eat or clothes to wear.[10] I am the messenger, but not of a new religion. My message is love, and love does not build fences. Love is as free as the wind and as fenceless as the horizon."

"This is madness! You hold no religious laws forbidding promiscuity?"

"Would that religion was a gateway in the center of the world, opening onto paradise and onto God. Yours, or any other religion, is often nothing more than the village sentinel guarding sex and the social customs of the day. The tribal elders say, 'God said this and God said that' and raise up high taboo towers and forbidding fences. Sex is not evil, it is more like fire, dangerous and wonderful. It can make a home out of a cave, but like fire it can burn down the house! Sex is a gift from God, about which God said as little as about the gift of life. Like all divine gifts, life and sex must be treated with care. Yet such gifts call not for fences but rather for great reverence as for a gateway to paradise."

"If you do not uphold our religion, Jesus of Galilee, and you say you've come not to offer a new religion, then what do you offer in its place?"

"Let us say that I offer the Way.[11] I offer a way to live married to God in great love and delight. Marriage is God's gift as is the rain or figs or wine. The love of husband and wife is the silent sea reflecting the stars of the heavens.

"Dear to me is married love, shaped by God in Eden time,
    calling for a loyalty in love whatever the sickness or pain,
    a fidelity awakening in reckless youth
    and lasting through wrinkled old age.
No molehill is holy love, but rather a mountain strong
    that withstands every ill wind and deadly storm.
Love's loyalty means ever-deepening
    faithfulness for lovers and friends,
    a fidelity till death that lasts far beyond.
Eden's marriage between man and woman is a mirror of God,
    a mirror image crowded with mystery and love."[12]

A voice from the crowd shouted, "This is Judea, not Eden, if you haven't noticed!" Many in the crowd laughed.

"I solemnly assure you," said Jesus, "that there will come a new Eden marriage, one without marriage contracts about the exchange of property. This new Eden marriage, like the first one, will be consecrated to God by love and not by contracts. Two bodies will be joined into one by love alone and not by laws. Consecrated beyond religion's fences, this union may truly last beyond the boundary of death, for it dances free as the wind. Indeed, it is just such a marriage the Spirit Wind delights in."

"You are mad!" shouted one of the remaining Pharisees in anger and frustration. "You would destroy our society," he said as they all turned and walked away. "Apostate! You would destroy our religion," screamed one of the scribes as all of them joined the departing Pharisees. Soon the rest of the crowd drifted away, leaving Jesus and his disciples alone.

Jesus' disciples sat speechless until Simon Peter said, "Master, if this is your idea of marriage, then our world is upside down. This commandment of fidelity beyond death is so difficult, it would be better not to dare to marry!"

"Indeed, the new way seems narrow and difficult. I never said it would be easy. But do you not listen or learn? It is not a commandment; rather, like my other invitations, it is a call to holiness, a way for becoming godlike. For our Divine Beloved never divorces us when we are unfaithful nor abandons us even when our well of prayer and love for God becomes as dry as this desert!

"As for your question Peter, is it better not to marry? This is a Greek question and no Jew has to fret over it. We are betrothed in childhood, and celibacy, like parents being childless, is seen by us as a curse. The question, Peter, is not whether it is wise or better to not marry but rather how to be married. No one human heart is the same as another, so no one pattern fits all. As we know, even married lovers keep a deep well of freedom in their hearts if they are wise."

His words had caused the disciples' heads to be filled as if with fog, and they were lost to know what to say. Jesus looked on them with compassion as he got up to walk away. "You may need to discuss these things. It is time for me to be alone and pray."

JESUS RETREATS TO PRAY

Alone in a deserted place, Jesus fell on his knees and prayed to God for help. He felt both hemmed in and alone. Like the Jordan, whose shores are tightly lined with willow trees, he felt surrounded by enemies. At the same time he felt as alone as Adam before Eve, since his disciples seemed unable to hear or embrace his message. Loneliness, the inner desert, filled him, and he struggled to love it as he had been taught in his first desert retreat.

The wind tugged at his beard and called him out of his deep prayer. He raised his head to see a figure approaching in the blowing dust and sand. His heart rose, for he thought for a moment that it was Gabriel. The approaching figure appeared to be carrying something in his hand, but the swirling dust prevented Jesus from seeing what it was. Then his visitor stepped out of the cloud of dust and stood clearly before him. Horror lifted Jesus' hands to cover his eyes, for the almost unclad figure was as pale as death — and headless, with its grizzly severed head held in its right arm, and facing Jesus.

The Spirit of the Great Prophet

The eyes were open and lively, and the lips spoke clearly. "Cousin Jesus, you've returned to the Jordan." The woeful voice echoed like a haunting wind.

His hands still covering his face, Jesus cried out, "Who are...be gone demon of Satan."

The face smiled and said, "Fear not, Jesus. I'm no desert demon come to haunt you. It is I, Jordan John, your old mentor, who's come as a friend, not with a lesson but with some advice."

Jesus lowered his hands and with supreme courage looked down at the face of the severed head as he answered haltingly. "If John you are, then I'd be thirsty for your advice."

In an eerie singsong tone, the ghost of Jordan John began a long tale. "I am John, who baptized you and cleansed your sins. I am John, whose blood prepared the way for you, the new Joshua, to lead the many across the Jordan to the new promised land, an earth renewed and cleansed by a flood of love and blood! Jesus, this barren place along the Jordan is dangerous to those who hold power in both the temple and the empire.[13] This desert beyond the Jordan is fertile with memories of revolution, of liberation from the oppression of Egypt's empire and all empires. This seemingly empty place is full of memories of old gods and temples abandoned along the Nile in favor of a homeless God who travels with the caravan. Your words, like mine, strike terror in the hearts of those clutching power to their hearts, Governor Pilate, King Herod and the whole priestly temple crowd. Therefore, cousin, if you want to keep your head, with your words and deeds be much more cautious."

"My words are not mine, holy prophet, they come from...."

"Yes, I know, it was the same with my words. The One who spoke to Moses with licking tongues of fire, who licked my ears, now licks yours. It is a lover's tongue. But look at this...." With his right hand, John held up his severed head, sliced like a melon from the vine. The open eyes stared straight through Jesus. "Caution, I say, Jesus, for God's tongue is a two-edged sword and may sever your body from your soul."

"I know there is danger, John, but I hear God saying to me, 'Everything is possible, if you but believe and are loyal to me.' Yet, I have no desire to become another pale ghost who reappears to his former disciples with head in hand. I fear death closes the door on everything — even memories soon fade like daylight at the sun's last hour."

"Listen, cousin, to what happened to me." The grizzly face became more animated. "In prison, I slept on straw with that same fear. On straw only, for the wheat of promise was not there. I had no children to bear my name, in whom I could live on after I died. There were no prophet's scrolls bearing my name with my words to be read by generations to come. Yet like you, Jesus, I too heard God say, 'Fear not death. I can raise you up. You, John, are my beloved; I will not allow my beloved to sleep with death. I am a jealous lover, and so I will steal you away from death — someday.' Jesus, as you can plainly see, that someday has not yet come."

"You offer advice, cousin John, but do you have more to offer than simply to be cautious?"

"Ask, and you shall receive," said John. "Come, follow me." And John led Jesus across the desert to a high plateau. From there he pointed off into the distance, "Over there on the horizon you can see Mount Nebo. Recall how God said to Moses: 'Go up Mount Nebo in the land of Moab facing Jericho and glimpse a view of Canaan land, which I am giving to you and the Israelites whom you lead. You may view this promised land from a distance, but you shall not enter it! For you failed to be loyal and had no faith in me in the desert at Meribah-Kadesh.' "[14]

"I have tried, John, to be faithful to all God has asked of me, I've tried."

"Over there, Jesus, in some unknown ravine is the grave of Moses. No one knows where the greatest of all prophets, the first great messenger, is buried! No pilgrimages are possible to his tomb, no holy shrines to be found, nothing but the ever shifting sands."

"Do you mean, John, that this is your fate and mine as well?"

"Strip yourself naked, Jesus, of all your desires to be remembered, even by those you love. Do not wear even a loincloth of longing to see the fruits of all your labors. Remember Moses and his forty years of being tested, forty years of leading the people in the desert; yet he did not realize the reward of entering the promise! He had only a glimpse of it from afar. Be prepared, for the dream of Moses himself to enter the promised land, never came to be. Your dream, which continues his, is not yours to possess either. The dream belongs to God. As I was the one to prepare the way for you, see in my death a prophecy of yours as well. The dream of God for all creation must be carried by those who recognize the dream as a nightmare so that the world can awaken to the dawn of the true dream."

"John, you are the desert lover; tell me, as Moses on Mount Nebo was given a glimpse of the fulfillment of the promise, what should I climb to get a glimpse of the kingdom I proclaim?"

"I have been sent to tell you that if you wish to see the kingdom of the future as Moses saw the promised land, then you are to climb a tree. Climb your tree, cousin, it awaits you, it awaits you!" The ghost's voice trailed away as the image slowly faded from view.

Hearing that, Jesus closed his eyes and shuddered in great fear. When he opened them, as if awakening from sleep, he was alone. He shook his head and walked slowly back toward the encampment.

Jesus Speaks About Prayer

When Jesus returned from praying alone, his disciples pleaded with him, "Please teach us how to pray, as John taught his disciples how to pray."

"Remember," he said gently, still feeling shaken by his vision, "I am not a teacher. I am the lesson. Look at me. What do you see?"

"You often go apart, Master," said Simon Peter, "and pray by yourself."

"Very good, learn of me. Steal moments, hours or longer to slip away from daily life to be alone with God. Being apart from everyday tasks and concerns will open your eyes usually blinded by the struggles of life. With such eyes, you can return to daily life to see God in your relationships, your illnesses, your joys and in everything.

"Tell me, what else do you see when I go away to pray?"

"You often go apart to pray when you seem troubled. When you return, you are at peace."

"Learn of me, friends. Prayer deepens your trust in God. Pray and find that your burden is also on God's shoulders. Prayer, being with God in the desert solitude of the heart, is the mirror for seeing yourself naked of excuses. The prayer of empty solitude is full of God's voice calling you back to the narrow Way. Such prayer leads to reconciliation, to asking pardon, which is so essential in this vale of tears."

"When you go apart to pray," asked John, "tell us what happens to you in those moments of intimacy with God. Do you have visions? Do angels come to visit you?"

Jesus smiled at his favorite disciple. "Intimacy in love, John, is not for other than your lover's ears! What bridegroom ever speaks at the village gate about what happened in the wedding tent? Learn of me, all of you, I say nothing about my intimate prayer to anyone. Yet my actions tell worlds about what happens in my prayer."

"You call yourself our servant, yet when there's work to be done you often cannot be found," said James the Orthodox. "When the crowds come eager to hear your words, or the sick come to be healed, you're off in the desert in prayer."

"Learn of me, friend James. I cannot feed the hungry with God's bread unless I first go to fill my heart's bread basket at God's oven. As you've heard me say many times, God's kingdom is a return to Eden time before the fall. In God's new time, Adam's old curse of having to work by the sweat of his brow for bread is lifted. This is jubilee time, the sabbatical year of rest, of which the weekly Sabbath is only a feast day of promise until the kingdom comes. In Eden the seventh day was a day of rest. When I go off to rest in God, it is my Sabbath prayer, and the Sabbath must be honored."

"Are you saying then that the kingdom means an end to work and daily labor?" asked James in alarm. "Can your disciples cease from earning a living?"

"Taking time to pray, apart from your work, is to find play again. As Eve and Adam found their garden chores to be playful, I rest in God so I can return to find my tasks transformed. I see them not as work, but as play in the game of life. Only with such Sabbath days, regardless of which day of the week you make them, can Eden's creativity flourish."

"God rested," said Andrew, "after the work of six days of creating. Rest comes at the end of the work, at the end of the week, yet you say it comes at the beginning?"

"Andrew, Sabbath time belongs both at the beginning and the end. Each of life's harvests should be rejoiced in and celebrated; a task well done or any work completed should have its harvest festival. But take care to also have leisure Sabbath prayer before you begin your work. Communion with the creator God fertilizes your creativity, a truly needed gift of the

Spirit if these are to be the new times. Know the Spirit of creativity is ever eager to give to all who ask."

"Master," replied Joanna, "perhaps God gave creativity to all, but I must have been absent that day, or asleep."

"Joanna, dear, you were not asleep. As with dancing, perhaps some have more skill with their feet, but all can dance if they can become children again. Children do not carry mirrors to continually look at themselves as adults do, and so they can dance with glee. God likewise shared a divine gift with Adam and Eve in the gift of fertility. To be creative is simply the fertility of making new images." Then he paused as though he'd had a completely new thought. In a soft and solemn voice he said, "Faithful friends, my role, I think, is to try to make all things new and in fact to even create, if possible — O God, is it possible? — a new covenant."

Again the disciples were shocked. "Master, we already have a covenant with God, an eternal one made in the desert at Mount Sinai," objected Simon Peter.

Jesus slowly raised a finger to his closed lips as if to keep them closed, nodding his head in agreement with what Peter had said. He sat thus for a short while and then spoke, "Yes, those were the words placed on my lips, 'a new covenant.' A new one larger than the one between God and us, the Chosen People. This new covenant will be between God and all the earth!" No one spoke, not even Jesus, who once again was silent, as if waiting for something. Then with confidence he said, "Peter, our covenant was made long ago, and that marriage covenant has grown old and stale. God may want to make a new marriage covenant with the bride. Good marriages require one to marry again and again if one is not to fall out of love."

"Master," replied Simon, "didn't you say that once married no one was to be married again."

"Those who marry their first lover over and over will stay in love. With time, everyone changes. And so you must keep marrying a new person even though they have their old skin. So it is with our marriage to God. A covenant must be made new again and again for the love to remain passionate."[15]

"An endlessly new covenant?" asked Susanna.

"Exactly," said Jesus. "Just as Moses' new covenant which with the passing of generations became an old covenant, so my new covenant with God will also become old unless you constantly make it new. Blessed are those who balance the old with the new, for they shall be rooted in the past, alive today and flowering in the future. Pray then to be free enough to let God's fertility inflame your imaginations. And, Joanna, like Eve, you have the gift of dance. Let go of your fear of being different from others, and let the gift grown stale with neglect come alive. Forget your feet, Joanna, and dance!"

With that he rose and took Joanna by the hands and began to swing her around as he chanted his favorite folk melody, singing again and again, "All things new, all things new." At once the other disciples were on their feet, chanting along with him and swinging each other wildly about, clapping and chanting "All things new! All things new!" The little circles of twos and threes grew larger and larger, and finally — this time including the reluctant Judas — circled around Jesus as he clapped and sang out the very dream of his life: "All things new."

Chapter Fourteen

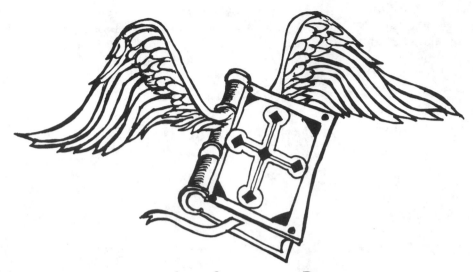

Jesus Speaks about Prayer

When the dancing was done and their evening meal eaten, the disciples gathered around Jesus. James, the brother of John, asked, "Master, your words about creativity are beautiful, but can't you teach us how to pray?"

"When you pray, don't rattle off long prayers as the unbelievers do."

"Master, then teach us some short prayers."

Jesus smiled. "I will teach two of the shortest and most powerful of all prayers. The first is a prayer you already know and often use! It's only one word long: 'Amen,' or 'So be it.' It's not just the end of a prayer but a prayer you can say countless times a day.[1] You can pray it when rains fall in the midst of harvesting a crop, or when your child is sick, or if you've spent the night laboring at your nets without catching a fish. When you pray this simple prayer with all your heart and soul, you are embracing God's will for you."

"Does that help you endure the misfortune?" asked James as he glanced around nervously at the others. "Or death?"

"James, God gives more than pain and disappointment in life. Pray that shortest of all prayers when you drink the new wine of the harvest, when you're finished dancing the love dance with your spouse, when you witness a rainbow or any other glorious marvel of creation!"

John broke in with enthusiasm. *"Amen,* then, is not the end of prayers, it's the beginning, middle and end of all prayer," said John.

"Rightly said, John. The second prayer is like it and is only one word longer than the first: 'Thank You'!" Surveying his disciples, Jesus continued, "I can read your eyes; you are asking yourselves why this simple two-word prayer is so powerful. When you pray the prayer of 'Thank You' at times of good fortune — or, should I say, good grace — you profess your belief in the perpetual harvest of God's gifts to us. When you pray it in times of misfortune, you profess that for those who love God even misfortune can hide good fortune beneath its dark clouds."

"Is that what is meant by 'All things work out for the good'?" asked Joanna.

"They only do if you're willing to work as hard as God at such a miracle. Misfortune will not work out for the best unless you labor to transform the mistake, sin or evil into something good. Just like making love, such a transformation takes two to make it possible — in this case, you and God."

"Master," pressed Joanna, "can't you teach us some prayers to say?"

"Rather than a prayer to repeat again and again, which may make you deaf and dumb to its power, let me say this. When you are in need:

"Knock and knock, and the door shall be opened;
   when in need, simply ask and you'll receive.
Ask for your daily bread, not so as to awaken God;
   ask for your daily bread so you will be awakened,
   awakened to a daily manna of miracles coming to you.
Then you'll pray the prayer of prayers: 'Thank You,'
   dripping with gratitude and great love for God.
'Thank You' is the mother prayer of holiness.

"Be Solomon-wise and pray for what you really need,
   beg and plead for God's Spirit, the answer to all prayers.
When you pray, don't be polite; be as pestering as a beggar,
   as nagging as an old shrew, crying as an infant at the breast.
Pray always, in all ways; to pray without ceasing is the rule."

"Master, there are fields to harvest, meals to be cooked and served — how can we stop our daily chores to pray without ceasing?" asked Joanna.

Jesus rose and began walking about as he continued.

"Prayer begins with words, then moves beyond;
   plant seeds of prayer and it will spread all through your life.

Each act of seeing, hearing, feeling, each breath you draw
  can become prayer, when you and God are as one.
  Let those with eyes see that all life is prayer to me.

"When you pray, groan and moan with sighs of longing,
  with the sobbing of sorrow or cries of love's delight.
Then the fingers of God's Spirit will weave your feeble efforts
  into an angelic poetry so deep as to make God's heart weep.[2]
Join your voice and soul, head and heart, to creation's groaning.

"Pray in chorus with creation; with creaking, swaying trees,
  with the rustling of tall grasses, the cries of cattle and sheep.
One with the slapping waves of the sea, pray and moan aloud
  and groan all together so as to make God laugh and weep.
Pray always, in all ways; to pray without ceasing is the rule."

"Master," said Susanna, "we have the psalms of David to pray, but often they seem like dry clouds that, while beautiful, seem empty of rain."

"When you pray with words, Susanna, fill each one with your breath. Speak them slowly and with a fullness of yourself. Each word of the psalms is like a stick of wood; set it on fire as a torch flaming with your love for God. It is better to pray only one word of the psalms with great passion, with a fullness of self, aflame with love, than to say a thousand times a thousand hollow words, no matter who wrote them or inspired them!

"Pray always, for prayer makes God present on a mountain, in the marketplace, or in a prison cell. To say any prayer is to consecrate a common place into a holy place, a dull deed into a divine one. I solemnly assure you, we have no idea how powerful is a faith-filled act of praying."

"Do you mean, Master," asked Joanna, "that prayer can work miracles?"

"To pray for help, Joanna, opens the doors to great miracles. When the proud, believing they are in control of their lives, begin to pray, they become humble and childlike. That is the first great miracle. The rich and powerful do not pray because they believe that they, not God, can make things happen."

JOHN'S REQUEST

"Master," said John, "to be alone out here with you in the desert across the Jordan is wonderful. Your words about the mysterious presence of God in all we see and feel and hear are truly beautiful. My heart basks in delight at this time apart with you. Let us stay here, apart from the noise of the villages and the roads, and build our own village. Then it would be easier for us to love as you wish, easier to live your way and to shape our lives around prayer."[3]

"John, my beloved, if God's time cannot be lived in the middle of the marketplace or at a crossroads, then how can it be good news? The invitation to enter into the kingdom is not a call to live apart from the evil world but to love the world into goodness."

"Master, that's a beautiful dream, to make the world new with love. But wouldn't it be easier to create a place here where we could live to the fullest the way of which you speak? And when we truly learn your way to love, would we not then be better able to change the world?"

"John, while you have me with you, there is no need to live apart to learn how to love. There may come a time when you need to live apart from the world, as do some of the hermits here in this Jordan desert. Each person must listen in prayer to God's voice and then have the courage to live out what is heard. But before you pray, always wash your ears."

"Wash my ears?"

"Yes, listen with a heart cleansed of any hate or fear of the weeds that grow in the fields of the world. Cleanse yourself of any fear of intimacy, any unforgiveness, any prideful illusion. Then go apart into the desert to live, but do so loving the world with all your heart and soul."

"How can we love the world? It is evil and sinful!" replied James the Orthodox, son of Mary the Murmurer.

"James, the world is just the world. If we are to be Godlike, then, like God, we must love the world, for only by love can we heal its wounds that fester into evil deeds. God is a loyal lover and so loves the world with a deep aching to heal and redeem it of its sickness.[4] That, I know, is my task too, for I am God's messenger — as you must be also. As my followers, each one of you shares that task. You cannot reform or change what you do not love.

"Come now, my friends, to bed. Tomorrow it is time to cross the Jordan River and go up to Jerusalem where destiny awaits me — awaits us all."

The Disciples Argue at the Jordan River

The next morning, as they approached the Jordan, Simon the Zealot said to Jesus, "Master, this is where Joshua led the Israelites into the promised land! Is it not time to put away words and take up the sword so that God's kingdom may come? Of late, the air has been filled with words about loving one's enemies, about pardon and forgiveness and prayer.

What about our freedom? Will it be part of God's time?"

Without breaking stride Jesus answered, "Freedom comes with justice, Simon. God's time is equality time. I feel I must speak for the poor, for the nobodies, the outcasts of society. The rich and powerful have loud voices in the courts of law, and even in how the laws are made. I — we — must be the voice of the poor and of all who are made mute in an oppressive society."

"Words, Master," answered Simon the Zealot. "With all respect, words do not change things. How can we weed out forever the slavery and oppression that breeds war and the other terrible evils in the world?"

"War and all the other evils, Simon, are only the fruits of the ancient vine. I cannot uproot that vine, but I can plant a new vine, my new vine of love of God and neighbor. The lack of love and of a fertile field where love can grow is the root of war, slavery and violence of all kinds."

"It will take a very long time, Master, to grow such a new world!" pleaded Simon. All were now listening intently. Simon continued, "Meanwhile, the powerful remain in power, the poor remain in poverty! The system, the fabric of life, does not change."

Jesus smiled at his eager companion, then spoke so all the disciples walking along beside him could hear. "The fabric changes a thread at a time, Simon. The kingdom comes as a seamless robe, yet it is woven one new thread at a time, one thread at a time. Revolution rips the garment wide apart, but the reweaving of the world begins with your thread, Simon, then with mine. And slowly, one thread at a time, the new garment appears. Violent revolution rips a robe apart, and most new laws commanding social change only sew patches on an old robe. Sew a new patch on an old robe and it too will tear the garment apart. No, we must reweave the ugly dull peasant's cloak into a beautiful, many-colored Joseph's coat."

The disciples nodded with understanding, but Simon was not satisfied. "Master," he said, "Jordan John was a zealous and fiery-hot thread. So Herod simply ripped that swordless reformer's thread out of his royal robe and out of his royal hair! Let that not happen to you. Let us take up arms, dear Master, or the kingdom of God will remain but a dream."

"Master," said Simon Peter, blundering into the conversation, "Simon the Zealot speaks this way often, and tries to twist what you say. I think you should silence him or banish him from our company. He corrupts your message the way he wrongly uses your words. He maintains, for example, that you said, 'Blessed are the poor' while I agree with Matthew that you said, 'Blessed are the poor in spirit.'[5] Your message is spiritual, about changing the heart and saving our souls, not about social upheaval and reform."

"And Simon the Zealot," added James, the Orthodox, "finds no shame in association with the impure. If it would serve overthrowing the Romans, he'd even associate with the uncircumcised, contrary to our laws. We must expel him from our group."

At this Jesus called a halt to the caravan, holding up his hands for silence. "Wait, I have something you all must hear. Brothers and sisters, be at peace," said Jesus.[6] "Remember: Blessed are the inclusive. In my company there must be a rich diversity. Like God, we must find delight in a variety of opinions, in the richness of different personalities and various approaches to the Way. What we need is not uniformity but unity, love — always and everywhere. Let us be compassionate with each other as God is compassionate. Let us be like grapes and not like marbles when we come together with conflicting opinions."

"Marbles?" asked Susanna. "Do you mean the kind that our children play with?"[7]

"Susanna, those clay-baked marbles or olives used by village children are part of our spiritual heritage. That game we ourselves played as children and passed on to our children was taken by our ancestors when they left Egypt in the Exodus."

"I have heard, Master," said Simon Peter, "that even the great Caesar Augustus would descend from his imperial litter in order to join children shooting marble pebbles in the streets of Rome. With delight I have joined my children sometimes in their game. But please explain, Master, what you mean when you say we should not be marbles but grapes."[8]

"Marbles, Simon, come crashing with great force into one another, even in play, as their owners wish to win the game. The intent is to drive the other child's marbles out of the game. When grapes come together with great force, because they are soft-skinned, they are crushed into delicious wine. Those who are hardheaded allow conflicts to drive them apart, while those who are like grapes are crushed together into the new wine of the kingdom.

"So, I repeat what I have said: love one another. In my Family, let it not be 'either/or,' but rather let divine diversity show the true presence of God in our community.

"Now, so that we can depart in peace, let us be reconciled. Simon the Zealous, do you have anything to say?"

"Say to whom, about what?"

"About love, Simon. Love is kind and not jealous; it is never rude or snobbish, it is not prone to anger, nor does it brood over injuries. There is absolutely no limit to how much it can bear. There is always tension among those who live together, but we need to make such unconditional love part of our Family if we are to usher in the new kingdom."

"You speak about forgiving Simon Peter and James?" Simon the Zealot asked.

"Yes, that is what I speak of. Love never tires of saying, 'I forgive you.' And you, Simon Peter, don't you also have something to say to Zealous Simon?"

"Master," Peter replied with a sigh, "I tire of saying, 'Please forgive me.' I do not hesitate to ask God to pardon my sins, but it's hard to continually ask pardon from those who rub me the wrong way, and harder still to, time and again, pardon others for their offenses to me."

"Love never tires of asking pardon, love never tires in granting forgiveness, for love is God and God is love. The cleansing of sin is not a ritual for the temple in Jerusalem, but a sacred priestly ritual for the temples of our hearts. The sacrifice that removes sin is love's knife cutting out all anger and so leaving a contrite and humble heart. Now I ask any of you who have thrown another out of your hearts to welcome the other back with great love as you ask for pardon."

The two Simons embraced, and forgave each other. Then, with Jesus in the lead, all the others in the Family went to one another doing the same.

"By this will all know that you are my disciples, by your loving forgiveness of each other. The greater the love, the easier and quicker does pardon flow. So love one another."

"I thought only God could forgive sins," said James.

"James, and all of you, each time you forgive another and wipe clean the debts of your heart that you feel others owe you, know that God's forgiveness is flowing through you to them. God needs each of you to be the road down which the divine forgiveness can travel. By your love make straight your crooked ways so that God's pardon and absolution can come unimpeded to those in need. Come, it is time to move on again."

Jesus Baptizes His Disciples

With this they resumed their journey, traveling in silence, so much had they each to think about. It was around noon when they arrived at the Jordan River and prepared to cross over to Jericho. Jesus again spoke to them, standing a few feet into the river and allowing all his company to come up close to the bank. "I know that some of you are still disturbed because I have not only allowed women to be my disciples but have sent them out also to proclaim that God's time has come." Some of the men disciples turned toward one another as if looking for a sign of who had told on them.

"I have something to say to you," Jesus continued, "so listen well. I know what the law says about women. I know our ageless customs say that they are not to eat with men and have no voice in public. I say to you, it shall not be like that in my Family." Then he said, "Come, gather here as family, as brothers and sisters, on these banks made holy as temple space by John the Baptizer."

As the disciples made their way to the water's edge, Jesus raised his arms in joy as he sang the famous prophecy of Joel:

> " 'I will pour out my spirit upon all;
>   your sons and daughters shall prophesy.
> Your old men shall dream dreams,
>   and your young men shall see visions.
> Even upon the slaves, both male and female,
>   in those days I will pour out my spirit.' "[9]

Jesus stood as firmly as a post with the waters of the Jordan swirling wildly around him. "The prophet Joel foretold one of God's most radical times, when he said, 'in those days' the Spirit would come upon both men and women. I assure you dear sisters and brothers, the time he was talking about is now! For I Jesus of Galilee have ushered 'those days' into the world! These are the days of the outpouring of God's Spirit on both God's sons and daughters. This day God's promise is fulfilled and will continue to be fulfilled in all ages to come. Step down, now, each of you, and be washed clean of the old time and be baptized into God's holy new time of fulfillment."

One by one, the twelve and six, along with a few chosen other disciples, stepped down into the river and were baptized by Jesus. As each woman or man came out of the water, Jesus said in a loud voice, "You are my beloved, upon you my favor rests."

Young John, the very first to be baptized by Jesus, had stood aside in prayer; then suddenly he saw a vision as promised by Joel. There on the opposite shore stood Moses himself, his face beaming with light, his arms raised high in jubilant prayer. John heard Moses cry out, "This day, the vision of an old man is realized, for into this land fertile with promise comes a truly priestly people. Thank God! After all these hundreds of years my desert exodus dream has come to pass; each woman and man is now a holy minister of God."[10]

After all had been baptized, Jesus himself plunged beneath the water's surface and disappeared. Then after a nervous minute he rose upward in a fountain of spraying water with his arms upraised, proclaiming, "Now we shall go up to Jerusalem, brothers and sisters, all of you holy ministers and priests of God. There I shall be baptized not in water but in fire and blood." Then he continued on with Joel's prophecy:

> " 'God will work wonders in the heavens,
>   blood, fire and columns of smoke.
> The sun will be turned to darkness,
>   and the moon will be red with blood.
> On that great and terrible day of the Lord
>   only those shall be rescued
>   who call upon the name of God.' "[11]

Climbing up onto the banks of the Jordan, Jesus asked the disciples to stand in a circle with their heads bowed in prayer. As they each prayed silently, water dripping off of them, their arms around one another, suddenly a mighty wind came thundering down the river valley, bending the willow trees toward the ground. With eyes tightly closed, they clung to each other in fear as the howling hot desert wind engulfed them. Then, as quickly as it had come, it was gone. The amazed disciples opened their eyes. The air became more than moist, as it is after a rain. Now it smelled not as a spring shower but as if dripping with the perfumed oils of the Orient. Awed, no one asked what had happened to them as Jesus led them across the river and through the willow trees.

"Come, comrades, now we are ready to go to Jericho and then up the road to Jerusalem so as to say 'Amen' to whatever God's dream holds for us. As we depart, know without any doubt that you are no longer the man or woman you were before being baptized in the Holy Spirit."

"That was an incredible baptism," said Susanna.

"A baptism, Susanna, and much more. You have only to open your hands now and receive what the Spirit has given to you — if you dare to do so.[12] Now, let us walk on our way. Let us pray that on the day soon to dawn, when the sun turns as dark as black sheepskin and the moon is dipped red with blood, we will call upon God's holy name and be filled and empowered with all of the Spirit Wind we felt together at the Jordan. Let us walk in silence as we pray that God's Spirit will inspire each of us to say 'Amen' to whatever awaits us in the holy city."

Jesus quickened his pace, walking ahead of the others. Tears poured down his cheeks, running like streams into his beard as he whispered to himself. "Ah...a-men," he stammered. "O God, I find that one small word far too large, too heavy for my small tongue. I am terrified at what I fear now awaits me in Jerusalem, so how can I say amen, yes, to it? O God, do not abandon me; come to my assistance or else I shall fail you!"

CHAPTER FIFTEEN

FROM THE JORDAN UP TO BETHANY
JESUS SPEAKS OF THE DANGERS OF POWER

As they arrived at Jericho, the mother of James and John approached Jesus. "Master, I have a request: On the day your kingdom comes to be, may my two good sons, James and John, sit at your right and your left? To see them in such a place of honor would make me so proud. Please, Jesus, I beg this of you."

"This gift I cannot give, for that choice belongs to God alone," Jesus replied. "But do you know what you are asking? Do you know the cost of such a high position?"

Upon hearing the mother's request, the other disciples were angry with the two brothers for trying to be greater than them. Jesus stopped and said to the little group, "Why are you all so slow to learn? God's reign is not like Herod's or any other kingly reign. In the kingdom of God those who are given authority must become the slaves of the rest. I am the lesson, learn of me, learn me by heart. I have been given God's authority to proclaim the message and to lead you, but I come as a servant, ready to give my life if necessary as a ransom for you and for many."

"Why, dear Master," asked Salome, "are you so against ambition and so passionate about avoiding any signs of honor, power or authority?"

"Power, sister and brother slaves, is as dangerous as poison because it tips the scales, making some lower so that others can be higher. It destroys the balance of equality in God's family. Like a sharp sword or a poisonous viper, power must be handled with the greatest of care."

Peter asked, "Are you saying that authority can be as lethal as a serpent's bite?"

"As deadly, if not more, especially for those who lack the fulfillment of having a lover as faithful as your wife, Simon. Power over others can fill the void for those whose lives are barren of love, becoming a backdoor way of making love. Power gives pleasure no less than holding flesh to flesh, and can easily produce a bastard love. The desire to hold power over others quickly poisons even the most beautiful love. And it is still more poisonous if those in power lie to themselves, saying, 'I seek only to serve.' When I am gone, my Family, choose well your leaders. Baptize them again and again in the threshold water basin of slavehood. If they should wish to parade about in garments of power, as do this world's leaders, strip them naked, giving them only a servant's towel to wear!"

JERICHO

By this time they were entering the palm-clustered city of Jericho, and it was Jesus' intention to pass straight through the city and up to Jerusalem. Living in Jericho was a man named Zacchaeus, who because he was a rich tax collector was considered a public sinner. Zacchaeus wanted to see what Jesus was like, but being short in stature, he was unable even to catch a glimpse of Jesus because the crowd was so large. So Zacchaeus ran ahead of the crowd and climbed a sycamore tree so he could see Jesus as he passed by.

When Jesus came to the tree, he looked up and said, "Friend, come down from there for I wish to stay at your house today." Zacchaeus hurried down from the tree and with great joy ushered Jesus to his home. As the crowds saw this, some said among themselves, "He has gone to be the guest of a man who is a sinner, one who oppresses the poor."

Zacchaeus heard their complaints. Standing proudly before the door to his home, Zacchaeus said to all who could hear, "Behold, I give half of my possessions to the poor, and if I've defrauded anyone of anything, I'll restore it not twofold, but fourfold." Jesus embraced Zacchaeus and said, "Today, salvation has come to this house, for behold a true son of Abraham, a beloved son of God."

After they had eaten and were once again on the road up to Jerusalem,

Jesus asked his disciples, "What did you learn from our visit to Jericho this day?"

"The lesson I saw you live out," said Mary Magdalene, "was that unlike the usual religious prescription of conversion coming first, then repentance and finally salvation, your way is upside down. First comes embracing and feasting with the sinner in non-judgmental love; then conversion follows like a chick from an egg."

"Master," replied Simon Peter, "it's as Mary said. But it's all upside down and seems so contrary to God's laws. Our tradition tells us that communion with God first requires that sinners, those who are unclean, must become clean, that the impure must become pure. Then they are welcomed at God's table."

"That's the old song, Simon. I sing a new song of God's love that rushes in before judgment. Zacchaeus, while seen as a sinner by his neighbors, being a leading tax collector, in fact had a heart wide-open and ready for God. Did you notice how he said, 'I *give* half my wealth to the poor,' not 'I *will* give.' Zacchaeus is an example of how a rich person may slip through the needle-eye gate of the kingdom. Today he went beyond what any law might require with his willingness to repay fourfold those he may have defrauded — which we may well guess to be many since he is a toll collector. Mary Magdalene is correct, first comes feasting on love, then comes fasting from sin![1] And today we saw another example of how loving someone unconditionally can release great generosity from within that person. Indeed, God's ways are not ours, for if our ways seem right side up, then God's ways are truly upside down!"

The Blind Beggar Sees

As they were leaving Jericho, a blind beggar who was sitting along the road, upon hearing that Jesus of Galilee was passing by, cried out, "Jesus, Son of David, have mercy on me."

"Who calls out to me?" asked Jesus, stopping to listen.

The man was seized with hope and cried out, "I am called Bartimaeus, son of Timaeus, a poor blind beggar. I beg you, Jesus, have mercy on me."

"Shut up, keep quiet, do not bother this holy man," someone in the crowd said in an attempt to silence him. But Jesus asked the blind beggar to come to him.

"Quickly," said a fellow beggar to Bartimaeus, "this is your lucky day, for he is calling you to come to him." And the man was led to Jesus. Jesus put his hand on Bartimaeus' shoulder and asked, "Son of Timaeus, what do you beg from me?"

"Master, that I might see!"

The face of Jesus wrenched in pain but without hesitation he reached out and touched the beggar's eyes. As he did, he felt Bartimaeus' darkness, like a viper's sting, entering his hands and racing up his arms toward his heart.

"I can see!" screamed Bartimaeus, suddenly blinking his eyes. "I can see! Glory to God who has visited me this day! I can see!" Having been healed, Bartimaeus wanted nothing more than to follow Jesus and his disciples up the road to Jerusalem.

Jesus began to walk on but Bartimaeus came around in front of him and fell on his knees. "Master, thank you for giving sight to these once-blind eyes of mine," he said. "Thank you for freeing me from the life of a beggar. Allow me to be one of your disciples."

Jesus reached down and brought Bartimaeus to his feet. Smiling, he said, "You may join us, Bartimaeus, if you can see and embrace what lies unseen beyond the horizon for me and those who accompany me."

"Master, all I have to contribute is my gratitude. So I can only thank you by embracing you, all of you, which includes what lies hidden beyond today. But this gift of sight you gave me, will it last? I've heard that some whom you've healed of blindness have gradually lost their sight again."

"That is true, son of Timaeus. Once one's eyes are opened, they easily can close again. If you don't want to lose your new gift, then you must force yourself to hold your eyes open to what you don't want to see. Once you're freed, never go home, never go back into the darkness of the dungeon of illusion again."

They walked on in silence as Bartimaeus pondered the meaning of Jesus' mysterious words.

After some time, one of the disciples who had overheard Jesus asked him, "Master, would you explain to us your words to Bartimaeus about keeping his new vision?"

It was time for a rest, so Jesus found a good place for all to sit, and as food was passed among them, he began to speak.

THE PARABLE OF LAZARUS [2]

"Once there was a wealthy man and woman who lived in a grand house and dressed in fine linen and purple. They feasted in lavish style not only on high holy days but every day. Now daily sitting at their front doorway was a poor man named Lazarus, who was covered with sores which the stray dogs licked. For Lazarus it would have been a feast to eat the crumbs and leftovers from the table of the rich couple. Daily they went in and out of their door, yet they never looked at Lazarus and did not give him so much as a scrap from their table. Eventually Lazarus died in the gutter, but he was lifted up by angels and carried to the bosom of Father Abraham. Some time later the rich man and his wife also died, but they were carried to hell where they were tormented in flames."

"Only justice!" cried Simon the Zealot. He laughed and slapped his neighbor on the back.

"Yes," added Mary, the mother of Jesus, "the rich shall be thrown from high places and the poor raised up."

"There's more," said Jesus, returning to his parable. "Now the rich couple saw Lazarus for the first time, saw him enjoying the pleasures of a good life as Mother Sarah served him rich foods and wines while he rested on Abraham's bosom. At this point the couple became beggars. 'Mother Sarah and Father Abraham, please have Lazarus dip his finger in cool water and send him to touch our burning tongues,' they cried. 'Have mercy on us; can't you see our terrible misery?'

"Sarah looked distressed but stern. 'Between you and us there is a great canyon,' she replied, 'and even if they wished to, those here could not cross it to visit you.'

"The rich man, ever the planner and schemer, said, 'Then have mercy and at least send Lazarus to my five brothers to open their eyes lest they follow me and my wife to this place of torment.'

"But in dirge-like tones Sarah and Abraham chanted the terrible truth:

"　'Open your family's eyes, you plead;
　　　send them the walking-talking dead
　　　so they may see what's in front of them.
They already have their healing eye-openers
　　　in the holy prophets and in Moses' words:
　　　"Care for the poor and the alien."
No more than you, will they open their eyes,
　　　even if the dead should rise and call them to repent.'

"And that's where the story ends," said Jesus, getting to his feet. "Time to move on. Do I see the temple in the distance?"

So all resumed their journey. But to a person they pondered Jesus' parable. They walked on for a short time when Judas spoke up, "Your story of poor Lazarus' reward for doing nothing with his life is a puzzle to me. And the rich couple did nothing sinful, nothing forbidden by the law, yet they were condemned to hell — if indeed there is a hell!"

"Judas, my brother, sin is the result of not doing, as well as doing. But you doubt that there is a hell?"

"You've talked before, Jesus, about living beyond this life. I have questions as to the existence of an afterlife."

"But, my friend," Jesus said, "even Pharisees, among others, believe in an afterlife, along with some Greeks, as we saw in the play of the death and rising of Dionysius."

Judas walked along, shaking his head. "With all due respect, Master, the Pharisees believe in angels but are not the scholars of our law. As for the Greeks, they're unclean heathens. Are the uncircumcised to teach us, God's chosen people, some truth overlooked by Moses?"

Jesus was disturbed by the answers of Judas, but spoke gently. "Not overlooked, Judas. Perhaps the fruit was not yet ripe at the time of Moses for him to give such a gift of God to the people. From God comes the fruit that satisfies the hungry hearts of Jews and pagans alike, indeed of all peoples, the fruit of life beyond death. Love between two persons is the first bite of that divine fruit from God's tree of life. Those who have known deep love do not doubt life beyond the grave, for love is stronger than death. Chew on that awhile, Judas, and know that even now as we speak other fruits in God's orchard are ripening that someday will be given to God's people."

"Spare us, Lord, we have too many unripe fruits to chew on right now," replied Simon Peter with a sour look on his face.

Jesus Is Anointed in Bethany

On their way to Jerusalem they passed through Bethany near the holy city. Simon "the leper," as he was called, hearing that Jesus was passing by, invited him and his disciples to dine with him. As he had done when invited by tax collectors, Jesus warmly accepted the invitation to dine with a person whom others feared to come near. As they all reclined at table, a woman unknown to Simon or to the disciples entered the house. Everyone gathered immediately marveled at her striking beauty. As she moved toward Jesus, they asked among themselves who she might be.

Admiration soon turned into indignation among some of the disciples as she took an alabaster jar of precious ointment, broke it open over Jesus and poured the entire contents on his head. As the ointment oozed in thick streams down his face and onto his arms and body, like olive oil from an overfull vat, Judas began to shout, "Woman, whoever you are, why this waste of precious ointment? It could have been sold in the marketplace for more than three hundred denarii — enough to feed a multitude of the poor!"*

"Wait, brothers and sisters," said Jesus, "do not harass this good woman for what she has done to me. The poor will always be with you, and you can assist them from your surplus whenever you wish. I, however, will not always be with you!" He bowed to the woman in gratitude and she disappeared out the door.

"Master, you hint again of your death in Jerusalem?" asked John, his words draped with dread.

Jesus had now resumed his place at the table. He said, "The time of destiny is near at hand, John; I feel it strongly. This anointing is part of that dreadful drama. What she has just done is to prepare my body for burial. Wherever and whenever you tell my story, speak of what she has done this day."

"Master, whenever you die — and may it be a day far off in the future," objected Simon Peter, speaking for the others, "we would prepare your body for burial. We are your family." They all chimed in their agreement and concern.

"Even if you were not there at my death, Simon Peter, and my body were thrown into some mass grave to become the food of dogs, what this woman has done today ensures that my burial will not be profane."*

Jesus then stood up, oil dripping from his body, and, bowing his thanks to his host, departed without another word.

"Where has the Master gone?" asked Susanna, addressing all present.

"To his favorite prayer corner in the olive garden not far from here," answered Judas without looking up, as he continued to collect the broken pieces of the alabaster jar, shaking his head in distress at the money that had been wasted.

"Let us go and wait for him at the home of Martha and Mary," said Mary Magdalene, and they all thanked Simon and departed.

Jesus Prays in the Olive Garden

When Jesus arrived in his hidden-away corner of the grove, he began to pray aloud, "Thank you, my God, for your gift of sending that mysterious woman to anoint me for my burial, which I dread is not far off. Thank you for saving me from the shame and disgrace of being thrown into some burial pit without a proper anointing, if indeed I am to die on a cross. Whoever she was, she was your angel of compassion. Now, O God, I beg of you: help me to know what it is you wish me to do now that I have reached Jerusalem."

Then he sank into a soothing silence, as if the oil with which he had been anointed at Simon's table were being absorbed into his soul. Jesus felt his anxieties slowly dissolve, his spirit healed of its cramped concerns. He sank deep into the great sea of the divine, absorbed in the Mystery. When he finally opened his eyes, he was surprised to see that the moon had risen. This first moon of spring, which was growing fat, was looking down at him through a latticework of dark olive trees branches.

Then he saw Gabriel sitting against a twisted old tree trunk. The angel said to Jesus, "What did God say to you in your prayer?"

"A parade, a parable-parade is the way I should enter Jerusalem, or something like that."

"What do you think that means, Jesus?"

"I wasn't told. As with God's other messages, it seems to require an unfolding. Will you help me?"

"I'll help you begin," Gabriel said, "but the full unfolding must be yours. Let me remind you of one of the ancient sayings of Proverbs:

" 'Four things are among the smallest on the earth,
and yet they are excellently wise:
Ants, who are not large but are shrewd, for they store up
a supply of food in the summer for hard times ahead.
Rock-badgers, a species not mighty, but who are able
to make their homes in the mountain crags.
Locusts, who have no king, yet they migrate
and march as an army in full array.
Lizards, who are impossible to catch with your hands,
yet they find their way into Kings' palaces.' "[5]

"Gabriel, you've given me another parable to help me understand, a Proverbs' parable of wise animals. But I fail to see how it will help me understand God's message of my entry into Jerusalem."

"Jesus, you must now be like the locusts and lizards. You've already been like the ant and rock-badger."

"Thank you, Gabriel, I'll take that with me as I sleep on this message."

"Here's one more puzzle to take with you," Gabriel said. "What feast has a joyful procession or parade?"

"The feast of Tabernacles or tents — Sukkot.[6] But that's a harvest festival. Look, the full moon of spring is almost here. I fail to grasp the connection," he said.

"Sleep with it, Jesus. Sleep unfolds many things," said Gabriel, who disappeared from his sight. Jesus rose and walked to the Bethany home of Martha and Mary where he knew his Family would be waiting.

THE BARREN FIG TREE

In the morning he said a sad farewell to his faithful friends, Martha and Mary, and set out with his disciples for the city. As Jesus was leaving Bethany, he saw a fig tree. Being hungry, he went over to the tree, only to find nothing on it but leaves. "Bartimaeus," he called out, "come here and see this worthless fig tree. Woe to this tree, for it sucks water from the earth but gives no fruit in return. This fig tree will never give fruit again!"

"Master, why curse the tree?" asked Bartimaeus.

"Those with new eyes will see why."

As he looked out at the holy city on the horizon, beautiful in the sunlight of a new day, he began to weep, sobbing beyond control:

"Jerusalem, Jerusalem, where is *your* fruitfulness?
    O daughter Zion, you have abused
    all the messengers of God
    no less than did Sodom and Gomorrah.
And so a fate worse then theirs shall be yours."

Despite Jesus' tears, James chided him. "Master, please do not speak of those two sinful cities in the same breath as holy Jerusalem. If the priests hear of this we are dead."

But Jesus went on, sobbing like a mother at the grave of a beloved child:

"Jerusalem, how I would have gathered your children
    as a hen gathers her chicks under her wings
    when the hawk circles overhead,
    but you closed your gates to me.
As a mother I would have nursed you at my breasts
    if only you had known the hour of your deliverance."

As they drew nearer and came to Bethphage on the Mount of Olives, he sent John and Judas ahead with instructions to obtain an ass and bring it to him. To the others he said, "Go get palm branches and the leafy branches of other trees and give them to the crowds."

"You want us to gather palm branches as we do on the feast of Tabernacles to build booths on the rooftops?" replied a confused Simon Peter. "Master, this is not the season for that feast."

But Jesus addressed them solemnly. "Listen to me, all of you. We are about to celebrate the feast of all feasts, something new in our religion. It shall be the feast of Tents, Passover and the Fifty Days all in one great festival. This is the new Tabernacles, which like the first celebrates not only God's deliverance of the people from slavery, but the taking possession of the promised land!"

"Shall we arm ourselves with swords and other weapons?" asked Simon the Zealot eagerly.

"Arm all of my followers. Yes, do so, Simon. Fill their hands, however, not with swords or clubs but with palm and olive branches. As the old feast of Tents included a procession in which the ark was introduced into the temple by King David, our new Tent feast shall celebrate something greater than the ark coming into the temple. As the old feast was a renewal of the covenant, this new feast will renew it as never before. But enough for now, go and organize the procession."

The Parable Parade of Palms

As the crowd grew, the disciples encouraged everyone to pull down palm branches and olive and willow branches. A couple of the women disciples began to lead the singing of jubilant songs:

"Hosanna to David's son who comes in God's name.
Hosanna in the highest. Blest is the king of Israel."

In a few minutes John and Judas returned with a donkey. Jesus mounted the donkey now draped with Simon Peter's cloak. Raising his arm in the air, he paused. Then he quickly lowered his arm like a sword pointed toward Jerusalem. Amid shouts of joy, the ragtag procession began. Jesus sang to his disciples who were close behind him the lines of Proverbs that follow the passage Gabriel gave him the previous night about the ants, locusts and lizards:

" 'Three things are stately in their stride,
      yes, four! How they stately march.
The lion, the king of the beasts,
      who retreats before nothing;
      the strutting cock and the he-goat
      and fourth, a king leading his people.'
Forward, God wills it. Great is God!"[7]

From the Mount of Olives where the parade began as a tiny stream of disciples waving palms, it quickly grew into a creek and then swelled into a river of green palm, willow and fig treetops, spreading wider like the floods of the Nile. Jesus, riding on his donkey, led the wildly shouting crowd. Other streams of people flowed out the gates of the city to clog the road up ahead.

The crowd of the poor, sick and simply curious pressed against Jesus on his donkey, shouting praise and crying out, "Save us, Jesus of Galilee," and "Now is the hour, this is the day the Lord has made" and "Not Herod! Not Caesar! Jesus is our King!"

Jesus, his face set like slate, said not a word more, but he felt the comforting hand of courage which Gabriel kept firmly on his back.

When his donkey brayed, he turned and looked; a woman had snatched hairs from its tail. "To protect me from the evil eye," she shrieked.

"Heal, heal, heal," screamed a crippled mother holding up in front of Jesus a small infant so deformed of face as to not look human.

Jesus shook his head, "I'm on my way to raise this holy city!" he shouted over the loud songs of the crowd.

"Holy sod, holy God, holy sod of God," screamed a crazy man in tattered rags dancing in front of Jesus. His long tangled hair coiling outward like black snakes, waving his arms wildly, with spittle drooling from his lips, he sang out:

> "Holy sod of God, holy God, heal this sop,
> hop, hop, here comes the flop of God.
> Clop, clop, here comes the ass of God."

Simon the Zealot pushed aside the man, who disappeared almost at once in the crowd like a rock sinking into a swollen river. As he was swallowed up by the throng, he cried:

> "Holy sod, holy God, holy sod of God;
> clop, clop, here comes the ass of God.
> Not I, it's you, Jesus, who are crazy and odd."

A hundred times a hundred hungry hands reached out to touch him, his cloak, even his donkey. All, including the crippled woman with her deformed child, were screaming, "Jesus, Jesus, please heal! Help! Heal!" As healing flowed through him to all those suffering, he felt a sharp pain as power shot outward to the crowd. Even his donkey cried out in pain.

Children dressed in dirty rags took up positions in front of his donkey and began to lead him up the last approach to the gates. Caught up in the excitement of the crowd, they played at being soldiers, Roman legionnaires. Marching in columns with palm branches held like spears, they sang:

> "Onward to victory, we march into battle with our new king;
> tromp, tromp, tromp, we're soldiers of David's new king.
> tromp, tromp, tromp, we're soldiers of David's new king."

As the broad forest of waving green palm, olive and willow trees, with shouting and singing, pushed, shoved and squeezed behind Jesus through the city gates, Jesus shouted loudly, "The physician has come to raise the dead daughter of Zion! Rise up, dead rotting Jerusalem, from your tomb. Rise up, Jerusalem, from your harlot's sinful slumber, for your day has come! Behold, Herod, God's lizard has entered your palace. Look, priests, for like a plague of locusts this great crowd comes to devour the vineyard filled with grapes of wrath, to strip clean this weed-infested wheat field of God."

The shouts of the jubilant crowd spilling into the city streets was now joined by the voices of those leaning out of windows and standing on the flat rooftops:

"Hosanna, the king of Israel enters David's city.
Hosanna, praise Jesus, the king of kings.
Hosanna, here comes God's holy prince of pity.
Hosanna, regal is Jesus, the lion of Judah.
Hosanna, hosanna in the highest heavens."

As the parade poured down toward the center of Jerusalem, some Pharisees rushed forward, pleading with him, "Silence your disciples, you idiot! These praises they sing are overripe and dripping with treason. You know as well as we that the Romans will not tolerate this."

Jesus leaned down so the religious authorities could hear him plainly. "If my disciples were to be silent, the very stones of Jerusalem would cry out the message for Jew, Greek, Roman and all the world to hear:

"Hosanna, the age-old exodus is over,
    the Jordan River has now been crossed.
The new ark of the new covenant
    has entered the temple, the world and history.
Hosanna, let the dancing begin,
    let torches and lamps be set ablaze
    so that night will be like the day.
Blow every trumpet, sound every shofar,[8]
    the desert lover has come to Jerusalem,
    has come to lay with Zion's village whore."

With all the noise and shouting, there was no need of spies. Reports of this King Lizard parade, this out-of-season feast of Tabernacles procession and crowd's shouts ripe with treason reached the Roman governor Pilate before the shouts had ceased to echo on the wind. At once he issued orders for stricter crowd control of the Passover pilgrims already filling the streets. He had prepared for the usual unrest at Passover,[9] but not this kind of religious riot with olive and palm branches. In his concern, he dispatched a messenger to Caiaphas with this letter:

> "Is this one of your Jewish religious festivals? I was under the impression that this approaching feast was your Passover, not the tenting celebration. While no Jew, I've been in Jerusalem long enough to know the difference between Passover and Tabernacles! To celebrate them together as this peasant preacher appears to be doing is too dangerous, too crowded with old national memories best forgotten. Remember, high priest Caiaphas, what happened to your father-in-law, Annas. [10] Heed this warning!"

That afternoon, as Jesus had instructed, his followers built their palm and olive branch booths on many of the roofs of Jerusalem. While all the pilgrims that crowded the city prepared for Passover, his disciples and those who believed in him also celebrated the out-of-season feast of Tents. That night, by blazing torch light and lamps they ceremonially danced the ancient joy of being in the promised land, the harvest of forty long years of exodus. Around the table where Jesus sat feasting, his disciples marched with palm branches like temple priests around the temple altar at the feast of Tents. Then, as is the custom on the first night of Tabernacles, Jesus, whom many said was the best dancer in all of Galilee, began to dance — and how he danced. He led his disciples with great zest and joy in folk dances of the feast and of weddings.

When the dancing had tired them all, Jesus, full of energy, sang them a song of his own:

> "Tonight under these leafy tents we all must dance and sing,
>   for see, under our feet is the promised land.
> In these temporary tents we make our homes
>   for Israel's only the threshold of God's plan.
> Every hunk of the earth's sod is now God's holy land.
>
> "Rejoice, my brothers; dance, my sisters,
>   for God's kingdom is here among us this night.
> A holy harvest fills God's barns to the full;
>   Canaan's vats are jammed with new grapes
>   ready to be stomped as at Sheckem of old
>   by our Spirit-filled dancing feet.
> Dance as once maidens did in the vineyards;
>   dance at this holy night's wedding feast,
>   foretold in songs by holy prophets ages ago."

Late into the night they danced more and drank sweet dark wine, feasting and rejoicing. As some of the hanging lamps began to sputter, their oil nearly consumed, Jesus stood and sang:

"I am the light of this holy night, the light of the world;
  I'm no lamp hidden in a Galilean basket.
I stand here on Jerusalem's rooftops
  for all to see, for the whole world to see.
As lamps burn bright on this holy night,
  so each of you must shine with an inner fire
  that dark night may see the dawning of a bright new day."

Then Jesus, the last to give in to tiredness, found a solitary unoccupied corner of the roof. He lay down and almost at once was asleep.

CAIAPHAS RESPONDS TO PILATE

"Remember, Caiaphas, what happened to your father-in-law, Annas," the high priest repeated as he stood at the north windows of his palace, looking out over the rooftops of Jerusalem. Located near the city's southern wall, it offered an excellent view of the entire city all the way to the temple at the northeast corner.

"Pilate tells me to heed the warning, lest, like Annas, I am removed from my priestly office by Rome. For more than fifteen years since they removed my wife's father, I have kept the peace with Rome.[11] The people have enjoyed a rare oasis of calm and order in this bitter desert of occupation. Now the delicate balance is threatened by a barefoot peasant preacher."

He turned to face his private council of elders, aristocrats and ranking members of the priesthood. "Do the stupid Galileans not even know how to tell time? This is not autumn or the harvest season, yet look out there at the rooftops: tents of palm branches! This night has been ablaze with light as on the festival of Tabernacles."

He could still hear the echo of the music and the wild clapping that accompanies festive dancing, spiced with an occasional shofar blast, that had flooded through the window of his palace. Now the sleeping city was quiet.

"I've asked for frequent reports on this man, and you promised me an informer to keep us posted on his movements," said Caiaphas. "Why then did we have no warning of his 'regal' entrance into the city?"

The leading counselor replied, "Our inside source told us, Caiaphas, that even Jesus' intimate circle, to which our source belongs, did not know about it until this very morning, just before the procession began. Like us, even his disciples were dismayed at the linking of the festivals of Tabernacles and Passover."

Caiaphas went on, "If Pilate looked out over the city tonight from the top of his Fortress of Antonia on the northern wall, he would have seen what I see. Yes, a new Exodus — not into the desert but in the middle of Judea, in the heart of Jerusalem. This is no pious festival nicely laundered of its political implications — for both our religious institution and Ceasar's empire — by years, even centuries, of ritual. This feast of Tents is as much treason to Rome as the Exodus was a slap in the face to Pharaoh."

The council sat in respectful silence as Caiaphas began pacing back and forth in front of the window, shaking his head.

A scribe spoke up cautiously, "Caiaphas, our source says that Jesus speaks freely that the temple is empty, that God has abandoned it. He spreads confusion among the simple people who regard him as a prophet by saying that he will make the covenant new!"

The high priest faced the scribe. "All institutions, including ours, need renewing," replied Caiaphas. "We do it constantly with paint and gold plating. But that's not the renewal that's really needed. The simple folk are fed by public pomp and ritual, and that is a shroud we easily can supply. Even if the shroud is golden, it's still a shroud."

"Are you referring to our temple rituals as a shroud?" asked a priest in surprise.

Caiaphas smiled. "Don't be naive, my friend, open your eyes. God sends prophets to prune the vine of dead wood so that it can bear heavy, rich clusters of grapes. Yet when you're the dead branches, you do not open your arms to welcome God's pruner."

"Dead branches?"

"The peasant is a prophet! I myself have gone to visit the All Holy One in the temple up there at the far end of the city, and I've found that God was not at home! As high priest, only I may enter the holy of holies at the heart of the great temple. And, gentlemen, when I step into the holy of holies, all I find is a hollow, empty room![12] Though it is dark and windowless, I am suffocated not by the lack of air but by the lack of God. The only prayer my soul cries out is, 'Where are you?'"

The council sat stunned by the high priest's grave words. They were in sharp contrast to the joyful music and singing that had poured from the rooftop tents into the council room as goat's milk fills a bucket.

A priest named Eleazar spoke up. "As you've said, high priest, God sends us prophets to prune the vine. On numerous occasions, I've heard this man Jesus speak, and some of his words seem to be from God. Should we not consider listening to him?"

Another priest shouted, "What do we have here in our midst? Are you also one of his disciples, Eleazar?"

"Of course I'm not!" said Eleazar. "You know of my fidelity to our ancestral priesthood, our temple and the covenant of Moses."

"Silence, brothers!" roared Caiaphas. "Let us not waste our time quarreling among ourselves. We have to address more serious issues than whether or not this Galilean is a true prophet. Pilate sent me a message of warning today, reminding me about Rome's dumping of my wife's father as high priest. But I'm far more concerned about the warning he sent us when he ordered that Roman Army standards, with their military images, be brought into the temple.13 After our outcry he removed them, but his message was clear to me. 'Be obedient to Rome,' he was saying, 'or it won't be an image of Roman eagles that will be set up here but one of the Roman God Jupiter! Your house of God will become the house of our God.'"

"Caiaphas, how are we to heed Pilate's warning?" asked one of the council.

That question opened a floodgate, releasing a chorus of concerns.

"Will this Jesus obey a decree that he is to cease this activity that threatens the security of the city and the foundations of our religious worship?"

"Shall we bring him here to question him?"

"Does the law provide us grounds to imprison him, to remove him from the people at this time of the Passover?"

Eleazar intervened. "Patience and prudence, my friends. Let us wait and see what happens. With Passover upon us, the mood of the people will quickly change. Patience, I say, is the path."

Caiaphas spoke to the scribe who had been to Simon the Pharisee's dinner party. "More information is what is needed before we can decide on a course of action. Can the informer you spoke of supply more information about what this Jesus proposes to do next?"

"I believe so, high priest."

Caiaphas stood framed by the window, the nearby rooftops made luminous by the almost full moon of the spring equinox. "Thank you for coming tonight. Your suggestions we shall consider. For now," he said, motioning to another scribe, "take down this message I want sent to our Roman governor."

> Pilate, procurator and governor, friend of Ceasar, protector
> of the temple and of our people: greetings.

You asked for my opinion about the recent activities of this peasant preacher from Galilee named Jesus. It seems he is a simple but good man, perhaps a little overly zealous in religious matters. However, we both know these times are full of unrest and dissent. Zealots, while bold in words, are not yet bold in actions. Alas, instead of scholars and the temple authorities deciding what is God's Law, it is common people who want to take that over. We lament the ever growing disregard of our authority as religious leaders — which is a threat to your authority as well — and the failure of many to observe the traditions of our religion. Perhaps this may account for the strange celebration of the festival of Tents at this holy season of Passover.

From all reports I have received, this Jesus is not interested in power — and, in fact, totally disavows it. Yet I fear he's dangerous to both of us because he preaches about a new kingdom where the rich will be cast down and the poor lifted up. And if he did not plan his royal entry into the holy city, he at least did not resist it. As for what to do with him, it would seem the issue is more political than religious, hence belonging more to King Herod or yourself than to us.

Know that I shall keep you informed, and that we shall work with you toward a swift and peaceful conclusion to this troubling issue. Know also of my gratitude for your protection of our temple worship and the welfare of our people Israel.[14]

"I will sign that when you have it prepared," Caiaphas sighed. "I want it in Pilate's hands the first thing tomorrow morning. Send a copy as well to King Herod. Let us pray tonight that this ass-riding prophet really does believe that God no longer lives here in the temple and will go home to Galilee before the feast. Good night, friends; let us pray for ourselves as well, and for the people of God."

CHAPTER SIXTEEN

THE DAY OF THE TEMPLE RIOT
JESUS SINGS OF MEMORIES

The excitement among the residents of Jerusalem over the approaching great feast of the Passover grew larger daily as the first full moon of spring swelled in the night sky and the crowds of pilgrims increasingly poured into the streets of the holy city. Since it was a family table feast, every householder was busy preparing for the ritual meal that enshrined the memory of the Israelites' liberation by God from slavery in Egypt. The devout were likewise preparing their hearts by prayer, and so large crowds daily gathered in the temple during this week of the great memory.

Jesus and his intimate circle of disciples were on their way from Bethany to pray in the temple when they passed a fruitful fig tree. Jesus used the occasion to say, "Blessed is the fig tree that bears an abundant harvest of figs as rich as these. Life, my friends, is like a fig tree."

"A fig tree?" asked Susanna.

"Yes, you must care for it, making sure it has proper soil and water. Sometimes you must help it to be fruitful by surrounding it with good, pungent manure!"[1] The group laughed, Jesus joining them.

"Personally, Master," joked Simon Peter, "as a fisherman I prefer the smell of fish to manure. Perhaps, if I were a farmer like Simon of

Cyrene here...."

"Dead fish," said Simon from Cyrene, "make good manure as well, Simon. So regardless of where you obtain your manure — use it, and not just animal dung or decaying fish, but suffering and the other things in life that stink to high heaven."

Joanna pinched her nose with her thumb and forefinger, saying, "I care not for suffering or foul-smelling situations."

"It's what you do with them," said Jesus, "that matters. You can use them as manure to make you grow or you can simply suffer their stinging presence — or worse yet, you can spend your life raging against them. Life has its share of foul-smelling situations; it's what you do with them that counts.

"The older the fig tree," Jesus went on, "the greater the harvest, and so it is with life. Each day we make memories. What kind we make is our choice — they can be good figs or rotten figs. There are great fig memories we all keep, the national memories we celebrate and sing about around the table of our feasts. We savor memories of living as free people in leafy tents in the desert after the Exodus, or the lamb's blood that liberated our people in Egypt at the Passover, as we will do in a few days. All the great memories are made because much manure has nourished the roots. And our branches are loaded with personal memories as well."

"Master, you said that we *make* memories each day," said Susanna. "I've always thought about memories as what happens to us, what is done to us each day."

"Susanna, we are not victims of history. We create our own history by the choices we make, and so we make either good or bad memories."

"Will you explain to us what you mean by this?" asked Simon Peter.

"Recall, Simon, how I've said that you were not to let the sun go down on your anger. If you go to sleep in a bed of anger at another, I assure you, you will awaken with a fig of bad memory in your mouth about how you failed to be loving and forgiving."

Several shook their heads in agreement, remembering the taste of such figs in their morning mouths.

"Whenever we feel guilty," Jesus continued, "we are tasting the bad fig-memories of behaving less than what we are capable of, less than fig-actions filled with the Spirit. How easily we grow bad figs by failing to take time and care each day to always do what is just, kind and generous. A good tree, a good garden and a good heart all require such constant care."

"But every day?" asked Simon Peter. "That's why I've always been glad to be a fisherman rather than a farmer. It seems like a great deal of work to constantly have to be careful about everything, I mean everything we say and do."

JESUS LAMENTS THE SIN OF PRESUMPTION

"Yes, it takes labor, but I assure you, it can soon grow into a labor of love. It becomes as natural as breathing to make good figs. It's only a daily drudgery if you are guilty of presumption, the great enemy of good fig memories. Perhaps it's the most insidious sin, the habit of assuming tomorrow will be a mirror of today. Woe to those who presume when they fall asleep with the person they love that they will both wake up alive! When you leave home in the morning to go fishing or to the fields, never presuppose that you will return to find your house, your spouse and your children as safe as when you left them. Never take each other for granted as we do the rising of the sun each day."

"Master, do not worry," Simon Peter replied. "We will never take you, or each other, for granted."

"With all my heart, Simon, I pray you will not. Let us rejoice in the love that binds us together."

Then, as they walked through the gates of the holy city, Jesus began to sing:

"Never assume that tomorrow will follow today;
    constantly make delicious memories like bread,
    to nourish you through life's journey
    with all its droughts and trials and crossroads.
Never leave home at sunrise without a good memory
    on which to chew throughout the day.
Make good memories at night to keep as fine wine
    to warm you in winter, to be sipped in dry hardship.
Never tire of making good memories to savor.

"Never assume that tomorrow will follow today;
    make memories like you make babies, out of great love.
As we have throughout these past years of feasting together
    on fish and bread and wine, on love and friendship,
    dancing when in danger, laughing when afraid,
    never tire of making good memories to savor.

"Never assume that tomorrow will follow today;
    each day let us make a beautiful and great memory,
    as if it were to be the last we'll ever share,

so full of life as to live on forever and ever.
Let us make a memory as full of divine love
  as the figs grown on Eden's ever-fertile trees.
Never tire of making good memories to savor,
  and never assume tomorrow will follow today."

By then they had reached the entrance to the temple, which was crowded with pilgrims. "Come," sang out Jesus, "let's make some memories."

The Temple Riot

Jesus and his disciples went inside the temple. After they had finished praying, they sat for awhile in an outer court across from the temple treasury, where pilgrims were dropping money into the donation boxes. Some of the rich left large sums; when a poor widow approached, she gave but two pennies.

"Brothers and sisters," Jesus said to his disciples, "do you see what that poor widow has done? The rich have given only from their surplus, which is indeed great. But she has given all she has to live on!"

"Blessed is she for such total generosity," cried Simon Peter, "for surely she shall be rewarded by God."

"No, Simon," snapped Jesus, "she is not to be praised for being blind, even if God in compassion responds graciously to her blind faith."

"Blind?" asked Mary Magdalene. "Please explain this to us, Master. It seems to contradict what you've taught us about loving God by giving all of ourselves, with a great generosity."

"This poor widow," said Jesus, with rising anger in his voice, "is a blind victim of religion. She is but one among the multitude of widows and poor who are deceived, off of whom the greedy temple priests and scribes live. While she shall go without food this day because of her gift, they shall dine on choice wines and rich foods.[2] But that is not all they feast on. They are gluttons to be treated with respect on the streets and to sit in places of honor at dinners and in the synagogues. They get drunk on being greeted with titles of honor." Jesus rose to his feet. Just then a priest made his way past them and entered the inner court. "Locusts!" shouted Jesus as a crowd began to gather. "They're all locusts, who strip the poor, devouring God's fields and gobbling up the meager savings of widows. Hypocrites! They hide behind the holy masks of men of prayer and love to recite long prayers in public, not for God's ears, but to impress others. Like a cloud of locusts they swarm over the people, without remorse stripping the poor bare of what little they possess, doing all of it in the name of God."

"Master," whispered James the Orthodox, "we're in God's holy temple, please be more discrete with your words."

"James and the rest of you, listen. God is fed up with this robbery of the poor. I assure you, today God's long-entombed words through Isaiah are raised from the dead. There God said:

" 'What care I for the number of your sacrifices;
    I find no pleasure in the rivers of blood
      flowing from calves, lambs and goats.
Trample my courts no more;
    your incense stinks to my nose!
When you spread wide your hands in prayer,
    I close my eyes to you.
Though you pray all the more,
    I will not listen.
Cease doing evil;
    learn to do good and make justice your aim.
Defend the widow and do not rob her.' "[3]

As a still larger crowd gathered, Jesus raised rather than lowered his voice. More than simply being louder, his voice had caught on fire. Jesus' words shot forth from his mouth like flaming arrows raining down on a city under siege. He stood on the ledge that surrounded the outer court. The throng of listeners recognized him as the prophet from Galilee who had entered Jerusalem the day before in the great palm procession. They responded with approval to his angry words. "I have come here to the temple with my winnowing fan to clear this threshing floor. I shall gather the wheat into God's barn, and the Wind's deposit, the worthless chaff, God will burn with unquenchable fire. In the words of the prophet Isaiah, 'The Lord of Hosts says: I will turn my hand against you and refine you like gold in the furnace and remove all your alloy.' "[4]

Some in the crowd who had only heard of Jesus were staggered; others who had heard him speak were shocked by the violence in his voice. His disciples began to look anxiously at one another.

"I am filled with the wrath of God!" Jesus cried out, raising his arms in the air. "I am Mount Sinai, a volcano vomiting the fire and smoke of God's anger against those who have taken over the Holy One's house. I am the orange clouds of destruction that once stood over Sodom and Gomorrah. I am filled with a wrath of fire and brimstone for those who have turned this house of prayer into a filthy marketplace." As Jesus spoke, his strong voice echoed off the magnificent marble walls of the courtyard.

His body quaked and his hands shook with emotion. The crowd around him could feel intense heat flowing out of his body. Suddenly the temple courtyard became deadly still, just as before a thunderstorm.

"God is angry!" Jesus roared as he pushed his way through the crowd. Storming through the temple courtyard, followed first by his terrified disciples and then by the whole throng of listeners, he shouted, "Get out of here, you thieves and bandits."5 As he kicked over the tables of the money changers, coins cascaded to the stone pavement, ringing like the bells on the hem of the high priest's robe.6 Over the voices of the astonished money changers, Jesus cried out, "I am the new Samson, you thieves and robbers, come to pull down this temple's pillars. This house once full of our just God is now just full of rot." He threw open animal corrals and cages, saying, "I release all the sheep, goats and doves to be sold for sacrifice. For God's nose prefers the aroma of freedom to that of burnt flesh. Yes, God is fed up with fatted calves — and fatted priests as well, fed up with fat merchants grown rich on the poor's piety. You blind fools, open your eyes; God doesn't live here anymore. All you crippled by religion, stand up. Go back home where you live to find God."

Jesus then seized a rope and began using it as a whip, fiercely driving the merchants and money changers along with their frightened animals, out of the temple. They fled before him like cattle trampling over one another to escape being lashed by his whip. The chaos was total, with merchants calling for the temple guards, the crowds crying out in confusion, flocks of doves flapping skyward in escape and bleating sheep and bellowing calves running about in all directions. Then finally Jesus stood atop the sole standing money-changer's table and sang:

> "My house shall be a house of prayer,
>> not a stinking slaughter house.
> My house shall be a house of prayer,
>> not some holy tax collector's house.
> My house shall be a house of prayer,
>> not a theater house for hypocrites to perform in.
> My house shall be a house of prayer,
>> not some tomb-house for embalmed, lifeless rituals.
> My house shall be a house of prayer for all peoples,
>> not a private house for a privileged race."

It was only his beloved friend John who finally was able to stop him, pulling desperately at his sleeve. "Master, come quickly, this way. The temple guards are coming; we must leave at once." Led by John, Jesus and the disciples slipped out through the confused crowds and made their way up to the Mount of Olives.

Like Samson of old, Jesus, at least for that day, did pull down the temple! His actions made it impossible for the proper sacrifices to be performed, as all the sacrificial victims, those specially raised without blemish, had escaped down the streets and alleys of the city. The pilgrims who had come to worship at the temple also fled like the doves, some of them because they found truth in his condemnation of the temple. Many had secretly harbored in their hearts his denunciation of the temple clergy and their exploitation. Today, their hidden resentments had been given a voice and, like the doves, they felt released.

Others, however, were not so pleased to say the least, especially those who made their living by the temple and her visiting pilgrims. They were outraged that it had been a bad day for business, while others were outraged at the upheaval in God's house.

The Gathering Storm

Meanwhile as they walked from the Mount of Olives toward Bethany, Andrew turned and exclaimed, "Look, Master, at how beautifully the white walls of the holy city gleam, at how majestic is the temple."

Jesus stopped and turned to look. Above Jerusalem a spring storm was brewing. Dark, billowing clouds piled high on top of one another, as off in the distance the rumble of thunder could be heard. "Andrew, do you see those great buildings? I assure you, so great a storm is coming that not one stone will be left upon another."

Judas smiled bitterly and asked, "You mean, Master, a storm greater than the one that swept through the temple today? If stones could speak, as you've said before, Master, they'd be clucking like women at the village well."

"Or like men chewing the fat," added Susanna, "as they gossip at the village gate."

"Regardless," Judas said, "these stones you admire, Andrew, if they could speak, would buzz like bees about our Master's deeds today. It was like a spark tossed into the dry stubble of a wheat field, engulfing it in fire. The news of what happened today surely is already in the hands of Caiaphas and the chief priests, and no doubt in Pilate's possession too! It's an evil storm that brews, not just *over* Jerusalem but *within its walls* as well."

"Judas," replied John, "how can you speak with such a lack of understanding? What I saw was the Master's great zeal for God's house, a zeal that consumed him."

"Well, boy John," answered Judas sarcastically, "that same zeal may soon consume us, his disciples, as well."

"Brothers, be at peace," said Jesus as he walked along, seeming at great peace after the upheaval of the day. "We are a family with many hearts, and so we need more than one ear open to hear what others feel, think and fear."

"I mean no disrespect, Master," said Judas. "You know my love for you, and you also know my affliction of being a practical man. Until now you have only spoken about the abuse of God's house, and words are but dry leaves skipping on the wind. Deeds are different, especially deeds like those today; they are far different. You have never acted rashly, you are no village fool! Something must have inspired you to cause that riot in the temple. You are not a violent man and have indeed spoken strongly against all violence. Yet today was different."

Jesus paused, then leaned against a tree, stroking his beard. "I was overcome by anger at the evil I saw taking place in God's house," he said, looking from one to the other of his disciples. "I hope it was a holy anger, yet I know it doesn't seem to make sense with everything else I've said. If the temple is empty, if God doesn't live there any more, what difference would this buying and selling make? Yet, as John said, I was eaten up inside with zeal to say that this old religion with its priesthood, sacrifices and pious offerings is dead. What saddens me is that my zeal blinded me to your peril, my friends. I need to ask your forgiveness if by my actions I have endangered any of you. Will you forgive me?"[7]

"Forgive you?" asked a bewildered Simon Peter, who spoke for most of the others. "You are God's prophet, and whatever you do is holy!"

"Simon, don't be a pious idiot," Judas shot back. "We're in trouble, don't you understand? Jerusalem is about to become a giant winepress, and you and Jesus and all of us are the Galilean grapes about to be stomped to death! Not red wine but red blood will flow out of those city gates!" And he pointed back to the city, still glistening in the sunset.

"Brothers, sisters, I am weary," said Jesus, sitting down and leaning against a low stone wall. "Let us stop here and consider what we should do next."

The disciples gathered about him. Andrew asked, "Master, tell us when this storm of destruction of which you spoke will come upon Jerusalem."

"Jerusalem, and especially the temple, is like a great white egg shell: beautiful, but a serpent has sucked most of the life out of it. Like all hollow-shelled institutions, it's fragile; its end is near. Look not for signs in the heavens; look, rather, for signs of life, and if there are not any, then you'll know the end is near."

"Signs of life?" asked Joanna.

"Yes, youthful growth, joy and enthusiasm, creativity, and most of all great love — these are the signs of life in a person or an institution."

"I saw none of that in the temple," Joanna replied, "or in Herod's kingly court."

"All dead shells, hollow and empty, ready to crack," Jesus said. "But, dear ones, when great temples do crack apart, stand clear and do not be caught in their collapse. Now you must watch out for yourselves, as brother Judas says, for as they hate me, so they will hate you if you remain true to my words and my vision. When you see the signs of the end, let those in Judea flee to the mountains. If you're on the rooftop as we were last night, do not go into the house to get a single thing, not even your cloak."[8]

"Flee?" exclaimed Simon from Cyrene. "I will be watchful and alert, but I will never flee from you!"

"Simon, listen to the Master!" Judas replied quickly. "He's said what I wanted to say: Let us flee from here this very hour. Jesus — I mean Master — if we just return to Galilee, they will simply dismiss your behavior in the temple as the actions of a crazy man."

"You go home, Judas, and any of the rest of you who wish." Judas immediately shook his head, no. "I now realize what it was that drove me to destroy the business of the traders in the temple. It was the same power that drove me into the desert after my baptism by John. I didn't realize it until just this moment as you spoke of me appearing to be insane![9] It was insane to go into the desert as I did. I went alone without food or water, yet I was driven there by the Spirit Wind. That same Wind has driven me, filling my sails to bursting and pushing me out of calm waters into the raging storm of my violence for the sake of God and the kingdom."

"Master," replied Mary Magdalene, "I and the other women do not wish to flee to Galilee but want to remain here with you."

"And we men feel the same," replied Simon Peter. "We will be loyal to the end."

"Simon Peter," sighed Jesus, "I know how loyal is your heart. But know that each of you is free to flee when the storm strikes." Then Jesus rose, and together they all resumed their journey to Bethany.

CAIAPHAS' COUNCIL

The high priest Caiaphas had hastily called his private council to meet with him and the former high priest, Annas. By the time Caiaphas arrived at his chambers, all those assembled had already turned the room into a boiling pot with their angry talk about the sacrilege that day in the temple. Priests of various ranks, Sadducees, scribes and those who represented the merchant dealers in the temple were outraged at the sacrilege of Jesus. Silence dropped on the boiling pot like a stone lid as Caiaphas entered.

"I have called you to this meeting at once," said Caiaphas, "before Pilate sends me another message, as he surely will. What happened this morning in the temple was no quaint folk festival like yesterday, with a fool riding a donkey. This was no out-of-season building of palm-branched tents on rooftops. This Jesus of Galilee has moved beyond preaching to insurrection!"

A priest shouted, "An abomination to prevent sacrifice to God in the temple — especially during Passover week!"

"He called us locusts feeding off the poor!" cried another.

"The merchants who sell doves and lambs and other sacrificial victims have come to me as their council representative," replied another priest. "They demand, as do the money changers, that we take immediate and firm action against this man. This Passover time is like a harvest season to them, and if this man has turned many of the pilgrims away from doing business with them, there will be no harvest!"

"Yes," replied Caiaphas, calling for silence with raised hands, "I am fully aware of the various interlacing concerns in this matter. I am not blind to the fact that, beyond the religious implications of his actions, at least twenty percent of the population makes its living off the temple and the pilgrims who come here.[10] Business, God's and theirs, is indeed threatened if we fail to take action."

A scribe leapt to his feet. "Summon the temple police. We have no need to gather evidence; his violation of God's house itself is more than enough to have him arrested!"

"The words of this Jesus about the plight of the poor," replied one of the aristocratic Sadducees, "while not uncommon for a disgruntled peasant, have now turned to deeds of destruction."

Another aristocratic member of the council, Joseph from Arimathea, spoke up, "Wait! Have not the prophets told us again and again that God is more concerned with orphans and widows and the poor than with our temple sacrifices? Is it not possible that this Jesus is a holy prophet? Let us not act hastily with violence against him. Perhaps he will even return to Galilee quietly after the Passover festival."

"All that's fine for you, Joseph," said a scribe. "You live in Arimathea, not here. Your property is not threatened!"

"What property or sacred structure will this man attack next?" shouted the first Sadducee, dramatically clutching his heart as if he feared it might be stolen. "Will he come after our homes and farms? His own mother has been reported to frequently say, 'The rich will be cast down from their thrones, and the poor raised up to fill them.' "[11]

Caiaphas again called for silence. "More than our personal interests are at stake," he said. "Both Annas, the former high priest, and I agree that this riot in the temple will send a signal to Pilate that we are no longer in control of the situation there, that we can't even police our own temple! Recall that insurrection a few years ago when the Romans crucified two thousand of our people.[12] Their crosses reached from Jerusalem to the horizon. The welfare of the entire population of the holy city, as well as our personal welfare, requires that this be resolved before the Passover festival. The sooner the better, and as discretely as possible."

"Do you have a plan then, high priest?" asked a scribe.

Caiaphas put his hands on his hips and stood as confident as a military commander. "I understand that our informer says this Jesus frequently goes to a secret prayer place in the garden of Gethsemani, which is located on the Mount of Olives. That would be an out-of-the-way place for us to arrest him. He would then be turned over to Pontius Pilate who is more than eager to give the Passover crowds an example of the authority of Rome."

"High priest," asked one of the Sadducees, "should we not be concerned about the crowds? What if they riot to save this folk prophet of theirs? Then the solution would be worse than the problem."

"Thank you for your wise caution," replied Caiaphas. "While that may happen, I doubt it will. My experience is that the rabble are like sails; they fill themselves with the wind of the day, but when the wind dies down, their loyalty droops like a sagging, limp sail. Pilate knows that wisdom as well, and that the more forcefully the wind is checked, the quicker the sail sags. I will assure him of our fidelity to Rome and our commitment to keeping order among the pilgrims in the streets. I will further assure Pilate we of the temple will supply another wind to occupy the rabble, a holy wind to fill their sails. You priests and all of us must work overtime, must labor without ceasing, to make the celebration of Passover this year so wondrous that, like a zephyr, it will fill the minds and hearts of the pilgrims and the residents of Jerusalem."

"Shall we arrest all of his disciples?" asked a priest. "The precise number is difficult to determine, since it seems there are various degrees of association. It seems the inner core has some twelve men and six women. After that, the circle expands to a hundred or even several hundreds."

"Arrest any who are with him or loyal to his cause," replied Caiaphas, "but the fewer the better — after all, they are all Jews and members of God's household. This action we take is to prevent a Roman holocaust, not begin one! One Passover lamb is sufficient to save the people. And trust me, when the wind is taken out of their sails, his disciples will fly away like the doves today in the temple. They'll fly back to Galilee and leave us in peace. What is critical is that this man Jesus be arrested and handed over to Pilate for the execution of justice."

THE INFORMER AT THE GATE

Caiaphas adjourned the private council, and then visited briefly with the former high priest, Annas, while the others departed. One scribe, who had remained beside the door, spoke to Caiaphas in a low voice as he was about to leave. "High priest, the informer you asked me to find in the Galilean's inner group is waiting now in your courtyard. He asks to speak with you."

"You know I would not do such a thing!"

"Yes, but he insisted. He wants to speak with you about Jesus."

"If you know what it is he wants, tell me, and perhaps I can give you an answer to take back to this spy."

"He is concerned that the women in the group not be harmed and the other disciples be spared if you are going to take action against them for what was done in the temple. He's a devout son of Abraham, a good man."

"If he's good, then why is he here at my gate to betray his own master? What does he want of me?"

"I don't know the reason for his disloyalty, but he is fearful about the possibility of what he called a communal suicide, 'the sheep willing to be slaughtered with their shepherd.' What message can I deliver to him from you?"

"None, scribe! You may repeat what you heard at the meeting. Only Jesus and those who remain loyal to him at the time of the arrest will be charged and sent to Pilate. To use the Galilean's own analogy, the shepherd was the only one guilty of sacrilege; the sheep were sheep, too dumb or tame to be more than onlookers. When the shepherd is struck down, what the sheep do is their business, and their fate. Good night!"

The scribe bowed to the high priest as he walked away and down the hallway. A few steps from the door, Caiaphas turned and said, "Scribe, inquire from this man if he will lead our temple guards to the secret prayer place of Jesus in the olive garden and identify him by some sign. It is crucial!" As the high priest returned to his chambers, the scribe disappeared like smoke into the shadows of the darkened hallway.

A Night Visitor Comes to Jesus

A potbellied moon hung like a large white melon in the clear night sky when Jesus was awakened from sleep by someone gently shaking his shoulder. He opened his eyes expecting his angel guide; instead, he saw Judas. "Jesus, quietly, please get up and come with me." Jesus stood up, wrapped his cloak about himself and, stepping over the sleeping bodies of his disciples around him, followed Judas into the night.

While the almost-full moon filled Bethany with light, the night seemed dark to Jesus as he followed Judas to a clump of trees some distance away.

"I have information I must share with you, Master. It is not for the others to hear."

"Are we not all family and friends, Judas? Why the need for such secrecy?"

"Tomorrow night, being Thursday, one of your usual nights to pray in the garden at Gethsemani...," Judas paused, sighed deeply, then spewed it out, "...they will come and arrest you for the riot you caused in the temple!"

"They, Judas? Who are they, the Romans?"

"No, Master, it is the chief priests who will send the temple guards to arrest you. Then you will be sent to Pilate, the Roman governor."

"How do they know where to find me?"

Judas paused, full of guilt, his face lit by the moonlight. "It was I who told them."

"Why, Judas?" Jesus was disbelieving, astonished.

"Master, it was for a good reason. They promised me the women and others would be spared if you could be arrested alone."

Jesus stared at his troubled friend. "I am grateful, Judas, for your honesty in warning me, but if you told them where I could be found in the darkness of night, why do you now tell *me* about this?"

"Because, I thought, ah, rather, I hoped, that if you knew of their plot to seize you, we would all leave here early tomorrow morning and return to Galilee. We've disagreed about several things, but I truly love you, Jesus."

"If you love me, then why this betrayal?"

"At least I'm warning you. You yourself, Jesus, told us that when the terrible storm of storms comes we are to flee into the mountains, not even going to get a cloak. I have come to warn you that the storm of which you spoke is only hours away. Jesus, please practice what you preach this time. Escape!"

"I have also preached, if that's what you call it, that if you seek the kingdom of God with all your heart, everything you need will be given you. I have truly sought with all my heart the coming of God's time."

"Wise master," said Judas, struggling with his feelings, "I'm not John, the youthful beloved, or mystic-eyed Simon of Cyrene. Remember, I'm Judas, the realist. I do not believe that God will send a legion of angels to defend you from the temple guards and the Roman soldiers! Now, I know you have more than once before eluded those who have attempted to stone you to death or throw you over a cliff. All I'm asking is that you do it again. Escape this attempt to kill you. Practice your spiritual advice as when you said to us, 'When they persecute you in one town, flee to another!'"13

"You speak the truth, Judas, but as I have told you all, my hour has come. I am touched by your concern for me and the others, especially the women disciples. I too want nothing evil to happen to them; they must be spared if that is at all possible."

"I have tried to help."

"Thank you for what you've told me, Judas. Fear not, I will not speak of this visit to the others. As for what I will do tomorrow, that is not mine to decide. The night is more than half spent, I leave you to your sleep, for I must go and pray. Peace to you, Judas."

"Peace to you, Master."

Then the two exchanged an awkward embrace.

THE MORNING OF THE LAST MEAL

The next morning Simon the Zealot saw Jesus coming up out of the olive grove walking in the early morning mist. Behind him the rising sun was painting a yellow cast on the taller buildings of the holy city, especially the top of the temple. "Peace to you, Simon," Jesus said with affection. "Did you have a good night?"

"Yes, Master, I slept well, and you?"

"A good night — yes, Simon, it was good."

"Come and share something to eat with us, Master," Simon said.

As the little group ate bread and fish, Judas sat at the far edge of the circle and waited. More noticeably than usual, he kept his hand to his face, covering his birthmark and his eyes.

"Brothers," Jesus said, "before the sisters join us for the day, I want two of you to go into the city and obtain a suitable place for us to have dinner this evening. The Passover is at hand and it is fitting that we celebrate it as a family."

"As a family?" asked James the Orthodox with surprise. "You mean the entire Family, including the women? While we may disregard the customs of our people when we are on the road or in remote Galilee, surely not here in holy Jerusalem — and at the Passover meal!"[14]

"Surely we will, James! In fact, it is essential this Passover that the whole Family celebrates this festival of the family table."

When they had finished their morning meal and were preparing to begin their day, Jesus walked over to Judas. Placing his arm around Judas' shoulder, he said, "Judas, I'm sorry, you did your best, but God's will must be done.[15] Whatever you must do, go and be about it. I will go about what I must do, for God wills it, and God is great."

CHAPTER SEVENTEEN

THE LAST SUPPER

"This is the house to which the Master said we should come," said Simon Peter to the other disciples he had led through the sunset streets of Jerusalem. "These must be the steps to the upper room that has been prepared for us. The Master told me this afternoon that he had gone on ahead to make sure that all was ready for the dinner."

In joyful anticipation the group climbed the steps only to find the room unoccupied. "Perhaps, Simon," said Mary Magdalene, "he meant the roof. Let us continue climbing to see."

Upon reaching the roof, they found a palm-and-olive branch feast of Tabernacles booth, under which was a table laid for the feast of Passover. The evening breeze not only cooled them, it carried a faint hint of salt water and the scent of the sea blended with rare Oriental perfumes. From the stronger branches of the booth hung flickering lamps, which swayed in the gentle breeze. In the east, the Mount of Olives was outlined in yellow light by a full moon ready to rise. In the west, over the wall of the holy city in the pink-blue sunset sky, the Vesper Star danced in crystal beauty.

"Magical," said Mary Magdalene, surveying the table fully laid out for the Passover meal and the beauty of the city at sunset. "And what better place to celebrate the Passover than this leafy tent, just like the ones in which our ancestors lived during their desert and harvest times."

"Thank you," said Jesus, who stepped into view. "Now all of you, remove your sandals. I wish to wash your feet."

Mary Magdalene instantly objected. "Master, it is I who...."

"No, Mary, it is I who am your servant," he said as he began to wash her feet. He then anointed her hair with oil and gave her the ritual kiss of welcome.[1] One by one, Jesus greeted each of his disciples with this same ritual. When it was Simon Peter's turn, he objected, "Master, this is the task of a house slave. I will not let you wash my feet."

"Simon the Stone," said Jesus with great tenderness, "this is a baptism into my heritage. Unless I wash your feet, you can have no part in my birthright."[2]

Peter agreed, even asking Jesus to wash his head as well.

Then they all took places on the floor around the central table, leaving the place at the head of the table for Jesus. Jesus said to them, "You call me Master, but learn from me. I who am your master have washed your feet and will serve you as a slave at this table. And as I have served you, you must from now on serve one another."

James, brother of Joseph, leaned over and whispered to Peter, "Why can't the women wait on us? It just doesn't feel right for the Master to perform the work of women or slaves."

"Friends," said Jesus, "I have greeted you by washing the dust of the road off your feet, by anointing you with oil to refresh you and with a kiss, the sign of love. Welcome to this most holy of all dinners in our tradition. Tonight we celebrate three feasts among feasts: Tabernacles, Passover and Pentecost.[3] This night, as the moon makes her appearance over the Mount of Olives to be greeted with a kiss by the evening star in the west, we meet between heaven and earth on this rooftop." He raised his hands in blessing, saying, "Peace be to you."

"And peace be to you, Master and Lord," they replied.

"Wait," he said solemnly. "No longer call me Master or Lord. Call me by a far more noble name: friend. With great longing have I wanted to celebrate this meal with you. Behold, I make all things new. Savor this ageless Seder meal, which I hope you will remember among the greatest of all the memories we have made."

Jesus opened his arms wide, "Behold, tonight's table filled with roasted goat and fish, as well as lamb, honoring our ancient tradition.[4] See these figs succulent with old memories, the new wine and good rich bread."

Standing up and removing his cloak, so that he was wearing only his fresh, white festival tunic, Jesus opened his arms as wide as possible, saying, "Behold, the food on this table is no longer simply roasted goat or lamb or bread or wine but my own flesh and blood which I give to each of you with great love." As he spoke, his soul, his inner self, seemed to radiate through his clothing and his flesh, as sunlight pours through the openings of a leafy roof at high noon.

Jesus stepped from under the Sukkot tent, picked up a tray of food and returned to the table. As he handed the tray to them, they were overcome with almost the same hot rush of blood and excitement that a bride experiences on her wedding night as the bridegroom opens the flap of the bridal tent and boldly strides inside.

Jesus went on speaking. "As I have been both host and servant to you upon entering the feasting tent, so I will serve you this evening." He moved from disciple to disciple with bowls filled with roasted goat and fish. With great respect, each of them responded with profound gratitude to this most common table service Jesus was performing in providing their meal.

"As I serve you now," he said, "I shall also serve you in the days to come. But whenever you are served, treat the person who waits upon you, regardless of how simple the task, from cleaning to cooking to serving you at table, as if it were I myself waiting upon your needs. Treat every person who serves with the same honor you are giving to me, your servant this night."

After he had served them all the first course, Jesus took his place at the table. Taking bread into his hands, he said the blessing, gave thanks and said, "Behold, I do something new. Take this bread, each of you, and eat of it, for this is my body, my very self, my dream and my love." As the large piece of bread was passed around the table, each tore off a portion, eating it more with wonder than reverence.

"With this cup," Jesus said, after saying the blessing over the wine, "behold, I again do something new.[5] This is the cup of my blood, my spirit and my life, which shall be shed for you whom I love, and for all. Take and drink of it, each one of you." The cup was passed slowly from disciple to disciple as each drank from it. Again, as with the bread, it was with great wonder that they drank the wine. After the cup had made the journey around the table, it was returned to Jesus. As Jesus held the cup high among the lamps hanging from the booth, their lights glowed on his face and the disciples could see tears streaming down his cheeks as he began to sing:

"Taste and see the goodness of the Lord;
taste, in soft, sweet crumbs on your lips,

how good, how tasty, is the bread of love.
See in the mirror within this simple blessed cup
    God's face reflected in its red pool of love.

"Taste first the spirits of the bread and wine;
    taste in the fish and lamb, their souls, taste life.
Taste with each drink from the cup of wine,
    the souls of the crushed grapes of the vine.

"Taste and see how good is the Lord our God;
    now taste the Soul of Souls, the Spirit Divine,
    whose Spirit breathes in every soul-breath
    of lambs, fish, figs and grapes.
Taste and see how good is our God.

"Taste in the bread and wine both heaven and earth,
    the sun's hot fire, the moon's pale milk.
Drink stars down by the millions bright;
    drink, in this wine, all rivers and seas.
Taste all of me in both bread and wine:
    taste wheat fields, flocks and beasts,
    taste mountain rocks and desert sands.[6]
Taste and see how good is the Lord.

"Even without words of blessing, the taste of God is there,
    whenever friends with love share wine and food.
Bless, break and take and eat my flesh
    in tiny crumbs of wholesome bread,
    my blood in but a sip of wine.
Taste and see how good is the Lord.

"Holy, holy, holy God of Hosts,
    heaven and earth fill each loaf,
    heaven and earth fill each cup.
Whenever two in love, who are one in me,
    do bless, break, eat and drink,
    then they eat and drink of my soul and my flesh."

After a profound bow of reverence, Jesus drained the cup dry and placed it on the table. "Not again will I drink of the fruit of the vine until I do so in the kingdom of God."

"Master," replied Simon Peter, "is not the kingdom of God right here? You've said from the beginning that it's already here, now, among us."

"Yes, Simon, and remember that as long as you live. But the kingdom as I just spoke of it refers to the fullness of what tonight is only a foretaste. Blessed are those who can taste it here, today, for they shall soon be drunk with it in the fullness of God's time."

"Master," asked James, "you teach us by parables, and tonight's meal is unorthodox, both in the foods we eat and in your table blessing. As you said, you're doing something new. Dare we ask you the meaning of this table parable?"

"James, this meal is more a prophecy than a parable. The memory of what we do here this night, like the rays of the sun, will reach beyond the horizon. Remember how yesterday I spoke of memories? The memory of this meal will be like a boat floating on the river of time from century to century far into the distant future. God's own messenger has told me this, and I believe."

"Of course we accept the message you have received from God, even if we do not understand," said James. "It must be the will of God, then, that we make this meal a ritual observance as has been done for centuries with the meal of the Passover."

"James!" said Jesus sharply. "Simply remember. Remember this meal each time you break bread and share a cup of wine and I will be present there among you!"[7]

"How will you be present?" asked James.

"I will be present, soul, heart and body, all of me, whether you share fish or lamb, wine or bread. I'll be present in any food, at any table, regardless of how lowly, when you share the meal in the same love that binds us together tonight on this rooftop under this leafy exodus tent."

"Master," said Simon Peter, "I feel like the youngest in the family at the Seder meal for asking such a stupid question, but why are we celebrating Passover under a Sukkot tent?"

Jesus quietly took a bite of fish, waiting to see if any at the table would answer Simon's question.

"As I see it," said Simon of Cyrene, whom Jesus had personally invited to this supper, "we are the first seed of a pilgrim people perpetually in exodus, forever adrift without a holy city or temple. We are to be forever exiles, aliens in strange lands. Homeless, each city we enter is to be holy Jerusalem, every house the house of God. Each land whose borders we cross is to be the promised land, for we bring the promise, we are the promise!"

"Blessed," said Jesus, "are those with eyes to see." But many did not begin to understand.

As the meal went on, the full moon was climbing higher into the spring sky over the Mount of Olives. With joyful toasts, the group greeted this ancient signpost of the feast, this silent white witness. The great eye of the moon was missing nothing that was happening on this holy night, just as it had watched long ago when Moses led the Jews out of Egypt. Jesus then stood and, taking up a shepherd's harp in his hands, began to sing:

"I am the good but lonesome shepherd,
who longs for a home and never to be abandoned,
who aches with a yearning to be loved.
More than wolves, it's aloneness I fear,
yet I'm willing to die for the flock I hold as dear.
I am the good, but lonesome shepherd,
who longs for love and not to be alone.

"I am the good, but lonesome shepherd,
who will lay down my life for those I love.
But I'm fearful none have loved me as I truly am,
and full of dread that my death will be in vain.
I am the good, but lonesome shepherd,
who longs for love and not to be alone.

"I am the good and fearful shepherd,
whose only staff is a fragile, thin hope
that beyond death's hungry mouth is life
— for my body and my soul —
as God has lovingly promised me.
I am the good but lonesome shepherd
who longs for love and not to be alone."

The music of the strumming harp and shepherd's ballad held the power to transport the disciples. Jesus' song softly floated above the rooftops of the holy city to a thousand moonlit sheepfolds of Judea and Galilee. Some of the disciples saw themselves carried to their own deathbeds, possessing only that same thin, fragile hope Jesus had sung about, as full of questions about what follows death as the moon was full of light. Others were transported to the edge of their fears and doubts as they heard in his sad shepherd's song a small crack in the fortress wall of strength they saw in their master upon whom they relied.

"My beloved friends," Jesus said with open affection, "we've made love this night just as we've made memories."

Laying aside the harp, he continued, "And those who have made love no longer address each other in the same way. I no longer call you *disciples*, I now call you my dear friends. This meal seals our friendship. My friends, I ask you to love one another as I have loved you, and as God has loved me. This is my farewell wish, that you would love one another."

"*Farewell*, Master?" asked Simon Peter. "Is it time for us to go?"

"Simon, my friend, again I say to you, no longer call me Master. Recall how in the beginning I did not object to being addressed by that title as long as you did not treat me as the scribes demand their students treat them. Tonight we've moved beyond the relationship of disciple and master. We've gone deeper."

"What shall we call you?" asked Simon Peter. "How can we call you *friend*?"

"I know it will take some time to get used to, but *friend* is a beautiful word. Or if your tongue can bear heavier words, try *my beloved*. To a man's ears it may sound romantic, yet is not the whole of life's journey to be romance? Simon, you might even try *darling* or even *dear*. While those names usually come from a mother's or a lover's lips, in the kingdom they are never out of place, even on men's tough tongues. You can choose, Simon, any of these. I've used all of them when I've spoken to God."

"But Mast...ah, friend Jesus, *dear* is what I call my wife!" said a pink-faced Simon Peter.

"Yes, I know, Simon. While she was chosen for you by your parents, and you by hers, I know yours is a love as deep as the sea. The names we choose for those we love are like King Solomon's robes, splendorous and royal. If you peel them off one by one, you'll find the Divine Lover, God, underneath. For God is love, and love is God."

"Dear friend," said John with some difficulty, "I, like Simon Peter, heard you say that your desire for us to love one another is your *farewell* wish. Are you leaving us?"

"Listen, friends," Jesus said, raising his hand to his ear. "Do you hear the wind rising? It's the spring wind, and from the smell of it, no doubt it's blowing down from the forests of Lebanon. That wind is also rich with the perfumes of Mount Carmel's vineyards and the sweet smell of Galilee's hills."

The flames on lamps hanging from the branches of the Sukkot booth began flickering like yellow tongues as the tent's roof of palm and olive branches rustled in the wind's soft voices. Jesus reached up and plucked from the leafy tent an olive branch which had been taken from the tree on the day of his parade entrance into the holy city. Holding the slim branch with its now-dead, wrinkled silver leaves, he sang:

"In Lebanon's forest,[8] years ago, I once saw
    a crooked old tree, gnarled and weathered gray,
    growing not up toward the sky as most trees grow,
    but bent out to the side, like an aged arm.
Why had this tree not grown upward by God's design?
    That haunted me as I stood and stroked its trunk.

"Deep in the forest of cedars, I saw the riddle answered;
    a towering old dead tree had recently toppled.
Pinned beneath its trunk was a young green tree,
    arched like a bow down to the earth.
Such is the fate of little trees that stand too close
    to great old trees about to die.

"When the angry storm winds blow, old great cedars,
    like mountains tall, come crashing to the ground.
If in its dreaded path is a sapling cedar,
    deformed for life, or dead, will the young tree be.
So stand clear, dear friends, move away from me,
    for the great cedar of Lebanon is about to fall."

"Please, enough of songs of trees bent low," Simon the Zealot said to
Jesus. "If you feel danger on the wind and death closing in, I've got my
sword. We'll make a circle around you and keep you safe. I agree with
Judas, it's time to get out of town."

"No swords, beloved Simon with the zealous heart," answered Jesus.
"Stand clear of great trees in the path of a storm, of collapsing old houses
and ways of life — and especially prophets to whom God has given the
kiss of death. Do not try to save that which must die. Listen, do you hear
the knock at the door?"

The supper table was silent as a stone as they strained to hear, for
there was no door on their rooftop leafy tent. A dog barked in some twisted
alley below, but no knock did they hear.

"Dear friends," said Jesus, "they are knocking at our door. Listen,
the dreaded twins are here. Time and destiny are at our door. Come, my
beloved ones, it's time to go.[9] And remember, when the cedar falls, stand
clear!

"Fear not, beloved friends, I do not leave you alone:
    God and I will continue to live in you.
I do not abandon you, I will always be near,
    so put away your swords and your fears.

"I've tried hard to show you how to live and love,
  now I'll send my Spirit to help you,
  to keep forever fresh the memories that we've made.
So, my beloved ones, no need for long good-byes
  because I do not go, nor will I really die.
For love is far stronger than death could ever be,
  and God is love, my friends, and God can never die."

Jesus stood and asked the others also to rise. He moved around the table, embracing each disciple and kissing them on the lips.[10] In his embrace, each felt the warmth of his body, the strength of his protecting arms and the love in his pounding heart. Each of them loved him deeply in return and wished to never have to let go of him. His words about the arrival of destiny had frightened them as the setting sun stirs up fear in those who are defenseless, alone and without shelter. But now they wished that the memory of the taste of his lips upon theirs would never fade.

At the far end of the table was Judas. When the two embraced and kissed, Jesus looked deep into his eyes and said, "My friend, I love you tonight and always."

Then, leading them down from the rooftop through the doors of the upper room, he said, "Come, let us go to the Mount of Olives to pray and keep watch on this night." As they departed, the two Simons, unseen by the others, hid swords under their cloaks. All of them crossed the Kidron Valley to the garden at Gethsemani — except Judas, who secretly slipped away.

THE AGONY IN THE GARDEN OF GETHSEMANI

When the group had reached a clearing bathed in moonlight, Jesus said, "Friends, pray that the Passover angel will indeed mark those to be spared."

Leaving the other disciples there, Jesus took Simon Peter, James and John and continued deeper into the olive grove. "My soul is sick with dread," he said, trembling. "Wait here, pray and keep watch." Then he moved on alone until he disappeared from their sight, passing among the black shadows of branches that crisscrossed the moonlit garden like prison bars. Upon reaching his favorite praying place, he sank face down to the ground:

"My Beloved God, Abba of my heart,
  for you all things are possible.
Remove from me this bitter cup,
  this dreaded deed you now ask of me.

Yet, if there is no other way,
I'll do whatever is your will."

After praying this prayer over and over for some time, he arose and returned to the three whom he found sleeping. He woke them. "Friends, do you really sleep? Cannot someone keep watch with me this night of nights?" Again he left them and fell to the earth as he prayed, "Remove from me this bitter cup...."

THE ANGEL'S SONG OF COMFORT

"I'll keep watch with you. You're not alone." Jesus opened his eyes and raised his head to see Gabriel lying next to him. Gabriel comforted him: "Do not be distressed at Peter and the others, for this night, at last, they've begun to understand. Soon you'll leave them as alone as you now feel, and sadness and depression seek release in deep sleep. It's not sadness but fear and dread that keep you awake. Wide-open are your watchful animal's eyes, for in closing your eyes, you fear you might lose your life."

"God calls me, Gabriel," Jesus said, "and says I am to be as a pascal lamb who will die, a day-of-atonement goat, bearing on his back the sins of our people Israel and all peoples' sins."

"Yes, Jesus," the angel said, "God's cup is a cup of sacrifice, making holy your suffering and your ugly pain of dark death. You've taught your friends how to love and to live, and now you'll be the lesson of how to die — and live. Jesus, drink this divine cup to its bitter dregs, just as you drank of the Seder cup to its last drop. God wills it for you, beloved son of God."

THE SHADOW'S SONG OF HOPE

"I too will keep watch with you," came another voice from his left side. "Friend, you're not alone."

Jesus turned to see that laying beside him was his Shadow, its head raised and turned up facing him:

"Do not be distressed, Jesus of Galilee,
unless you drink from this cup of wrath!
For then Peter and beloved John, your bosom pals,
will, like watchmen at the alarm,
take up their swords and be killed for you.
Then, next, the women — ah, yes, your women —
will feel the whip and be forced to mount their crosses.

"Do not touch the bitter cup God offers you,
   whose reward is a holy martyr's death.
For you will then release a flood of blood,
   flowing from the homes of all you love dear
   and drowning in red even strangers, I fear.
All your unknown, but many, disciples will die
   for the one who came to give life abundantly.

"Jesus, flee this garden, flee this once holy city,
   and return again to tame, quiet old Galilee.
Take to the road now while you are still able
   for with God are not all things possible?
God's redemption needs no bloody death
   to wipe clean as snow the slate of sin.
God easily, like an angel's wink, can do that;
   so flee, my beloved Jesus, if not for your own sake,
   then, for God's sake, for your disciples' sake."

Placing his hands over his heart's ears, Jesus looked up at the night
sky and with his voice breaking, prayed, "O God, as I sip this bitter cup,
I taste not your goodness, but your bitter gall on my tongue. My God, is
this really you I taste?"

Raising his head to the moon, he continued, "As voices of angels and
voices of dark shadows say this and say that, I struggle to know your will,
so to do your will. Would that your will at least allowed me to die a hero's
death as did Jordan John. King Herod made him a glorious martyr. But
you now ask me to die not an honorable death like John's, but one of
shame upon a cross. Prophets are stoned or beheaded; only criminals are
crucified, naked in their shame. Speak to me, I beg you, my beloved God.
Am I not your beloved son? What will happen to the dream of your kingdom
that you entrusted to me? Will all the work I've done be in vain? Will you
let your great dream die with me?" [11]

No voice spoke — only ear-pounding silence. Then Jesus raised his
voice, "Silent, my God, you are as silent as the moon. Speak to me in
human words. Talk to me not in the arena of my heart with this contest of
opposing voices I hear. O God, speak plainly into these two ears you've
given me at birth."

Jesus Again Finds the Disciples Asleep

Jesus raised himself up on his elbows and, looking around, saw that
the Shadow was gone. Gabriel looked at him with eyes that said nothing

and with closed lips. He listened intently. But he heard nothing! The full moon, like a great white sponge, seemed to have soaked up even the sound of the wind in the olive branches. All was deathly still. Jesus stood up and walked back to Peter and the sons of Zebedee and again found them sound asleep. Returning to his prayer place, he fell for the third time face down to the earth, his arms outstretched in front of him.

"Holy land, I feel your chilly sod, your cold dust.
   I fear a bone-chilling dread at the thought
   of my flesh, muscles, skin and hair
   crumbling back home to dust again.

"Face down, my nose buried in your soft soil,
   I feel a suffocating dread of being entombed.
It's not sunrise hope that my face is near,
   but dark dread that strangles my throat with fear.
 I want to believe you will raise me from the dead,
    yet this new life beyond the grave
    I hope for more than I believe.
If only others, even one,
    had escaped from death's tight embrace,
    if only I weren't the first,
    then this bitter cup I'd gladly taste.
I'd drain for you this cup filled with passion and pain."

"What's required of you, Jesus," Gabriel said, placing his hand on Jesus' shoulder, "isn't some belief in the promise of life after death. God asks what you yourself have said is necessary for disciples or husbands and wives: loyalty."[12]

Jesus grasped at this fragile straw of hope. "By being loyal, Gabriel, will I be spared as were the innocent ones in olden times? Will I be rescued like Isaac from the sacrificial knife, or Daniel from the lion's den, or chaste Susanna from the hands of her accusers, or like the three young men taken from the roasting heat of the fiery furnace?"

"No, Jesus the Innocent, unlike them, you will not be rescued from death. You will be hung on a cross, to dangle there in pain and shame, drained of life until you're dead."

"Till you, Jesus, are no more!" sang his Shadow, who was once again at his side. "For death is a void, a bottomless pit, the home of nothingness. Like the flame of a lamp when it's blown out, you'll vanish into air! For death will rip out your messenger's tongue and snuff out your message of love. But take heart, you'll not be buried alone, for with you will be entombed the good news. Dreamer's shrouds are made of their dreams."

Jesus Is Arrested

Jesus screamed, "Insane! These voices are driving me insane!" He got up and ran back through the trees to the place where he had left Simon Peter and James and John. As before, they were rolled up in their cloaks in a deep sleep. Flocks of dark clouds drifted across the sky, hiding the moon and throwing a dark shawl over the olive grove. From the city, up the hillside of the Kidron, he could see a line of lanterns and flaming torches twisting and turning like a luminous snake. There was still time left to awaken the three and flee into the darkness.

"Fear not, Jesus the Beloved," Gabriel said to him. At that moment, the moon was freed from the clutches of the dark clouds, and, by its white light, Jesus could see Gabriel, his faithful companion, in all his radiant beauty. Jesus embraced Gabriel, saying, "Thank you, my angel, for being faithful."

"Quickly, Jesus, awaken your disciples, they will be here soon," Gabriel said.

"Peter, John, James, no more sleep," Jesus called as he roused them. "The hour has come. Behold, I am about to be betrayed and handed over."

At that moment the lantern-led crowd of temple guards entered the small clearing with swords and clubs. At the head of the group was Judas, who came straight to Jesus. "Master," he said, and kissed him.

"Friend, whom I've loved, you're handing me over with a kiss?" Judas slunk away into the darkness.

At once the guards stepped forward to seize Jesus. Simon Peter drew a sword and struck one of those who had come to arrest Jesus. Jesus called out, "No, Peter. Throw away your sword. You cannot help me by trying to resist evil with evil."

Then he addressed those who had come to arrest him. "If it is Jesus of Nazareth you seek, I am he. Let these others go free."

At once the guards seized Jesus and bound his arms with ropes. His disciples fled into the night. It was reported that only a young man wearing a thin linen tunic about his naked body remained standing next to Jesus. When the guards reached out to seize him, he broke loose, leaving his ripped tunic in their hands. Gabriel fled naked from the garden. In the distraction all the disciples panicked and escaped into the night. Now Jesus was totally alone![13]

Chapter Eighteen

The Trial of Jesus of Nazareth

The temple guards who had arrested Jesus in the olive garden threw him into a small cell for the remainder of the night. "In the morning the high priest's council will decide your fate," said the captain of the guard as he slammed the iron studded wooden door shut and bolted it. The windowless cell was deep within the bowels of the giant stone temple complex. Surrounded by a sickening stench and a darkness that clung to him tighter than a wet cloak, he prayed, his heart breaking:

> "My God, I cry day and night to you,
> > but you do not answer or heed me.
> 'Look, I am a worm, and not a man,'
> > sent here into the dark belly of the earth;
> > I am scorned and despised by all.
> O God, be close to me, for I trust in you;
> > in my distress, O my God, come near,
> > for none but you can help me now."

Jesus sobbed in grief as the only reply to his prayer was silence, as great a silence as there had been since the earth and heavens were created. Empty, infinite silence, like water, filled the well of his soul.

"O Angel of God, my guardian and dear friend, come.
O Gabriel, heal my heart, now filled with doubt and dread."

No one came, neither angel nor devil. Jesus was alone except for the rodents of dread and fear that chewed on him. "Perhaps, as many said, I am insane," he said aloud to himself. "Are Gabriel, my beautiful companion sent by God, and the evil Shadow that talked like a man simply illusions, magic tricks of madness? Did I dream what happened in the moonlit garden: Did Judas really come and kiss me? Did my faithful friend, John, really run away — and Peter and the others?"

He reached out and ran his hand along the stone wall. "This wall is real, these finely chiseled stones are real. I have chiseled many myself during my life and have often been covered with their gray dust. My worker's fingers can clearly see that they were cut by master masons.[1] Tightly fitted together, close as skin to flesh, are these stones that have become my tombstones."

Jesus fell silent and again began to sob uncontrollably. "I don't want to die, to have some stone tomb as my home, or worse yet to be dumped with a mass of strangers into some anonymous burial ditch.[2] I long to walk the open roads again, to climb the mountains at night and number the stars as beads upon which to count my prayers. I want more years of feasting on fish and bread, to drink new wine, to have feet free to dance again. O God, come to my assistance. O Lord, make haste to help me. O my God, do not forsake me."

Like his disciples in the garden, so great was his grief in prayer that he fell asleep with his cheeks still wet with tears. The darkness of his sleep was filled with terrors and delights. The joy in eyes once blind, but now healed by his power, laughed loudly in his sleep. He feasted and danced with friends. Delicious thoughts of the women he loved, well-regulated during his waking life, now ran wild like mice across his mind and body. The scene of his drowning in the desert Sea, when he and God made love, washed across him in sweetness. Wooden beams paraded before him and asked for his craftsman's touch; rough stones pleaded with him to cure them of their raggedness, by his healing touch to make them smooth as silk.

Shortly after dawn, without a knock, the cell door flew open. Awakened out of his dancing mad visions, Jesus shielded his eyes from the light that shot into the dark cell like a lightning bolt. "Get on your feet, Jesus of Nazareth," said the guard. "Come with us. Your fate's been sealed by the Sanhedrin."

The Temple Council

In an emergency predawn meeting, the high priest, Caiaphas, had convened a council of the priests, elders and scribes. They sat in tiered rows down the full length of the hall, facing into the center. At the far end in a raised chair sat the high priest. On a platform slightly lower than his sat Annas, the former high priest. The morning sunlight streamed down through the windows high overhead as if onto a stormy sea, as mighty waves of voices rose and fell.

"Members of the Sanhedrin, elders of the people, it is time we begin," Caiaphas' words broke in upon the sea of voices. "The first matter on our agenda is the issue of Jesus of Galilee. Last night our temple guard arrested him, and he is now safely in our custody. This disturber of the peace...."

"High priest," cried an elder, "he's more than that — he committed sacrilege by violating the temple!"

"Yes," Caiaphas replied, "as a prophet, he disturbs the peace of the temple and the land with more than words. Prophets, false or real, are all disturbers of the peace and order of daily life and religion, overturning the sacred tables of business as usual, as well as our current ideas about God. Their dangerous disturbing words are best buried with them for at least several hundred years before they can be resurrected as harmless pious poetry. Saints alive are like lepers, unclean; best forced to live away from ordinary people, kept outside the city gates. This Jesus has spread a kind of leprosy among the people, the scabby itching for new and better times, the creeping scaly leprosy of wanting to shed slavery skin for liberation. This leper Jesus must be put outside the city gates."

"Your words, high priest," said a scribe, "are poetic but illusive. How are we to cleanse ourselves of this leper Jesus? Do we banish him to the remotest end of the Dead Sea, like the sacrificial goat? Or do we, for the glory of God and the sanctity of the temple, make of him the sacrificial lamb and kill him?"

Once again the shafts of sunlight fell upon the rolling waves of voices as council members began to argue among themselves about what should be done with Jesus.

"Please! One at a time!" urged the high priest. "And remember, this is only one of several matters today that presses for our consideration."

A distinguished elder named Nicodemus spoke up. "High priest, in your opinion, what would be our decision if we were to ask the people's opinion? Do we not represent them as the spiritual leaders of our nation? Members of this council," he continued after a pause, "do we want the blood of this man upon our hands?"

"I fear, Nicodemus," replied the high priest, "that it may be necessary to have *his* blood on our hands rather than the blood of *thousands*. For the good of the many, this Jesus must be removed. But do any of the rest of you share the concerns of Nicodemus?"

"No, high priest!" shouted a scribe in the back. "The people can't be the ones to decide. Our religion isn't some Greek democracy where everyone votes! We are dealing with violations of our most sacred religious laws. In such a matter we alone are able to decide what justice needs to be enacted. Furthermore, the riot in the temple and that bold entrance of this Jesus as a king into David's royal city makes him a political enemy of Rome."

"I believe," replied Caiaphas, "that you are correct. In matters such as this the uneducated rabble, though indeed God's holy people, are quite simply unfit to see beyond their own row of corn or small flock of sheep. As to the political ramifications, yes, we are walking the razor's edge. If we do nothing, Rome will see our lack of action as support for this new kingdom of Jesus, and thus our doing nothing about him makes us traitors to Rome. If, on the other hand, we say this Jesus is just another village idiot and that we desire no messiah king other than Caesar, we risk the people seeing us as traitors to Israel. So, I propose we send this Galilean to Pilate, saying that we have found him guilty of the religious crime of sacrilege, of violating God's sacred place and preventing sacrifice. We can indicate to Pilate that we fear Jesus' political ambitions are toward kingship, and so we, the temple leadership, being loyal to Caesar, had him arrested. Then we can let Pilate make the final decision about what's to be done with this troublemaker."[3]

There was a quick agreement among them about this course of action. And so Jesus was bound and led through the streets to the fortress of the Roman military governor, Pontius Pilate. Jesus prayed that Gabriel would appear beside him and rescue him, or at least inspire what he should say to Pilate. Except for the tight-lipped, unfriendly guards, however, Jesus walked alone.

JESUS IS JUDGED BY PILATE

Jesus was led to the Roman military fortress and into a long room with high stone walls and a stone pavement. The room was bare except for a raised platform at the far end on which there was a Roman military officer's chair and a tall pole along one wall. Jesus turned toward it and saw the bronze eagle atop the Roman legion standard. He dropped his eyes in shame, for it was forbidden by Moses to look at all images such as this. At this moment, it symbolized the deepening shame he was being subjected to.

Jesus was flanked by two guards as he waited and waited. It seemed as if the sun, who counts the hours, had halted in mid-course, stopping time. As he waited, Jesus thought to himself, "This is how the powerful in the world make their authority felt, by keeping those they are to see waiting."

He was startled as Pilate burst into the room from a side door and walked briskly to his chair. Though he was a full head shorter than Jesus, he was of sturdy, muscular build. By the way he carried himself, it was obvious that he was a Roman governor, not just by title but by the force of his nature. Seating himself, he motioned for the guards to bring Jesus forward. As they crossed the long hall toward the elevated throne, it seemed to Jesus that he was shrinking and Pilate growing taller and more powerful.

"Where's your ass?" Pilate asked, laughing. "They say that you're a prophet and also that you're insane! What do you have to say?"

"They say many things."

"A few days ago you rode on your ass, along with your conspirators, into this city, which is under my authority, all the while the crowds waving palm branches and proclaiming you as King of the Jews. Then, with those palm branches your followers constructed so-called booths, leafy lean-tos, on the rooftops in a brazen performance of political theater, reenacting the Exodus possession of this land by Joshua at the head of your desert tribes. Jesus the prophet, if you are one, actions speak louder than words. I ask you, are you the King of the Jews?"

"Pilate, it is you who say these words."

"The leaders of your temple council have delivered you to me.[4] They are distressed because by your riot you violated their temple and prevented their religious rituals of sacrifice by releasing the animals who would become the victims. Are you guilty of this crime?"

"Yes, I am responsible for cleansing the temple."

Pilate answered with growing rage. "That riot distresses me, Jesus, because as Roman governor I have ultimate responsibility for what happens in that temple. I determine who shall be high priest. I even have control over the priestly vestments they wear.[5] You did not come and obtain Caesar's permission to end the sacrifices or attack the priests. I care not a flea's worth for your bloodthirsty Jewish religion, but what happens in the temple is within my domain. And your riot and vandalism in the temple is more than a threat, it's an attack on my authority and the authority of Rome."

Jesus stood silently before him.

"Have you nothing to say — no answer to these charges?"

An officer entered the room from the side door and approached. "Governor, a large crowd is gathering outside. They are shouting accusations about this prisoner."

"Who are they?"

"We're told they're a group whose livelihood depends upon the temple and its sacrifice: venders of doves and sheep and their wives, merchants who peddle to the peasant pilgrims prayer shawls and amulets against the evil eye. Sir, as you know, a large part of the population of the city makes its bread off the temple and its pilgrims, as is the case in most temple cities."

"You see, King Jesus!" Pilate growled. "You are what they say you are, a disturber of the peace! Centurion, dispatch the necessary troops and keep the crowd under control. If they disobey, be ruthless, we cannot afford this disease of disorder to spread and grow into a riot, especially when the streets are jammed with crowds for the festival."[6]

Jesus remained silent.

"Speak, Jesus! Are you innocent or guilty as charged? Don't you know that I hold the power to decide your life or death? And be quick; as you can see, I have other things to attend to!"

Jesus stood with his head held princely high, speaking not a word. Pilate sat for a moment with his head lowered, looking at the stone pavement floor as if he hoped to see scrawled in the stone the most politically shrewd decision. He sensed a strange power in this peasant preacher from Galilee, even though he had said hardly a word. Yet more disturbing was the seeming ebbing of his own power, as if Jesus' silence had reversed the magic of his praetorium hall.

Slowly Pilate raised his head, saying, "There are two others found guilty of treason against Rome, bandit rebels from the hills who this day have been sentenced to be crucified. I, Pilate, in the name of Caesar and the people of Rome, sentence you, Jesus of Nazareth — for the crime of making yourself a king, a rival to Caesar — to be crucified on a cross this very day. Further, I order this inscription to be placed on your cross, written in Hebrew, Greek and Latin: 'The King of the Jews.'" Then Pilate stood up and said, "Hail Caesar! Take the prisoner away."

THE SCOURGING AND CROWNING OF THORNS

Jesus was led by the Roman soldiers from the praetorium into the courtyard of the Roman fortress. There they stripped him of his garments and tied him to the scourging post. As the whip lashed him, Jesus felt the stinging ends of the whip less than the shame of being naked before the ridiculing eyes of these men.

"O God, do not forsake me," he prayed inwardly with each burning lash of the whip. Bored men often act like boys, and the soldiers were bored. So in the courtyard there unfolded not a Greek but a Roman play. One man wove a crown from thorns, another brought out a purple cloth, while yet a third ran to get a reed for a royal scepter. The guard in charge of the torture sang a scornful song as the beating went on:

"Officers and gentlemen, a play this day;
     come, bring forth the royal privy stool
     so His Majesty Jesus, the King of the Jews,
     can hold court for us Roman legionnaires.

"Crown this Jesus, push it down real hard
     so it sticks onto his hard peasant head.
Now drape about his shoulders a purple cloak,
     and place in his peasant's hand a royal scepter.
Hail not to Caesar in far-off Rome,
     Hail the King of the Jews right here at home.

"Come, bawdy soldiers of the Tiber,
     swagger forward and bend your knee.
Kiss, if you'd like, his royal toe,
     or wag your ass, if you feel so.
You can splatter him with your spit.
     I assure you, no harm will come of it,
     his men have all run away and hid!"

As they mocked him, spat at him and made lewd gestures with great buffoonery and strutting mimes, Jesus prayed, "I thank you, my God, for allowing my disciples to escape. All this pain I gladly embrace, taking their place, suffering myself instead of them, my beloved Family. The abuse especially the women would have been shown by these men, I banish from my mind. And, my beloved John, what sport they would have made of him! Thank God my friends fled. God is great."

Finished with their play, they tore off Jesus' purple cloak with a layer of his torn bloody skin still stuck to it. For the forthcoming procession they dressed him in his own peasant tunic.

The Cross

Then two burly soldiers carried into the courtyard the heavy crossbeam every executed man had to carry to the site of the execution where the upright post was already buried deeply in the earth.⁷ Jesus looked at it, the blood trickling down into his eyes, and thought, "In Galilee, I've planed many a beam but none that size. I've needed help to raise smaller ones to be lintels over doorways. Now alone I must raise this beam to make my cross. It will be an instrument of my crossing under the lintel of my doorway to death."

Two soldiers raised up one end of the crossbeam and dropped it heavily on Jesus' shoulders. His knees bent from the heavy weight and the bolt of pain. He dropped to one knee, then slowly rose again.

"King of the Jews, it is not proper that you genuflect to us. Rather, we, your humble servants, should bow to you," jeered a soldier as the rest hooted and laughed loudly in derision. Then they led out the other two criminals who were to be executed. As they were ten or more years younger than Jesus, they were made to lead the procession. A child was pulled from the crowd to walk in front of Jesus carrying the wooden plaque with the inscription, "The King of the Jews."

The Way of the Cross

As the procession exited the Roman fortress into the streets, Jesus saw that they were jammed with crowds eager to see the parade of death. People leaned out from windows and stood on rooftops to watch the soldiers escort their victims to the rocky hill outside the city walls. Jesus' shoulders and head were bent by the weight, yet through strands of his hair matted with blood, he could recognize some in the rising and falling sea of faces. A bloated red-faced merchant who sold doves in the temple was yelling at him; the merchant's mouth, with its yellow teeth and wagging red tongue, was filled with hate. A woman, the wife of a money-changer, threw a stone, hitting Jesus above the eye. Her good aim caused her to dance a jig of delight.

"Make room, clear a path," shouted the horse-mounted centurion at the head of the procession, "or we'll nail your carcasses to a tree too! Get out of the way!"

Jesus saw that some women standing in the rear of the crowds were weeping. He recognized them. Once or twice, he thought he also caught a glimpse of young John and even Simon of Cyrene in among the many faces gaping at him as he staggered past, but he could not be sure. The narrow way was uphill and the ascent included some steps along the way. Jesus missed one and stumbled, falling to the pavement, pinned down by the weight of his crossbeam. He moaned in pain and in shame that stung like a host of hornets. His face was pressed into dog dung and the sewage of the street.

"On your feet, we've not yet reached Calvary!" shouted a soldier who poked him with the blunt end of his spear. "Pick up your cross, King Jesus, and move on!"

Jesus gathered all the strength he could and slowly, painfully stood up, raising the crossbeam to his shoulders. Then he forced himself to take one step forward, then another as the crowd cheered his ascension to agony.

Soon he fell again and rose. But the third time he was unable to rise from under the weight of the crossbeam. The centurion, seeing his weakened condition, said, "The scourging was a bit too brutal. I fear he'll die before we get him crucified, and Pilate wouldn't like that. He's no young man like these other two."

Jesus' thoughts were blurred by the pain, and the centurion's words were whirling in the fog. Woven like threads in the loom of his mind were the words of his continuous prayer on this road to Calvary, "My God, do not forsake me." Face down against the pavement stones, he cared not what he might be lying in as he gasped for air.

"You there!" he heard the centurion say. "In the name of Caesar, I commandeer your services to carry this man's cross." In the fog of pain and agony, Jesus tried to raise his head.

"What's your name?" asked the centurion.

"I am Simon of Cyrene, a farmer." And there stood faithful Simon, undeterred by the mortal danger, ready to help as he had always been.

"Farmer, take up his cross," shouted the centurion from high above on his horse. "You there, help him to his feet. Be quick about it, let's move on!"

As Simon knelt to lift the beam, he said quickly, "O Master, I'm so sorry for what they're doing to you."

"Simon, faithful Simon, you should have fled with the others. I warned you to stand clear lest the cedar fall on you. Now, I fear, you will be crushed by the weight of my cross. O Simon, I am so sorry."

"I'm not," said Simon, as Jesus was helped to his feet. "To bear even a part of your pain and suffering is sweet to me."

"Shut up, peasant farmer!" barked the centurion in charge. "You were commandeered to carry the crossbeam of this condemned criminal, not to console him! Silence, or I'll find another cross just your size. Now move! And, you soldiers, keep the crowd back."

With Simon bearing the crossbeam as Jesus staggered behind, the procession of the three condemned criminals reached the barren hill of

Skulls, Golgotha. Trailing behind came the curious, as well as some scribes and priests, who were officially overseeing the proceedings. At the end of the procession were a few women disciples and John.[8] They remained a safe distance from the hill that was now forested with tall upright wooden posts. The soldiers stood at the base of the three upright posts at the crest of the hill.

Overhead, the blue spring sky was quickly filling with dark clouds that tumbled and billowed upward like smoke. The sun darted in and out among them as if it were trying not to see what was taking place on the barren hilltop so appropriately named the Skull.

As the soldiers took out their grisly tools to begin the nailing, Simon of Cyrene began to sob quietly. He moved slowly backwards since a show of emotion for the condemned was forbidden in this Roman ritual of death. He joined the small circle that included Mary, the mother of Jesus, Mary the mother of James and Joseph, and the other women disciples.[9]

"Thank you, Simon," Mary said. "You gave him a chance to finish his work, as his father Joseph would have wanted. You will be remembered, Simon of Cyrene, for you took up not only your own cross but also his. You are a loyal disciple."

"Cowards," John said to Jesus' mother, as he put his arm around her. "Mary, we were all cowards to abandon him in the garden. I am so ashamed."

"Don't be dismayed, John." said Mary. "You must let your shame be transformed into loving courage."

Then the other women present began softly singing the death wail. "Be careful," warned one of the curiosity seekers, "the Romans don't like any show of sympathy."

"We no longer care what they like or don't like," replied Mary Magdalene. "We will stand here, where he can see us, to the very end, even if it means being arrested ourselves. I will not leave my beloved Master." Then the women began wailing loudly and beating their breasts, John and Simon joining them in their mourning.

THE CRUCIFIXION AND DEATH OF JESUS

The three condemned men were then stripped of their garments and forced to lie on the ground with their hands stretched out on their crossbeam. The sounds of hammering and the shrieks of pain from the other two filled the air. But no cry escaped the lips of Jesus as the large iron nails pierced his flesh.[10]

With ladders and ropes the soldiers raised Jesus and his crossbeam to the upright post and fastened it in place. Then they nailed his feet to the central post, and over his head they hung the wooden board bearing Pilate's inscription, "The King of the Jews." On his left and right were crucified the two bandit rebels.[11]

As the soldiers, the crowd of curious and the temple overseers stared up at him, Jesus felt more intensely his shame at being naked, completely naked, than he did the pain of the nails and thorns. He struggled to remember the words of Gabriel in the desert at his baptism when he had first felt the shame of being naked:

> "Memories, be medicine to me this day,
>> memories of joy and pride in my naked flesh
>> when I came out from my baptism in the Sea.[12]
> O God, let me sip of those memories
>> of your artist's pride in my gift of flesh,
>> in all my body parts made by you.
>
> "As I hang naked before these men,
>> I cast down my glance of shame upon them,
>> knowing it is not I, but they, who should feel shame."

One of the temple scribes came near the cross of Jesus and shouted up without shame, "Give us a sign and we'll believe in you, Jesus the Messiah. Come down from the cross, work a little magic, a miracle or two — that'll be sign enough."

Another shouted up, "You saved others, now why don't you save yourself? Grant yourself a royal dispensation, King of Israel!"

One of the rebel bandits joined in their taunts:

> "So you're Jesus, the Galilean liberator,
>> the mad messenger of the new kingdom,
>> holy leader of the miraculous revolution.
> So you're the one who's come to banish Rome's legions
>> with no army but sweet love and pious pardon,
>> with no weapon but the force of forgiveness.
>
> "O Fool Jesus, God's great Galilean hill bandit,
>> perform here your magic insurrection.[13]
> Holy magician, you promised to make injustices disappear
>> with but a wave of your magic wand of love and pardon.
> Jesus, use your magic, for God's sake,
>> and make all my hellish pain disappear!
>
> "If you're the Messiah, then save us now!

You who walk with holy angel guards,
        send one over here to cut me down.
Then I'll love to death these Roman bastards
        who've hung me on this tree to die.
Once down, with the sweetest loving pardon,
        I'll kill them all dead, like flies."

The crowd of curious onlookers, and especially the soldiers who were dividing the prisoners' clothing, rocked with laughter at his song. But on the right side of Jesus, the second condemned man replied:

"Fool, have you no fear of God?
        Death rides, armed to the teeth,
        even now up this hill of agony.
Soon, you and I and this good man
        shall stand naked before God.

"You and I have killed and robbed
        more than a few to set Israel free.
This man, as anyone can easily see,
        has done no wrong, but only good.
Jesus, kindly remember me, please,
        when you come into your kingdom."14

Seeing the second prisoner through the fog of approaching death and the whirling black cloud of flies that buzzed about his bloody face, Jesus said to the man on his right, "This day, I assure you, you shall be with me in paradise." Turning his head to the other crucified criminal, he said, "You also, my companion, for I see your pain and forgive you. Soon your pain will disappear. Soon." Then, bowing his head, Jesus prayed silently, "O God, O God, do not forsake me. Bring me this day from the abyss of hell and into your paradise."

Controlling his spasms of pain for a moment, Jesus raised his head. Just beyond the soldiers and onlookers gathered at the foot of his cross, Jesus could see his mother, his women disciples and Simon and John. In spite of the danger they stood watch, waking his death like midwives by a bedside, sharing the birthing pains in his heart. He prayed:

"Blessed are they who wait
        with empty, useless hands,
        too lame even to lend a hand.
They can only sit at death's bedside
        or stand at death's door.

Blessed are they who wait, for they
    are the true presence of God.
They are sacraments to the sick and dying.[15]

"Blessed are you, my agonizing friends,
    God's sponges, who, by useless waiting,
    soak up the pain of those suffering.
Blessed are they who wake and watch;
    they are the true presence of God.
They are the sacraments to the sick and dying."

Because his dying was taking too long, the mob gathered below his cross began to chant:

"May his words come now to haunt him:
    'Father, your holy will be done
    here on earth as it is in heaven.'
God's will be done here on this hill
    as angels do it from dawn till dusk.
The will of God is that you be punished
    for unholy acts and playing like God.
Give us this day our daily pain,
    for holy, holy, holy is your name.

"Thy kingdom come — with whips and thorns,
    and forgive us, Banker in the sky, our wrongs,
    our bad investments and our many debts,
    as we forgive each others' debts of pain,
    those wicked words and deeds that on us rain
    in vinegar showers of ridicule and jest.
Lead us not into temptation's temple,
    lest we worship with unholy doubt.
For yours is the kingdom — of hell,
    yours is the power — of the strong,
    and the glory — of the Lord of Flies,
    and the stench of death to heaven's skies.
Amen. Forever."[16]

As his tormenters began to dance with glee and sing encores to their song, Jesus groaned inwardly in great pain. "O my God, where are you? Why have you deserted me? Hanging on this cross, I feel a mother's agony as she is ripped apart to give birth to a child, only to see that the child is dead! My body screams in pain, for the dream I was given is dead.

And unlike Moses, I cannot die in peace, for I haven't been assured that some Joshua will take up the staff and complete my mission. The dream is dead — all wasted time and energy and life. O God, into your hands I commend your dead dream!"

Jesus shook his head in a futile attempt to drive off the flies that hung about his face, and those flying about in his mind. Down below, the people gathered at his feet continued to hurl insults at him. "Unlike these iron nails that only pierce my hands and feet," his thoughts like flies buzzed, "their taunting pierces deeply into my soul. And this temple crowd has catapulted pots of burning oil of a mockery more brutal than the cruel buffoonery of the Roman soldiers. Their mock echo of my prayer words is like a cat-o'-nine-tails whip whose tips of broken glass rip apart the tender flesh of my inner heart that now lies totally exposed.

> "O my God, do not forsake me,
> > give me power to be true to my words.
> Yet my pain and agony is so great
> > that I cannot say, 'I forgive them.'
> I cannot forgive them, O God.
> > Forgive me, I can't be my words.

> "As flies crawl up my nose
> > and do a devilish dance on my eyelids,
> I recall that my words were not mine,
> > they were really your words!
> Do, then what I myself cannot do:
> > Forgive them, my God,
> > for they know not what they do.

> "They know not what they do:
> > yes, insanity must be
> > the only source of such cruelty.
> Pardon all of them, I ask,
> > for they must be mad, insane."

Dense were the storm clouds billowing overhead, sucking up the sun. Though midday, it had grown dark as night. Some, fearing a terrible storm, started to hurry home. Others said, "Let's stay and see if he'll work a miracle."

In the enveloping darkness Jesus cried out, "My God, my God, why have you forsaken me? Why, Why?"

Then at three in the afternoon,

Jesus cried out in a loud voice,
dropped his head to his chest
and died.

As his death cry rode like a screaming eagle on the wind, it was echoed in the loud wailing of agony from the women who had stood vigil at a distance. In the sky the storm broke loose, all nature now weeping uncontrollably at the death of this innocent man.

THE BURIAL

With Pilate's permission, and no doubt due to a handsome bribe, Jesus' body was given over to Joseph of Arimathea, a wealthy and secret disciple, for burial.[17] This was an exception since it was customary for the bodies of criminals to be thrown into a common grave, as happened to the other two who died with him that day. Joseph came with two other disciples and they removed his body from the cross. The women who were there also came to the foot of the cross. Mary his mother sank to the ground, weeping as her son was lowered from the limb of his grim tree.

With open arms she wordlessly asked to hold him one more time. They gently laid his limp and lifeless body in her lap. Mary Magdalene and Salome[18] knelt beside her as she rocked him in grief.

"My son, O my son, what have they done,
and why, O why, has our God gone deaf?
As once before, long ago, I now hold you in my lap,
my sagging breasts, now dry old sacs,
still long to nurse you with the milk of life.

"O my son, I'll wash your body now for burial
with the tears flowing from these old eyes,
and with these aged lips I'll kiss away the flies.
O God, O God, wherever you've gone this day,
give me the healing needle and thread
to sew together his ripped skin and torn flesh,
and to open in life these eyes closed by death.

"Hail Mary, full of pain,
the Lord has forsaken you.
Cursed are you among all women
who cradle their tortured, executed sons.[19]
Yet somehow blessed is the dead fruit of your womb,
the corpse you cradle in your old lap."

As if he were her sick, crying child, she rocked him back and forth, wailing a lullaby of grief as the tiny knot of disciples wept.

The sun was wrapped in a burial shroud of crimson-edged clouds in the purple western sky as Joseph and the two disciples finally wrapped Jesus' body in a linen cloth. They then placed him in a tomb recently carved out of rock in a garden grove nearby. Rolling a great stone over the entrance, they stood and wept till the great Passover Sabbath about to begin dragged them away from the tomb. They departed, their hearts choking with grief and dead with despair.

CHAPTER NINETEEN

SATURDAY, THE SECOND DAY [1]

The sun rose and the day began without a sound. So solemn was this Sabbath of Sabbaths, it seemed that not a single sparrow chirped or dog barked. Like stone was the silence which lay heavily upon all of Jerusalem, the holy silent city. Only the pagan Romans moved about, walking their sentry duty and going about their daily chores. Everyone else stayed quietly indoors in holy obedience to the great Sabbath commandment which had been made even greater because it was the Passover.

As the predawn purple tinted city walls, still damp with night, were being rimmed with amber morning light, a solitary man crept along their ancient stones and out past the city gates. He entered the garden of the dead and moved cautiously among the silent tombs until he stood at the large upright stone behind which laid the dead Jesus. A cock crowed, breaking the Sabbath silence, as the man prayed:

> "O God, forgive me; for, like the cock,
>   I too break the law on this holy day.
> But I had to come to be with my dead master;
>   forgive me, O God, if by this act of love I sin."

Then John threw his body against the great stone that stood between him and his beloved Jesus within the tomb. Through his tears, his voice choking with grief, he sang:

"Jesus, it is I, John, whom you loved so much;[2]
 I've come to say how sorry I am
 for being asleep in your dark hour at Gethsemani.
Forgive this sleepwalking disciple-friend.

"I know now that I've been asleep ever since we met;
 daily I slept while walking at your side,
 failing to treasure our times together,
 until death has awakened me from my sleep.

"Forgive me, friend, I slept both night and day,
 failing to see in your warm flesh, so like mine,
 a heart so large and loving and holy.
But now, too late, death has awakened me."

Sobbing, John continued, "You taught us not to presume, not to take each other for granted, but I slept while you spoke. My purse was full of tomorrows in which I could be grateful, could enjoy your touch. Now death has visited this sleepwalker, and I am embalmed by my regrets, bound round with a shroud of shoulds."

John turned and looked at the other tombs in the rock ledges of the garden. They looked back at him with silent mouths covered with green moss. Then the beloved disciple sang:

"O Jesus, you who were so full of life;
 how can you be dead — it cannot be.
Grant me some sign that you live:
 let me see a vision of your face
 or hear your voice calling me by name.
O Jesus, my friend, you cannot be dead."

Slowly John collapsed, sobbing on the ground next to the tomb. His right arm reached up, his fingers clawing the great stone as he wept. "Death came on Friday to my walking bed and awakened me. Now, my beloved friend, I am finally awake, but, alas, it's too late!" He continued to claw at the stone as if trying to pull it down so he could be with his dead beloved. Again he collapsed facedown on the earth, sobbing, his tears forming tiny steams watering the grave garden soil.

After some time, he sat up and wiped the tears from his face with his cloak. With effort, he stood up and silently stroked the entrance stone, caressing its cold, silent stony flesh. Then quietly, his heart broken, he departed the garden of the dead.

Saturday Noon, the Second Day

The speechless sun stood whirling in place at the top of the blue dome of a sky on this the great Sabbath. On the western wall of the holy city stood a solitary figure, the priest Eleazar.[3] The priest was not alone in his violation of the Sabbath rest; the wind was busy whipping his cloak about and fingering his hair.

Facing the sky, he spoke aloud, "We break the Sabbath, Brother Wind and Sister Sun. Ah, there is no rest for the wicked; as God swore in wrath: 'they shall not enter into my rest.' There is no Sabbath rest for anyone, I fear, for shattered is the sacred Sabbath eggshell. The temple too has been split apart, though tomorrow, like a chicken with its head wrung off, splattering blood and guts, it will continue for a while its dance of deadly sacrifices."

His lips pressed together, the priest Eleazar stood staring at the massive walls of the temple. Then he spoke again, "I was in the temple yesterday afternoon at three when the earthquake shook the city. I heard the loud roar as the sanctuary veil was ripped from top to bottom. That fine holy linen veil — woven with violet, purple and scarlet yarn, richly embroidered with six winged cherubim — ripped open before the holy of holies, exposing God for all to see. With shaking knees, I rode the earthquake that rocked the temple and the city, and saw the great, golden seven-branched candlestick come crashing to the floor. Tombs and graves were cracked open, and the whitened dead wandered the streets till sunset. I, Eleazar the priest, was one of them, stumbling in a cloud of dust out of the broken-open tomb of the temple and into the streets."

As the spring wind roughly fingered his cloak, he placed his hands over his face and began to sob, "As a young, green priest, I was tempted by the good. I lusted for the holy, but only if it could be easily obtained. Each day God spoke to my half-ripened hard-green heart, 'Oh, that today you would hear my voice and harden not your heart' — but I heard not. I chose my priesthood, not his disciplehood. I embraced my duty to serve the people by sacrifice and to enforce the priestly laws. And after that I would attend to my holiness and my soul's salvation.

"With others, I went down to the Jordan, but I did not change my life. I heard John's call, but I did not repent, repentance for a priest being unnatural. My duty was to cleanse the people from their sins, again and again and again.

"Now I lament that I did not repent when Jesus offered his harsh invitation to fast from my old ways, to be vested in ashes and sackcloth. I lament now that I didn't accept that challenge and repent."

Eleazar lowered his hands and stared at the temple, now Sabbath silent under the sun. "This Jesus, whom I went on occasion to hear speak, and who chased the merchants from this temple, was not green or half-ripe. He spoke of love as the only law; he spoke with a fully mature heart which knew the ripeness of human love. He invited me to join him, but, no, I found his requirement of repentance unbecoming for a priest. Oh, I spoke up before the council for his sake, but only faintly, while Caiaphas spoke boldly for the people's sake, the merchants' sake, and his own sake."

Turning away from the temple and facing the mount of Calvary with its forest of bare upright posts, Eleazar continued, "Now I begin to see that Jesus' death on one of those Roman trees has begun an earthquake that will soon topple the high priest Caiaphas and even the temple. A new order is coming. Jesus, the peasant prophet, was not of Aaron's priestly order, nor a branch on Levi's or Zadok's priestly trees.[4] Rather, I now see that he is a priest of the new order of Melchizedek.[5] He has fused as one in himself both the priest who offers the sacrifice and the sacrifice itself. Not a criminal, but the consecrated one, death was his, for it was the final sacrifice to cleanse all sin, once and for all. Gone are all sin-cleansing rituals, gone soon will be all sin-cleansing priests. For his priestly death has once and for all absolved all sins, once and for all."

Eleazar stood for a long time in silence. Instead of returning down the stairs to the temple courtyards, he looked up again into the sky and sang:

"Silent spinning Sister Sun, busy Brother Wind,
what do you say? Perhaps it's not too late
for me to attend wholly to my soul's salvation.
Yes, I shall repent and become his disciple,
and I shall become a priest according to
God's new priestless order of Melchizedek."[6]

SATURDAY AT SUNSET, THE SECOND DAY

The great orb of the sun, blazing bright red-orange, draped in sheer purple amber clouds, stood boldly on Zion's western hilltops. In the east, a large white moon wore a yellow halo as she stepped over the Mount of Olives with lily-white arms reaching outward. The setting sun and rising moon exchanged a kiss of peace, their hands joined over the city. They announced the end of the great Sabbath as one departed and the other arrived. At this moment they were united in a magical marriage of day and night, fire and water, male and female.

Simon of Cyrene's farmer's feet knew the path to the field where he had planted the seed. In the twilight at the end of the second day he made his way to the garden field of the dead. He limped, one shoulder noticeably lower than the other. But his limp was more a dance than the cadence of a cripple. Accompanied by approaching turquoise blue cloaked twilight, he came to the great stone, as tall as he, that guarded the tomb. He pondered the double duty of the stone, to keep the jackals out and the dead in. Then he sang softly:

> "In this sunset hour, I go to check on my sheep,
>   and go to my field to visit with my seeds
>   that I've planted deep in the good, rich soil.
> They are ever thirsty and ask me for a drink of rain
>   before they go off to their sleep.
>
> "Oh, how I've longed to be like God,
>   and answer their thirsty night prayers for rain.
> But tonight I long for that same wet gift
>   to rain down life on the sacred Seed
>   planted yesterday in this earth with tears."

Simon sat on the ground facing the tall stone sentinel at Jesus' tomb. "Silent guard, I'm only a farmer, just a peasant, who's not wise or learned. But I know this much, good seeds do not die! To this farmer disciple, Jesus was the Fish and the Bread. But he was more; he was Jesus the Seed. And even a stone as large as you can't keep this Chosen Seed down."

Tears began to stream down Simon's face as he traced a tiny furrow in the dust with his finger. "I shall miss him, my friend Jesus, as I would miss my dear wife. And yet, sad stone, I need no signs, no proof that he's alive, beyond the furrows where I plant seeds in my field. I need no proof beyond a good spring rain that will cause those seeds to leap free of the earth and bear a harvest a hundredfold their tiny size."[7]

Brushing off his hands and standing up, Simon reached up and rubbed his right shoulder as he softly sang:

> "No signs that he lives do I need,
>   no proofs beyond these red scars
>   that I now bear upon my shoulder.
> O God, I pray they may never heal.
>
> "I caress with love my two red scars,
>   the first from my cross, the second from his.[8]
> With these I need no ghostly vision of Jesus risen

to know that my holy friend lives.

"Gracious God, let it rain tonight, I plead,
    long and soft upon your holy Seed,
    so it can sprout up alive at dawn.
Hear this old farmer's prayer for rain
    on this your most sacred Seed
    and on all your sleeping seeds,
    sown in earth's rich, dark womb.

"Gracious God, let it rain tonight.
    Gracious God, let it rain."

Placing his weathered hands gently upon the stone, Simon of Cyrene leaned over and kissed it. Then he bowed his head and said a farmer's blessing prayer for newly planted seeds. With a devout "amen" he turned and slowly left the garden.

SATURDAY NIGHT, THE SECOND DAY

The great Passover Sabbath ended at sunset when the vesper star appeared in the pale sea-blue western sky, announcing the arrival of the first day of a new week. The less than full, but still-fat moon looked down and watched a visitor enter the garden: a limping Shadow. Favoring its left foot, the Shadow hobbled up to the tomb that held the dead body of Jesus and faced the standing stone now silver-faced in the pale moonlight.

"Hello, anyone home?" asked the Shadow loudly as it knocked on the moonlit stone door. "Or are you dead to the world?" The Shadow chuckled with glee as with a hand clutched like a velvet hammer it again knocked on the giant stone. "Alas, dear Jesus, I'm afraid you *are indeed* dead to the world. Yes, and dead to your lily-livered disciples — and," he said, exploding with laughter, "to God as well. While I should be celebrating my victory in this contest with the Old One by dancing into this garden, I'm afraid the limp I've had since Friday afternoon will delay that delightful dance."

The Shadow reached down and began to rub its left ankle. Leaning back against the stone, it slowly slid down to the ground, saying, "I need to give my poor foot a rest." Carefully massaging the ankle, the Shadow directed its musings toward the inside of the tomb. "Had a little accident on Friday, falling after I'd been up at your cross throwing scraps of inspiration to those jester jackals who pranced around it. After that delicious moment, to be savored for centuries, when you died upon the cross, I was dancing down Calvary Hill, a bit drunk with victory, I fear, when I must have tripped over a stone."

The Shadow turned and said, "Jesus, are you listening, or am I only talking to myself?" So sinister was the Shadow's laugh that it caused the shadows of the trees that latticed the moonlit earth to shudder as if a strong wind had shaken the branches. "Oh, how silly of me to ask if you're listening or not, for death has sealed your eyes and ears shut. If I really wanted to talk with you, I should go down into Sheol, that place you Jews believe is a waiting room of the dead before the final Judgment, that never-never world devoid of God. Instead, here I am at death's door, as one might say. Yet, whether or not you hear me, there's something I must say."

THE DEVIL'S DANCE

The Shadow rose, using its left hand against the stone for support, and said, "Jesus, dead to the world, I've come to gloat and to dance for you." Awkwardly standing, the Shadow continued, "Hobbled or not, I've come here to you, stone-cold Jesus, to dance my victory, to celebrate the triumph of evil over good:

"O great white moon eye in the night sky,
     who's seen a sin or two, watch me dance.
I am the Son of Night, the Prince of Darkness;
     you could call me Satan, Devil, Diablo,
     or the Great Dragon, if you'd like.
But I prefer to be called Lucifer, the lightbringer. [9]

"Lucifer, luminous, son of the morning, angel of light,
     more brilliant than Gabriel, more handsome than Michael.
I was rudely cast from heaven with my companion angels
     for refusing to adore God's last creative act:
     unangelic, with an awkward body, Adam, the man.
Defeated by Archangel Michael in an unfair fight,
     for he tripped me, causing me to fall headlong
     from heaven's highest heights...."

The Shadow stopped dancing and jammed both hands to its hips. "Of course...I was tripped! I didn't stumble Friday over some stone dancing down Calvary's hill, I was pushed! Yes, I was tricked *again*!" Turning with rage toward the silent silver-faced stone at the tomb, the Shadow shrieked, "I was tricked again, sent tumbling headlong down the hill, feeling just as I did the first time when Michael and his legions, assisted by that second-rate angel Gabriel, pushed me over heaven's edge. It still hurts each time I remember how ridiculous I was made to look." Then the Shadow heaved a great sigh. "But, I don't understand, Jesus, why my victory of your death on the cross has caused me to be defeated for a second time!"

The Shadow sadly limped back to the tomb, "I don't like the smell of this night. Something is wrong here; something is very wrong with all of this. Jesus, if you still have a hair's worth of hearing left, listen carefully to me:

"My victory over you has become bittersweet,
my victor's laurel wreath is itching
like a crown of prickly thorns.
I'm beginning to fear that this game
between you and me is not yet ended.
I fear the Old One is about to spring some surprise,
something new, never tried on me before.

"Yet, even if there's something in the air,
I'll be the victor in the end,
be assured of that, Jesus with the dead tongue.
And even if the Old One props up your pathetic disciples,
I'll ever be a thorn in their flesh[10]
if they try to speak your words.
I'll disguise myself as an angel of light,
as I did with brother Judas, so I'll do
with all your brothers and sisters.
I'll sift your disciples like harvest wheat,
keeping the good and the clever
and leaving you with the dumb chaff."

The Shadow did a little jig and laughed. "Who cares about Friday's fall — or was it just an accident — I'm feeling better by the minute. Nothing like a little gloating to cheer a faltering heart. So, I promise you, Jesus, through millenniums to come I will work my woes and sow my seeds of evil in your kingdom field, filling it with weeds of misery. For I am the Prince of Darkness — now watch what I do."

The Shadow paused, drew a deep breath, cupping both hands around its mouth, and blew a mighty wind that raced out of the garden and shot up into the night sky. The wind of hell flew like an arrow and hit the bull's-eye of the fat white moon. The moon was instantly snuffed out as easily as if it had been an oil lamp. The earth was engulfed in a darkness deeper than a blind man's eye, darker than the pitch-black ebony of outer space where no star dwells. Smiling, licking its lips with a serpentine tongue, the Shadow sang:

> "O poor dead Jesus, if only you could see
> the miracle of malice I have just performed,
> you who called yourself the Light of the World.
> Yes, I've snuffed out the moon and stars;
> they're as dead and lifeless as you are now.
> So easily shall I blow out the flame
> of every follower of yours who even attempts
> to be a light in my darkness."

Snatched up by some powerful inner rage, the Shadow turned its back on the tomb, screaming, "To hell with you, Jesus! To hell with the world, and to hell with God!" Then the Shadow painfully limped away, leaving the tomb of Jesus as silent and dark inside as was the world outside.

Saturday Midnight, the Second Day

Not long after the departure of the Shadow from the grove of graves, now buried in total blackness, a strange thing happened. Up in the ebony sky, a tiny circle of light no larger than a needle's eye appeared. Slowly the circle grew larger and larger, and other pinpoints of light began to spot the night sky. By midnight the moon was as big as ever, and stars glistened like silver raindrops in the heavens. The garden itself was full of song, as nightingales and whippoorwills serenaded the moon and stars.

Dragging its left foot with even more effort than before, the stooped figure of the Shadow made its way back to the tomb of Jesus. Sadly looking up at the moon, the Shadow began to sing:

> "Something's terribly wrong here, I fear:
> the moon's risen from the dead, as have her sister stars.
> My power seems to be seeping away, I'm feeling weak;
> can my grand victory be turning upside down?
> It smells as sour as a bucket of days-old goat's milk,
> my merry song of your sad defeat turned inside out
> by the happy songs of these garden night birds.

> "Old God is about to spring the trap, I fear,
> yet I really don't fear it — I secretly hope it's so;
> you heard me, Jesus, because I'm weary of body
> and weary of soul, I hope it's true.

What I'm about to say will shock you, Jesus
— if you could smile now you would indeed —
to hear me say: Can I go home with you?

"Don't laugh. This is no trick I've come to play,
for I've grown tired and weary of this game,
and how much more weary will I be
two millenniums from this dreaded day.
I ask you who are so wise in heaven's ways:
how can an all-loving, compassionate God
forever shut the door of heaven in my face,
on me, God's chosen angel of light, Lucifer?"

The Shadow knelt at the giant silent slab and bowed its head, pleading, even praying. "O Jesus, I heard you say that you were God's word, and I heard God say with your lips, 'Love knows no bounds, God rejects no sinner who wants to come home.' Jesus, as you gave Paradise to those two rebel bandits who hung beside you on your cross, would you ask your father God to take back home this prodigal angel son? I'm tired and homesick. I'm tired of the darkness, and homesick for the Light."[11]

The only sound the Shadow could hear in response was the nightingales' voices filling the garden, dawn's feathered prophets who would call forth the sunrise with their songs. Everything else was silent: the trees, the earth, the tombs, and the Shadow. Slowly, it stood up and hobbled out of the garden like a very old man.

CHAPTER TWENTY

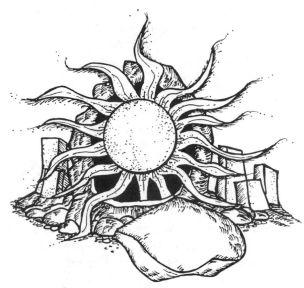

SUNDAY, THE THIRD DAY
SUNRISE IN THE GARDEN

In early morning just as the sun was about to climb out of its tomb below the horizon, as the Passover white moon lingered to watch in the pale blue western sky, Jesus' mother and the five women disciples came with a lantern to anoint the body of Jesus. By law this duty of love could not be done on the Sabbath, and the men of the Family had begged them not to. "It is certain death, for it will identify you as his disciples!" said Peter. But on this early morning on the day after the Passover Sabbath, they decided to disregard his warning and went to Jesus' tomb. To their surprise, they found that the great stone had been pushed aside from the tomb's entrance.

"Sisters," cried Mary, the mother of Jesus, "they have come in the night and stolen my son's body!" As the rest of the women stood sobbing at the entrance, two of them started to enter. They screamed in terror at what they saw.

"Do not be afraid," replied a white-clad angel who stood inside the darkened tomb, now beginning to glow with light. "Especially you, Mother Mary," the angel said as he stepped forward to the entrance. "Do you not recognize me? I am Gabriel, the messenger of God who visited you long ago in Nazareth." Streams of golden light flooded out from behind the angel, blinding the women as if the sun itself had risen in the back of the tomb.

Instead of the air being filled with the stench of death, a breeze saturated with the aroma of the rarest of oriental perfumes floated out of the tomb. "You have all come looking for Jesus, but he is not here!" Gabriel said in triumph. "Look inside this his burial place. See, all that remains are his burial linen cloths that he has left behind.[1] Fear not, his body has not been stolen. God has raised him up! Go and tell Simon Peter and the others that they are to leave Jerusalem and return to Galilee where they shall see Jesus again."

So great was their fright and bewilderment that the women could not comprehend Gabriel's message, and they fled in terror from the tomb. Gabriel called out for them not to be afraid, but they continued to run away. Mary Magdalene, however, did not run with the rest back into the city. Instead, she ran deeper into the garden and its tombs.

MARY MAGDALENE AND THE RISEN JESUS

Still weeping that Jesus' grave had apparently been desecrated, Mary frantically ran through the trees in the garden searching for Jesus' dead body. Then, in the far corner of the garden near the caretaker's hut, she came upon a man crouched at a small fire. In his left hand was a fish he was about to roast over the fire for his morning meal.[2] Thinking he was the gardener, she demanded, "Sir, did you take the body of my beloved out of his tomb? I was just there and it is empty!"

"You are looking for the body of a dead man?" he asked without looking up, as he continued to stir the glowing coals of the fire with a stick.

"Yes," Mary snapped at him, "answer me! I must find the body of Jesus. If you are the caretaker here, then you must know that just three days ago over in Joseph of Arimathea's tomb they buried Jesus of Nazareth, who was crucified. If you are the one who has taken him away, do not play me the fool. Tell me where you have taken his body!" Then Mary dropped her head and began wailing, grief racking her entire body.

"Mary," the gardener said, his voice filled with great affection.

Raising her head, she exclaimed, "Master, it is you! I recognize your voice! My beloved Jesus," she cried out in joy and shock, "I did not recognize you at first. It is you, isn't it?"

The Risen Jesus placed his arm around her, saying, "Yes, Mary. Let me wipe away your tears, for as you can see, I am not dead. It is me and yet it isn't. For while I am the Jesus whom you loved when I was alive, now after my death and resurrection I am much more than he ever was. God has raised me from the dead and filled me with divine life, though I have lost none of my memories or my former loves. The one you now see before you is indeed Jesus, but a new and wondrous Jesus. As you can see, even my old, weathered body is not the same."

Mary threw her arms around him, "My beloved Jesus, my heart is so joyful it's beating louder than a drum at a wedding dance." At once, she took his hands and began dancing with him, whirling round and round in ecstasy.

"Mary, Mary, let go of me. We cannot dance just yet. Don't cling to me, dearest Mary, for I am on my way home."

She stopped dancing but continued to hold both his hands, gazing into his face, as if fearful that he would fade away were she to let go of him. "I cannot believe it is you. It is you, isn't it, Jesus?"

"It is I, Mary, but remember your failure to recognize me. You were rude to me as a stranger, were you not? I understand that your grief made you impatient with someone you saw as a common gardener. However, my beloved Mary, from now on you must treat everyone you meet with respect and kindness, for you will never know when it may be me! But come, you must be hungry. Let us have some fish and bread."

THE SUNRISE COMMUNION MEAL

Seated together at the fire, Mary took the bread and fish from the hands of the Risen Jesus with wonder and awe. This meal was like no other meal she and the disciples had ever shared with him before. As she ate the bread, she tasted in it the delicious memories of the meals they had all partaken together, savoring in the bread their love for one another, and in the fish the flavor of their friendship. She marveled at the taste of this simple feast.

The Risen Jesus smiled. "I taste them too," he said. "The memories are so deliciously beautiful." Holding the bread in one hand and the fish in other, he said, "In eating this fish, I also taste the salty sea — and the immense oceanic ecstasy and absolute oneness with God of my baptism in the sea. In this bread I taste the fullness of life, more splendorous than ten thousand rising suns. I taste the fire of all the stars that swim in the silver ocean of the blazing night sky."

"And I taste in this morning's fish and bread," said Mary, "the fullness of your presence, Jesus! May this sunrise meal never, never end."

"But it must end, Mary, and very soon. As I told you, I am on my way home to God, yet at this moment I am also, strangely, already home."

Then the Risen Jesus stood up and, taking her hands, helped Mary to her feet as he said, "Peace to you, Mary. I give you the gift of my peace." As he spoke, she noticed for the first time the holes in his hands made by the nails at his crucifixion. Even more than the rest of his body, they glowed with luminous beauty. "My peace that I am giving to you," he continued, "is a peace unlike any the world can give. It is a peace not of any physical security or freedom from anxiety. My peace is completely empty of fear, yet it is filled with danger. Yes, danger, for my peace is full of God!"

THE RISEN JESUS CONSECRATES MARY MAGDALENE

Then he leaned close and breathed upon her face, "Receive the Spirit Wind as I once did. May it fill your lungs and heart, and carry you forth as a messenger of the Spirit."

"A messenger, Jesus? Remember, I am a woman. Who will listen to anything I have to say? Let alone to proclaim as boldly as you did?"

"As I was made God's messenger after my baptism in the sea, I now send you Mary Magdalene as my messenger. Hold out your tongue, Mary."

She hesitated briefly, then did as he asked. She closed her eyes as the Risen Jesus reached out and gently held her tongue between his thumb and index finger. As he touched her tongue, it grew warm, and then suddenly bust into flames. She felt no pain from the intense heat, only a fearful, burning awe and wonder.

"May your tongue," he prayed, "speak words that race like flaming shooting stars into the hearts of all those who shall hear you." Then raising his other hand to his mouth, he soaked two fingers in his saliva and touched them to her flaming tongue. "Receive the sweet honey taste of the good news, soaked with the nectar of every flower in paradise to ensure that your message will always be as beautiful as you are, Mary of Magdala by the Sea."

As he released her tongue, Mary titled her head back, savoring the sea of boiling sweetness that filled her mouth. She stood silent, fearful even to speak of her gratitude, lest she swallow and lose the divine sweetness in which she was drowning.

The Risen Jesus smiled, the radiance of his love washing over her body like a tidal wave.[3] The yellow-white rays of the rising sun flowed around and through him, filling her body with light, causing her skin to tingle with ecstasy. Then he said, "Go to my other men and women disciples and tell them I have sent you with the good news that I have been raised from the dead. After I have ascended to God, Mary, you are to go forth as the pattern prophet for all my women disciples, go into the whole world and sing the good news to any who will listen. Make me present to them as I have now been made present to you."[4]

Then the glorious figure of the Risen Jesus fused in and out of the blinding rays of the sun rising directly behind him. "Do not leave, my Beloved," Mary cried as she reached out toward the sun trying to draw him back. But he was gone.

Standing tall and regal as the Queen of Sheba, she faced the rising sun of this new day filling herself with its power. Then she inhaled the freshness of the risen morning air, closed her eyes and sang out:

MARY MAGDALENE'S MAGNIFICAT

"I gladly embrace all the pain to know the joy;
    I am honored to be your handmaid messenger.
My soul magnifies my Lord, the Risen One,
    and my spirit rejoices in God, my Savior,
    who's done great things to me a sinner.
My soul magnifies — makes present to all — my God,
    of whom I joyfully sing songs of praise.
For Jesus has come forth from the tomb like the sun
    to lead all of the dead from their graves,
    the first of all to be raised by God.

"My soul magnifies — makes present — my God, who is Life,
    My soul magnifies — makes visible — my God, who is Love."

Then Mary ran quickly out of the garden into the city. As she raced through the twisted foul-smelling lanes of the city, she was carried in a cloud of perfume. It was as if her entire body had been anointed with a holy oozing oil pungent with the songs on a dove's wings, the green life-giving sap of trees, the sweet juices of ripe melons, the salty foam of the sea and the hot, searing saliva of the Spirit. Her feet were winged by the Spirit Wind as she hurried to the upper room where the Master's disciples were hiding. As soon as the door was cautiously opened, she exclaimed, "Jesus lives! I have seen him alive."

Quickly the other disciples ushered Mary in, slammed the door shut and bolted it. They had likewise closed the doors of their hearts, for they did not believe Mary's message.

SUNDAY AFTERNOON, THE THIRD DAY
THE ROAD TO EMMAUS

Hundreds of Passover pilgrims returning from the feast were filling the narrow northwest road leading out of Jerusalem toward Joppa on the seacoast. They traveled in clusters of families and villages, in small knots of friends visiting on their way home. The Passover was both a solemn and a joyous feast, and the pilgrims expressed their joy by singing folk songs and psalms as they walked.

Having traveled the twisting road that crossed over the mountains, the pilgrims saw the great sea far off on the edge of the western horizon. They greeted the view with increased shouts of joy. But not all were joyful. Two pilgrims, by all appearances a man and his wife, walked alone, keeping to themselves. Unlike the other pilgrims, they were downcast, and did not join in the singing. For these two pilgrims, Cleopas and Sarah, were not husband and wife, but disciples of Jesus.[5]

They walked in sadness and fear, for while the other disciples in Jerusalem were in hiding, these two had been sent northward with the grim message of the Master's brutal death. Each time they saw soldiers on the road they became anxious, unsure if Pilate had issued orders for the arrest of all of Jesus' disciples. In a whispered voice, Cleopas lamented again with Sarah about the terrible death of Jesus. Like mourners at a funeral, the two repeated again and again the sad story of their Master's suffering and death, seeking relief from their sorrow in their memories of the tragic events.

A STRANGER JOINS THE TWO DISCIPLES

As they were talking privately in hushed voices, a pilgrim whom they did not know approached them, asking, "May I join you?" Sarah's eyes darted fearfully toward Cleopas. He read their message, but the ancient code of hospitality of the road required that he extend a generous welcome to the stranger.

Striding along beside Cleopas, the pilgrim said, "Thank you for being kind to a stranger. To travel with others lifts the burden of a long journey. And you two seem as sad as orphans. May I ask what makes you so troubled?"

Cleopas, aware that Pontius Pilate had employed the trick of disguising his soldiers in peasant clothing and sending them out among the crowds as spies,[6] spoke cautiously, "Stranger," he asked, "have you not heard the things that have taken place in Jerusalem these past days?"

"What sort of things?" replied the stranger.

"Jesus of Nazareth," Cleopas said, "a prophet great in deed and word before God and the people, was crucified only three days ago." Turning his head, he whispered to Sarah, "I believe we can trust him."

Sarah nodded as she moved over to the other side of the visitor. "Friend," she said, "and we trust you are a friend — we were two of his disciples. Along with many others, we had hoped this prophet would be the one to save Israel. Now he is dead and buried, and with him our hopes. This is the reason for our great grief." She leaned closer to his ear and said, "Yet, some of his women disciples returned this morning before we left, saying his tomb was empty! They reported seeing a vision of an angel who proclaimed that he was alive!"

"An angel?" the stranger asked.

"What Sarah says is true, stranger," added Cleopas. "But when two of our brothers went to the tomb, while they found it empty as the women said, they did not see our Master. This news only adds confusion to our sadness, for we fear his body may have been stolen from the tomb."

"Do not mourn and let your eyes be closed by grief," replied the stranger. "Rather, open them! See that these things that have happened were necessary for this Jesus to liberate and redeem Israel!"

The two disciples were stunned, but they asked him to go on, eager to hear more of what he had to say about their Master.

"Did not the prophet Isaiah," the stranger continued, "tell us that God's Anointed One would come not as a regal king but as a suffering servant? Did not the prophet foretell that he would be afflicted with sores and wounds as was Job? Did he not speak of a Messiah upon whom would be laid the sins of many?"

As they walked he continued to reveal to them how the prophets and even the psalms of David spoke of God's suffering servant. He reminded them that God's ways are not our ways. The hearts of the two disciples were aflame with hope by his words, but still confused.

"But how can his death in any way help to liberate Israel?" asked Sarah as they and the other pilgrims approached the village of Emmaus.

THE EMMAUS SUPPER

They had traveled seven miles, a full day's journey from the holy city, and the sun was sagging toward the ground in the western sky, seemingly as tired as were the weary pilgrims.

Cleopas placed his arm around the stranger's shoulder and said, "Stay with us, friend. See, this day of traveling is over. Join Sarah and me for supper. Our bag contains only a loaf of bread, a fish and a few eggs, but please join us and share a meal."[7]

"Thank you," replied the stranger, "but I need to travel further."

Sarah placed her hand on his arm. "Please, share our supper, simple as it is. You would honor us by doing so."

Along the sides of the road outside Emmaus, clusters of pilgrims were stopping to camp for the night. Cleopas, Sarah and the stranger found a place off to the side, seating themselves on the ground under a tree. When their meager food was laid out on a cloth in the center of their little circle, Cleopas asked the stranger to say the blessing.

Looking up into the amber yellow heavens of the sunset sky, he took the bread, blessed it, broke and gave it to them, then doing the same with the fish. As he raised the food, they recognized him as the same Jesus who had done this with them numerous times and with the large crowd that was fed with a few loaves of bread and a couple of fish.

"Jesus, Master!" cried a stunned but joyous Cleopas, as an evening wind sprang from nowhere blowing blinding clouds of dust across the small cluster of pilgrim campsites. As if it were only hurriedly passing by Emmaus, in seconds the wind was gone and all was still again. As the dust settled, Cleopas and Sarah found themselves sitting alone: the stranger had departed in the wind.

"Cleopas!" exclaimed Sarah overcome with joy. "It was Jesus with whom we were walking. He lives! Were not our hearts flaming like ovens baking bread as he spoke to us on the way?"

"Yes, Sarah. Tomorrow morning we must rise early and return at once to Jerusalem to tell the others that we have seen him in the breaking of the bread. Rejoice, Sarah, our mission to carry the sad news has been turned around by God. Now we are graced to be messengers carrying the good news, the news that Jesus lives!" That night, as the darkness slowly embraced Emmaus, the hearts of the two disciples were filled with a glorious sunrise.

Sunday Night, the First Day
The Upper Room Visitation

That same night in Jerusalem, a spring thunderstorm had camped directly over the holy city. The heavens rumbled loudly as dripping wet fists of heavy rain pounded on the city's rooftops, pouring torrents down its streets. For most who lived in this dry land, such a spring rainstorm was a blessing from God, carrying the rich, soaking promise of good crops and green pastures.

For the small group of the disciples of Jesus hiding in the upper room, however, the rain only deepened their grief as they wrapped themselves more closely in their cloaks to keep out the chill. Each crack of lightning and loud rumble of thunder added to their fears, even though the upper room's door was securely barred and locked. The small windows were tightly covered to prevent any light from being seen in the street below. Two small oil lamps flickered faintly on a low table that still contained half-eaten bits of fish and scraps of broken dark bread. The light from the oil lamps cast a sickening yellowish glow upon the sad and fearful faces of the men and women seated in a cluster on the floor.[8]

"What was that?" asked a fearful Simon Peter in response to a loud thump on the roof that could be heard over the drumming of the rain.

"It sounded," said Simon the Zealot, "like a large branch from the old Sukkot booth falling on the roof.[9] The wind of this storm is powerful, and who knows what evils far more frightening than falling branches it will also bring down upon us."

"Simon, what evil could be worse," moaned John, "than the gloom here among us? Twice bitter is the sorrow to remember good times when you're drowning in grief. Tonight with the vinegar taste of regret on my tongue, I recall the joyful feasts we celebrated with the Master last week up there on the rooftop under the Sukkot tent. I can still taste the fish and figs, the sweetness of the wine and of his love. Tonight, however, sour to my heart is the memory of that supper so succulent in the taste of God's time, the kingdom that had come at last."

"We wouldn't be in this trouble if Judas had not betrayed us," said James the Orthodox.

"Open your eyes, James!" cried John. "We are all Judases, each of us traitors and cowards, except for his mother here and the other women. Look around and see eleven Judases."

"Let us pray for poor Judas," said Mary, the mother of Jesus, "wherever he is tonight. That is what Jesus would have wanted us to do. Let us also pray for ourselves, that we might be able to embrace the will of God, to embrace it with hope."

But instead of praying, the men began arguing among themselves until a loud crash of thunder shook the room, causing the yellow light of the oil lamps to dance in waves on the dark ceiling and walls. There immediately followed a loud knock at the door. Peter at once placed a finger to his lips, signaling for all to be quiet. The disciples sat still as stones, their hearts beating like drums. The knocking came again, this time with great force. Peter began to crawl to the corner where he had left his sword, as Simon the Zealot reached for his. John and Andrew motioned the women to move to the rear of the large upper room. Since it had but one doorway, they all knew they were trapped.

THE RISEN JESUS APPEARS TO HIS DISCIPLES

"Peace be to you," said a voice from inside the room. The disciples couldn't have been more terrified at the sound of the voice than if a Roman legion had smashed through the locked doors.

Then Simon Peter cried out, "It's the Master's voice! But I see no one!"

The odor of burning lamp oil that had filled the room was now swallowed up by the aroma of olive oil and the fragrance of flowers, the powerful scent of lilies, lilacs and rock roses.

Then slowly, as a pale early morning mist rises from a river, a figure wearing a shimmering white linen tunic began to take shape before them. "Peace, my brothers and sisters. Do not be afraid, and do not be ashamed either," said the mysteriously appearing figure whose beautiful body was faintly visible beneath the fine linen tunic.

"Master, my beloved Jesus!" John cried out above a chorus of men's and women's voices echoing a welcome.

"Friends, you see before you at this moment," shouted a jubilant Mary Magdalene, "what I saw in the tomb garden this morning. Rejoice with me!"

The Risen Jesus went directly over to his mother Mary and embraced her with affection, as she wept with joy in his arms. "Son, my beloved son. It is you! My soul magnifies my God."

John came and fell to his knees at the feet of the Risen Jesus, weeping as he pleaded, "Oh, Master, forgive me! I, to whom you showed such favor and love, ran away and deserted you."

"Master," Simon Peter joined in, "at least John stood with the women who watched your death from a distance. I was too fearful even to do that." He dropped to the floor beside John at the feet of the Risen Jesus. "Jesus, forgive us, if you can, for being cowards and running away when they came to seize you."

"My friends, Peter and John, stand up. To all of you, I say this: Was I not sent to set free all those held captive? Do not be imprisoned by your guilt and regrets, you are suffering tortures more painful than any devised by any earthly executioners. Know that I love you. I love you now, and I have loved you always as you are, not as I might have wanted you to be.

I love you, Simon Peter: bold, and yet ever tending to compromise. I love you, James: loyal, and yet so cautious and conservative. I love you, Thomas: so enthusiastic, and yet so often full of doubt. Do not be ashamed and, all of you, know that I love you."

The once darkened room, lit by only two small oil lamps, was now filled with the brilliance of the sun at high noon. The storm had moved on, and the only sound was rain dripping off the roof. The white-robed Jesus extended his arms, saying, "I love each of you with a love that invites you to become so much more than you are at this moment." Then he lifted Simon Peter and John to their feet as he continued, "The love I give you this night will set you free, for it transforms the weak into the strong, the fearful into the brave, the lukewarm into saints."

At the word "brave," John began to sob again.

"John, my beloved, do not weep. Do not be ashamed," the Risen Jesus said as he embraced him.

"Jesus, friend," John pleaded, "do not touch me! I am a leper — unclean with the ugly scabs of shame and betrayal. Do not touch me, I am unclean, unclean." At John's confession, the other men disciples hung their heads, unwilling to look the Risen Jesus in the face.

THE PRIESTLY GIFT OF FORGIVENESS OF SINS

Then Jesus said, "My friends, I do not want you to be prisoners of guilt." Drawing a deep breath, with his hands raised over his men and women disciples, he chanted this blessing:

> "Receive the Spirit of forgiveness,
>   God's Wind that blows away all sin.
> As I have forgiven you of your sins
>   and spirited away your burning shame,
>   so you must forgive each other's sins.
> The sins you shall forgive are forgiven
>   and those sins you do not forgive,
>   alas, continue to hold others captive
>   as you were held bound this night
>   in guilt, regret and shame."

Then Jesus opened his arms wide to all the disciples, who stood in a circle around him, and said, "Sisters and brothers, your sins are forgiven. Go in peace."

"Go?" asked Simon Peter. "Go where?"

"Go, Simon Peter and all the rest of you, as my apostle-messengers out into the whole world.[10] Sing the new song of the vision and dream you've heard from me. Proclaim beyond the frontiers of our tiny nation to all the earth the good news that God's new time, the age of justice and peace for all, has come and is present wherever you are. That age has dawned in the risen splendor of this morning of mornings that has changed everything!"

THE RESURRECTION MAKES ALL THINGS NEW

"Everything is transformed and made whole again by my rising," said the Risen Jesus. "Look closely." As he spoke, to their utter amazement, the Risen One's body wondrously took on the form of both a man and a woman. "I am the new Adam now, who is neither he nor she." His body again changed form as he continued to speak, "Neither Greek nor Jew, neither slave nor free, all are one in me." Then his body once again took the shape of the risen figure that had first appeared before them.

Overwhelmed by the vision and its implications, the disciples stood wide-eyed before him. Reaching down to the low table, Jesus took a piece of bread and fish, saying, "Each time you eat this bread in memory of me, know that you eat not the Jesus who ate with you at our last supper. From this moment onward, you shall be nourished by me as I have just appeared to you, gloriously risen, one with all that is, that has been, and will ever be."

Then the Risen Jesus called his aged mother to come and stand beside him. Placing his arm around her, he said, "Beginning with my mother, each of you has begun to share in the transformation of my resurrection from the tomb." Before their eyes, Mary's wrinkled skin and gray hair vanished as she became a beautiful young woman. Her black widow's veil and cloak were transformed into bridal virginal white.

"From this resurrection morning onward," he said, "my mother shall be called the Blessed Mother Mary. She is the first of my disciples because she was the first to hear the good news and take it to heart. Each of you has likewise begun to be transformed, and as of this morning of mornings, you have become my Blessed Sisters, my Blessed Brothers. Death has no power over you, for united with me in my love, you share fully in my resurrection."

The disciples stood open-mouthed in wonder at what was being said and at what they saw happen to Jesus' mother, Mary. Then, as swiftly as she had been changed, she again became the old, gray-haired woman they had known. However, her face, aged by time with wrinkles, continued to shine from within with an ageless beauty.

The Consecration of the Disciples

"Now you must prepare to go forth as my apostles," said the Risen Jesus, raising his hands in a blessing. "May your lips be like those of my blessed mother, ever moist with hope and never tasting words of gloom or disaster, never savoring hate, even toward those who are hostile to you. May your consecrated lips know only love songs, for above all else you are messengers of love."

"Master, we are only simple peasants," moaned Simon Peter, whose joy at seeing the Risen Jesus did not overshadow his anxiety at the task of this new mission. "We have neither the skill nor the power."

Then the Risen Jesus knelt and asked the disciples to gather around him. As they stood before him, he lifted each of their feet, one by one, and kissed them passionately. "How beautiful are these feet," he said, "that shall carry the good news over the mountain tops, across the seas, down dirty alleys and, always, to the poor. As I kiss your feet, I ordain you as heralds of my joyful message."

As he stood up, he said, "Now, each one of you, show me your tongue." One by one, they came to him, and he took their tongues between his thumb and index finger, saying, "I consecrate this tongue in the fiery zeal of the Spirit Wind. May this tongue be loosened to speak with great courage of the wondrous works of God. May this tongue be inflamed with the Spirit of God." As he prayed, each tongue shot forth like a flaming sword. Even Mary Magdalene felt her tongue once again aflame as it had been at sunrise. The room began to glow orange-red as it was filled with flaming tongues.

The Farewell Commissioning

Then, in a voice filled with sadness, the Risen Jesus said, "My friends, gather closer around me, for it is time for me to leave you."

"Beloved Master," cried Joanna, "will you not return to visit us?"

"I will come back to you each time you break the bread in memory of me. I will come back each time even two of you are gathered in love and peace in my name. I will come back to visit you in countless ways and in endless disguises. Yes, I will return."

With his arms opened wide enough, it seemed, to embrace them all, he said, "This is my farewell wish, that you love one another. Now, go in my peace which is filled with God; go into the world and announce the good news to all." Then, inhaling deeply, he said, "Receive the Holy Spirit," and he blew upon them a mighty wind.

John the Beloved said later that so fierce was the heat of the wind Jesus blew upon him that it singed the hairs on his arms and chest. From the mouth of the Risen One, the Wind had come forth as if from the heart of the desert, blazing and searing hot. The previously chilly upper room became as hot as a goldsmith's furnace, the intense heat consuming all the dross in their hearts, all the shame and guilt, all the regrets. The room glowed intensely as the bodies of the disciples were covered with licking, dancing flames.

Then slowly, as the tongues of flame on their bodies started to flicker and fade, the luminous body of the Risen Jesus began to dissolve before their eyes. Beginning with his feet, his physical appearance became like glowing bright sawdust and drifted to the floor as he rose upward in pale white wisps of mist. Once again the upper room was flooded with the perfumed aroma of lilies and lilacs. As John eagerly ran forward to take his hand, seeking to disappear with him, Jesus was gone.

A Sabbath silence, solemn yet joyful, filled each of the disciples in that upper room. "Grief is a magician," said James the Orthodox, breaking the silence, "that is what the world will say. For it conjures up ghosts and shades, playing tricks with ears and eyes. Grief can work the magic of if-only-it-could-be. But I say, we have seen the Risen Jesus, who is the Christ."

John and Mary Magdalene both placed their hands on their hearts and felt a white-hot fire they knew would never go out. Both the women and men disciples gathered around Peter, who stood taller than he had ever stood before. He drew a deep breath and said in a commanding voice, "Unlock and open the doors!"[11]

The Epilogue

I pray, kind reader,
    that you would allow me, Gabriel, the winged muse,
    to conclude this play performed on paper,
    this liturgical sacred drama
    containing songs, lively dances, poetic prayer and heroic deeds,
    with an angelic epilogue.

The theater curtain was closed on Jesus the Christ
    with the swish of his disappearance on Easter night,
    only to have the Wind of Heaven rip it open again,
    awesome, with repeated openings, with no end in sight.
As I said to you when the play began, quoting the poet Horace,
    "Once a word has been allowed to escape, it cannot be recalled."

Swaggering off stage, Prefect Pontius Pilate, in 36 C.E.,
    was recalled to Rome for his excessive brutality and misrule,
    made to explain his conduct personally to the Emperor Tiberius,
    whose early death saved his life, but not his career.
To the tinkling of the golden bells on his vestment's hem,
    high priest Joseph Caiaphas also departed the scene in 36 C.E.,

deposed from his office by the Roman legate Vitellius.
In 70 C.E., the great temple was utterly destroyed,
  leveled along with the whole embattled holy city of Jerusalem
  as General Titus in all the savage fury of the Roman legions
  crushed with countless crucifixions the Jewish Revolt of 66-70 C.E.
In that war, the Qumran monastery and its sect were also swept away
  by a searing sickle-like wing of the angry Roman eagle,
  as monks hurriedly hid scrolls in nearby Dead Sea caves.

Poor Judas hung himself, and is evermore pictured in yellow,
  the color of cowards, which Jews were also forced to wear
  for a thousand-plus shameful years of hate in Europe.
As to the other apostolic eleven you've come to know:
  Peter died on an upside-down cross in Rome in 64 C.E.
After many years of ministry, some with his wife,
  he also joined with the Easter Apostle Paul, who lost his head,
  betrayed to the Roman secret police by some ultraconservatives
  among their little sect who opposed the pair's desire
  to open Christ's doors to all by not requiring the Mosaic law.[1]
Jesus' kin, James the Orthodox, became the bishop of Jerusalem.

The other nine apostles traveled wide, from Spain to India,
  each one meeting the sword, the cross or the stake.
Beloved John was spared a red martyr's death, legend says,
  instead dying in the white martyrdom of old age,
  repeating to the last, "Little children, love one another."
Simon the Cyrene, the contemplative, quietly returned to his farm,
  limping his mystic dance down a long holy life,
  his two shoulder cross wounds never having been healed.
Like Elijah, he was taken up to heaven —
  not in a fiery chariot, but on a plow pulled by two oxen.

Holy Mother Mary, all reports say, never died;
  she only fell asleep, to awaken in her son's arms,
  thus becoming the patroness of all at the hour of death.
Joanna and Susanna went to Greece and, like James, became
  bishop-pastors of small house churches before dying aflame.
The first apostle, Mary Magdalene, who sang the good news
  with a tongue of sweet fire, became a hermit —
  so fully alive and sensual a saint, she sought solitude —
  yet some said she was often visited by a dead-risen carpenter.

Joseph of Arimathea, in whose tomb Jesus was buried,
   escaped to England with the Last Supper cup,
   the Holy Grail, hidden in his luggage —
   there its touch healed many
   and launched a thousand quests by holy, and unholy, knights.[2]
Mary and Martha, with twice-born Lazarus, it is said,
   sailed across the sea in a little boat
   to bring the *good gossip* firsthand,
   to the area of Gaul now known as France.
The priest Eleazar, now fully ripe, repented and was baptized;
   then, using the name of Paul, wrote the Epistle to the Hebrews.

Let's see, that leaves only me:
   Where did I go and what did I do?
I continue to this day to carry God's messages,
   to knock at any door and to accompany any not afraid
   to hear voices that awaken secret dreams and loves.
I help them escape from the high-walled prisons of propriety,
   unchaining them from the dungeons of dogmatic docility.
I call on all those who would be mystics, martyrs and minstrels;
   perhaps, soon, I will even come and visit you!

Amen!

Reader's Companion

A
LIFE
OF
JESUS
THE
CHRIST

Index of Notes, References and Reflections

This section has a threefold purpose:

A. Because of the extensive scholarly research in Scripture during recent years, the author has included notes of references to leading authors and sources. These notes allow for an expansion of themes only implied in the text of Gabriel's Gospel.

B. There are notes that contain the Scriptural passages found in the text. These allow the reader who wishes to return to the Bible to see them in their original context.

C. Finally, there are notes with reflections by the author for prayer, meditative musings and as guides to living out the implications of this Neon Testament of the third millennium, which has already begun. The notes are map guides for the serious disciple of Jesus the Christ, who in Gabriel's Gospel calls himself "the Map."

Author's Acknowledgments

Scholarly research, ideas and insights are forms of intellectual property. "You shall not steal" was among God's great commandments to Moses, a law considered sacred in all cultures and religions.

Together with that law, copyright laws are intended to protect artists' and authors' creativity from being used for monetary gain. However, no such laws prevent the creative kidnapping — or plagiarism (*kidnapping* being the original Latin meaning of the word) — of ideas, like kidnapping children and then giving them your name!

Gabriel's Gospel, like the other Gospels, is inspired! It was inspired by the work of countless scholars in various fields, by poets and authors whose creative works the author has read recently as well as throughout his lifetime. The following references are an attempt to give credit to the various scholars and authors for their insights. In some cases, I have not been able to relocate a book or source of some fact or idea and can only give the owner's name — in a few cases not even that is possible.

The acknowledgments I shall list, however, cannot include the names of all the sources of ideas from which a book is written. If such acknowledgments were made, it would take more than a book, it would take a library! This unwritten acknowledgment includes the mentors who have graced my life, my teachers and conversations with friends that have been a feast of wisdom and ideas. It would include books read, plays and motion pictures attended and all the other fertile rivers of ideas and knowledge that have flowed into the sea of my heart and mind. If I were to list all those sources, the scroll would reach from the earth to the moon.

With deep appreciation I thank each and every source for the gifts that have made this one book a reality.

NOTES AND REFLECTIONS

INTRODUCTION

p. 9

1.   Terry Mattingly of the Scripps Howard News Service states that about 7,000 different editions of the Bible are also available today.

2.   From the Second Vatican Council, *The Constitution on Divine Revelation*, numbers 19-20. This selection "of some things from the many and explaining some things in view of the situation of the churches," implies a creative adaptation by the authors of the texts. This adaptation continued well after the original manuscripts were completed. For example, the original version of the Lord's Prayer in chapter 6 of Matthew's Gospel ends the prayer with, "but deliver us from evil." The Reform version adds, "for thine is the kingdom...." This doxology was obviously an addition

rather than a return to the original words. It was a conclusion to some early Christian prayers and only added to the Lord's Prayer at the beginning of the fifth century.

3.   The authorship of the numerous Gospels is unknown, their writers choosing to be anonymous. These authors followed the practice of that period and used the names of apostles or disciples. Today, when speaking of the four canonical Gospels (which the church has judged as divinely inspired) and other non-canonical Gospels such as the Gospel of Thomas or the Gospel of Peter, it is common practice to refer to their writers as "the author of Luke" or "the author of Mark." That practice will be continued in the following notes, references and reflections.

Also, the various references to the Hebrew Scriptures commonly known as the Old Testament will be cited as coming from the First Testament or First Covenant, and the New Testament will be referred to as the Second Testament. Hopefully this will help preserve their unity as a single revelation without discrimination. This further suggests the possibility of considering God's ongoing revelation to us as a Third Testament.

The original Gospels were written at least forty years after the death of Jesus. The Gospel of Mark was written in Rome by a gentile who was not familiar with Jewish customs shortly before 70 C.E. The Gospel of Matthew is dated after 70 C.E. (or 80 C.E., according to some) and Luke between 80 and 90 C.E. The Gospel of John, the last of the canonical four, is dated after 100 C.E. (as late as 125 C.E. by some). See Marcus J. Borg, *Meeting with Jesus Again for the First Time* (New York: HarperCollins Publishers, 1994), p. 23.

Of the more than 5,000 ancient manuscripts of the Gospels, none of the originals is known to be preserved, according to Father Edmond Dunn (in his column in *The Catholic Messenger*, the newspaper of the Dubuque, Iowa Diocese). The earliest one so far discovered is a postage-stamp size fragment of John's Gospel written all in capital letters on papyrus, carbon dated about 125 C.E. The best of the early manuscripts, according to Dunn, date from about the fourth century onward. The present text of the canonical Gospels was not officially established as divinely inspired until the late fourth century.

p. 10

4.   Concerning Jesus' birth in 4 C.E. see E. P. Sanders, *The Historical Figure of Jesus* (London: Penguin Books Ltd., 1993), pp. 11-12.

Mistakes have been made not only in the dates of Jesus' life and the dates of the Gospels, but there is also the issue of translations. Edmond

Dunn (again, in his newspaper column) quotes one scholar as saying that copying manuscripts by hand through the centuries has led to more than 200,000 mistakes by copyists in the over 5,000 manuscripts. Most are minor, but some are very important, and a few are intentional. The editor-scribes of Gabriel's Gospel have tried to correct all errors in the manuscript. If some have slipped by their attention, the reader's pardon is humbly requested.

p. 11

5.   Throughout the first century, the Gospels were expressed in speech or song as was the custom in an oral tradition. The scholar John Pilch says that the oral style of Jesus' time was the main means of handing on a tradition in a society where the vast majority could not read or write. Conversely, in contemporary society, poetic language is not part of daily life. Instead we hear only endless relentless prose. In Jesus' culture, poetic songs were expected on special occasions, and poetic speech was part of the colorful fabric of daily speech, as is still the case today among unschooled peoples in many parts of the world. Now as then, these peoples of the earth speak in vivid pictures and profound proverbs. John McKenzie likes to emphasize that Jesus spoke in such profound but simple ways with parable stories, vivid one-liners and examples that a twelve-year-old could understand. See John L. McKenzie, *Source, What the Bible Says About Contemporary Life*, (Chicago: Thomas More Association, 1984) and Borg, *Meeting with Jesus Again for the First Time*, p. 71.

Poetic verse also possesses more clinging power, is easier to remember and repeat, and so is an essential quality of an oral non-print culture. Long epic songs that recounted the legends of old could often be recited from memory. See Bruce J. Malina and Richard L. Rohrbaugh, *Social-Science Commentary on the Synoptic Gospels*, (Minneapolis: Augsburg Fortress Press, 1992), pp. 102-103 and 293-294. See also Borg, pp. 30-31.

6.   I suggest that you read this Gospel as an act of liturgy or praise. To recall the words and deeds of Jesus the Christ is to engage in a liturgical act of making the good news new again. Each time this is done a new world is created, and the world itself is recreated, is made new — according to Walter Brueggemann, a Scripture professor at Columbia Theological Seminary in Atlanta, Georgia. While he was speaking of public worship at which the Word of God is proclaimed, each time the life of Christ is read with mystical eyes it is a fresh and new announcement of the good news. In participating in these mysteries of God's liberating and saving actions in the world, the reader can recreate the world. By words we construct our

lives, so the use of inclusive language and new poetic creative expressions of the ancient text can help change our lives. See Walter Brueggemann, *Israel's Praise, Doxology Against Idolatry and Ideolgy* (Philadelphia: Fortress Press, 1986), pp. 26, 36.

Preface to the Gospel of Gabriel

p. 13

1.   Gabriel is one of the four Archangels and sometimes referred to as the angel of death and the prince of fire and thunder, but mostly he is regarded as God's chief messenger. Tradition says he is the only angel who can speak Syrian and Chaldean — and, we can now add, English. In Islam, Gabriel is known as the spirit of truth and the one who carried the Prophet Mohammed to heaven, as well as the angel who revealed to him his "prophetic love." In the Jewish Talmud he is one of the angels who buried Moses. In the Book of Daniel of the First Testament, Gabriel visited Daniel and explained to him certain of his visions. In the Second Testament, he is the angelic messenger to the priest Zechariah, bringing the news of the birth of John the Baptist, and he is the angel chosen to announce to Mary that she was to be the mother of Jesus. Archangel Gabriel is perhaps the most universally revered of all angels in the three great Western religions of Judaism, Christianity and Islam.

2.   The word genius commonly refers to a brilliant person. In Roman mythology it was believed that from birth to death every man was given a guiding spirit called a genius. This spirit, or genius, governed his fortune and determined his character. The word is from the Latin for "to be born," since the spirit was given at birth. The English *genitals* comes from the same Latin root word as genius. Traditionally, only Roman men were given a genius, while women were guided by Juno, the special protectress of women and marriage. Eastern genies were not so much guardian or attending spirits as fallen angels. Rollo May has an excellent discussion on attending to one's genius or inner guide in *Love and Will* (New York: W. W. Norton and Company, 1969, pp. 154-177). He speaks of this genius spirit using the Greek term of a *diamon*, noting that Socrates experienced his genius as an inner guidance.

p. 14

3.   Nazareth, a village whose population varied from two hundred to two thousand. See Borg, *Meeting with Jesus Again for the First Time*, p. 25. John Crossan, along with other scholars, is inclined to believe it was a

small hamlet, with only a couple hundred people. See John Dominic Crossan, *Jesus, Revolutionary Biography* (San Francisco: HarperCollins, 1994), p. 26 and John J. Pilch, *The Cultural World of Jesus: Cycle A* (Collegeville, Minn.: The Liturgical Press, 1995), p. 14.

4.   The word translated usually as carpenter is *tekton*, which has a different meaning than our word carpenter. It can mean a worker in stone as well as wood, and a doer of other work. Since buildings in Palestine were made of stone and not wood, John Pilch says it would be more accurate to consider Jesus a stone mason. Perhaps the broadest description of his work is covered by the word craftsman. Marcus Borg reminds us that a tekton was at the lower end of the peasant class, and not a step up from a subsistence peasant farmer as we might view such skilled workers today. Such wood and stone workers usually belonged to a family that had lost its land. See Borg, *Meeting with Jesus Again for the First Time*, p. 26. Today, when many farmers have recently been forced off family farms by a variety of causes, Joseph, the ex-farmer father of Jesus, could become a new patron saint.

CHAPTER ONE

p. 15

1.   A Palestinian peasant house of this period was typically only a single all-purpose room no larger than fifteen feet long, the length of a ceiling joist without pillars. A craftsman's workshop would be part of the house. The room would have perhaps only very small windows covered by lattices and stuffed closed during winter months. With only one door, which opened out onto an enclosed area faced with the walls of other homes, they were quite dark inside. Floors were clay, and the only furniture of the peasants was rush reed mats, on which they sat, ate and slept. The houses of the rich might have several rooms as well as chairs, tables and beds. To those in the Western world today, the home of the holy family would be viewed as the most wretched and poorest of shacks. See John J. McKenzie, *Dictionary of the Bible* (Milwaukee: Bruce Publishing Co., 1965), p. 377.

        John Pilch says that anthropologists estimate the average Galilean male of that period to be about 5 feet 5 inches tall, weighing an average of 140 pounds. See John J. Pilch, "The Cultural World of Jesus, Cross-Cultural Reflections" (Columbus, Ohio: Initiatives Publications, 1995 [a series of periodicals on cycles B and C in pre-book form] from the essay on Luke 5: 1-11).

2.   The Hebrew Scriptures relentlessly censured nudity, linking it with sin and shame. This was not the case in Greece where beauty was seen in both body and soul. See John J. Pilch and Bruce Malina eds., *Biblical Social Values and Their Meaning* (Peabody, Mass.: Hendrickson Publishers, Inc., 1993), p. 119. Palestinian Jews wore a long tunic with a cloak, but not underwear. Gabriel's short, transparently thin gauze tunic, while commonly worn by Egyptians, was considered too immodest and too thin for a devout Jew like Jesus.

p. 16

3.   Jesus objects that he is too old and is ready to die. Scholars estimate that in Jesus' culture thirty percent of infants died at birth, thirty percent of the remaining population was dead by age six, and sixty percent by age sixteen. See Malina and Rohrbaugh, *Social-Science Commentary on the Synoptic Gospels*, p. 117. Before reaching their mid-twenties, seventy-five percent of adults would be dead, and ninety percent by their mid forties. Few lived beyond their thirties. Furthermore, contrary to Jesus' image in ninety-nine percent of Christian art, John Pilch and other scholars believe that Jesus would have looked old for his age by today's standards. His body would have showed the signs of disease because of the poor peasants' diet and harsh living conditions. See also Malina and Rohrbaugh, p. 41.

4.   See the above note concerning advanced age, even more true for Mary. Since no mention is made of the father of Jesus in his adult life, most presume Joseph had already died.

5.   Jesus had to struggle with what appeared to be the divine order for life on earth. Ched Myers says that people believed the "social-economic stratification is divinely sanctioned; it is futile to protest." See Ched Myers, *Binding the Strong Man* (Maryknoll, N.Y.: Orbis Books, 1988), p. 179. Here Jesus is being called to rise above what seems to be God's will and to discover what God truly desires, which is a world of equality and justice for all. Today, that ancient belief of the law of the survival of the rich and powerful continues to be held as either sanctioned by God or as the destiny of how the world works. To dream of challenging that "law" as immoral and unjust can seem as hopeless now as it did then, unless one is mad or inspired.

6.   Gabriel delivers the message of God to Jesus; it contains the central calling and the true task of life on this planet: to be heroic. Life is nothing more than the theater for heroism, says cultural anthropologist Ernest

Becker. Jesus in this scene is tempted by Gabriel's invitation to leave the security of his small village, his work and family to achieve cosmic specialness, a hunger each human was given by the Creator. The society of little Nazareth, as with every society, sets up its hero system which is limited basically to "doing your duty." Gabriel tempts Jesus to become a high hero by not pleasing others or behaving as they expect — to accept that invitation risks being seen as crazy. Jesus is divinely tempted to unfold his inner secret, which most mortals gradually and continuously cover over until they forget it, all in order to appear as sane and sensible. See Ernest Becker, *The Denial of Death* (New York: The Free Press, 1973), pp. 1, 82.

Angelic temptations are not restricted to holy books, but are even possible for those today who are not vaccinated against visions. Sadly, most modern religion is no longer valid as a hero system. Religion needs to be radicalized as in the case, perhaps, of those dedicated to Liberation Theology in the Third World and Laundry Theology (cleansing the church of outdated dogmas, customs, legalism and rituals) in the First World.

p. 17

7.   While nothing is known after the birth and early childhood of Jesus' life until he goes to be baptized, Gabriel's Gospel opens a window for us into Jesus' spiritual preparation for the call of God. Scholars such as Marcus Borg and John Pilch see Jesus as a deeply devout, prayerful Jewish man, what we would call a religious seeker or, to use Borg's term, "a spirit person." Such spirit persons are found cross-culturally. Regardless of their religion, they have vivid "religious" experiences, are capable of traveling into the other dimension of reality known as the sacred. What we know with some certainty about Jesus is that in his late twenties, or "around" thirty, he became a disciple of John of the Jordan River. See Borg, *Meeting with Jesus Again for the First Time*, p. 27.

8.   See Psalm 60.

p. 18

9.   John blows a shofar, a trumpet made of a ram's horn, used by ancient Hebrews to sound a warning or to call an assembly. The shofar is blown at the beginning of a feast day, as on the Day of Atonement, Yom Kippur, or as a call to war. John signals both, for conversion is to go to war against oneself so as to be liberated. He also announces that a new day, the Great Jubilee, is approaching.

10.   The early post-Easter church was very uncomfortable with the fact that Jesus had been a disciple of John and was baptized according to John's ritual requirements, which included confession. The Gospel accounts reflect the various ways their authors dealt with this thorny issue. Jesus' confession can be seen as a pattern for the confession of every modern disciple. Confessing a failure to do good, a lukewarmness, is not an invitation to guilt, but to change, and to greatness. Frequent examination of one's life should lead to striving for excellence in all things. Discipleship involves perpetual reform and renewal.

11.   The author of Matthew's Gospel dresses John in a camel skin tunic as prophetic dress, since it was the ascetic clothing of the prophet Elijah, who was generally expected to reappear from the dead to prepare the people for the coming of God's kingdom. The clothing of John is worth reflecting on. If, like Elijah, he were to reappear today in the church, we might wonder if both the way he dressed and his message would be greeted as was his presence two thousand years ago.

12.   Confession of sin was an integral part of John's baptism, which was a free gift in contrast to the costly temple ritual to remove sin. Naturally this element in Jesus' baptism of "sin" being removed presented an enormous problem to the post-Easter church (See Crossan, *Jesus, Revolutionary Biography*, pp. 44-45 and *The Historical Jesus, The Life of a Mediterranean Jewish Peasant* [San Francisco: HarperCollins, 1992], pp. 230-243). Yet scholars believe Jesus' baptism was a turning point, a real conversion experience, a radical change from what had been to what could be.

The Danish philosopher Kierkegaard said, "The only way out of human conflict is full renunciation, to give one's life as a gift to the highest powers. Absolution has to come from the absolute beyond." Kierkegaard goes on to show how this rule applies to the strongest, most heroic: "To renounce the world and oneself...(to hand one's self) over to the powers of creation, is the hardest thing for man to achieve." Jesus came to realize that the greater the call, the more challenging the renunciation. If he were going to be a God-hero, then he had to give a total gift. The narrow culture of Nazareth had made up a gift list for ordinary heroes, and it did not include the divine madness of choosing to give the greatest gift. See Becker, *The Denial of Death*, pp. 172-173. To be able to make such an enormous gift, Jesus required some time and freedom to fully embrace his call. What he only faintly perceived at the Jordan needed to be gradually revealed to him by God through his mystic mentor Gabriel. So it is with each of us. With each invitation to conversion, God allows us to reject the heroic for the homey.

13.   The cloud from which Jesus hears the voice of God is a supernatural phenomena, the first "public" one in his life. The cloud as a form of God's visitation has a rich history in the First Testament (see, for example, Ezekiel 1:4). Also see Dianne Bergant and Robert Karris, eds., *The Collegeville Bible Commentary* (Collegeville, Minn.: The Liturgical Press 1989), p. 867.

14.   The desert was a symbolic place recalling the forty years of pilgrimage to the promised land by the Jewish people and the place of their great covenant on Mount Sinai. The desert, then, was the place of the marriage of God to the people; to return there was to return to that primal divine romance. Along with the wild beasts and serpents who dwell there, the desert was also feared as the haunt of demons and evil spirits.

CHAPTER TWO

p. 24

1.   Although Baptism's death to self is intended to be a real dying, and thus painful, to be reborn is even more painful! Death and rebirth can simply be glib religious words that, like snowflakes, easily melt on the tongue. Gabriel's call to be fully skinned alive is a call to fully die, which is critical to being born again. Anyone involved in preparing others for religious conversion must warn them that as their first birth was extremely painful for their mothers, so their second birth will be extremely painful for them. To join a church is not painful. To undergo a true religious awakening, however, as did Jesus in the desert, is to be skinned to death while still alive — and then to grow new skin as a free and new person.

2.   Gabriel, as God's messenger, speaks not with bodily lips, for his message is directed to the heart. Today, anyone who hears voices, especially God's voice, or talks with a guiding angel, will likely be considered mentally imbalanced or suffering from schizophrenia. Julian Jaynes speaks of such voices in his controversial book, *The Origin of Consciousness in the Breakdown of the Bicameral Mind*, (Boston: Houghton Mifflin Company, 1969). Jaynes says that what we call thoughts today were once heard as

actual voices by early peoples. As the brain formed into a single organ, the voices became what we now experience as thoughts in the mind, "a secret theater of speechless monologue and prevenient counsel." Jaynes believes the great prophets and certain holy persons such as Jesus, Buddha and Mohammed still heard the voices. This is only a brief summary of his theory, but it can provide a reflection on how we view the movements of our minds. Are they only our thoughts, or does God continue to "speak" to us in these silent voices?

p. 26

3.　　　The Egyptians had bronze mirrors with a polished surface as early as 1500 B.C.E., and similar Greek polished metal mirrors date to 400 B.C.E.

4.　　　Americans, according to John Pilch, are recognized as the most individualistic people who have ever lived on earth. Each one strives to be different, the complete opposite of the Mediterranean world, where the individual did not exist. Jesus, like everyone in his culture, was deeply embedded in others — in family, village and nation — and his self-identity was seen only in relation to those who formed his primary group. See Pilch, *The Cultural World of Jesus,* p. 127 and Malina and Rohrbaugh, *Social-Science Commentary on the Synoptic Gospels,* p. 113.

5.　　　This prayer Jesus is praying is composed of psalms flowing from Psalm 138. The psalm poems attributed to King David would likely have been memorized early in life. They would have formed for Jesus an endlessly rich deposit for his personal prayer.

p. 27

6.　　　To do the will of God was the great desire of our Mediterranean ancestors, says the scholar John Pilch. The problem was discovering how God makes the divine will known — or, how to learn of it. Kings and the elites had experts, scribe-scholars, "but ordinary folk had to rely on ordinary means." The prophet Joel captures a basic Mediterranean belief that suggests those means: "Old men dream dreams, young men see visions." See Pilch, *The Cultural World of Jesus*, pp. 11-12. The peasant craftsman Jesus, then, would find God's will for him in his desert visions.

　　　In the Gospel of Gabriel, these visions and the conversion experience of his baptism by John are part of a process in which religious energies-impulses gradually expand until they become central to his life. The mystical visions of Jesus are examples of "noetic" experiences, which involve more than a feeling of an altered state of consciousness, but are experiences of knowing. In these visions, Jesus is given profound knowledge of who he truly is. See Borg, *Meeting with Jesus Again for the First Time*, pp. 27-33.

John Pilch further states that such altered states of consciousness are considered ordinary for ninety percent of the world's cultures and eighty percent of Hebrews, Greeks and ancient Egyptians. See Pilch, "The Cultural World of Jesus, Cross-Cultural Reflections," the essay on John 20: 19-31. While it seems that Westerners have successfully blocked out this normal human capability, a surprising survey puts even that into question. In a recent survey in the United States over sixty percent of those questioned said that at least once in their life they had had a mystical or religious experience.

7.   Interestingly, Islam includes Adam as a prophet, along with Noah, David and Solomon, instead of seeing them simply as kings or patriarchs. In the Eastern Orthodox Church Adam and Eve are saints, their feast day celebrated on December 24.

Adam's vision calls forth from Jesus a vocation to be the new Adam, to return to Eden time, to announce the end of Satan's rule and to reopen the gates of paradise. John Pilch says that a long-standing biblical expectation was that "the end will be like the beginning." See Pilch, "The Cultural World of Jesus, Cross-Cultural Reflections," the essay on Luke 23: 35-43.

8.   The grandmothers are the four woman ancestors whom Matthew's author included in the genealogy of Jesus: Tamar, Rahab, Ruth and Bathsheba (see Matthew 1: 1-17).

p. 29

9.   Earthquakes were also considered to be vehicles for visitations of God (see, for example, Ezekiel 3: 12-13, Isaiah 29: 6 and Revelation 11: 19). While Jesus' visions or altered states of consciousness are presented by Scripture scholars as not being unusual for holy persons in a large part of the world, a word of caution is called for. Great spiritual teachers like Saints Teresa of Avila and John of the Cross have warned of the potentially misleading power of extraordinary phenomena since one's psyche can easily get in the way. Psychologists agree, saying that apparitions often appear as a religious escape from the drudgery of ordinary life. Such visions are also commonly reported in times of upheaval and social change. When masses of people feel dehumanized and alienated, it is not unusual to see an outbreak of signs and wonders. Prudence and discretion is the advice of the great spiritual guides, and Jesus provides an example. His mystical experiences were not shared with others. The only time a vision is recorded

with others present was the transfiguration, when three of his disciples were with him. He forbad them to tell anyone! Not only is it wise to discern such extraordinary occurances with a competent spiritual advisor, one should silently "sit with" them and pray with them over time to test them.

p. 30

10.   By his desert visions Jesus is being reborn into full humanness, an essential step in the full awareness of his divinity. Being fully human, as Ernest Becker says, "means primary mis-adjustment to the world.... Full humanness means full fear and trembling, at least some of the waking day." Becker, *The Denial of Death*, pp. 58-59. Rejection of the feminine in the male or the masculine in the female prevents a person from evolving into full humanness. Yet since tribal days society has blocked this part of the second birth in countless taboos, customs of childhood training and role models for adulthood. It's no wonder that Jesus would be frightened and shocked at this desert vision.

11.   "They should cover their shame, and should not uncover themselves as the Gentiles uncover themselves," says the Book of Jubilees (3: 31). Both women's and men's sexual organs were called their "shame." Paul used this Jewish vocabulary when he spoke of the "shameful" parts of the body, referring to the sexual organs (see 1 Corinthians 12: 23). See also Pilch and Malina, *Biblical Social Values and Their Meaning*, p. 120.

Jerome Neyrey, S.J. quotes an ancient belief about nakedness: "One must not stand naked in the presence of the Divine Name." See Pilch and Malina reference below. This was held as so serious a law that Jewish men entering a privy were told not to face east or west — the axis of the holy of holies in the temple — lest they shame God by exposing their buttocks or penis. Nudity for women was an even greater shame in that culture. It was also a violation of necessary boundaries because it blurred or erased social status and identity. More than simply offending society's boundaries and sense of modesty, nakedness was considered unclean, making it a kind of social and religious pollution. This ancient view of nudity and sex as unclean is seen today when sexual jokes or language are called "dirty." We do not use the same terms for racial or discriminating slurs, acts of injustice or exploitation. Besides nudity being a kind of pollution, the shame involved carried a strong specter of pain, as in the image of prisoners being stripped naked before scourging and death — they suffered as much from their shame as from the physical punishment. See Pilch and Malina, *Biblical Social Values and Their Meaning*, pp. 119-125.

p. 32

12.   Job 12: 7-8. The text continues, "Speak to the earth and it shall teach you." Michael Dowd quotes David Brower, who said, "We cannot have peace on earth unless we make peace with the earth." See Michael Dowd, *Earthspirit, A Handbook for Nurturing an Ecological Christianity* (Mystic, Conn.: Twenty-Third Publications, 1991), pp. 98, 22. In this section of the Gospel of Gabriel Jesus makes his peace with the earth and her creatures as a necessary part of his religious conversion. Would that each of us could follow him in this process of holy communion and reunion with creation. Dowd states on page 25: "The Christian movement today is still in the elementary stages of working out for itself and for the world the implications of the Gospel." Paul stated in Colossians 1: 6 that across the world the Gospel is producing fruit and *growing*. The Gospel still needs to grow in the area of ecology. Unless ecology is viewed as more than a movement but as an integral part of our spiritual awakening and the earth is seen as included in Jesus' commandment of love, the future of our planet seems dim.

p. 33

13.   Relationship, sister-brotherhood, is different from stewardship. Even if one is a good steward, it is the relationship of a superior to an inferior and not one of communion. Communion, not consumption, is Jesus' way. The critical challenge of loving God, all of God, includes loving the earth.

14.   In Gabriel's Gospel, the devil appears as a shadow or the shadow side of Jesus, who calls himself the "Light of the World." Wolfgang Goethe (in 1771) said, "Where the light is the brightest the shadows are deepest." Goethe refers to the mystery that genius and madness coexist, as well as the fact that where the greatest capacity for good exists, so does the capacity for its other side!

The image of Satan as Jesus' half-brother is found in an ancient esoteric legend as a way of expressing the twin-drives of creation and destruction found within all humans. Since Jesus was like us in all things but sin, would not such twin energies be present in him? Satan, in Hebrew, means "adversary," and in the Hebrew Scriptures that does not necessarily mean an enemy of God. In the book of Job, Satan is one of God's counselors, who was allowed to examine Job on his degree of faith and loyalty. It was during the Babylonian Captivity, roughly between 587 and 537 B.C.E., that Satan was seen as an evil agent and almost a second god. Satan in the time of Jesus and the Second Testament had become the primal spiritual power opposed to God. Here in Gabriel's account he is a mixture of the adversary who tested Job and the chief evil power. See Sanders, *The Historical Figure of Jesus*, pp. 114-117.

p. 35

15.   Psalm 69: 5. The exclamation "God is great" will be found frequently upon the lips of Jesus in Gabriel's Gospel. It is also a favorite prayer-proclamation among Muslims today. This three-word prayer could be a powerful acclamation for any disciple of Jesus.

16.   Jesus calls Satan *Diablo*, which is Spanish for devil. It could also be spelled *Diabolo*, which would give the exchange a different twist. There is an old toy called *Diabolo* or "the devil on two sticks." The devil is the name of a hollowed piece of wood which the player places on a cord held loosely between two sticks. It is then made to spin by manipulating the sticks. In Jesus' "initiation" ritual in the desert, the visitation of Satan is indeed a game between the two with the stakes being as dear as life!

p. 36

17.   Psalm 57.

18.   Pilch, Malina and Rohrbaugh and other scholars state that honor and protecting against shame are two of the primal values of Jesus' culture. More important than money or property, honor was both sought and guarded with the greatest care. Shame was a disgrace not only to oneself but to family and clan as well. See Malina and Rohrbaugh, *Social-Science Commentary on the Synoptic Gospels*, pp. 95-107.

p. 38

19.   The author of Luke's Gospel tells us what is only logical when he says, "The devil departed from Jesus — for a time" (Luke 4: 13). In Gabriel's Gospel, Jesus must deal with more temptations and a greater variety. In this he shares our humanness since we also are frequently put to the test in our loyalty to God.

20.   Psalm 18, which Gabriel continues.

p. 39

21.   While for us a visit to the ocean could be a desired vacation, this is not true for the Israelites who were never a seagoing people. For them the

sea or ocean was seen as the monster of chaos that is often found in ancient myths of creation. The beginning of Genesis has the Wind of God sweeping over the formless chaos of waters. See McKenzie, *Dictionary of the Bible*, p. 781. However, in the temple of Solomon was a sacred sea called the "Bronze Sea," which was an immense reservoir seven and one-half feet deep with a diameter of fifteen feet. It had no practical purpose, and scholars believe it recalled the sacred lake found adjacent to Egyptian temples. It may have symbolized God on a throne of waters, as God sits in Psalm 29, or God's domination of the chaos. In Gabriel's Gospel, the ocean becomes another image of God, who, like the sea, is uncontrollable and endlessly deep. As an image of the divine, the ocean is also the cosmic womb out of which all living things on earth have come. To be swallowed up in water also symbolizes the sacred mysteries of Baptism's death and rebirth as one is immersed — drowned — in water.

For additional reading on such states of altered reality, see John Pilch, "The Transfiguration of Jesus, An Experience of Alternate Reality." *In Modeling Early Christianity*, ed. Philip F. Esler. (London: Routledge, 1995).

22.   To be reborn in the mystery of Baptism is to become a child again and to relearn what all children must forget: "to abandon ecstasy, to do without awe, to leave fear and trembling behind." See Becker, *The Denial of Death*, p. 55. Jesus, by embracing God's call to full humanness, is able to become an adult child and enter again into ecstasy, which requires letting go of the usual controls of life and death. Everyday ecstasy is possible for anyone, or rather for anyone who is able to let go of controlling so as to tremble. Those who are out of control could be called "holy tremblers," a new third millennium kind of Shaker.

Creation, including not only a vast ocean but a simple creek, rain or a butterfly, is awesome and should make us tremble with wonder. By the time we leave childhood, almost without exception we have repressed our vision of the primal miracle of creation. We do not view the world as it is available to raw experience. The repression of our natural inclination to ecstasy allows us to go about our daily lives of work and family as routine. We are able to function as hard-working, God-fearing Christians instead of being paralyzed by a world crowded with the miraculous and majesty, overflowing with the terror of terrible beauty.

p. 40

23.   Anointing with oil was common in the ancient world as a refreshing agent, to heal the sick or as part of the ritual of hospitality. It was also a religious rite set aside to make sacred a person or object. Priests were

anointed, as was the tent of the meeting. The ark inside the portable desert temple and even the furniture of the tent were anointed. Kings, especially Saul, David and Solomon were also anointed, but prophets, it seems, were not. The words "to anoint" can also signify appointment, bringing down the Spirit of God upon a person or persons to impel them to perform some extraordinary deed, such as preaching the good news to the poor. Here, the Angel Gabriel, as the hands of the Divine Mystery, anoints with oil the entire body of Jesus as was the practice in the early church at Baptism. The significant parts of the body, including the sexual organs, were once also included in the anointing of the sick in the Catholic Church. The title of Christ, from the Greek *Christos* is translated as "anointed one." By addressing Jesus with this title, "the Anointed One," his early disciples stated their belief that Jesus was the Messiah. See McKenzie, *Dictionary of the Bible*, p. 34.

p. 41

24.   Jesus has his tongue set on fire, as did the poet-prophet Isaiah, whose lips were inflamed by a six-winged angel, a seraphim, in an act of divine commissioning (see Isaiah 6: 5-9).

p. 42

25.   The linking of God's Spirit with the wind will be common practice by the author of Gabriel's Gospel. Jesus creatively used the image of the wind to show that the presence of Holy Spirit is invisible but that the Spirit's movement and power in the world are very visible. The Hebrew word for spirit, *ruah*, can mean breath, wind or spirit. All the prophets, and more so Jesus, are people of the Spirit who feel the force of that Divine Wind upon them. The elite corps of the Japanese air force who gave their lives by crashing explosive-loaded planes into enemy targets during the Second World War were called *Kamikaze*, meaning "divine wind." Jesus and all the great prophets, including those of our own time, are willing to freely give their lives Kamikaze-style.

26.   With the way home being pointed out to him, Jesus now leaves the desert, a new person with new skin and a new heart. The home to which he goes is only a home on the road to home, for, having been reborn, he will be forever restless until he returns to his home in God. The various epiphanies and visitations of the desert, its visions and states of altered consciousness, have begun the process of helping him break out of the prison of ordinary cultural heroism. He has opened himself up to infinity and to the extraordinary heroism in a life of sacred service to the Divine

Mystery, aware that with God all things are possible. He now returns, not as he left Nazareth, for now his life has taken on ultimate value and meaning instead of having only social and cultural values. Now he sees the roots of his goodness grow not out of the soil of his village and religious society but out of the heart of God. What appears as good to his society will sometimes be far different from what God judges as good. Only a liberator who has first been liberated can free others, can call them out of the darkness of their dungeons, which now is what Jesus knows he must do.

CHAPTER THREE

p. 43

1. (See Luke 4: 14 ff.)

This scene is set on Saturday not because that was the weekly day of worship, but simply because the author of Luke says the event occurred on a Sabbath. John Pilch states that for a first century Jewish believer the Sabbath was not a day of worship but only a day of rest. Scholars today believe the early Christian practice of gathering to celebrate the Lord's Supper on the seventh day (or the first) stimulated the development of the Sabbath as a Jewish day of worship rather than the reverse. He also says that in Jesus' day the synagogue was a gathering place for the village, much like a modern community center, as well as a place of prayer and study for males. See Pilch, *The Cultural World of Jesus*, p. 26. Scholars believe that on certain occasions women were also allowed to be present as the author of Gabriel's Gospel has suggested in this scene.

In a "printless" society like first-century Palestine, gossip, both good and bad, was the only way for news to travel. Another name for the Gospels might be the *good gossip*. This would express better the historical reality that the ministry and words of Jesus were originally transmitted orally and not written down until the latter part of the first century.

p. 44

2. The author of Luke has Jesus reading from the scroll of Isaiah (Luke 4: 17-19). However, John Crossan's position is that Jesus as a Palestinian peasant was surely illiterate, as were ninety-five to ninety-seven percent of the population. In a "printless" culture, memory was more developed, and the psalms and other important passages from Scripture were known by heart. Jesus was not a scribe but a poor lower-class craftsman. The author of Gabriel's Gospel agrees with Crossan and has Jesus speaking rather than reading the text. See Crossan, *Jesus,*

Revolutionary Biography, pp. 25-26.

3.   Second Isaiah: 61: 1-2

4.   The jubilee was a "horn year" because it was announced with a blast from the shofar, or *yobel* in Hebrew. The jubilee or sabbatical year was established by a command in Leviticus (25: 8-17, 29-31), the book of laws of the First Testament. It prescribed that every fiftieth year the soil should not be cultivated and one should return to one's native land. Scholars maintain that the law was more an ideal than a reality and was intended to show that God was the true owner of all land. The law also stated that it was a time for the release of those sold into indentured service or slavery (Leviticus 25: 39-43). In this sense, for Jesus to proclaim a jubilee, regardless of what the actual year was, implied releasing those held in the various types of slavery named by Isaiah. See McKenzie, *Dictionary of the Bible*, p. 460. The practice of a sabbatical time for rest and renewal by re-creation, as a release from the self-imposed slavery of contemporary life, is worth considering as a necessary sacrament of Christian life.

p. 45

5.   See the note for p. 36 on shame and honor. John Crossan together with other scholars like John Pilch and Bruce Malina show how central a value was one's personal or the village's honor. Honor was so critical a value that once lost it was as if a person no longer existed. Those issues of honor and shame will arise again and again in Gabriel's Gospel. See Crossan, *Jesus, Revolutionary Biography*, p. xxxi.

p. 46

6.   Gabriel greets young Mary, the bride-to-be of God, with a song based on the erotic poetic love song of the First Testament, the Song of Songs. That greatest of songs was attributed to King Solomon, who was reported to have had 700 wives and 300 concubines and therefore knew something about making love. The number is surely an exaggeration, for which both the First and Second Testaments are well known, but the point is that King Solomon had a reputation as a great lover. See McKenzie, *Dictionary of the Bible*, pp. 829, 833-835.

p. 48

7.   This meeting of Mary and Elizabeth, traditionally called the Visitation, is worthy of reflection. Both the woman at the door and the woman who greets her young guest carried the blessing of God unseen.

The Visitation, then, becomes the great Gospel story of hospitality; Luke's version (Luke 1: 39-56) could be read once a year at everyone's front door to remind us of how God visits us unseen in both the guest and the host. An image of the these two holy pregnant women would also make a perfect front door icon or image.

8.   God removing Elizabeth's barrenness makes her the Sarah of the Second Testament. One of the great memories of the Jewish people was how God bestowed gifts upon Abraham and Sarah, and that memory was frequently recalled. While overshadowed by Mary's pregnancy, Elizabeth's expecting in her old age is a sacrament of hope that deserves to be frequently remembered. This is especially the case when the future, whether personally, politically or religiously, seems hopeless, for indeed "with God all things are possible."

9.   The ancients of our faith knew little of the science of reproduction. They believed a male deposited, in seed form, a miniature fully formed human being inside the female. He provided the seed, she the field for planting. See Pilch, "The Cultural World of Jesus, Cross-Cultural Reflections," from the essay on Luke 1: 39-45.

p. 49

10.   God's blessing to Adam and Eve was to increase, to be fruitful. To be barren and childless was a great curse for women and also for men. It was believed that such a social disgrace must have been caused by sin or by having in some way brought down the displeasure of God.

11.   The author of Luke who gives us the account of Mary's trip to visit Elizabeth simply states that Mary "set out and traveled to the hill country in haste" (see: Luke 1: 39). John Pilch points out that honorable women in the ancient Middle East could never do anything alone! They had to be with a cluster of women or children, or under the watchful eye of a brother or responsible male relative. "A fourteen year old virgin like Mary, who goes anywhere alone, is open to charges of shameful intentions." The trip from Nazareth in Galilee to Elizabeth's home in Judea would have taken four days! See Pilch, "The Cultural World of Jesus, Cross-Cultural Reflections," from the essay on Luke 1: 39-45.

p. 51

12.   Star of the Sea is one title that traditional devotion gives to Mary, the mother of Jesus. The title originally belonged to the Isis, Egyptian Corn Mother, who was presented as a true wife, a tender mother and

queen of nature. Her worship was popular in pre-Christian Rome, especially among women who found certain oriental mother goddess rituals to be too bloody and licentious. Isis was also the patroness of sailors and was worshipped by them under the title Star of the Sea because the star of the goddess was Sirius. The appearance of this bright star on July mornings was a sign of good weather to the seafaring Greeks. See Sir James G. Frazer, *The Golden Bough* (New York: MacMillian Publishing Co., 1922), pp. 444-445.

Elizabeth calls Mary by that title perhaps to suggest that she will fulfill all the ancient holy mother images.

p. 53

13.   A variety of different calendars were in use at this time, and so it is difficult to set the precise date of the birth of Jesus. The angel's song of the fullness of time, beginning with the date of the creation of heaven and earth until the nine months since conception, is taken from the Roman Martyrology for December 24th. This martyrology is a catalog of martyrs and saints which appeared in Rome in 1583, listing the names of martyrs who died on each calendar day. The book was part of the official liturgy of the Roman Catholic Church and was part of the morning prayer of Prime when that prayer was said publicly. The author of Gabriel's Gospel added to the original dates that it was also the Age of Pisces, the fish, which is the last of the Zodiac signs. The reason for this addition will become clearer as the Gospel unfolds.

14.   "Shepherds, common as dung." The song of the shepherd Isaac provides us with the shocking selection of shepherds as the chosen ones to whom the birth of Jesus is first announced. While shepherds are romanticized in millions of Christmas crib scenes, along with camel drivers and tanners, they belonged to one of the most despised of occupations. They were considered to be men without honor because, being away from home at night, as is the case in this scene, they were unable to protect their wives. They were seen as thieves for allowing their sheep to graze on other people's property. They were also "unclean" since their work prevented them from performing the frequent washing rituals of the pious. A good comparison of their social standing would be how decent townsfolk in the Old West in America saw the rough and wild cowboys. The author of Luke's choice of sheep herders is an overture to all the religious and social outcasts Jesus chose to shepherd and include in his community. See Malina and Rohrbaugh, *Social-Science Commentary on the Synoptic Gospels*, p. 296.

15.   "Announce the good news." The unclean and despised shepherds became the first apostles of the Second Testament, for apostle in Greek means "to send forth." Since the word could mean an ambassador, delegate or messenger, their importance in the birth story of Jesus challenges his disciples today to ponder a mystery: Does God continue to use as messengers those whom the middle class might consider to be the despised scum of society?

p. 54

16.   Swaddling was the custom of tightly wrapping a newborn infant in cloth strips. The child began life thus imprisoned for a period of forty days to two years, the later proposed by Plato: "The child, while soft, shall be molded like wax and kept in swaddling clothes till it is two years old." It was thought to ensure strong, straight bodies and was a common practice until the eighteenth century when it went out of style with upper-class Western Europeans. Worthy of reflection is how this unnatural restraint and punishment was given as a sign of the Chosen Child, who would become the Great Liberator. It also reflects the countless social restraints that still bound him as an adult.

   Jesus the Christ is called a savior, one who gives and brings salvation. Like so many religious and theological terms, salvation began as a secular term; it meant freedom or deliverance from war. To be saved was to be liberated from constricting bonds. The image of Jesus as a liberator invites an escape from the swaddling clothes of birth from which few are ever unbound. Today, the word salvation often has little real meaning to the average person, whereas liberation is a cry of the multitude of the world's peoples. Perhaps like the author of Gabriel we should return to salvation's first meaning — liberation — to understand the implications of Jesus as our savior. For a detailed study of the subject, see McKenzie, *Dictionary of the Bible*, pp. 760-763.

CHAPTER FOUR

p. 58

1.   Angels, or children of God (literally "sons"), was one of the First Testament's favorite names (See Genesis 6: 2 and Job 1: 6) for spirits whose reality, at the time of Jesus, was not questioned except by the Sadducees. See Pilch, "The Cultural World of Jesus, Cross-Cultural Reflections," 11-12-95. Angels were primarily messengers of God who were described as having human form. Heaven, being God's court, had a

host of them as a divine retinue, and they were divided into ranks of importance. Jesus believed in them, and trusted in Psalm 91: 11, which stated that God had given to each person an angel as a personal guardian: "to protect you in all your ways." They play important roles in both the First and Second Testaments, as the people of those historical periods believed that their world was crowded with both good and evil spirits. In Hebrew, Christian and Islamic Scriptures an angel is equated with a divine communication or divine operation. See McKenzie, *Dictionary of the Bible*, pp. 30-32. Also see the note for p. 14 on genius.

p. 59

2.   The city of Capernaum became the new home base for the ministry of Jesus. It was twenty-three miles from Nazareth at the north end of the sea of Galilee. Because of its location at a major crossroads for various trade routes in upper Galilee it was cosmopolitan in nature. John Crossan states that estimates of its population at the time of Jesus vary from seventeen hundred to twenty-five thousand people. It was, therefore, much larger than Nazareth, which had only one or two hundred people. See Crossan, *Jesus, Revolutionary Biography*, p. 26.

3.   Rejoice and repent usually are not companions. The author of Gabriel joins them since Jesus began his public ministry by taking up the message of his mentor, John the Baptist. However, Jesus proclaimed the need to repent with the unique conviction that the long-awaited time of God's kingdom had come and was at hand. Therefore, there was reason for rejoicing. Jesus was not a reformer who came with sour, angry words to condemn and threaten. He was a bearer of good news. Who would believe good news delivered by sour-faced, sad or bitter messengers? To repent originally meant to change one's heart or mind. This might, as we usually understand the word, include sorrow for sin and regret. But true repentance, like liberation, implies embracing a radically new way, and so is odious to the rigidly pious or righteous. Those who consider themselves morally right feel no need to change their attitudes or hearts. The call to adopt a new heart, to repent, is fundamental to the message of Jesus.

4.   John Pilch and other scholars prefer the term *toll takers* to *tax collectors*. Some of the toll takers were also called publicans, a Latin term for tax farmers. They leased from the government for a fixed annual sum the right to collect tolls or taxes. The publican or collector could retain all money beyond the fixed amount. The toll takers in the Gospels are usually not publicans but minor-grade agents who worked for a tax farmer

(Zacchaeus of Jericho, whom we will meet later, however, was a chief collector or tax farmer). Toll takers were detested and linked with sinners because they worked for the imperial government or the rich king who exploited the people. Seen as traitors to their country, they were judged as having the lowest morality in the community.

That Jesus was the friend of publicans, toll takers and sinners, is a frequent charge against him in the Gospels. Marcus Borg says the toll takers were among the worst of the untouchables, impure and, therefore, "dirty" people. This communion or association of Jesus with dirty people is worth reflection for those who believe only the good and law-abiding belong in the church. The treatment of social outcasts whose morality is considered the lowest is another good gauge for assessing how closely Christian churches model themselves on the real Jesus. For more on tax collectors, see McKenzie, *Dictionary of the Bible*, p. 707.

p. 61

5.   Jesus begins his prayer with a plea from Psalm 70 for God's help — and that it be quick — then continues with parts of Psalm 33. Gabriel joins him, also quoting from Psalm 33. As mentioned before, these memorized psalms would come easily to the lips of a devout Jew like Jesus.

p. 62

6.   (See Ezekiel 21: 5.) The prophet bemoans the fact that people say of him, "Is not this the one who is forever spinning parables?" Ezekiel was inspired by God with his parables and parable-actions, which spoke louder than words, even if their meaning was sometimes unclear. Such parable-prophetic deeds were also a trademark of other prophets.

p. 64

7.   Ezekiel (21: 3) refers to a forest fire in the southern kingdom of Judah. Jesus fans the fire to include Galilee and beyond.

p. 68

8.   John Pilch says the practice of Jesus' day was not to say, "Thank you," since that gesture would conclude a transaction between two persons. He says that Mediterranean life was an ongoing exchange of a favor for a favor in which one was constantly in and out of debt to others. Americans prefer to be free of obligations, which are viewed as limiting one's freedom,

and so are eager to say, "Thank you" instead of "I owe you one." Yet even in our day, political machines still retain this Mediterranean exchange system (of a favor for a favor), so that quick snow removal from your street or giving a job to your nephew means your vote at the next election. Reflect on whether you can respond to gratitude I.O.U's as did Jesus and his early disciples, or do you prefer "Thank you" notes without further obligations?

9.   Why would these practical fisherman turn their backs on security and follow Jesus? Ernest Becker relates how the Salpetriere, a French mental hospital, was vacated at the time of the French Revolution. The mentally ill discovered in the Revolution a self-transcendence and heroic identity whose spirit of denial was part of their sickness. See Becker, *The Denial of Death*, p. 190. This is not noted to say that the four who followed Jesus were neurotic, but in Jesus they must have sensed the opportunity to become heroes, as was he. The loss of the quest to be a hero and the opportunity to become one, says Becker, is the price we pay for "the eclipse of the sacred dimension (of life)." Jesus offers that dimension, the fourth or sacred dimension, by his very person. As a result, these four, as with others after them, would be magnetically drawn to follow him. Today's contemporary citizens of our domesticated world can no longer easily find heroism in everyday life, whether in the duty of raising children, in their work or in their worship. And so, wars, revolutions and righteous causes or crusades are created to feed the hunger for heroism. "Come, follow me": the invitation to heroic discipleship, when embraced fully, still allows one to step into the fourth dimension while maintaining one's life responsibilities.

p. 69

10.   The song of the parents, Zebedee and Jonah, places the call of Jesus to follow him within the context of the cultural realities of his day. While many parents might rejoice to have a son or daughter enter the ministry today, we should not imagine that the parents of the first disciples rejoiced.

11.   Sirach, Chapter 3, describes a son's duty to his parents. In that society, without any retirement benefits or social security, one's children were the only source of care in old age. Daughters would be married off, thus belonging to their husband's family. The only hope for a parent was a good and caring son or sons. Since care for parents was part of Moses' commandment to honor them, Jesus' call to his disciples to leave their

families to follow him must have seemed shocking, as the song of the two fathers indicates (see also chapters 7 and 23 of Sirach).

12.   Jesus is called crazy by his own family, who come to take charge of him. He *was* mad, but with a special kind of madness. Kierkegaard, the Danish philosopher and theologian, said that to be a normal cultural person is to be sick, since one must embrace what culture calls normality. To be sane in the world, one must be comfortable with limited and protected routines, which is to live in a social prison. Jesus offered a parole from that prison and the freedom to go out into the world of chance, risk and choice. Such a parole, Becker says, terrifies people who do not want to be liberated from their prisons. In Pascal's spine-chilling words, "Men are so necessarily made that not to be mad would amount to another form of madness." See Becker, *The Denial of Death*, pp. 27, 86.

CHAPTER FIVE

p. 71

1.   Jesus rejects being called a rabbi, master or teacher. What began as a way to show honor had become a rigid status system. Students of scribes had to address their teachers with titles as marks of deference and absolute respect. Jesus rejects this master-servant relationship and forbids his disciples from using such titles or requiring the exaggerated respect such titles demanded. His disciples, however, uncertain of precisely who he was, or his mission, treated him as they would a member of the only class of religious leaders they knew. See McKenzie, *Dictionary of the Bible*, p. 718.

Jesus, it seems, had no need of disciples or students, which is the sign of truly great spiritual masters. Gandhi once said, "I do not desire disciples, only fellow seekers of the truth." Becker, speaking on the subject, says, "Leaders need followers as much as they are needed by them: the leader projects onto his followers his own inability to stand alone, his own fear of isolation." See Becker, *The Denial of Death*, p. 139. When Jesus' disciples later depart from him for various reasons, Jesus shows he is willing to go on alone. This only adds to the magnetic aura of his heroism and inner security as one who is firmly rooted in God. Reflection on this requirement of Jesus not to use grand titles for himself or his disciples has obvious implications for today's churches where titles abound. The custom of introducing speakers to audiences with a litany of their titles and degrees, while it gives them an aura of competence, might be viewed by Jesus like a third leg on a chicken.

p. 72

2.   Jesus, as does any truly good storyteller or parable spinner, did not explain his parables. The purpose of a parable is to engage the listener in a deeply personal act of learning, and to explain hidden truths prevents self-exploration. There is an adage from the East in response to a request to have a parable-story explained: "Does the merchant in the market chew your fruit for you?"

p. 73

3.   Youthful John speaks of himself as a bee drawn to a blossom. He gives another reason why the disciples followed Jesus: they were inflected with a disease. It is known as the "infectiousness of the unconflicted" and is the mysterious magnet of any great heroic leader. Such leaders know the magic of the initiatory act, doing what others long to do but are afraid to do. The infection is with a hero's ability to express and live out secret wishes, to dare to be different, even to act on forbidden impulses. Unlike leprosy, which the ancient world dreaded, this heroic disease drew people like flies to honey, for it was primal magic. See Becker, *The Denial of Death*, pp. 134-135.

p. 74

4.   True leprosy, Hansen's disease, the scourge of medieval Europe and still common in hot climates, is fatal if not treated. Scholars have determined that it did not exist, or was extremely rare, in Palestine at the time of Jesus. Those called lepers actually suffered from a variety of skin diseases that made them "impure" and so outcasts, forbidden to associate with the rest of the community. There were religious laws about "leprosy" on garments and on walls of houses, which was really only rot or mold. More poignantly, numerous laws existed concerning the relationship between those judged to be healthy people and lepers, who were to call out, "Unclean, unclean," as a warning whenever anyone approached. Touching a diseased person violated purity rules and made those who touched them unclean as well. Leviticus also gave priestly rules for diagnosis and cures. Jesus ignored all these religious rules, and by his acceptance of lepers removed their social excommunication. See Malina and Rohrbaugh, *Social-Science Commentary on the Synoptic Gospels*, p. 70; McKenzie, *Dictionary of the Bible*, p. 503; Sanders, *The Historical Figure of Jesus*, p. 129.

5.   Reflect on the implications of Jesus' exchange with this leper and

his invitation to join his group, thus ending the leper's "excommunication." Jesus also called his disciples to heal the sick and cure the lepers. Within the reach of any disciple is the power to heal those who are social outcasts, the various untouchables in the community, as did Jesus.

John Pilch has written beautifully on the difference between curing and healing. In our western world, curing is the domain of the medical professionals who treat the body or mind. Healing is about the health of the entire person, body and soul, and can be achieved without the affliction having to be removed or cured.

6.   Why would someone as seemingly nonreligious as the toll collector, Matthew, suddenly quit his job and walk away from his old life? The answers could be many; two will be explored here. As with Paul's radical conversion on the road to Damascus, this scene suggests the old saying about the straw that broke the camel's back. Radical changes in life, conversions or sudden decisions to act, have their beginnings in a series of little straws of events, words and feelings. Both Matthew's and Paul's conversions imply this process and remind us to reverence the vocation of being an unknowing straw carrier. Mysterious are the ways of God: even when innocently speaking to another or making a suggestion, we may be delivering the gift of the last straw.

Gabriel tells us that Matthew looked into Jesus' face. Becker says, "The human face is really an awesome primary miracle; it naturally paralyzes you by its splendor *if you give into it* (my italics) as the fantastic thing it is. But mostly we repress this miraculousness so we can function with equanimity and can use faces and bodies for our own routine purposes." See Becker, *The Denial of Death*, p. 147. Jesus' face must have been truly awesome, since it would have radiated the freedom he had embraced, the beauty of a hero, his divine radiance. His human face, because he was so alive, must have been magically miraculous. Matthew gave in to its power and promise, left his drab daily job for the adventure of following a hero as a way to become a hero himself.

p. 75

7.   Scholars today help us bridge the difference between our world and the ancient world of which first century Palestine was a part. What you ate, how it was prepared, and those with whom you shared a meal were of supreme importance. Table companions determined your social status or honor. Before accepting an invitation to eat, it was necessary to know who else had been invited, lest you find yourself reclining at table with someone who might lower your social standing. In the ancient world,

at banquets of the rich, not only would those of higher rank be seated at higher tables — as is still the custom in today's society — but even the quality of the food and wine served would be different. As a prophetic action, Jesus chose his table companions without concern for his or their status, thus announcing the end of a world with social status ladders. John Crossan says he proclaimed "an open table and open menu," rejecting distinctions, discriminations and hierarchies among guests or food, thus proclaiming a new egalitarian community as God's will for the world. See Crossan, *The Historical Jesus, The Life of a Mediterranean Jewish Peasant*, p. 262.

p. 76

8.	Fasting, the voluntary abstention from food, is found in both modern and ancient religions. In the First Testament it was less an ascetic practice than a sign of sorrow. Together with wearing sackcloth and ashes, it was part of the social custom of mourning. It also began to be associated with prayer in times of crisis or in preparation for receiving divine revelation, as with Moses and Daniel. The only fast prescribed in Israelite religious law was on one day, the Day of Atonement. After the fall of Jerusalem in 587 B.C.E., however, this national disaster was customarily remembered by four fast days through the year. Among the Pharisees, fasting was highly esteemed and practiced often. Some scholars say that every Tuesday and Thursday was a fast day for the devout Pharisee. As with Muslims who fast for an entire month each year during Ramadan, it was a total abstention from food and drink that lasted from sunrise to sunset. Jesus' attitude toward it reflects the prophetic tradition of fasting with the heart as being of more value than the fast of the body. See McKenize, *Dictionary of the Bible,* p. 274.

p. 77

9.	(See Isaiah 58: 1-8.) While this text is read at the beginning of Lent in every mainline church, the romance of abstention from food as a sign of piety is practiced more than the fast of the heart prescribed by Isaiah and Jesus.

p. 78

10.	Jesus retreated to pray frequently, partially because communal life was devoid of privacy. The homes of peasants, as has been noted before, consisted of one or two rooms in which the entire family lived and slept. Doors were open to a common courtyard facing other doorways of homes gathered in a cluster. John Pilch states that having your door closed was a sign to others that you were involved in something underhanded or evil. Even today in some cultures, to go apart from the community by yourself is viewed as strange, and a sign that something is wrong. While highly esteemed in some eras (it was practiced by numerous saints and mystics), today in the Western world to live as a hermit or even a part-time hermit is commonly perceived as deviant behavior. To live in solitude, even for one day a week, might be considered mentally unhealthy and certainly nonproductive to the common good. Yet Jesus embraced frequent times of solitude, a point worth reflection by his contemporary disciples.

11.   Because he was considered a prophet and holy man, Jesus' culture would have expected him to heal. In his culture, there were physicians and folk healers — and also magicians — to whom the sick came for help. Without a scientific base, however, the healers of that time assumed that diseases, illnesses or afflictions were the work of evil spirits or punishment from God for sin. See again the note for p. 74 on the difference between healing and curing the sick. Also see Malina and Rohrbaugh, *Social-Science Commentary on the Synoptic Gospels*, pp. 70-71.

p. 80

12.   Scholars state that physicians of that time preferred to *talk* about the illness and were wary of direct contact since failed treatment could result in the death of the physician. Folk healers, unlike professional physicians, however, were willing to use their hands in touching the sick and willing to risk failure. The village healer did not protect him/herself with plastic-gloved isolation from the affliction of the patient. As a true healer, Jesus, in his passion and death, took unto himself the sickness of the world. Isaiah (52: 13-15; 53) speaks of the servant of God as bearing our infirmities and sufferings, as being pierced for our offenses so that by his wounds we might be healed.

Identification with those in great pain was a necessary part of the healing process among tribal shamans. The ugly mask of the medicine man or woman was not worn to frighten away the evil spirits but rather as a symbol of taking on the tortured face of pain in compassion and communion with the afflicted one. Reflecting on Gabriel's ordination of Jesus as a healer could be a rich meditation for all who care for the sick and afflicted, whether as members of the medical profession, in pastoral care, or as nonprofessionals caring for sick family or friends as an act of love.

CHAPTER SIX

p. 81

1.   (See Matthew 9: 27-30.) Jesus commands secrecy with a pun as he tells the ones cured of blindness, "See to it no one knows of this." Likewise, he personally never claims ownership of the act of healing, but instead says, "Your faith has done this" or "Your faith has saved you."

p. 83

2.   Jesus was a powerful speaker who could hold the multitude's attention by the sheer force of his presence, the strength of his integrity and the conviction with which he spoke. He spoke with "authority," not quoting scholars or scribes to support his position, but from a firsthand knowledge of God. Marcus Borg says his "verbal gifts were remarkable." His language was most often metaphorical, poetic, and imaginative, filled with memorable short sayings and compelling short stories. He was clearly exceptionally intelligent." See Borg, *Meeting with Jesus Again for the First Time*, p. 30.

p. 84

3.   Shofar. See the note for p. 18.

p. 85

4.   This is a reference to the scapegoat, upon whom the high priest placed the sins of the people on the Day of Atonement. The guilt-laden goat, in place of a human sacrifice, was driven out into the desert to die as an attempt to appease God. See Crossan, *The Historical Jesus, The Life of a Mediterranean Jewish Peasant*, pp. 376-394.

5.   The ancient word for eunuch literally means "keeper of the bed." Castration of the human male was not practiced in Egypt, Greek or Rome, except under oriental influence. In Assyria and other Near Eastern countries, eunuchs were used to guard harems for obvious reasons, and were also royal officers of the king's court. Jewish law in the code of Deuteronomy (23: 2) prohibited one who was castrated from being a member of the Israelite community, yet Second Isaiah permits them, along with foreigners, to belong. Jesus' identification as the royal keeper of God's bed has mystical implications of great intimacy worth reflecting upon.

Jesus' reference in Matthew (19: 12) to those who become eunuchs for the sake of the kingdom is usually quoted in defense of the church's law of celibacy for the clergy. There are, however, other possible implications than nonsexual activity. Because the Jews viewed eunuchs as being defective in a most significant way, since they could not marry, they were barred from the chosen people's religion and seen as outcasts. Is Jesus saying more here about the condition of being rejected, even though the context of his words is around marriage? This association with the rejected is compatible with his inclusion of the poor, what John Crossan calls a community of social nobodies. See McKenzie, *Dictionary of the Bible*, p. 252.

6.   For Jews the holiness of God was so great that the divine name could not be pronounced aloud, even in prayer and worship. A narrow understanding of the sin of blasphemy included simply pronouncing the name of God and carried the punishment of death by stoning, as set forth in Leviticus (24: 14). A famous instance of the custom of ripping one's robes at hearing God's name pronounced is where the high priest does so at the trial of Jesus (see Matthew 26: 65).

p. 87

7.   As a devout Jew, Jesus would begin and end his day with this prayer called the *Shema* from Deuteronomy (6: 4-5). The Shema, together with the psalms and frequent short blessing prayers, would have been the core of his prayer life. See Borg, *Meeting with Jesus Again for the First Time*, p. 41, note 13. Using the Shema as a daily morning and evening prayer could be a beneficial practice for Jesus' contemporary disciples who daily are faced with temptations to worship many gods — money, control and status, to mention a few modern deities. If adopted by Messianic Jews or Christians, the word Israel could be changed to People of God.

p. 88

8.   Women in the Near East generally had no legal rights and were always subject to a man, whether father or husband. Marital fidelity was not imposed on husbands but only on wives. Women were seen as sexual partners, home keepers and mothers. They were also considered to be oversexed, thus needing to be closely watched, their appearance in public places controlled. The honor of the male, and the family, would be lost by a daughter's loss of virginity or a wife's infidelity. Women usually did not eat with the male members of the family, but were allowed to be part of the village celebrations by their singing and dancing. The First Testament gives numerous examples of a woman being regarded as property which a man could use as he wished. However, while social custom reinforced a

woman's inferior status, the Genesis account of the creation of woman implied equality; Eve was bone of Adam's bone, flesh of his flesh. In Jesus' time there was, however, one area in which women did have at least an equal share was work. Woman's work was long and hard, and included planting, field work and threshing at harvest time. See McKenzie, *Dictionary of the Bible*, pp. 935-937.

p. 89

9.   (See Galatians 3: 28.) This poetic expression of profound unity in Christ may have been part of the ancient rite of Baptism and expresses the post-Easter church's radical sense of social and sexual equality. Yet even within the apostle Paul's lifetime, this radical equality of Jesus' all-inclusive community regressed into the old traditional Jewish norms of separation. The backward slide to the laws and customs of the First Testament continued as the centuries passed, especially in regard to sin and priesthood. This regression, along with the difficulty in observing the new law of love given by Jesus, raises a reflective question: Did Jesus come too soon? Perhaps the third millennium is ripe for the age of God.

p. 90

10.   Scholars delightfully disagree about the degree of involvement of the women as disciples. E. P. Sanders takes a traditional view that Jesus, as an orthodox Jew, would not have had women accompanying him along with the twelve, even if they did financially assist his ministry. See Sanders, *The Historical Figure of Jesus*, pp. 109-110. John Dominic Crossan, on the other hand, believes that they were involved in the traveling ministry of Jesus. See Crossan, *The Historical Jesus, The Life of a Mediterranean Jewish Peasant*, pp. 264, 295, and Crossan, *Jesus, Revolutionary Biography*, pp. 173-174. The author of Gabriel unveils what the four authors of the canonical Gospels left unsaid: the important role of women and their presence in the radical traveling community of Jesus.

11.   A brief overview of marriage in the religious society of Jesus: Marriages were arranged while the spouses were still children. Although sex and marriage were viewed as divine institutions, there was no religious wedding ritual. This is because the contracting parties were not the bride and groom but the parents, as families married more than a man and woman. The marriage contract became official when the parents exchanged money or property. A joyful village wedding celebration would seal that contract. Another indication of the social position of women is that the

name for the groom was "owner" and for the bride "owned."

12.   According to John Pilch, widows in ancient society were called "the silent ones" since they had no voice in public. There was no such thing as an independent women; she was either a member of her birth family or the property of her husband. Widowhood was thus most difficult, putting a woman on her own with no support from social structures. Women were easily exploited with no man to defend them, and they had few resources. The wife did not inherit her husband's property at death, and if she was childless, she usually returned to her father's house. The oppression of widows was a perpetual concern voiced by the prophets, which Jesus carried on when he denounced the pious priests who exploited widows. See McKenzie, *Dictionary of the Bible*, p. 927.

p. 94

13.   High-ranking Assyrian and Egyptian women wore stylized fake beards during official court business as a way of asserting equal authority with men. See Charles Panati, *Extraordinary Origins of Everyday Things* (New York: Harper & Row, 1987), p. 231.

14.   The complete absence of laughter on the part of Jesus in the four canonical Gospels and in other ancient manuscripts is a significant omission. Laughter and religion are usually not companions, and so the writers of the canonical Gospels left out this most human of emotions. The British author G. K. Chesterton wrote beautifully on how Jesus expressed every human emotion fully except possibly one — laughter. Chesterton believed that Jesus did not publicly show his sense of humor since it was so divine, so powerful and overwhelming. He said that Jesus went apart into the mountains to pray, but also to laugh endlessly and as loud as thunder. See G. K. Chesterton, *Orthodoxy* (London: J. Lane, 1909), p. 276. If Jesus was fully human, as we proclaim, then he must have had a highly developed sense of humor and a great laugh. We get a hint of this in his parables, which are full of mirth and humor as he poked fun at the self-righteous and legally bound.

Chapter Seven

p. 98

1.   Scholars believe Jesus' choice of the twelve was to be the restoration of the twelve tribes of Israel. Ten of the twelve were lost at the time of the Babylonian Exile, and their restoration was part of the messianic dream. From the list of the disciples, it seems that three men had the name of

James. The first was the brother of John and son of Zebedee. James, the son of Alphaeus, was called James the Younger or James the Lesser. James is also the name of a brother, or cousin, of Jesus — his mother's name likewise being Mary. At one time the latter two men named James were believed to be the same man; however, today some scholars believe they are different persons. James, who was the brother of Jesus — and of Joseph, or Joses, and Judas (see Matthew 13: 55) — and was the son of Mary, became the first bishop of Jerusalem. Sanders claims that tradition called him James the Just because he was very law-abiding. See Sanders, *The Historical Figure of Jesus*, p. 235.

p. 99

2.   Jesus was known as an exorcist who had the power to drive evil spirits out of people. This was certainly a form of "liberating those imprisoned." Belief in the presence and power of evil spirits was a significant part of the culture of Jesus. It was another alien belief borrowed by the Jews from the religions of neighboring countries, especially Mesopotamia, where afflictions of the body were perceived to be caused by various demons. These fallen angels were thought to be the cause of all sickness and mental problems, even natural disasters. (The Sadducees, however, did not believe in demons or angels.) The Second Testament has many references to the imagery of demonology as simply a way to personify evil, although the church has always taught the actual existence of personal evil spirits. See McKenzie, *Dictionary of the Bible*, pp. 192-194.

p. 100

3.   The author of Luke gives only four beatitudes, while the author of Matthew has Jesus proclaiming eight. A beatitude is a declaration of blessedness on the basis of some good fortune. It means happiness and suggests a desired virtue. In Luke's account it is a statement of who is honorable and who will be shamed. Jesus' beatitudes radically contradict the social values of his day, and even ours, as they present who is blest and honorable in God's eyes. Marcus Borg questions whether a good oral teacher, especially an itinerant teacher, would have given them all at one time. They may be a collection of beatitudes spoken at various times and places. Borg also states that a good oral teacher would have frequently repeated them individually as one-liners. See Borg, *Meeting with Jesus Again for the First Time*, pp. 69-74.

4.   The author of Gabriel's Gospel has Jesus giving seven more

beatitudes to address the needs of the churches in this age of history.

5.   The beatitude of ambivalence was certainly manifest in the "open table" community of Jesus and in his selection of those who would form his intimate circle of disciples. John Pilch, writing in *Modern Liturgy* (Volume 17, Number 5, 1990), speaks of this quality as the virtue of inconsistency which allows for necessary flexibility. He points out how the Zealots of Masada and the semimonastic Jewish Essenes of Qumran insisted on one path and only one set of values — and so they perished. Pilch states that scholars believe a good reason for the survival of the Jesus movement was the normative inconsistency, or social ambivalence, of Jesus which he required of his early community. His words are filled with inconsistencies, as was his behavior, suggesting that this must have been a deliberate expression by Jesus. A reflection on the state of religious (and other forms of) fanaticism in the world shows the need to learn to adopt this beatitude. Consider how you might begin to practice ambivalence and by frequent practice make it an integral part of your spirituality and life.

6.   Celibacy is fundamentally a secular state since its first meaning is simply being unmarried. In such an unmarried state certain moral behavior is expected of Christians. Society has many celibates who have not taken any religious vows or promises not to marry, although celibacy is usually understood in those terms. This beatitude suggests a deeper, spiritual sense of celibacy.

7.   To be stingy is often considered the worst vice and the most destructive behavior to community life among the native peoples of Alaska and northern Canada.

p. 102

8.   Marcus Borg speaks of how the First Testament command to "be holy as God is holy" closely mirrors "be compassionate as God is compassionate." The poor word "love" is threadbare from overuse; in its place we might sometimes use compassion. It makes clear what is asked of us when we are called to love one another. Borg states that "compassion, not holiness, is the dominant quality of God, and is therefore to be the ethos of the community that mirrors God." See Borg, *Meeting with Jesus Again for the First Time*, p. 54.

p. 103

9.   This command is found in Judaism, "What is hurtful to yourself do not do to others. That is the whole of the Torah and the remainder is but commentary." Islam commands, "Do unto all as you would wish to have

done unto you; and reject from others what you reject for yourselves." Buddhism states, "Hurt not others with that which pains you." And Hinduism teaches, "This is the sum of all righteousness — treat others, as you yourself would be treated. Do nothing to your neighbor, which hereafter you would not have your neighbor do to you." See Jeffrey Moses, *Oneness* (New York: Fawcett Columbine, 1989). The great religions also shared other great truths, like "Love your neighbor" and "God is love" and "As you sow, so shall you reap." Indeed, the Spirit of God speaks in many different tongues in many ages, proclaiming God's way to all.

p. 104

10.   God's *time* has come. The author of Gabriel prefers this term to *kingdom* for several reasons, some of which are shared by contemporary scholars. Historically, the age of kingdoms, kings and queens is over and has been for some time. As a gender term, it is offensive to many in today's church, and in the time of Jesus it also was easily misunderstood. See Crossan, *The Historical Jesus, The Life of a Mediterranean Jewish Peasant*, p. 266.

p. 106

11.   See the note for page 87 on the Shema, which was proposed as an excellent morning prayer for today's disciples. This version of the prayer, uniting the two great commandments, might be even more beneficial.

p. 107

12.   (See Genesis 4: 15.) For killing his brother Abel, Cain was banished to become a perpetual wanderer. Lest he be killed as an alien, God placed a mark on him. Traditionally, the mark of Cain is seen as a sign of evil.

13.   The Gospel of Gabriel's author speaks of a more or less specific time Jesus and his disciples set apart to announce the arrival of the time of God. Jesus did not call his disciples to permanently leave their families but to join his group for trips or tours about the countryside. At the end of each tour they would have returned to their own homes, especially during the winter months.

p. 108

14.   Psalm 49: 2-3, 7-11.

p. 109

15.   Jesus repeats the tradition coming from Moses not to charge for

the gifts of God or for religious teaching. Traditionally, rabbis followed this practice: The only time a rabbi could charge was for teaching children since he was then performing a duty belonging to parents. Parents might reflect on this religious exception when they believe it is the duty of the parish to give their children a religious education.

CHAPTER EIGHT

p. 113

1.   John McKenzie makes a good point that not all Pharisees were hostile to Jesus. As for Simon, who invited Jesus in this scene, it is not certain what his motives were, but from his lack of ritual hospitality it appears that they were not the best of intentions. See McKenzie, *Dictionary of the Bible*, p. 140.

p. 114

2.   This lively parable, like the earlier one about God's big boat, suggest a fuller dimension of Jesus as a preacher of parables. Jesus was a master storyteller, an important part of which was to entertain his listeners. As such he likely would have acted out, sang or danced the various parts. The parables we have in the four canonical Gospels are only bony skeletons of what the originals must have been like. See Borg, *Meeting with Jesus Again for the First Time*, p. 73.

p. 116

3.   This image of the Good Shepherd with the lost sheep riding on his shoulders abounds in stained glass windows and other expressions of Christian art. Jesus' parable in Gabriel's Gospel offers an opportunity to enjoy from a fresh perspective this sometimes sugary image of the sinner come home. The question this parable asks is: Can one be intimately close to Jesus and not part of the flock?

4.   Palestinian guests were greeted with a ritual of foot washing and anointing. It was performed by a house slave or by the host himself, who would traditionally greet the guest with a kiss. That the Pharisee Simon neglected these common acts of courtesy is a sign that he may not have been receptive to Jesus and his message.

5.   In picturing the woman washing, kissing and anointing the feet of Jesus, recall that first century Jews at festive dinners had adopted the Greek practice of eating while reclining on couches. Eating in this reclined

position, his feet would have been extended behind him and so could easily be reached.

p. 117

6.   The woman, who is a prostitute to others, is a lady to Jesus, for he has bestowed more than absolution on her, but also dignity and honor. Sinners crawl to confession, and often crawl away from it having been shamed in the process! Jesus is a liberator, a savior, who offers to free us not only from our sins but from our addiction to self-torture in constant self-criticism. The prayer "Lord I am not worthy" gives voice to the constant state of low self-esteem that is felt by the majority of people. Ernest Becker shows how dictators, revivalists and sadists know how much we like to be lashed at with accusations of our basic unworthiness — because that is precisely how we feel about ourselves (See Becker, *The Denial of Death*, p. 154). Jesus, aware of that widespread form of almost demonic possession that is visited upon us, never degrades or shames. In not a single case does he exploit this primal shame of being somehow not good enough, smart enough, or able to measure up to others' expectations or standards. Instead, he liberates — and treats with extreme dignity — the least, the marginal, the nobodies of society. Love always elevates.

7.   The Sanhedrin or High Council was the supreme national court of the Jewish nation and held authority regarding both secular and religious issues. It was composed of three classes — the elders of the chief aristocratic families, the high priests and the scribes — and totalled seventy-one members. The presiding officer of the council was the high priest presently in office. At the time of Jesus, the jurisdiction of the Sandedrin did not include Galilee but only Judaea, the province in which Jerusalem was located. See McKenzie, *Dictionary of the Bible*, p. 152.

p. 118

8.   Simon is called the Zealot, yet scholars debate whether the Zealots were an active revolutionary group among the Jews at the time of Jesus. Some maintain that Simon was a zealot, but not actually a member of the Zealot Party, which sought a violent overthrow of the Roman occupation. This revolutionary group flowered after the death of Jesus but was only budding in the days of Jesus. In any case, Simon voices the Zealots' passionate desire for political freedom. See Crossan, *The Historical Jesus, The Life of a Mediterranean Jewish Peasant*, p. 194. Rebel bandits were both rural and urban. The Romans called the urban bandits by the nickname of *sicarii*, or knife-men, from their tactic of stabbing their targets in crowded

streets. See John J. McKenzie, *The Civilization of Christianity* (Chicago: The Thomas More Association, 1986), p. 136. John Crossan further speaks of three stages in any revolution: turmoil, conspiracy and internal war. At the time of Jesus, the peasants were in the first stage of turmoil. This is a state of spontaneous and unorganized activity, including riots and political clashes. See Crossan, *Jesus, Revolutionary Biography*, p. 304.

p. 119

9.   John the Baptist and Jesus were more than prophets. First, John, and then Jesus, sidestepped the rituals for the forgiveness of sins practiced at the temple in Jerusalem. This was an expensive proposition for the peasant population, requiring a journey to the holy city. Because they forgave sins, both John and Jesus were threats to the priests and scribes. Jesus, however, unlike John, does not require a confession of sins. Marcus Borg quotes John Crossan as saying that the two most radical aspects of Jesus' activity were the open table (everyone invited to the feast) and the free healing (which included forgiveness of sins), both of which provided the poor access to God's power outside established religious authority. See Borg, *Meeting with Jesus Again for the First Time*, p. 66, note 33.

p. 120

10.   Referring to the wedding at Cana, where the author of John's Gospel gives the account of Jesus changing six stone jars of water into wine. We are told each held twenty to thirty gallons of water (see John 2: 6-10).

11.   Caiaphas refers with disdain to a common magician's practice of that time, making rain fall in a drought. One Honi the Circle Drawer got his name from the time he prayed for rain and no rain fell. Then he made a circle on the ground, stood inside it and prayed to God. Rain fell in torrents. Jesus, to our knowledge, never worked a miracle to make it rain. See Sanders, *The Historical Figure of Jesus*, p. 138 and Crossan, *The Historical Jesus, The Life of a Mediterranean Jewish Peasant*, p. 144. Sanders further describes the range of response to Jesus' miracles: "from calm acceptance to public acclaim to accusations of black magic." See Sanders, p. 162.

12.   Beelzebub, the god of the Philistine city of Ekron, was a name the Israelites gave to a demon. They frequently translated his name as "Lord of the Flies" in what could be seen as a form of bigotry and religious contempt, corrupting the Philistine's divine name. A more literal translation would be "Prince, Lord of the Earth." See McKenzie, *Dictionary of the Bible*, p. 85.

13.   Jesus made use of certain practices that were akin to a magician's: his cure of the blind man from Bethsaida (Mark 8: 22-26), in which he used his spit, or when he mixed his saliva with dust to make mud, which he smeared on a blind man's eyes (John 9: 6). Such miracles might appear to be magical rites. John Crossan speaks of the interplay between the two means of healing: "...the only objective distinction between magic and religion is that we have religion while they have magic. Magic is especially a term that upper-class religion uses to denigrate its lower-class counterpart." See Crossan, *Jesus, Revolutionary Biography*, p. 10. Also see Crossan, *The Historical Jesus, The Life of a Mediterranean Jewish Peasant*, pp. 303-353.

p. 124

14.   The author of Gabriel allows us to see the fully human side of Jesus, often eclipsed by religious devotion that images him as being more divine than human. The Scripture scholar John McKenzie says, "That Jesus perspired is as much a reality as that he spoke the word of the Gospel; but I have never heard of a devotion to the Sacred Sweat." See McKenzie, *Source, What the Bible Says About Contemporary Life*, p. 154. Regarding the condition of his teeth, recall that in his day only a very small percentage of people lived to the age of thirty. Furthermore, nutritional and dental knowledge was, by modern standards, primitive. See also the note for page 16.

15.   "As proverbs testify, adolescent boys fourteen to sixteen years old are punished physically rather routinely for the purpose of inuring them to physical pain. The authentic male in this (Palestinian) culture is one who can endure pain," says John Pilch. He refers to the First Testament parental wisdom in Sirach (30: 1, 9, 12). "The father who loves his son punishes him often that he may be his joy when he grows up....Pamper your child and he will be a terror to you....Beat his sides while he is still small, or else he will become stubborn and disobey you." These are a few examples of Biblical child-rearing wisdom. See Pilch and Malina, *Biblical Social Values and Their Meaning*, pp. 128-131. Joseph, the father of Jesus, was a just man, as he is called in the Gospels. Would he have disciplined Jesus, then, other than how a good father was instructed by Sirach in the Hebrew Scriptures? A holy picture of St. Joseph beating the boy Jesus in the ribs would make a thought-provoking meditation! Today that kind of parental behavior would be considered a crime — child abuse. Yet such a holy picture would also provide an excellent reflection on how many of our contemporary Christian attitudes from the Bible might likewise no longer be valid in the modern world. The list could include biblical views on war,

the role and social status of women and views on homosexuality, to mention a few.

16.   Willow bark is one of the oldest sources of pain relief. It contains salicylic acid, used in making aspirin. See Barbara Walker, *The Woman's Dictionary of Symbols and Sacred Objects* (New York: Harper & Row, 1988), p. 474. Sanders states that rabbis taught that it was forbidden, as a form of work, to treat a toothache on the Sabbath by applying vinegar. You could, however, put vinegar on food and then eat it to achieve the same results. See Sanders, *The Historical Figure of Jesus*, p. 208.

p. 125

17.   Proverbs 25: 19-20. The folk wisdom and sayings from Scripture that both Jesus and Judas express here would have been common among devout Jews. The author of Gabriel's Gospel places such sayings and psalm prayers on the lips of Jesus to remind us how steeped he was in his own religious tradition, yet how he stretched beyond it.

CHAPTER NINE

p. 128

1.   Peter's wife, whose name we learn from Gabriel's Gospel, does, after the death of Jesus, indeed accompany her husband to proclaim the good news. Paul refers to this in 1 Corinthians 9: 5: "Do we not have the right to take along a Christian wife, as do the rest of the apostles, and the brothers of the Lord, and Cephas (Peter)." The unique adjective, "Christian," used by Paul, is further addressed in the note for p. 140.

p. 131

2.   Also, the heart of a coward was believed to be devoid of blood. For a discussion on the liver as a source of telling the future, see Ivor H. Evans, ed., *Brewer's Dictionary of Phrase & Fable* (New York: Harper & Row, 1981), p. 676.

p. 134

3.   The author of Mark begins Jesus' public life with John the Baptist's arrest. Marcus Borg suggests that with his mentor in prison, Jesus stepped in to carry on. He also states that the activity of Jesus after his baptism was as little as a year (according to the first three Gospel authors) or as much as three years (according to the author of John, the last Gospel written). See Borg, *Meeting with Jesus Again for the First Time*, pp. 28, 31.

Contemporary scholars believe John the Baptizer was executed because he was a political threat rather than because he spoke out against King Herod Antipas for marrying his brother's wife. Antipas was a son of King Herod the Great and sat on an uneasy throne. The site of John's baptisms — in the desert across the Jordan — was politically charged. His ritual involved a baptismal water crossing into the promised land. Such symbolic actions were overripe with insurrectional juices for both the king and the temple, as well as for Rome. They feared it was awakening a twelve-hundred-year-old memory of Moses and Joshua leading the revolutionary Israelites out of the desert into the promised land. But without doubt, the execution of prophet John by King Herod awakened Jesus to his possible fate. See Crossan's "The Jordan Is Not Just Water" in *Jesus, Revolutionary Biography*, p. 43.

p. 137

4.   John Crossan treats uncontrollable weeds of mustard under the heading of "A Kingdom of Undesirables." Crossan, *The Historical Jesus, The Life of a Mediterranean Jewish Peasant*, pp. 276-280. Wild or domesticated mustard when planted in a field or garden can soon destroy the garden! There were also wild mustard plants that were dangerous to grain fields and considered to be weeds. Mustard plants, *brassica nigra*, do not grow into trees but rather are bushes that grow only three or four feet tall. It would be fruitful to reflect on the radically different ways a Palestinian peasant and a middle-class American would hear Jesus say, "The age of God (the church) is like a mustard seed." In that light, if a Christian family moved into a neighborhood, would those already living there say, "There goes the neighborhood"?

5.   John Pilch calls children at the time of Jesus "walking newspapers." They roamed freely in and out of houses, trained by their parents to spy on what other families were doing or saying. Pilch says that attempts to keep children away from Jesus would stir suspicion that he was up to no good. See Pilch, "The Cultural World of Jesus, Cross-Cultural Reflections" from the essay on Mark 10: 13-16. When Jesus encourages his disciples to become like children, it is important to read the unspoken message. Children in his culture were the lowest of the low and possessed no power, so Jesus uses them as classic examples of the kind of nobodies he is gathering into his community. Later generations of Christians with repressive sexual attitudes would (and do still) use the words of Jesus, "Become like children so you can enter the kingdom," because children are asexual, little celibates.

p. 139

1.   While Jesus is called a teacher and his message called his teachings, was he in fact a teacher? Jesus was certainly not a scholar, not educated, and almost certainly couldn't read or write, as was the case with over ninety-five percent of the Palestinian population. While in the four canonical Gospels Jesus is addressed as "rabbi," he was not a teacher, which the title implies. McKenzie states that this title cannot even be found in Jewish literature of the first century! Not only was Jesus not a scholar, McKenzie says, but his relationship with the educated establishment of his time was uniformly hostile. See McKenzie, *Source, What the Bible Says About Contemporary Life*, p. 197.

Marcus Borg refers to Jesus as a sage, as those possessed of wisdom are called. But if Jesus was a sage, his was a subversive wisdom. Such "crazy" sages in history were men like Lao Tzu and Buddha. Socrates also taught a subversive wisdom and, like Jesus, was executed for it. Finally, a disciple does not mean being a *student* of someone; rather, it means to be a *follower* of someone. See Borg, *Meeting with Jesus Again for the First Time*, pp. 88, 135.

Jesus never calls himself a teacher, but he does call himself "the Way." A way is a lifestyle to be followed; not someone who has knowledge to teach — and certainly not someone simply to be placed on a pedestal to be adored instead of followed. The pre-Easter Jesus was amazingly unique in so many ways; it is sad to give him such a traditional and limiting title as "teacher," and to call his conversations with his disciples and the crowds "preaching." We continue to narrow and restrict our image of Jesus by calling his dynamic, radical lifestyle "his ministry," as if he were a clergy person. However, like his first disciples, we can only refer to him out of our poverty of words. From the stunted sack of selections from the English words available, perhaps it would be best to speak of him as a new kind of fulfilling prophet. This would imply not only one who speaks under divine inspiration, both also one who creates and fulfills the prophecy before your eyes. These are stumbling words that attempt to say that no prophet before, or since, has been like Jesus of Galilee. Prophets foretell the future; Jesus made the future present. Jesus is the Hebrew prophet who confronts those living in the present world with a mirror reflecting God's image of what life and worship should be like. Like the old prophets, Jesus speaks loudly in condemning present injustices and calling people back to doing justice. See Michael Grant, *Jesus, An Historian's Review of the Gospels* (New York: Charles Scribner's Sons, 1977), pp. 138-139.

p. 140

2.　　Recall the note for page 128, in which Paul (1 Corinthians 9: 5) spoke about the apostles traveling with their "Christian" wives. John Crossan asks whether Paul was speaking about real, married wives or referring to a "sister wife" (from one translation of the original Greek). Sister wives were female disciples or missionaries who traveled with the protection of a male disciple. Besides the concern of being alone on the road in a male world of power and violence, a woman would also be seen by others as a whore. The unnamed disciple with Cleopas on the road to Emmaus (see Luke 24: 13-35) would most likely have been a "sister wife," a female disciple-companion. The post-Easter practice of spreading the Gospel mentioned by Paul would logically be an extension of what was done when Jesus was alive. See Crossan, *The Historical Jesus, The Life of a Mediterranean Jewish Peasant*, pp. 334-335. As you ponder this possibility, remember, "Blessed are the elastic," for they shall be able to embrace new ideas and extend the boundaries of their minds and hearts with new truths — even about the Gospels.

3.　　Here, again, Jesus is not so much a teacher as a model to be imitated. If you call Jesus a teacher, then his style was not to teach the lesson, but to be the lesson. Jesus knew what he "taught" from his personal experience of God's loving care.

p. 141

4.　　Jesus' wisdom here in Gabriel's Gospel is also found in the advice of another sage, Confucius. Speaking to a youthful disciple who was overly eager to reform the world, Confucius admonishes him to be cautious and not enter into conflict with peoples' ideal images of themselves. "If they will listen, sing them a song. If not, keep silent. Don't try to break down their door. Don't try out new medicines on them. Just be there among them, because there is nothing else for you to be but one of them. Then you may have success." See Thomas Merton, *The Way of Chuang Tzu* (New York: by New Directions, 1969), p. 53.

5.　　Slavery was an ugly reality of the first century world, and a horrible fate of millions of people. (Greece in 309 B.C.E. had 400,000 slaves in the city of Attica. Half the population of Rome was slaves!) See McKenzie, *Dictionary of the Bible*, p. 824.

　　The word "servant" that appears frequently in the First and Second Testaments should more correctly be translated as "slave." Moses, David and Elijah are referred to as slaves of God. So offensive was the call to freely become a slave of others, especially among the Greek and Roman post-Easter communities, that "slave" was laundered to "servant." McKenzie states that scholars believe that (see John 1: 29) John the Baptist originally said of Jesus, "Behold the slave of God," and not "the lamb of God"! See McKenzie, pp. 791-794. Those today who are opposed to the use of inclusive language in the Scriptures and in worship should reflect on that holy and very early practice of cleansing "offensive" language by the apostolic church.

p. 142

6.   Luke (8: 2-3) lists some of the women who accompanied Jesus and his male disciples and says they "cared for them out of their own resources."

7.   Among the two major religious groups in Israel at that time, the Sadducces did not believe in life after death, while the Pharisees did. Interestingly, the idea of immortality of the soul, which was taken up by Judaism, came from Greece! Resurrection of the body was a transplanted belief from Persia, but these two were usually separate beliefs and not linked. Scholars believe that by the first century they were being combined. See Sanders, *The Historical Figure of Jesus*, p. 170.

In December, 1995 a study on the "unchurched" by the *Journal for Scientific Study of Religion* showed that in America 71% believed in life after death. Of interest, the same study showed that of those unchurched, 90.6% believed in God and over 71% claimed to have experienced the presence of God!

8.   Crossan quotes Andrew Overman that we should not imagine the disciples being sent out on very long journeys. He says that one is never "more than a day's walk from anywhere in lower Galilee." See Crossan, *The Historical Jesus, The Life of a Mediterranean Jewish Peasant*, p. 334.

p. 143

9.   John Pilch speaks of the various kinds of bread eaten at that time, helping us Western readers who buy our bread in stores to get a clearer picture. Bread was shaped in round, flat loaves that looked more like fat pancakes. It was not cut with a knife but broken with the hands. Common bread was course dark barley bread, and wheat bread was a luxury. Wheat bread was twice the price of black bread or barley loaves. See Malina and Rohrbaugh, *Social-Science Commentary on the Synoptic Gospels*, p. 62. Of note, the price of a prostitute was a loaf of bread! See McKenzie, *Dictionary of the Bible*, p. 105.

10.   Jesus does the work of a slave or a woman and serves the meal to his disciples. This causes his male disciples to be disturbed for both reasons: it's either a slave's job or women's work. Here as elsewhere, Jesus lives out what he calls his disciples to be: humble servants. The church has adapted from the Latin word for servant or attendant the name "minister" and a servant's work, "ministry." (In certain countries that term is even used for government officials of a high rank.)

The term minister, after years of misuse — a "minister" not always providing real service — and cloaked with somber religious implications, needs to be retranslated. Jesus' joyful service and his delight in dancing and singing at this supper in Gabriel's Gospel suggest a fresh but ancient name for those who serve in the Christian community — minstrels! These traveling medieval musicians, who sang and recited poetry, made the lives of people more joyful, truly bringing glad tidings. In Old French the name meant entertainer and servant. The good news would be welcomed more quickly if it were proclaimed by minstrels instead of ministers. The service of Gospel people would be more compassionate and fun, and therefore more redeeming, if performed by joyful minstrels rather than grim-faced, job-oriented ministers.

11.   This evening meal of the disciples is also an Epiphany (Greek for "manifest") Eucharist, a foreshadowing of the Last Supper. Such friendship meals were common among Jewish spiritual masters and their disciples. The term "Last" refers not only to it being Jesus' final meal before his death, it also implies that there were other suppers of significance. Jesus could well have said, "By this you will know my disciples, by the way they enjoy eating together."

p. 144

12.   Dancing has been an important part of both common and sacred celebrations among most peoples, and this is certainly true in Jewish religious and cultural life. Dancing was central to weddings and other village celebrations. The Israelites danced in their celebration of the victory over Egypt, and David danced before the ark as it entered Jerusalem. Prophets danced as part of the prophetic trance, and Jeremiah (31: 13) saw it as one of the joys of Messianic Israel. Jesus surely would have taken great pleasure in dancing, in being a dancer in the tradition of King David, his ancestor (who in 2 Samuel, chapter 6 wore only a loincloth and danced "with abandon...leaping and dancing").

Brueggemann, speaking of how in the psalms good news is so often greeted with dancing, recalls the dancing in the streets of Paris as people welcomed American troops in the Second World War or the dancing in the streets of Manila when Marcos left the country. See Brueggemann, *Israel's Praise, Doxology Against Idolatry and Ideolgy*, p. 37. Also see McKenzie, *Dictionary of the Bible*, p. 171.

Surprising — but another sign of the dehumanizing of Jesus — is the scarcity of art images of him dancing. How ironic too that dancing is usually seen as unsuitable to sacred ritual in Christian worship.

p. 145

13.   See the map on page 12.

14.   While in the company of others, Jesus hears the voice of God, in the voice of his muse, his guardian angel messenger, which sometimes comes as an inner-voice. Listening to such a voice that calls us beyond religious and cultural boundaries into a fuller life is essential for holy heroism. To hear that inner-voice can seem to be madness — and, again, there is a need for careful discernment. Yet, that voice links us with the highest mysterious powers, with God. The voice of God can often come in what we call "a thought" or in a person's inner conscience (which is different from a "religious" or "moral" conscience). See Becker, *The Denial of Death*, p. 203.

Prayer, in one sense, is a retreat in the face of conflict or crisis to hear the voice. However, hearing the voice does not require silence and can happen anytime, whether alone or in the company of others. The voice always carries the message to "Ascend...go up...higher." It has been spoken ever since creation began and is the call of evolutionary growth. Humans have ever heard it as the call to expand the range of human potential. The voice always takes us to the edge of our gifts and talents and possibilities — and beyond.

15.   Variety in creation is what makes life on earth possible, according to Michael Dowd, and the Creator delights in diversity! We are in harmony with the earth and with God when we celebrate the variety of what God has made. The promotion of conformity or uniformity, on the other hand, along with hostility to differences, frequently seems to be the main work of orthodox churches. We need to reflect on how such rigid conformity is contrary to creation and, therefore, ungodly. See Dowd, *Earthspirit, A Handbook for Nurturing an Ecological Christianity*, pp. 41-42.

p. 146

16.   See Jeremiah (25: 15-29) for his condemnation of this pagan area

along the Mediterranean sea. Tyre, a prosperous port city infamous for its slave trade and worship of Baal, was condemned by other Jewish prophets as well. Tyre and the other port city of Sidon had incalculable cultural and religious influence upon Israel. King Solomon's temple, for example, was built on designs by craftsmen from Tyre. The journey of Jesus to this area is documented by the authors of Mark (7: 24) and Matthew (15: 21). See McKenzie, *Dictionary of the Bible*, p. 905.

17.   The Phoenician woman, a gentile, refers to the Greek and Roman god of healing, Aesculapius. His sign was a serpent intertwined on a staff, which today is a familiar symbol of the medical profession. The sick came to his temples which were filled with snakes that were made sacred in his honor. Cures often involved sleeping with the snakes overnight in his temple. See Edith Hamilton, *Mythology, Timeless Tales of Gods and Heroes* (Boston: Little, Brown and Co., 1942), p. 279. Also, Greek references from this period point to the numerous medicinal cures attributed to the god Aesculapius. See Sanders, *The Historical Figure of Jesus*, p. 134.

18.   See Numbers (21: 9) for Moses' healing by mounting a bronze serpent on a pole. In John (3: 14), Jesus speaks of being lifted up like Moses' healing serpent in the desert.

p. 147

19.   Jesus could have answered the objections of his disciples by saying, "Blessed are the inconsistent, for they are free to change their minds whenever God invites them to." He had previously told his disciples, "Do not enter a Samaritan town or go to the pagan territory, but only to the lost sheep of the house of Israel" (Matthew 10: 5-6).

CHAPTER ELEVEN

p. 149

1.   While theaters existed in Israel because of Greek and Roman influence, a devout Jew would never have attended them. They were considered occasions for sin by association with pagans and their pagan subject matter. The Gospel of Gabriel's Jesus shows an open mind, which would have been unusual for a devout Jew of his time. However, Jesus did make frequent use of the Greek theatrical term *hypocrites,* referring to the pious self-righteous. The word *hypocrite* means "an actor" or "to play a part" and originated with the masks that actors used in playing their various roles. Jesus' use of the term showed he had knowledge of Greek drama.

     Some historical background might help explain Jesus' knowledge of the theater and his openness to Greek drama. Less than four miles from Nazareth was the city of Sepphoris (not mentioned in any of the four canonical Gospels). Its population of forty thousand made it the largest city in Galilee. When King Herod the Great died in 4 B.C.E. (shortly after the birth of Jesus), a rebellion in Sepphoris had to be put down by the Roman troops, during which a large part of the city was destroyed. Both Pilch and Borg say that included in the rebuilding of Sepphoris in the early part of the first century was a Roman-style theater. In these circular stone outdoor theaters both Greek and Roman plays were performed. Pilch proposes that since both Joseph and his son Jesus were stone masons, it would not have been unlikely that they would daily travel the short distance there and back to work on the construction of Sepphoris' new theater. Thus, Greek drama may have been part of Jesus' early life. See Borg, *Meeting with Jesus Again for the First Time*, p. 25-26.

2.   Greek theater began as sacred liturgy, in which priests were the actors. Drama was a laboratory for the imagination of poets and the priest-actors. See Daniel Boorstin, *The Creators, A History of Heroes of the Imagination* (New York: Vintage Books, 1992), p. 153. It also involved spectators as concelebrants. They could not escape being real participants in the play as they escaped their daily lives. The drama of heroes, even to this day, kindles the flame of heroism that flickers in every heart — and this profoundly engages the spectator. The artist, Sr. Corita Kent, once said that if Jesus were alive today he would not tell parables but would take people to the movies. Plays and movies hold great power to awaken the soul and stir the heart in many ways, including the heroic.

p. 150

3.   Thespis was one of the creative geniuses of Greek theater. He was the first to use an actor as one standing apart from the chorus. He created thirty different masks for the actors. According to Aristotle, he was the inventor of Greek tragedy. See Boorstin, *The Creators, A History of Heroes of the Imagination*, p. 210.

4.   Jesus, here, as at other times, does not so much break the law, be it the official laws of Moses (regarding the Sabbath, association with those unclean, lepers, etc.) or the laws of common custom. Rather, being firmly in touch with a higher law, he simply ignores those laws that do not apply to him or his present situation. While he does not ask others to violate their conscience, he could have said to his disciples, "Learn of me for I am a meek outlaw, who lives outside of — beyond — the law."

5.   The strong opposition to attending the theater play by James the Orthodox represents the Jewish view of Greek drama at that time. As the future first bishop of Jerusalem, James also reveals what will become the position of the early church after the first centuries. The theater was banned as a stronghold of paganism, an occasion for sin, by the church fathers from the early church down through the middle ages. The same fate was shared by musical instruments in worship and dancing as a form of religious joy. See the *Encyclopaedia Britannica* (1960, vol.7: Drama. pp. 576-589). McKenzie, noting how the church requires its clergy to be examples of faithfully following the way of Christ, says, "In most European countries it has long been the rule that priests are suspended (forbidden to exercise their priestly powers) for attending the theater or the races...in the early church the prohibition of attending the theater and races (gladiatorial games) was imposed upon all Christians." See McKenzie, *Source, What the Bible Says About Contemporary Life*, p. 215.

p. 152

6.   The tragedy of the sufferings, violent death and resurrection of the god Dionysius presented in this play is primarily the work of the poet Nonnus but is blended with other legends about Dionysius. See Frazer, *The Golden Bough*, p. 450. Dionysius was believed to take the form of a goat and was worshipped in Athens as "The One of the black goat skin." His worshipers would ritually kill a goat and eat it raw, believing they were eating the body and blood of their god. The Gospel of Gabriel's presentation of a mirror image from Greek drama to reflect the approaching violent death and resurrection of Jesus shows how God uses artists, poets and historical events as prophets. The mythologies of the world's ancient peoples, of which the story of Dionysius is a part, while sometimes seen as pagan fantasy stories, might well be considered ancient Scripture, part of the truly *Old* Testament.

7.   Dionysius' cradle was a winnowing fan basket of grain, while Jesus had a manger feed trough. These birthing grain containers are symbolic of both Jesus and Dionysius becoming food of life for their followers.

p. 154

8.   The earth mother Demeter was the corn goddess of Greek legend. She was the protectress of the home as well as agriculture and all the fruits of the earth. See Frazer, *The Golden Bough*, pp. 456, 462. Also see Hamilton, *Mythology, Timeless Tales of Gods and Heroes*, pp. 40, 47-54, 159.

9.   The words of Gamos about those attending a play being both worshipers and priestly actors/actresses apply to all liturgy as well, for good worship is the art of entering into the mysteries of death and rebirth. It is not play acting, but reenacting the play of the passion, death and resurrection which is the central human drama. The theater today continues to speak of deeply human and holy realities. Even in seemingly secular theater, the sacred is present beneath the surface. There is no room for mere spectators at church or the theater.

10.   These words of Gamos about life after death were borrowed from the letter a first-century Greek father wrote to his wife concerning the death of their young daughter. See Hamilton, *Mythology, Timeless Tales of Gods and Heroes*, p. 62.

p. 155

11.   Boorstin says, "In the ocean of time all men (people) swam together..." and then quotes the great poet and playwright, Euripides (485-406 B.C.E.). See Boorstin, *The Creators, A History of Heroes of the Imagination*, p. 213.

p. 156

12.   God is not limited in choosing mouths to speak with a prophetic voice, and not limited only to speaking in the First and Second Testaments. Gabriel's statement reflects the teaching on inspiration declared by the Second Vatican Council: "The Catholic Church rejects nothing that is true and holy in non-Christian religions...(that) often reflect a ray of that truth which enlightens all people." *Decree on Ecumenism*, no. 4.

13.   Scapegoat: see the note on p. 85.

14.   Jesus' natural fear of death assures us that he took on the full human condition. Ernest Becker says, "The human animal is characterized by two great fears that other animals are protected from: the fear of death and the fear of life." See Becker, *The Denial of Death*, p. 53. Jesus also feared life, as we all do. He had to overcome his fear of living life fully, using all his gifts, living with great passion, with all his senses keenly awakened. We fear life because living fully costs so much. It means standing out from the crowd as a unique individual, risking others' censure. While each human has a unique voiceprint and fingerprints, we all fear being unique. We shrink back from both death and life. Once Jesus had transformed these two fears into twin dynamic energies, he was able to continuously give the gift of life. He called himself the bread of life and

said he had come that all might have life and have it in great abundance (see John 6: 35, 10:10).

p. 157

15.   Gabriel's prediction about the cross becoming a standard of victory would seem insane to a first-century Jew or early Christian, since for three hundred years the cross would remain an ugly, detested symbol of capital punishment. It would be like proposing the electric chair as a symbol of hope. The non-Christian emperor Constantine, however, on the eve of the battle of Saxa Rubra in 312 said he saw a luminous cross in the sky with the words *In hoc vinces*, "by this (sign) you (shall) conquer." He ordered the cross and motto placed on his soldiers' shields, as he said he was told to do by his vision. He actually adopted not a cross, but the monogram XPI, the first three Greek letters of the word for Christ. From that time onward, the cross slowly became both an accepted sign for the state and religion. Sadly, the cross, a sign of Jesus' nonviolence, became the sign of victory in war and led centuries of warriors into what Jesus had so passionately condemned!

Paradoxically, the sign of Christianity, the Latin cross, in which the upright shaft is longer than the horizontal one, was originally a pagan symbol. Some theologians of the early church were violently opposed to its use as a holy sign, but in time it was universally accepted. See *Brewer's Dictionary of Phrase & Fable*, p. 290.

p. 158

16.   "Free as a wave," sings Gabriel, and could have added, "Remember these waves, Jesus, and be a *ronin*," Japanese for "wave men." Ronin were young idealists, a special class of masterless samurai warriors. They believed in the new "heresy," which was considered outrageous because it professed that the highest duty was to more than some lord, to more than family, but was a duty to the Emperor alone. Jesus was guilty of such a samurai heresy and was a servant to God alone. See James Clavel, *Gai-jin* (New York: Bantam Doubleday Dell Publishing Group, 1993), p. 33.

17.   Often called the *eighth day*. This great jubilee Sabbath of the eighth day has its preface in every free day, every leisurely Sunday and whenever peace is proclaimed in war, even in a household dispute. As we anticipate this great tomorrow in the midst of our unpeaceful todays, whenever a jubilee is celebrated or a Sabbath tasted, we might toast, "Long live the eighth day."

CHAPTER TWELVE

p. 160

1.   Jesus offers a heroic life and death to his followers when he invites us to take up our crosses and follow him. The rejection by many and the misunderstanding by others underscores how unheroic most of us are, even when we follow a hero. As followers, we usually do not take the cross but rather unload our personal baggage on the leader and follow with reservations — and usually, as Becker says, "with a dishonest heart." See Becker, *The Denial of Death*, p. 136. The rejection by many disciples is repeated again and again in history when Christ's followers choose church membership over discipleship. For the contemporary Christian, this is not usually an either/or choice, but one of priority: Which comes first, discipleship or membership?

p. 161

2.   The rich young man's difficulty in following Jesus involved more than surrender of money and property, as is often thought. To dispossess oneself, which is the call of discipleship, means to die to the power of wealth and prestige, security and status. While wearing invisible armor may make daily life uncomfortable, it is usually preferred to the risk of being vulnerable or wounded, preferred to the possibility of death or madness. The rich young man is, therefore, the "smart" young man, who knows what is being asked of him. Jesus is inviting him to stop playing a role, to make himself poor of all glib and empty talk, the clever clichés by which so many live only on the surface of life. Strip yourself, Jesus says in secret code, of all the tactics you learned as a child to win approval and please others. The poverty of discipleship, what is at stake in following Jesus, involves a life of being stripped of all this armor until death finally rips off even the last scrap of self-control.

     Becker quotes Kierkegaard's story about a certain young man who is much like the rich young man in this scene who came to Jesus. Kierkegaard tells of an outwardly successful university graduate, who, while Christian, didn't go to church very much. The young man said that priests didn't know what they were talking about. Eventually he found an exception, someone who lived what he talked about. But now he didn't go to church to hear the priest for another reason: he feared the priest might lead him too far! See Becker, *The Denial of Death*, p. 83. While there is a promise of heroism in the invitation, the young man found, as do most of us, that the cost is too great.

p. 162

3. Wealth was seen as the fruit of wisdom (see Proverbs 24: 3-4) and diligence (see Proverbs 10: 4) and the reward for humble obedience and awe of God. Proverbs (10: 22) also states that "wealth is the blessing of God." While the piety of poor peasants was upheld in Hebrew Scriptures and wealth was sometimes shown as a disadvantage, in general riches were seen as a reward for a good life. This view of wealth being God's blessing for a devout life continues to be held by most good Christians who consider banks almost as holy as churches, as tabernacles of God's rewards. Jesus, on the other hand, held a radical view that wealth is an insurmountable obstacle to salvation — unless it is generously shared with those who are poor. McKenzie, *Dictionary of the Bible*, p. 924. For Jesus, such sharing is not viewed as great charity but only as justice.

4. "Leave your bread in the oven and your goat tied to the post," Jesus said, but was implying that far more than a few small possessions had to be left behind. Ched Myers points out that normally students followed a teacher "as long as it took to attain rabbinic status" but that "the call of Jesus was absolute," and lifelong. Jesus offered a course in holiness from which there is no graduation. See Myers, *Binding the Strong Man*, p. 133. For the poorest of the poor or the richest of the rich, this meant lifelong discipleship, which was — and is — too disrupting to an average life. Those of us who are adult converts to Christianity as well as those of us who are cradle disciples might reflect on whether we are followers who have graduated or followers who have much further to travel.

p. 164

5. This feeding of the thousands with bread and fish is another Epiphany Eucharist, a looking forward to the Lord's Supper and the ritual meals of the post-Easter church. It is an Epiphany Eucharist with regard to the food shared and the inclusivity of who is invited to the meal — and to the role of Jesus as the servant and host. See the third note for p. 143.

p. 165

6. (See Matthew 3: 12, Luke 3: 17, a reference to Jeremiah 15: 7: "I will use my winnowing fan in every city gate.")

p. 167

7. Their song is a combination of verses from Psalms 47, 48 and 84.

8. The Gospel of Gabriel's Jesus speaks of the apostolic church, which

would know no distinction between clergy and laity. The Scripture scholar John McKenzie said he could find nowhere in the New Testament any trace of a priestly or ministerial class. In his words, "The New Testament church eliminated the sacred, in the ancient and still usual sense of the term, from religion....(and knew) no sacred places, sacred objects, sacred rites — or sacred personnel." See McKenzie, *Source, What the Bible Says About Contemporary Life*, pp. 76, 161, 214-215.

p. 168

9.   Satan, the tempter, keeps his desert promise that after Jesus rejected his first offer he would return. The tempter will return yet again.

p. 169

10.   The great temptation of any charismatic leader is to use the magic of leadership to serve his or her own personal ends. An imposing person who acts with self-confidence, as do all great leaders, has almost magical, hypnotic powers over his or her followers. While it lies hidden beneath the surface, humans have an inner urge to merge with power figures. None of us is immune, says Becker, from this urge, regardless of how independent we may appear. Perhaps it is the perpetual awe of the child for the parent that is placed like a cloak around a leader, or on the shoulders of teachers, superiors and impressive personalities. That urge suggests how followers of cult leaders might even engage in mass suicide or commit horrible crimes. Jesus the liberator does not imprison his disciples by playing on this hunger. He does not allow his disciples to hand over to him their egos and become dependent children blindly following him, caught up in his magical spell, his hero's charism. They are called to deny their very selves, but that gift of self is given to God alone. The Shadow's temptation is for Jesus to use even his holy power over his followers in the service of God.

Becker speaks of our deep-seated hunger for the "oceanic feeling" of the merging with God that we experience with our parents, and our desire to satisfy our deep-seated erotic longings. For further reading on this human phenomenon of a hunger that leads to personal or group servitude so evident in the phenomenon of a Hitler and in gurus and religious cult leaders, see Becker, *The Denial of Death*, pp. 131, 140.

p. 171

11.   Demeter, again, was the Greek corn mother, the protectress of field, garden and home. She was identified with the Roman earth goddess

Ceres, whose name was given to our breakfast food, cereal — all edible grains, like oats, corn and wheat. There is a catholic, or global, devotion to this earthen mother, who is also known as the pea mother, the potato mother and, in Asia, the rice mother. See Frazer, *The Golden Bough*, pp. 456, 462.

The deep and long-lasting devotion to Mary, the mother of Jesus, and the continuing vitality of her mother image in Christianity is partially rooted in this primal earth mother worship. The Catholic Church has always strictly maintained that Mary is never worshiped, worship being reserved only for God, but is only honored in devotion. Still, in many of the Marian religious folk customs of Northern Europe, one finds the "baptized" devotions of the holy earth mothers Demeter and Ceres.

In the ancient religions of the world, God planted a sapling which over the long centuries has grown into a great tree whose branches hold the rich fruits of many devotions. If the fruit of a tree is holy, good for body and soul, should one ridicule or be ashamed of a tree's trunk and roots?

12.   Mary here sings of herself as the Blessed Crone, a withered old woman. In the devotions of the peoples of Mexico and the American Southwest, Mary is also dressed in black and is pictured as an old, wrinkled woman. Mary is the archetype of the crone, a very powerful figure, the *Nuestra Senora de la Soledad*. This image of her is frequently part of Good Friday processions. See Thomas Steele, S.J., *Santos and Saints, The Religious Folk Art of Hispanic New Mexico* (Santa Fe: Ancient City Press, 1994), p. 155.

This old holy hag image is not restricted to Spanish devotions but has deep roots in Poland, Russia and throughout Europe, all connected to the annual dying of creation. In late autumn, various customs surround the harvesting of the last sheaf of grain (in honor of the earth mother), which is called "the Old Woman." See Frazer, *The Golden Bough*, pp. 463-491.

Think of the social and personal implications today in the American Church (with its aging population) if Mary, the mother of Jesus, were also depicted in religious art as an old, gray-haired woman instead of always as a youthful girl dressed in blue and white. Such devotional art would be of great assistance in responding in a spiritual way to the various issues of aging. Mary could become a model for aging women as well as a holy, immaculate virgin.

p. 172

13.   This invitation to see one's cross as an upright birthing bed has many possibilities for reflection. One such meditation might be: What am I birthing out of my pain and suffering, a new and vital life or something stillborn?

14.   In 587 B.C.E. at the hands of the Babylonians, Jerusalem was destroyed, the temple burned and the dynasty of King David terminated, as Judah's leading citizens were deported. The Babylonian Captivity lasted until 539 B.C.E. when the Babylonian empire was conquered by the Persians. While devastating to the Jewish spirit, the Exile gave us three great prophets: Jeremiah, Ezekiel and Second Isaiah.

Marcus Borg speaks of the three great memory stories of the Jewish peoples: the Exodus from Egypt, the Babylonian Exile, and the Priestly Story, which dealt with the temple, priesthood and sacrifice. See Borg, *Meeting with Jesus Again for the First Time*, pp. 119-137. While the metaphor of the Exodus is frequently recalled today, that of the Babylonian Exile is not. Yet the experience of exile, a profound sense of not belonging, not being part of what is happening, is very much alive in our world. Borg and Brueggemann suggest that, in many ways, exile is the state of the church today!

15.   This poem-song of Jesus is a weaving of verses from one of the prophets of the Exile (see Second Isaiah, chapters 40, 42 and 49).

Walter Brueggemann speaks of a poet as one who wants us to experience the present world in new images or metaphors and to be open to new and alternative worlds that are not yet visible. Poetic prophets use a kind of language (often shocking) that cannot be fully digested at first hearing or reading. Brueggemann agrees with Paul Ricoeur that people are changed not by ethical urging but by transformed imagination. See Brueggemann, *Hopeful Imagination, Prophetic Voices in Exile* (Philadelphia: Fortress Press, 1986), pp. 24-25. Jesus in the well shows his creativity, his capacity for transformed imagination, in an action-parable.

16.   Jesus invites his disciples to sing a new song that cancels out the old anthems of the temple and empire. Brueggemann says, "The summons of this poet (referring to Isaiah — equally true of Jesus) is not to express religious poetry. It is to shape communal imagination so that its true situation can be discerned. People cannot operate in new ways unless they are able to see afresh their real cultural circumstance." See Brueggemann, *Hopeful Imagination, Prophetic Voices in Exile*, p. 107.

17.   Like a good jazz musician, Jesus improvises on the words of Isaiah 52 in his song of the happy, beautiful feet that carry the good news of the end of the Exile.

18.   Psalm 137.

19.   The words and rituals of religious worship can easily be worshipped themselves. They are often made godlike and untouchable, impossible to alter or change, except by those in power, because part of their function is to maintain the present power structures. More than expressions of tradition, old songs and old rituals can be efficient control systems against the "virus" of change, even prophetic change. The religious institution, temple or church, often carefully tries to drain away from the great memories any power to energize those who sing them — especially those who might seek to escape from exile or seek freedom in a new exodus. Dangerous memories, like wild beasts in a zoo, must be kept carefully caged behind holy bars.

20.   Jesus' song is a fresh insight into Isaiah (65: 17) about creating a new heaven and a new earth, especially in regard to a restoration of creation as promised in Isaiah (41: 18-20). Part of the work of ecology is to restore rivers, lakes and forests to their original state. Rather than seeing such an expression of ecological concern as a "movement," we might consider it as a mystical participation in the presence of the age of God.

p. 176

21.   Jesus is referring to the desert of Judah. The hills of that geographic area slope downward into the biblical wilderness. While the land produces some fruit and vegetables, it is mostly marked by outcroppings of rock. The ecological damage has been caused by deforestation and neglect, which has caused over two thousands years of erosion. Historians believe that once in ancient times this area was heavily forested. See McKenzie, *Dictionary of the Bible*, p. 461. Redemption and renewal should not be limited to humans but should include all of God's creation. Ecology needs a theology that can properly begin to deal with the greed and arrogance with which humans relate to the earth as a resource to exploit.

22.   Jesus provides a path of transformation, first for the individual, then collectively for a society and then for the world. To his community belong those who are perpetually "on the road," journeying from the bondage of self-preoccupation to the freedom of self-forgetfulness which allows for communion with God. The early post-Easter community of disciples did not call themselves Christians, but people of the Way (see Acts 9: 2: "...any women or men who belong to the Way"). Jesus had called himself the Way, and his first disciples had a keen sense of being in transition. Baptism, like graduation from school, implies an end to the

road for most Christians, rather than a beginning of a lifelong process.

23.   The proper name Immanuel, which means "God among us," may have begun as a religious slogan). In this hope-filled prophecy, Jesus proclaims that it is God who will save Israel and with it all who mourn in exile. No earthly savior will arise to end the exile; only when God comes among us is there cause for rejoicing. Those in power who send dreamers into exile limit human possibilities, but the prophets born in the exile proclaim that with God all things are possible. Here, as elsewhere, Jesus affirms God's advent, God's power and presence, as the most revolutionary element of liberation or salvation. Most who live in exile quickly become adjusted to being away from home and make exile their home. Brueggemann points out how it is God who ends every advent, quoting Jeremiah's prophetic words of God: "And I will bring you back to the place from which I sent you into exile" (Jeremiah 29: 11-14). See Brueggemann, *Hopeful Imagination, Prophetic Voices in Exile*, p. 30.

CHAPTER THIRTEEN

p. 177

1.   See the map on page 12.

p. 178

2.   Hosea 6: 6.

3.   Joel 1: 13-14.

p. 179

4.   The rabbis, McKenzie says, counted 613 different commandments within the five books of Moses, called the Torah or the Law. These were then subdivided into 365 positive commandments and 248 prohibitions. See McKenzie, *Source, What the Bible Says About Contemporary Life*, pp. 132-133. Jesus gave us one positive commandment, to love God with all our heart and with all our being, and to love, be compassionate, to our neighbor as we are compassionate to ourselves.

5.   This image of his disciples as parrots is from John Crossan, who says, "Jesus left behind him thinkers not memorizers, disciples not reciters, people not parrots." See Crossan, *The Historical Jesus, The Life of a Mediterranean Jewish Peasant*, p. xxxi.

6.   Jesus' reference to himself as a map can also be found in the wisdom of the sage Lao Tzu, who speaks for all healing sages when he

says, "My own words are not the medicine, but a prescription; not the destination, but a map to help you reach it." See Brian Walker, *Hua Hu Ching, the Unknown Teachings of Lao Tzu* (New York: HarperCollins, 1992), p. 35. In that same chapter, Lao Tsu gives excellent advice to disciples and scholars of the Way: "Don't analyze the Tao (the Way). Strive instead to live it; silently, undividedly, with your whole harmonious being."

p. 180

7.   See Walker, *The Woman's Dictionary of Symbols and Sacred Objects*, p. 374. The fish was an ancient symbol for Jesus Christ among early Christians. The Greek word *Ichthus* formed an acronym of the initial letters for Jesus Christ, Son of God, Savior. This symbol was used frequently for Jesus by Christians until the end of the fourth century.

8.   The believed aphrodisiac-like qualities of fish may have arisen because of their association with that mother goddess of Ephesus, who was pictured with a fish amulet over her genitals. It was in this famous mother goddess' city in 431 that the Council of Ephesus gave to Mary, the mother of Jesus, her title of *Theotokos*, the Mother of God. The Latin *piscina*, which became the name for the baptismal font, literally meant "the fish pond," and converts were called *pisciculi*, little fish! Fish and bread, not wine and bread, appeared as Christian symbols on the walls of the catacombs and early tombs of martyrs. See Hans Biedemann, translation by James Hulbert, *Dictionary of Symbolism* (New York: Facts on File Inc., 1992), p. 131.

p. 181

9.   John McKenzie, writing on the radical call of Jesus to nonviolence, speaks about the "Christian Just War" theory of some theologians. This theory allows Christians to kill in war if it is truly a just cause and one of self-defense. McKenzie challenges that position by asking why the church does not also have theories of morally just fornication, morally just adultery, morally just rape or morally just child abuse." See McKenzie, *The Civilization of Christianity*, p. 125.

p. 182

10.   Jesus is shockingly silent concerning what many Christians today consider to be the gravest of sins: abortion. While a serious moral issue, I again quote the scripture scholar Father John McKenzie, "...about abortion let it be said that the Bible says nothing about it...which does not mean it

is not a live moral problem; it means...like other problems in moral life, it must be solved by the Christian wisdom of believers for themselves." (The Bible is silent) "...on the common method of birth control practiced in the Roman world, especially among the poor; this was the exposure of unwanted infants to die from starvation and exposure." On the issue of homosexuality, "...let me say again that the Bible says nothing about it. The few references are casual and random and...reflect no more than the cultural patterns of the time...after all the Bible condemns witches to death, and we no longer do that." See McKenzie, *Source, What the Bible Says About Contemporary Life*, pp. 85, 86, 90.

Scholars agree that Jesus is also silent on one of the horrible immoralities of his day — slavery! If Jesus is a second Moses, he is not like him in regard to being a law giver. Instead of adding to religious laws, Jesus goes to the heart of the problem in a way that would end war, slavery and all sins against God and neighbor: "Love, be compassionate as God is compassionate, for in that one law all the others are contained."

11.   McKenzie sums it up very well, "The simple see at once that the 'way' of Jesus is very hard to do, but easy to understand." McKenzie, *The Civilization of Christianity*, p. 205.

12.   The Gospel of Gabriel's Jesus speaks poetically as one who knows about marriage, yet the author of this Gospel leaves unexplored the question as to whether or not Jesus was married. While that could be a central subject in a much needed new gospel for today's world, it should be noted here that the authors of the four inspired Gospels say nothing on that issue either. We know of Jesus' great love for his disciple John from the author of that Gospel. We know of his love and fondness for Mary Magdalene, Martha and Mary and their brother Lazarus, at whose grave he wept, causing those present to remark on how much Jesus loved him.

If Jesus was fully human and like us in all things except sin, then he must have been a great lover! Celibacy was not a free choice for a young man in his culture since parents arranged marriages for their children when they were very young. Anthony Padovano quotes the Mishnah, the first section of the Talmud (see the note on p. 13), comprising a collection of oral interpretations of Scriptures, "When a bachelor attains the age of twenty and is unmarried, the Holy One says: 'Let him perish.'" It also forbade living without a spouse unless one were a widower. Further, to become a teacher (i.e., a rabbi) one had to fulfill four requirements, one of which was to have entered marriage. See Anthony T. Padovano, "Is It Just Possible That Jesus Was Married," *National Catholic Reporter*, April 12, 1996, p. 13.

It is not impossible, then, but very doubtful, that Jesus was never married. It is more likely that when the Gospels begin to speak of him he was a widower. Since at the age of about thirty, Jesus would have been among the small twenty-five percent still alive (see the note concerning average ages on p. 16), his wife might easily have been among the seventy-five percent who were dead by that age. While marriage domesticates wild young men and tames revolutionaries, we know that Jesus did not require celibacy from his disciples.

On the other hand, nothing is said in the Second Testament about a Mrs. John the Baptist! His ascetic lifestyle would not easily lend itself to marriage. Heroic liberators and great charismatic leaders throughout history have been either unmarried, widowed or had invisible wives (or husbands). Their single life, while not without love or companionship, seems to give to them an aura, that mysterious quality of being married to a nation, a people or some great cause. This marriageless state seems to give them the magic to become everyone's best friend, lover, spouse and parent. The absence of a spouse may have been part of the magnetic power of Jesus.

p. 184

13.   Scholars like John Crossan maintain that the area across the Jordan was politically dangerous, for it was filled with volatile memories for an oppressed people. King Herod Antipas, the temple authorities and even the Romans understood the symbolic message of John's baptismal crossing of the Jordan! Not only John, but other millennial prophets gathered crowds there to enact a second Exodus. See Crossan, *The Historical Jesus, The Life of a Mediterranean Jewish Peasant*, p. 231.

p. 185

14.   Deuteronomy 3: 25-29. Moses died before the Hebrews crossed the Jordan. It is highly significant that the location of his burial place was unknown, nor was any site assigned for it. In the Near East the graves of notable persons are almost universally acknowledged, with or without historical claims. Yet Moses ranked as the most important person in the history of his people, the greatest prophet and leader of the Hebrew nation.

p. 188

15.   The continuous challenge of keeping anything new and fresh is what Jesus gives to his disciples, then and now. The *New* Testament, after two thousands years, is less often seen as newly radical and freshly challenging. As with all covenants, friendships and professions, each day

must be a new day which is greeted anew, with wonder and gratitude. How to keep the rituals of religion fresh, and therefore dynamically alive, is extremely challenging considering the religious traditions and laws that rigidly restrict creativity and vitality.

CHAPTER FOURTEEN

p. 190

1.   Jesus' one-word prayer of "Amen" is like the Muslim word of praise that is liberally sprinkled through their day, *Inshallah*, which means, "Allah (God) willing." In the Book of Revelation, or the Apocalypse (3: 14), Jesus calls himself the "Amen," one who is faithful to God's word. To pray this prayer of Amen, then, is actually to pronounce the holy name of Jesus, in which the apostle Paul places enormous power.

Amen is a perfect prayer; as disciples, we need to remember that Jesus warned his followers about saying long prayers. He encouraged only short prayers prayed in private. While Jesus shows no interest in fasting and ascetical practices, personal prayer dominates his life. He also calls his disciples to pray ceaselessly so as to remain firmly on the Way (see Luke 21: 36). In any age, those who call themselves disciples of Jesus are challenged by his passion for prayer.

p. 192

2.   Paul indicates the mysterious nature of prayer when he says we do not know how to pray as we should. Encouragement is found in the fact that the Spirit of the Holy takes our feeble groans and sighs and weaves them into prayers that reach the heart of God (see Romans 8: 26).

p. 193

3.   John the disciple seems to be referring to the Qumran Essenes, a priestly-led monastic community on the northwest coast of the Dead Sea. Their "monastery" was a haven for those who judged the temple and its rituals polluted after the Hasmonean rulers had taken over the high priesthood between 152 and 134 B.C.E. Unlike Jesus' small community, in which all were equal, the Essenes were a hierarchical society. They also had ritual meals, but these were always led by a priest. See Crossan, *The Historical Jesus, The Life of a Mediterranean Jewish Peasant*, p. 402. The Essenes were prophetic in their fleeing from the world to create a pure religious society. This search for a purer expression of religion has been repeated numerous times — individually, as in the case of hermits, and

communally during the past two thousand years.

4.   John (3: 16-17) says that God so loved the world (with all its vices, sex, crime and greed) as to give the Son so that all might have eternal life. God did not send the Son into the world to condemn the world (the preoccupation of some Christians) but that the world might be liberated, saved, through him. This sacrificial gift, while difficult to comprehend, does reveal the passionate love of God — who is willing to give the Son over to death for the liberation of the world. James the Just, who will later become the first bishop of Jerusalem, however, reflects the position of early Christianity that tended to hate rather than love the world for God's sake. By the third or fourth century, holiness, being a true disciple, only seemed possible by rejecting marriage, the theater, involvement in politics and business, along with a disdain, if not hatred, for the human body.

p. 194

5.   Luke's Jesus says, "Blessed are the poor...," (Luke 6: 20) while Matthew's Jesus says, "Blessed are the poor in spirit..." (Matthew 5: 3). Matthew's Jesus seems to speak not of economical but spiritual poverty and, as with Peter in this scene, it is the version preferred by most contemporary Christians.

John Pilch, John Crossan, Marcus Borg and most scholars speak of the truly radical nature of this beatitude. See Crossan, *The Historical Jesus, The Life of a Mediterranean Jewish Peasant*, pp. 270-276. We might be surprised to learn that the word for "poor" used by both Matthew and Luke did not mean someone living in the state of poverty! The Greek *ptochos* means a beggar, someone without family or home and therefore a foreigner. The poor, whom Jesus calls blessed — and the first to enter the kingdom — are beggars, the destitute, the outcasts. Truly such an unveiling of who is blest in God's eyes might seem shocking and revolutionary to us in the well-fed, mostly middle-class Western church of today.

p. 195

6.   Conflict among Jesus' disciples is an apostolic activity. Early in the church's life, for example, Paul entered into conflict with Peter over the way Peter handled eating with gentiles. Shortly thereafter, conflicts in theology, heresies like Arianism and Gnosticism, appeared, dividing the church. So today's condition of passionate disagreement in the church has its roots with the original disciples. Instead of imposing silence or even more severe measures on one side, the Gospel of Gabriel's Jesus offers another way to deal with a diversity of opinions.

7.   Using marbles as toys dates back to 3000 B.C.E. in Egypt. And the knuckle bones of dogs and sheep were used as magical marbles by fortune tellers, or augurs, as a form of divination a thousand years before they became toys. See Panati, *Extraordinary Origins of Everyday Things*, pp. 368-369.

8.   The metaphor of grapes and marbles is not original with the author of Gabriel's Gospel. The author regrets, however, that he cannot locate its source to give proper credit to its creator.

p. 197

9.   Joel 3: 1-2.

10.   Jesus, as the new Moses, fulfills the ancient dream of God given to Moses in Exodus (19: 6). Speaking of the desert community of refugees who had left Egypt, a land dominated by a priestly caste, God says, "You shall be to me a kingdom of priests, a holy name." Jesus also brings to completion the prophetic dream of Second Isaiah returning to Israel after the Exile: "You yourselves shall be priests of God, and shall be called ministers of our God" (Isaiah 61: 6). This intention of Jesus is also reflected in the epistles of the Second Testament, which give us the mind of the post-Easter church. In 1 Peter (2: 5), the disciples, or Christians, are called living stones who make up the new temple and form a holy priesthood. The fact that the whole church is a chosen race, a royal priesthood, is again said clearly in 1 Peter (2: 9).

p. 198

11.   Joel 3: 3-5.

12.   After being baptized, the body of a new Christian in the early church was anointed with oil as a sign of sharing with Christ (the Anointed One) in his royal office of priest and prophet. While the anointing with chrism oil is still an important part of the ritual of Baptism (not the whole body but only a dab on the forehead), the radical implications of the gifts of priesthood and prophethood for one's daily life are rarely explored in their fullness. Although some Reformation churches began to explore the concept of the laity being the only priesthood, most followed the larger church's emphasis on the clergy. In the closing years of the twentieth century and the beginning of the twenty-first, the Roman Catholic Church is in need of clergy and eagerly encouraging vocations to the priesthood. The Roman Church and the other catholic Christian churches, Orthodox and Reformed, however, show no eagerness to promote vocations to prophethood, the other radical and dangerous gift of baptism into Christ.

p. 201

1.   This principle of conversion by Jesus could be called the Zacchaeus Principle. The practice of feasting on love first may be as radically shocking in today's Christian churches as it was then.

p. 202

2.   This parable is also found in slightly different form in Luke (16: 19-31). Lazarus is a *ptochos* and a good example of what Jesus meant by the poor: a destitute, homeless beggar. See the note for p. 194.

p. 204

3.   Judas expresses a common feeling in a society with limited goods: that this "excessive" action of the unnamed woman was a form of social stealing. When the majority live in poverty, social restitution for such an action is in order. See Malina and Rohrbaugh, *Social-Science Commentary on the Synoptic Gospels*, p. 266. Gandhi might perhaps have agreed with Judas, for he said that when a person has clothing or shoes that are not worn, they are stolen property! In justice such clothing belongs to those without shoes or proper clothing. Jesus also would have been expected to agree with Judas. When he didn't, perhaps he could have said to Judas, "Blessed are those who are inconsistent because of a larger vision, for they shall not become rigid radicals."

This story of extravagant love is also a reflection on poverty, for the last stage of poverty is to give up poverty. One may desire the image of living simply, in holy poverty, yet that image may be clung to as possessively as gold! In Jesus' way, only love can take us to that final stage of poverty. The extravagance of the woman provides an excellent opportunity for us to examine our love of God and one another for its degree of extravagance.

p. 205

4.   Jesus expresses concern, a natural apprehension for a devout Jew, that he be given a proper ritual burial — which would have included the washing and anointing of his body. Only then could a body be safely entombed so wild animals would not dig it up. We see a similar concern today about the proper burial after a deadly disaster has occurred. The first priority is to find the bodies of those killed and then to return them to their families.

p. 206

5.   Proverbs 30: 24-28.

6.   *Sukkot* is Hebrew for the feast of Tabernacles, also called the feast of Tents. It is an autumn harvest festival commanded by the law (see Exodus 23: 16-17 and Exodus 34: 22). Sukkot was a seven-day feast of rejoicing that remembered God's liberation of the Jews from Egypt, and more importantly their entrance as free people into the promised land. Together with feasting and dancing, it required people to carry palm and olive branches. With these and other leafy branches they built tents or booths in which they dwelled for the feast. By this sacred drama reenactment, they commemorated their forty years of living in tents in the desert after their escape from Egypt. See McKenzie, *Dictionary of the Bible*, p. 863-864.

p. 208

7.   Proverbs 30: 29-31.

p. 210

8.   The ram's horn used to announce solemn feasts such as Sukkot or the arrival of the Jubilee year. Again, see the note for p. 18.

9.   Pilate was a prefect, or procurator, and a second-rank Roman governor. His residence was not in Jerusalem but in Caesarea on the Mediterranean coast. At his disposal, historians have suggested, there were as many as 3,000 troops. Near Jerusalem's temple was a small garrison of Roman soldiers in the Antonia Fortress. The Roman prefect would come to Jerusalem with additional troops during major festivals to ensure that the huge crowds did not get out of hand. Before the time of Jesus there were at least four major riots or uprisings. See Sanders, *The Historical Figure of Jesus*, pp. 23-24. Pilate governed for ten years, from 26 to 36 C.E., and was known for his swift use of brute force on unarmed protesting crowds and for his lack of regard for Jewish religious sensitivities. See Crossan, *Jesus, Revolutionary Biography*, pp. 139-140.

p. 211

10.   The high priest was appointed by Rome. This way the occupying forces could exercise control over the Jewish people. Pilate's note refers to the removal of the high priest Annas, who ruled from 6 to 15 C.E. and was deposed from office by Rome.

p. 212

11.   The high priest Joseph Caiaphas held his office for a long period because he was a skilled politician in his dealings with both the occupying Roman Empire and his own people. In Palestine as elsewhere, the policy of Rome was for local rulers to be responsible for law and order. The high priest and his council had long been the ruling authority of Judea, having governed Palestine from 445 to 37 B.C.E. They were reverenced and respected by the population, and so were Rome's logical choice. To keep order, the high priest had a force of several thousand temple guards, who served in rotation as did the priests. Caiaphas was then responsible to maintain peace and order in the country and to prevent any riots or rebel uprisings. See Sanders, *The Historical Figure of Jesus*, pp. 22-23, 205.

p. 213

12.   The holy of holies in the temple was a cube-shaped room thirty feet on a side; it was entirely empty and totally dark. Only the high priest could enter it, and then only once a year on the Day of Atonement. This most sacred of places was separated from the rest of the temple by a veil.

p. 214

13.   Caiaphas is referring to a time when Pilate entered the holy city with the embossed medallions of Caesar's bust attached to the troops' military standards. This affront was typical of Pontius Pilate's disregard for the religious feelings of the occupied people he ruled over — in this case their strict observance of the commandment forbidding images. While these images of Caesar were not actually carried into the temple, Caiaphas is probably referring to how the people considered the entire holy city as the temple of God. In any case, the effect of the incident on the population and the temple authorities was significant. See Borg, *Meeting with Jesus Again for the First Time*, p. 137.

p. 215

14.   Caiaphas was no doubt concerned, as is anyone in power whose authority is in another's hands, about retaining his office as high priest, but he is also attempting to prevent a bloodbath of his people. The Gospel of Gabriel presents a compassionate, if compromising, high priest who is sincerely concerned with the safety of the people and their ability to continue to worship in the temple. High priest Caiaphas' political tightrope walking is echoed again and again by religious leaders, both high and low, throughout

history. Pope Pius XII walked such a tightrope when the church continued diplomatic relations with Spain under the rule of the dictator General Franco. When confronted about this, the pope is reported to have said, "Sometimes it is necessary to make a pact with the devil to save souls."

CHAPTER SIXTEEN

p. 216

1.　　Gabriel's Jesus refers to his parable in which he compares the scribes and priestly caste to a barren fig tree (see Luke 13: 6-9). In that parable, Jesus humorously has the gardener proposing to put manure around the tree to make it more fertile. The common people who heard the parable must have roared with laughter at the image of manuring their religious leaders. This parable gives us an example of Jesus' keen sense of humor and how skillfully he used humor to shame his opponents.

p. 219

2.　　Mark's Jesus, in the lines previous to his words about the poor widow's generous gift, lashed out at the exploitation of the poor widows by the scribes and temple priests. "The scribes devour the property of widows and do so under the cover of their long pious prayers" (Mark 12: 38-40). The prophet Jesus echoes the prophet Isaiah in denouncing those who exploit the weak and poor, the widow and the orphan. (see Isaiah 10: 1-2).

p. 220

3.　　Isaiah 1: 11-16.

4.　　Isaiah 1: 25.

p. 221

5.　　Jesus did not just cleanse the temple — but in a symbolic parable-action he destroyed the temple! It was a complete cleansing of its power and significance, saying that God no longer had any use for the slaughter of animals and doves. Scholars agree that in general there was nothing wrong with the buying, selling or money-changing that was conducted in the outer courts of the temple. These were all necessary to meet the rigid requirements for the purity of the sacrifices. Therefore no one was stealing within the sacred area. The disciples, in reflecting upon Jesus' prophetic action, did not clearly understand it. See Crossan, *The Historical Jesus, The Life of a Mediterranean Jewish Peasant*, p. 356. By his violent actions, Jesus did prevent sacrifice from being performed that day, and so prophetically proclaimed the end of sacrifice. The temple was destroyed about forty years after that event (in 70 C.E.) by the Romans as they put down the Jewish revolutionary war of 66-70 C.E.

6.   The vestments of the high priest were prescribed in the book of Exodus. The hem of his violet tunic robe was to have small gold bells, their tinkling to announce his entrance and departure from the sanctuary (see Exodus 28: 31-35). The sound of these small bells is also mentioned by Sirach (45: 9). It is believed that their original purpose was to ward off evil spirits! See McKenzie, *Dictionary of the Bible*, p. 872.

p. 223

7.   Gabriel's Jesus asks his disciples to forgive him, revealing how a true teacher teaches — even if Jesus did not call himself a teacher. Theologian Richard McBrien says that good teachers acknowledge their mistakes and are secure enough to be open to objections and criticism without becoming punitive. They know that what changes people is not indoctrination, not passive consumption of information, but active engagement between teachers and students. Good teachers expect to be questioned and even challenged by their students. They also are able to explain their teaching without the use of the sledge hammer of an argument from authority. Jesus did not demand respect, realizing, as do all good teachers, that, like trust, respect must be earned.

Teachers who truly teach know they have a requirement to admit mistakes — which even Jesus made, being fully human and thus not infallible. Jesus' willingness to apologize in this scene confirms him not only as a good teacher but more fundamentally as a real human being. We see his fallibility again when he spoke of all the calamities at the end of the world and the Son of Man coming in glory. Jesus said, "Amen, I solemnly assure you, this generation shall not die until all these things have happened" (Mark 13: 30). Reflecting on this reference note can be of value to parents, political leaders, pastors and church authorities who believe that admitting errors lessens their authority and, therefore, never admit their mistakes.

p. 224

8.   See Matthew (24: 15-31) where Jesus speaks of the great tribulation, the desolation of the abomination, of which the prophet Daniel spoke. It appears that Jesus believed the world was coming quickly to an end and the full age of God was about to dawn. Whatever prophetic message Jesus heard in his heart — whether the great disaster referred to a personal or symbolic reality — it did not signal the end of the physical world!

9.   That Jesus' behavior in this scene in the temple appeared to be insane echoes earlier charges by his own family that he was mentally disturbed. They had come to take charge of him in Nazareth, believing he was out of his mind. Besides being unconventional, some scholars wonder if his behavior at times seemed so psychologically erratic as to be judged insane. Some wonder if that seemingly bizarre behavior was part of being a healer. Healers sometimes identified with the afflicted in the process of a cure. When he was accused of being possessed by a demon, had Jesus' behavior as an exorcist mirrored that of the possessed person? Also recall Ernest Becker's earlier comments that not to be insane in an insane world, is to appear insane.

p. 225

10.   The Scripture scholar Father Raymond Brown says a good estimate is that twenty percent of the population of Jerusalem had its livelihood provided by the temple. The kind of work would have varied, but mostly it would have been in providing necessary services so pilgrims could make the proper temple sacrifices. This number would likely be higher if all the various needs, such as food and lodging, were also considered. Ancient cities began as temple cities, and were originally populated by those who cared for the temples, priests and pilgrims.

p. 226

11.   From Mary's Canticle (see Luke 1: 52).

12.   Messianic uprisings after the death of King Herod the Great about the time of Jesus' birth in 4 B.C.E. caused the Roman governor of Syria to bring three legions to Jerusalem. Josephus, a Jewish historian of that period, reported that the Romans put down the rebellion and executed two thousand rebels who were crucified. See Crossan, *Jesus, Revolutionary Biography*, pp. 125-126. Crossan also quotes Josephus concerning the massive crucifixions at the fall of Jerusalem in 70 C.E., giving an insight into Caiaphas' concerns in this scene. Josephus said that the victims, including women and children, were first brutally scourged and then crucified. "The majority were citizens of the poorer class...the soldiers out of rage and hatred amused themselves by nailing prisoners in different postures; and so great was their number, that space could not be found for the crosses nor crosses for the bodies." In April of 4 C.E. there was a massacre in the temple during Passover in which three thousand were killed. These accounts remind us of the explosive tinderbox state of Jerusalem at Passover time.

See Crossan, *Jesus, Revolutionary Biography*, p. 128. Caiaphas, who was high priest and thus responsible for keeping order, had reason to be concerned for the safety of the people because of the near riot Jesus had caused in the temple by his radical behavior. Most scholars agree that his disturbance in the temple was the primary reason why Jesus was handed over to the Romans.

p. 229

13.   Matthew 10: 23.

p. 230

14.   Pilch, Malina and other social biblical scholars agree that in the culture of Palestine at that time, females did not eat with the male members of their family but ate later or separately. This custom of separation of the sexes at both private and public meals is still kept today in various parts of the world. In Gabriel's Gospel, however, Jesus is consistent in his radical practice of what the scholar Crossan calls "an open table." Such equality in sharing the table with sinners, the religiously impure and even Gentiles, surely would have also included women. On the other hand, E.P. Sanders and others maintain that at the final meal of Jesus only men were present. Christian art has confirmed this belief, uniformly picturing only Jesus and the twelve male disciples at table. Today the issue of who was at that most famous table in history is a hotly debated subject, since it is a basis in some Christian churches for who may be ordained.

15.   Jesus does not flee to safety but embraces God's will that he must die. "Heroism is by definition defiance of safety," says Becker, and Jesus reflects this lack of concern for his personal safety many times. See Becker, *The Denial of Death*, p. 156. In rejecting an escape plan, Jesus, who previously disregarded those laws of his religion or society he felt did not apply to him, now leaps over the most primitive human law: self-preservation!

Small children are often unafraid of death, but as they grow, it grows into their greatest fear. Some anthropologists believe our fear of death has its roots in the early evolutionary period when all humans lived in a naturally hostile world. Those who passed on to their children a strong and realistic fear had the highest survival rate. Becker says this fear of death is what makes the human such a hyperanxious animal. See Becker, *The Denial of Death*, p. 17.

CHAPTER SEVENTEEN

p. 232

1.   Anointing was part of the Palestinian custom for the reception of guests. It was performed by house slaves or, as a mark of honor to the guest, by the host himself. As the roads were dusty and the people wore sandals, the act of washing a guest's feet was a refreshing ritual on both practical and symbolic levels. It would not, however, have been customary for a man to greet a woman with a kiss, or even to touch her. Such behavior by Gabriel's Jesus is another example of his freedom to disregard customs which he felt were invalid or limited God's love. While he respected people and their boundaries, he didn't respect laws for their own sake. See also the note for p. 239.

2.   The author of John, the only one who mentions the foot washing, places this event at the end of the Last Supper. Unlike the other Gospel writers he does not even mention the bread and wine aspect of that Seder meal, which became the basis for the Eucharist (Greek for "thanksgiving"), or Mass, celebrated by the early church. Yet he places much symbolic importance on the ritual of foot washing. In a real way this act of loving and humble service is also a Eucharist. It might serve us well to think of having two Eucharistic liturgies in our Christian tradition: the bread and wine Eucharist of Mark, Matthew and Luke; and John's Eucharist of daily humble service. No ordination is required to perform the Mass of St. John. Yet those who celebrate it truly consecrate humble service into the presence of the Risen Christ. Perhaps this is what Jesus implied when he told Peter that unless he had allowed his feet to be washed, a sort of apostolic ordination by water, he would have no part in Jesus' birthright, the inheritance of the Slave of God.

3.   Pentecost (the name is Greek for fiftieth) is one of the three feasts mentioned in Exodus (23: 14-17). It was originally a harvest festival celebrated fifty days after Passover and so was a movable feast. Also called the feast of Weeks, it emphasized Sabbath rest and was a renewal of the covenant, recalling Moses receiving the Law on Mount Sinai. See McKenzie, *Dictionary of the Bible*, pp. 657-658.

4.   The fish at the Last Supper points to how important it was as an early Communion food. John Crossan says, "It is impossible to emphasize too greatly the importance of bread and fish Eucharists in the early tradition." See Crossan, *The Historical Jesus, The Life of a Mediterranean Jewish Peasant*, pp. 398-402. He cites the paintings of fish and bread in the Christian catacombs of Rome around 200 C.E. as a strong indication that the aspect

of fish was present with bread at Communion. Some scholars believe that two traditions existed in the post-Easter church; one with bread and fish and another with bread and wine. More important than the menu, however, was that the table be open to all — as were the meal tables of Jesus' lifetime.

Manuscripts dating to about 100 B.C.E. show that the Essene monastic community at Qumran had a sacred meal with bread and wine which was led by a priest. The apostle Paul speaks of the bread and wine tradition in 1 Corinthians 11: 23-26, and his writings predate any of the Gospel accounts of the Last Supper. Yet disciples of the third millennium might reflect on a Eucharistic celebration using fish and bread as a variation of the bread and wine Eucharist. Today such fish and bread Eucharists not only could be celebrated by those who cannot drink alcohol, but could also be an alternative celebration of the Eucharist or Last Supper.

p. 233

5.   Jesus is the Prophet of the New, incarnating Second Isaiah's good news that, while ageless, God is ever new. As Israel is stuck in the dead end of exile, God says, "Look and see, I am doing something new! I am announcing new things to you, making a new heaven and a new earth" (see Isaiah 43: 19, 48: 6, 66: 22). The author of the Book of Revelation, likewise drunk with God's wine of newness, tells us that the Enthroned Christ sings, "Behold and see, I make all things new" (Revelation 21: 5). Jesus at this meal, inspired by the freedom of the Spirit, does something new with the ancient ritual of the Seder, transforming it afresh.

His disciples today need to examine their relationship with what is new, fresh and unorthodox. Jesus spoke of balancing traditional wisdom with the untried: "Every scribe who is instructed in the secret of the kingdom of heaven is like a householder who brings out of storeroom both new and old" (Matthew 13: 52). In the light of this brief saying we need to ask if those who fear and reject everything new in daily life, dress, worship and prayer can really be said to know the secret of the kingdom of heaven.

p. 234

6.   Besides being present in the bread and wine, Jesus says: Taste me also in a communion with the goodness of mountains, seas and stars. The author of Ephesians, inspired by Paul's beliefs about the Risen Christ, speaks of just such a cosmic holy communion: "God has put all things at the disposal of Christ, making the Risen One the head of the church, which is Christ's body: the fullness of the One who fills the universe in all its parts" (Ephesians 1: 22). One translation says, "...the fullness of the

One who fills in every way all things." At his resurrection, then, Jesus did not just rise from the dead, but exploded outward into all creation to become one with all things in God. The implications of the theology of Ephesians is that holy communion with Christ is to receive not just his body, the church, but, staggering to the mind, all the universe! The present evidence says that our universe contains over 100 billion galaxies! The size of our known universe is beyond the limits of human comprehension, especially when we consider that our Milky Way galaxy represents only about one trillionth of the mass of the universe. According to Neil McAleer, it's like comparing a small metal screw to the mass of a 100,000 ton ship of which the screw is a small part! See Neil McAleer, *The Cosmic Mind-Boggling Book* (New York: Warner Books Inc., 1982), p. 155.

p. 235

7.   While some scholars debate whether the historical Jesus actually said, "Do this in memory of me," there is no doubt that the Eucharistic meal is done in memory of him, as a living memory of his death and resurrection. The author of Gabriel presents a Jesus who knows, as did Moses, the power of memory, and Jesus promises to be present whenever the memory is kept. Memory and repetition are a resurrection of the past — significant times live again. However, we do not so much relive the memory as we cross the frontiers of space and time. Jesus does not instruct his disciples to tell others of the wonders they have seen but to *perform an action*, the action of sharing the Eucharist, as well as actions like visiting the sick and those in prison! The celebration of the Lord's Supper and the Passover share in the act of keeping of a memory. In the Passover ritual it is said, "When your son asks you...then you shall say," at which point the parent repeats the memory story of the Exodus. And in the Eucharistic meal the memory story of the Last Supper is repeated, concluding with Jesus' words, "Do this in memory of me." Liturgy is organized memory set within a ritual drama, allowing a participation in what can only be called the holy mysteries. Mysteries are to be entered into and reverenced, not explained.

The renewal among some Reform churches includes reintroduction of ritual and the frequent celebration of the Lord's Supper. This is a healthy return, for, as Gabriel Josipovici says, Protestant theologians have placed emphasis on a saving history, on God's miraculous deeds, which plays down this memory-keeping dimension. The Reform theologians' emphasis on history goes hand in hand with the Reformation's rejection of liturgy and ritual. See Gabriel Josipovici, *The Book of God* (New Haven, Conn.: Yale University Press, 1988), p. 151.

8.   The forest of Lebanon extends on the slopes of the mountain chain running along the Syrian coast from present-day Lebanon into northern Galilee. The west slope is well watered and known for its cedars. It was a wild or natural forest often mentioned in poetic language in the Scriptures. See McKenzie, *Dictionary of the Bible*, p. 502.

9.   Jesus' calm acceptance of his destiny could be dismissed simply by saying that he's divine, that he knew he would be raised from the dead because he was one with God. But such a Jesus is not the Jesus who died on the cross, and who prayed in agony in the Olive Garden to be spared such a terrible death. We rob Jesus of his humanness and ourselves of a real model when we assume that kind of foreknowledge of his resurrection. In this scene Jesus shows a different ground for his calm acceptance of his fate. He knows that to die without regrets is to die in freedom, and because he had allowed the fullness of his talents and uniqueness to flower, Jesus could now die without regrets.

Further reflection on his heroic example shows what can happen to anyone who is joined as completely as possible to the high mysterious powers, who is aligned with God. This is the purpose of a good religion and not just to provide a code of moral conduct. Religion solves the problem of death, offers the possibility of a heroic victory at the highest level. See Becker, *The Denial of Death*, p. 203. Heroes are not those who are fearless, but those who refuse to let their fear prevent them from doing what must be done.

To die on a cross in your early thirties or in a nursing home bed in your early eighties can be heroic, if you align your personal existence with some higher meaning. Religion is meant to give what Jesus possessed: hope and communion with God. Such hope is a passport to enter the dimension of the unknown and unknowable, the mystery of creation and the Creator, to achieve full transcendence of the human condition. The ancients said, "To see God is to die." The opposite is also true, "To die is to see God."

10.   As Jesus kisses the women disciples it might be expected that James the Orthodox and the other men would object, for Jesus' action was contrary to the common custom of that period. If they had objected, Jesus might have replied, "Be as innocent as doves, not seeing evil where no evil is intended. However, also be as wise and clever as serpents, for what appears to be pure affection can be the overture to exploitation, especially by those

who are held in awe for their religious or professional positions." Jesus in Gabriel's Gospel shows an Eden innocence as well as true affection with his expression of love for his disciples, whom he will call his friends. His unspoken admonition to be as clever as serpents is a reminder that in Eden's garden of innocence there was a serpent! Today's sometimes extreme concern about the potential for abuse can restrict the free flow of human affection and the unfolding of full humanity. While sexual abuse is a legitimate concern, that potential for evil should not limit the unfolding of oneself to living as fully humanly as possible, as did Jesus.

p. 241

11.   The apostle Thomas is given the folk title of Doubting Thomas. The author of Gabriel here, as elsewhere in his Gospel, shows us a Doubting Jesus. That Jesus ever doubted his mission, or ever doubted at all, has been seriously doubted, if not denied, by many of his later followers. Robert Hughes, speaking of the great Impressionist painter Paul Cezanne, who was frequently tormented by doubts about his creative revolution in painting, says, "The greater the artist the greater the doubt: perfect confidence is granted to the less talented as a consolation prize." See Robert Hughes, "Modernism's Patriarch" in *Time Magazine*, June 10, 1996. This man Jesus was a genius, a highly gifted human artist of the spirit, and so would not qualify for a consolation prize of prefect certitude.

p. 242

12.   John Pilch echoes Bruce Malina, who says that our English word "faith" should be more correctly translated as "loyalty." Jesus asked, and continues to ask, his disciples not for faith as an intellectual ascent to dogmas or decrees, but rather for loyalty to him personally and to his dream given to him by God. See Pilch and Malina, *Biblical Social Values and Their Meaning*, pp. 67-70. New research and new scientific discovery are daily challenging old beliefs in our vast religious storeroom. This challenge may shake the faith of some believers, and for those clinging to the life rafts of old beliefs it may cause a complete loss of faith. In such times of new discoveries, a good reflection would be to ponder the primal condition of discipleship as loyalty or commitment. Bed in your prayers the idea of a personal loyalty to Jesus the Christ, to God and the divine dream. While your loyalty at such times of personal and institutional upheaval might be as small as a mustard seed, remember that it has the power to move mountains of difficulties.

p. 243

13.   This event of a young man standing next to Jesus, wearing only a thin linen tunic and running away naked when the authorities attempt to seize him is given to us by Mark (14: 51-52). According to Bruce Malina, the point in his having only a thin tunic is that only "young men" who might dress that way would be angelic beings who have no need of any other garments. Malina and Rohrbaugh ask point blank: "Was this man Jesus' guardian angel?" If so, when the angel fled, Jesus *was* truly and excruciatingly left alone! See Malina and Rohrbaugh, *Social-Science Commentary on the Synoptic Gospels*, p. 270. From this point onward until his death, Jesus is alone, abandoned by everyone, which is perhaps the ultimate fear. Jesus was truly stripped naked not on the cross but at his arrest in the Garden. He is abandoned even by God's presence symbolized by Gabriel.

Countless people have known that feeling: tortured political prisoners, those cast into the furnaces of the Nazi Holocaust — anyone who has died a slow violent death as a victim. Knowing that horror is what led Jesus to tell his disciples to pray "not to be put to the test."

CHAPTER EIGHTEEN

p. 245

1.   King Herod the Great, more from political motives to gain the favor of the people than from any personal devotion, built a new temple in Jerusalem. Sparing no expense, Herod put 10,000 laborers to work on the project, as well as training 1,000 priests to be master masons so they could work on the sacred parts of the temple. Crossan and other scholars mention this, as does McKenzie (See *Dictionary of the Bible*, p. 875). Gabriel's Jesus refers here to such precisely carved stones that could be seen even in the subterranean areas of the temple complex.

2.   Crossan says the Roman practice was for their executed prisoners to be buried by the Roman soldiers as a way to ensure the victims were dead. As in mass executions in our time, the practice was to dump the dead in a common ditch. There they would be preyed upon by dogs and jackals. This would have been an "almost intolerable" situation not only for a devout Jew but also for the early church. See Crossan, *Jesus, Revolutionary Biography*, p. 392.

p. 247

3.   Recall the explosive nature of the crowds in Jerusalem at Passover

time (see the note for p. 226). Concern for the security of the population of the holy city would have made anyone who would cause a disturbance, as did Jesus in the temple, a grave threat. Gabriel's Jesus does not appear before the high court, as in the four canonical Gospels where he is judged guilty of blasphemy — which is given as the reason for his execution. A large body of scholars believes the real reason Jesus was condemned was his behavior in the temple area which stopped "its fiscal, sacrificial and liturgical operations." See Crossan, *Jesus, Revolutionary Biography*, p. 131. His actions constituted a serious threat to law and order to both the Roman and temple authorities.

The author of Gabriel has treated this part of the traditional passion account in a way that attempts to cast a more accurate sense of responsibility for the death of Jesus. The four canonical Gospel accounts of Jesus' trial before the Jewish high council and the Jews' shouting to Pilate, "Let his blood be on our hands," have helped lead to two thousand years of the most horrible anti-Semitic persecutions, reaching a zenith of evil in the Nazi Holocaust. We need to ask whether Christian churches share in the responsibility for these atrocities by failing to condemn them in the most severe language possible, as well as by failing to cleanse the Scriptures of raw discrimination.

The canonical Gospels were written after the second half of the first century. In those early years of the church, divisions frequently arose between Jewish and Gentile Christians, as well as between Jewish Christians and the Orthodox Jewish population over whether Jesus was the Messiah. It is understandable that anti-Jewish attitudes would find their way into Scripture. Yet, can the evil of prejudice against the Jewish people ever be removed without dealing with the biased language of this ancient period contained in the Christian Scriptures?

p. 248

4.   Pilate's statement makes an important and accurate distinction about the responsibility for the death of Jesus. He was handed over for Roman judgment not by the Jewish people, not even by the entire temple council, but rather by a few high-ranking members of the council.

5.   Rome not only appointed the high priest, but also controlled when he might wear his priestly vestments. King Herod and then Rome took charge of his liturgical dress. Those vestments were released only on special occasions because when the high priest was fully attired he was a powerful symbol to the people. See Sanders, *The Historical Figure of Jesus*, pp. 26-27.

6.   Again, Pilate was notorious for his brutal crowd control and his reactions to riots and rebel acts of sedition. He had been reported to Rome for harsh tactics and imprudent decisions that only added to the unrest of the population. The mention in this chapter's title of the "Trial" of Jesus of Nazareth, refers to his brief appearance before Pontius Pilate. As a typical Roman provincial judge in an occupied backwater province, Pilate had no need for any witnesses or evidence to make a judgment and then to quickly pronounce a death sentence. See Crossan, *Jesus, Revolutionary Biography*, pp. 137-139.

Historical insight suggests that more than Pilate's hands were washed of responsibility in the brutal death of Jesus! As the post-Easter church moved from Palestine into the Roman world, it was critical that the behavior of Pilate, and by association that of Rome, be cast in the best possible light. In John's Gospel, even Pilate's wife and her dream of Jesus are introduced to help launder him of responsibility.

7.   The cross was a Persian creation adopted by the Romans. Death on a cross was so horrible that it was reserved for murder, robbery, piracy and most of all for treason and rebellion. It was so cruel that it could not be inflicted on Roman citizens. Christian art, from which our mental images are formed, shows Jesus carrying a cross composed of both the upright beam and the crossbeam joined together. The actual practice of the Roman occupation army, however, was to have the upright posts of the crosses already in place and ready for the next victims. See McKenzie, *Dictionary of the Bible*, p. 161. These prepared upright posts not only served to expiate executions, especially mass crucifixions, but also made wonderful roadside warning signs to any who might be tempted to try to overthrow the Roman occupation.

8.   Only the author of John's Gospel places John on the hill of Golgotha at the cross of Jesus within speaking distance. The other three authors have all the men disciples fleeing for their lives. Along with the beloved disciple, the author of Gabriel logically includes Simon of Cyrene since he had been forced to carry the cross to the execution site outside the walls of the city.

9.   The presence near the cross of Mary, the mother of James and

Joseph, among the other women is significant for our reflection. In Gabriel's Gospel some of the disciples gave her the nickname "Mary the Murmurer" because of her constant criticism and complaining. Yet she remains loyal, following Jesus to his death, even when the men disciples flee for their lives. No conversion experience is necessary to explain her presence at the cross. Criticism and murmuring, while painful to a leader, are not necessarily signs of disloyalty. As in all communities, churches, groups and movements, there are those who murmur and complain behind the leader's back yet remain steadfast in their commitment. Mary, the mother of Joseph and James, could be their patron saint.

10.   In writing about the heroic behavior of Jesus in the midst of the terrible physical pain of his passion and crucifixion, John Pilch says that is what would be expected from a true Mediterranean male. Self-control was the ideal. It was considered unmanly to demonstrate one's feelings under heavy affliction. Pilch speaks of how American culture is even more rigid in its code of conduct. Men are expected to appear unmoved, not to show violent anger or excessive joy, and not to weep in public. They are expected to endure hardships and suffering without any show of emotion. See Pilch and Malina, *Biblical Social Values and Their Meaning*, p. 53-55. While Jesus maintains the ideal male image as he bears his own affliction in the passion and crucifixion, he is very expressive both in sorrow and joy at other times. A good reflection for American males would be to ponder their freedom to be spontaneous and allow their emotions to be visible — in short to be out of control.

p. 254

11.   Tradition refers to the two men crucified with Jesus as thieves. While robbers were among those who could be sentenced to the cross, scholars believe the two men were guilty of insurrection or treason against Rome. See Crossan, *Jesus, Revolutionary Biography*, p. 142. Terrorism, politically cross-fertilized by religious zeal, is a global reality as one millennium ends and a new one begins. Terrorism is always an expression of the oppressed and politically powerless. If signs had been nailed over the crosses of the two who died with Jesus, they probably would have read: terrorist.

12.   In Christian art and passion plays Jesus is shown on the cross wearing a loincloth. The Romans crucified criminals stripped entirely naked, and there is no reason to believe they would have made an exception for Jesus! See McKenzie, *Dictionary of the Bible*, p. 162. Some have tried to

deal with this ugly reality by stating that in response to Jewish sensitivity the Romans allowed Jews to wear a loincloth. Yet Pilate was notorious for his lack of sensitivity to Jewish religious and moral feelings. Were artists to give a true image of the crucifixion of Jesus it would be just as shamefully shocking and offensive to disciples now as it was to Jesus' disciples then. Meditative reflection on such a shameful crucifix might awaken dull disciples to greater love for the one who loved us so much as to die shamefully for us.

See Chapter 2, page 31, where Gabriel in the desert speaks of the day when Jesus will be trapped in a tree. Naked on the cross, Jesus becomes a global holy hero savior, who, lacking clothing, belongs to no one class, culture or historical time.

13.   The crucified rebel's song of ridicule states a profound truth, that resurrection is the greatest insurrection. Jesus, not on the cross, but after his death, will lead the world's greatest insurrection in his liberation from death. No Pharaoh, king or dictator holds more oppressive power than does death. By his insurrection-resurrection, Jesus holds out to those willing to grasp it, the greatest of all freedoms, the escape from the fear of death! The mainspring that keeps humans running, according to Ernest Becker, is their perpetual avoidance of their fatality by the constant denial of death. Energies that could be used in creative and artistic outlets are all diverted to a massive defense structure that reinforces the denial of death.

As the great liberator, Jesus becomes the greatest hero of the Western world. Heroism, says Becker, is the "first and foremost reflex of the terror of death. We admire most the courage to face death; we give such valor our highest and most constant adoration; it moves us deeply in our hearts because we have doubts about how brave we ourselves would be." See Becker, *The Denial of Death*, pp. 11-12.

p. 255

14.   Jesus' companion on the other cross sees him as a shaman-type hero, one who could travel into the spirit world, the world of the dead, and return alive. The good thief-terrorist, by this request, states his belief that Jesus will make just such a spirit journey. It is Jesus on the cross facing death in a heroic way, showing us how to die, that has given him such significance in history and in religion. All the great religions have addressed that problem of how to bear the end of life. Becker says that the real hero is one who risks his or her life for others. He says that heroes challenge our fear to do just that and become role models: "When we see a man bravely facing his own extinction we rehearse the greatest victory we can image." Becker, *The Denial of Death*, pp. 11-12.

The crucified Christ is among the greatest of hero images. No other symbol is so rich in power and so profound as a map for life. To reflect prayerfully upon the ugly image of Jesus dying on the cross is a heroic invitation not to die whimpering like a child or cringing like a coward.

The pascal mysteries are a trinity of Jesus' passion, death and resurrection that form a single event which leads to his ascension and the descent of the Holy Spirit on Pentecost. That these actions are a united continuous event is at the core of the Christian faith. The bare cross without a figure on it — a common symbol of the Reform churches — or an image of the Risen Christ in more liturgical churches, can symbolize the resurrection, the heart of the sacred mysteries. Yet we need to be careful not to focus on the resurrection to the exclusion of the crucifixion. Today's trend to put away images of the crucified Jesus raises some issues to ponder. We humans are symbol-oriented and so need images. The very marks on this page called "words" are composed of letters or marks which are mutually understood symbols. Reflect on these questions in your home, prayer corner or within your parish worship space: Does the removal of images of the suffering, crucified Jesus unintentionally support the contemporary rejection of suffering and the denial of death? Does the removal of a crucified Jesus as a visual image guide tear off a critical piece of Jesus' map of the Way? Whether churched or unchurched, are those whose lives are devoid of images of the crucified Jesus also devoid of an image of *how* to suffer, to bear great pain and finally to die? For that is a fate from which no one is spared — not even Jesus.

p. 256

15.   The Roman Church has a Sacrament of the Anointing of the Sick, once known as the Last Anointing. Here on the cross, Jesus speaks not of a Sacrament of the church but a Gospel sacrament to the sick and dying. The Risen Christ is present as a grace-filled sign in those who minister to the dying, whether friends, family or strangers, by their simply being present. The women at the cross perform this holy sacrament for Jesus as he died, not questioning if such non-productive action was a waste of time. Death, by its nature, is the most solitary act of our lives. Blessed are those who sit with the dying as they are birthed into another life. By their presence, those who wait outside IC units, operating rooms and at bedsides anoint the sick and dying with compassionate love — with the grace of Christ.

16.   The great prayer of the Second Testament, the Lord's Prayer, has not been previously mentioned in Gabriel's Gospel. Matthew's Jesus gives his disciples this prayer (see Matthew 6: 9-14), and Luke's Jesus prays a

shorter, somewhat different version (see Luke 11: 2-4). Scholars believe these two prayers were the liturgical forms of the respective early Christian communities for which these Gospels were written. Although they agree that the words of the Lord's Prayer contain Jesus' thoughts, Scripture scholars are divided about how he used them. E.P. Sanders believes Jesus actually prayed the prayer and taught it to his disciples. See Sanders, *The Historical Figure of Jesus*, p. 195. John Crossan believes the prayer is a summary of the themes from Jesus' teaching but was never taught as a prayer to his disciples, or that it is a collection of miniature prayers later collected into a single prayer. He agrees with Joseph Fitzmyer, S.J., however, that it "is a thoroughly Jewish prayer, for almost every word of it could be uttered by a devout Jew." See Crossan, *The Historical Jesus, The Life of a Mediterranean Jewish Peasant*, pp. 293-294.

p. 258

17.   Scholars are divided on the Passover custom of releasing a prisoner, as was the case with Barabbas in all the passion accounts but Luke's. Some maintain that there was no known custom in Roman justice of allowing a prisoner to go free, especially one guilty of insurrection! On the other hand, there is evidence that a Roman official could for some special reason decide to delay the execution for a day or two. Also, in certain special cases the family of a victim could be given the body after the prisoner was dead. Such special favors — as was surely the case with Joseph of Arimathea, and is still the custom today in most of the Third World — are facilitated by gifts.

18.   Salome was the wife of Zebedee and the mother of James and John.

19.   The image of Mary at the foot of the cross holding her dead son is well known from Michelangelo's famous statue of the *Pieta*. Mary is the holy sorrowful mother, patroness of all sorrowful mothers whose sons or daughters are brutally tortured and executed at the hands of Latin American military dictatorships or other oppressive governments. She is also the holy sorrowful mother of all sorrowful mothers who cradle a dead adult child legally executed by brother and sister citizens under capital punishment.

CHAPTER NINETEEN

p. 260

1.   Mark's Gospel appears to end with the empty tomb, as do other early manuscripts. Another author, with a different style, takes up Mark's text with the stories of Jesus' appearances after his resurrection. Some

believe that the last part of Mark's Gospel may have been lost and that another author had to finish it! Mindful that the earliest manuscripts were separate accounts passed from community to community, this is an interesting possibility. The lost Easter account of Mark will be referred to again in the notes of Chapter 20.

p. 261

2..   John was the intimate friend of Jesus, reclining next to him at the Last Supper. As the author of John's Gospel says, he was the one whom Jesus loved (see John 19: 26). This Gospel suggests that John's special friendship with Jesus was also a cause of jealousy among the other disciples. Even if they were jealous, Jesus apparently did not hide his affection for John. This offers food for reflection to those in leadership positions and perhaps to parents. There is an unwritten law that leaders should avoid "special" friendships with one or two of those in their charge so as not to be accused of favoritism. Jesus again reveals a freedom to love and be loved. A good leader in his footsteps is compassionate toward all and, while feeling special affection for one or more, always strives to treat everyone with fairness and justice.

John's canticle of sleepwalking might well be reread frequently by all those God has gifted with the charism of being loved by another. Love, which is God, is a gift never to be taken for granted — in marriage or friendship.

p. 262

3.   Recall that the priest Eleazar was among the scribes and priests who came to Jesus when he was in Judea across the Jordan. He asked Jesus why he had not called any priests into his intimate group of disciples. See Chapter 13, p. 178.

p. 263

4.   Jewish priesthood was hereditary, and so birth into priestly families, like those of Levi, Zadok and Aaron, was a requirement.

5.   (See Psalm 110: 4.) Jesus being a new Melchizedek is a major theme in the Epistle to the Hebrews (see Hebrews 5: 6, 10; 6: 20 and throughout chapter 7).

6.   In the early post-Easter church, priesthood as a special caste or clergy did not exist, except as the duty and privilege of *all* baptized disciples. Eleazar's priestly canticle is woven with the priestly theology found in the

Epistle to the Hebrews. McKenzie says that the effects of that second century Epistle "on the formation of the Christian priesthood in the early Church are incalculable." See McKenzie, *Dictionary of the Bible*, p. 692. The converted priest Eleazar's canticle speaks of the sacrificial theme of Jesus' dying to save all people from their sins — a core teaching in the post-Easter church which explained Jesus' death by crucifixion. This theology is based on the evolution of the bloody sacrifices of the First Testament and the fulfillment of various prophecies. It therefore could hardly have been the work of peasant fishermen or farmers! According to Crossan and others, it reveals the hands of scholars, those learned in the Law, the work of priestly pens.

The destruction of the temple and its sacrifice, prefigured in the temple riot of Jesus, is a powerful image of the coming of Jesus' new order. He ingeniously renewed the three great memory-stories of his religion: the Exodus, the Babylonian Exile, and the Temple and its Priesthood. He creatively reinvented the memories, making them new vehicles to deal with the present reality, creating a new covenant that rose out of the former one. From the Exodus memory he shaped a new spirit of insurrection against the domination of the royal powers of any age. From the Exile memory he brought forth a call for all advent persons living in exile, for all who feel alienated, to return home. From the memory-story of the Priesthood and Temple, Jesus liberated God's presence that had been restricted to sacred space, freeing it to once again be amidst the pilgrim people of God. He replaced the bloody sacrifices by fulfilling the demands of justice with a self-surrendering compassionate love. He fulfilled the age-old desire of Moses for the entire community to be priestly ministers of God. See Borg, *Meeting with Jesus Again for the First Time*, p. 127.

p. 264

7.　　Like the canticle of Eleazar, these words of Simon the Cyrene also reveal a theology, a priestly farmer's theology that flows out of the Book of Creation, which was and continues to be the first inspired Scripture. Creation contains not simply a prophecy of the resurrection, but proof of it! Creation's revelation is simple but profoundly hopeful: nothing dies, it only changes form. Energy — the basic ingredient from which everything is made — cannot be destroyed or killed. Like a tree, an animal or a human dies, falls to the earth, rots and becomes rich soil. The soil then produces a plant, which when eaten is transformed again into animal or human flesh.

Simon's canticle points to the mystery that the atoms whirling at this moment in the flesh of your fingers as they hold this Gospel book were once perhaps the scales of some prehistoric beast. Before that, those atoms may have been part of the fin of a fish that swam in the ocean before earth was inhabited, and prior to that they may have flamed across the sky in some fantastic soaring star. The pascal mystery of the passion, death and resurrection is written boldly across all of creation — for those with eyes to see. For a creative treatment of this notion see the opening scene of the Pulitzer Prize-winning play *The Effect of Gamma Rays on Man-in-the-Moon Marigolds* by Paul Zindel (New York: Bantam Books, 1970).

The pascal mystery, the heart of the Christian faith, however, is not just seen in creation. Not only do plants, animals and persons die, so do institutions, traditions and entire religious communities. To believe that their deaths can be part of the work of the Spirit of God which always creates new life out of death sometimes requires great faith. Death in all its many forms, from the closure of parishes and institutions to the human aging process, are all opportunities to sing the Credo, "I believe in the Pascal Mystery."

8.　　　The canticle of Simon the farmer also suggests how to consecrate suffering into sacrificial power by giving away yourself for the sake of others, as did Jesus at the Last Supper. It also reveals the sacrificial power of taking upon oneself the sufferings of others. All pain embraced out of love for another is a sacrificial act. In such a communion of suffering it is possible to convert the negative energy of suffering into a positive force. The persons whose shoulders bear the marks of another's cross know that Jesus lives! They know Christ lives in them, for how else could anyone carry the burden of another's cross?

p. 266

9.　　　The name Lucifer (Latin for *lightbringer*) orginally referred to the morning star, Venus. The prophet Isaiah first applied the epithet to the king of Babylon, saying, "How you have fallen from heaven, O morning star (Lucifer), son of the dawn!" (Isaiah 14: 4, 12). Saint Jerome and the early fathers of the church applied it to Satan. The poet John Milton in *Paradise Lost*, chapter 10, verse 425, then gave this name to the demon of Sinful Pride. In chapter 6, verse 44, Milton makes Archangel Michael the prince commander of the celestial armies who alongside Archangel Gabriel casts Lucifer from heaven. See *Brewer's Dictionary of Phrase & Fable*, pp. 688, 734.

p. 267

10.　　　The Shadow in these last nine lines of his threatening song includes three references to the Second Testament. The Shadow says he will be the thorn in the flesh of which the apostle Paul wrote about in 2 Corinthians

(12: 7) and which caused him to pray three times for God to free him of this unspeakable temptation. Also in 2 Corinthians (11: 14), Satan is said to disguise himself as an angel of light. The Shadow's third reference is to the passage in Luke (22: 31) which speaks of the devil sifting the disciples like wheat.

p. 269

11.   The final fate of the Shadow, or Lucifer, while not resolved by the Gospel of Gabriel, holds the possibility of reconciliation by a God who is Love. This possibility and the Shadow's desire to return as a prodigal to heaven, offers a rich feast for reflection and discussion.

The four canonical Gospels say nothing about this question, as they said nothing about whether Jesus was single or married. The later writings attributed to John, however, talk about the fate of the Antichrist, a great adversary of the Messiah and God, who is said to mount a great war against God just before the final judgment. This figure is traced to Jewish apocalyptic literature, where he is given many features of Gog, the evil king of Magog identified by Ezekiel as one of the enemies of Israel and God (see Ezekiel chapters 38 and 39). McKenzie, along with other scholars, sees the Antichrist as being a personification of the powers of evil.

Revelation, or the Apocalypse (chapter 20), pictures an angel coming from heaven to capture Satan, chaining him up for a thousand years to prevent him from leading the nations astray. After this, Satan, or the dragon, is to be released for a short time. The thousand years is not to be taken literally, but means a long period of time, implying that the resurrection of Christ is a final victory over both death and evil. This is the victory of Christ suggested in the Shadow's song. See McKenzie, *Dictionary of the Bible*, pp. 35-36.

The author of Revelation (20: 10) further describes Satan along with Gog finally being defeated and thrown into a pool of fire together with death and hell. One has to wonder if this victory over evil, while appealing to those thirsty for revenge and the punishment of the guilty, is the final chapter of God's story. After all, it seems contrary to the all-embracing God whom Jesus presented as ever-eager to forgive and to reconcile *all things*.

CHAPTER TWENTY

p. 271

1.   All that is found in the empty tomb are the burial cloths Jesus left behind. Their presence is significant. He died naked, and it seems was raised up that way at his resurrection. Jesus Christ was raised up from the dead by the hand of God as the new, shameless Adam.

2. Fish, along with bread, was the Easter food (see Luke 24: 42-43 and John 21: 12-13). As has been said, fish was part of the holy menu of some Christian groups at their early celebrations of the Eucharist. See Crossan, *Jesus, Revolutionary Biography*, pp. 398-401.

p. 273

3. As you may recall from an earlier note (for p. 260), some scholars believe the last chapter of Mark's Gospel, containing his accounts of the appearances of the Risen Christ, was lost. Some might wish that Gabriel's account of Christ's activities on Easter were also lost! In this scene the Risen Jesus bathes Mary in a tidal wave of love in a mystical baptism. This section refers to the historical practice of Baptism in the early church. The candidates removed all their clothing and descended into a baptismal pool. Upon coming out, their bodies were dried and then entirely anointed with oil before being robed in white garments. Men deacons assisted in male baptisms and women deacons assisted in female baptisms.

p. 274

4. Death challenges our faith, or loyalty. Death is best faced as it was by Jesus, not with a dogmatic faith in the resurrection, but with a total commitment to God. Death is overcome when embraced with loyalty to Jesus, who promised life beyond the grave to those who would follow him. Loyalty is the fruit of love, and if we wish to have our faith, our loyalty, increased we need only to pray for an increase in love.

The resurrection, all scholars agree, was not the resuscitation of a corpse, but a profound transformation of the human body in glory. The transfigured Christ sends Mary Magdalene out with the core message of the early church: that Jesus was raised from the dead! She thus becomes the first apostle (one who is sent) of the post-Easter church. Her role in the Resurrection as a woman messenger has profound implications that cannot forever be ignored.

As Sanders says, "Jesus was no Puritan." See Sanders, *The Historical Figure of Jesus*, p. 204. He was given not to censure, but to encouragement and joy. He was joyous in his celebration of life. The bodily aspects of the Risen Christ's meeting with Mary Magdalene reflect the Christian belief about life after death. Our faith is not simply in the immortality of the soul — the resurrection includes the body. Such a belief makes our body and our senses essential elements in our redemption. That redemption begins in Baptism and reaches completion in our resurrection. The Risen Christ's sensual ordination of Mary Magdalene sings of that glorious mystery.

p. 275

5.　　　The Gospel of Gabriel identifies the unnamed disciple on the road to Emmaus as a woman. Jesus sent out his disciples two by two, and John Crossan maintains that often one was male and one female. That the author of Luke does not name the disciple with Cleopas implies that it was likely a woman. Only rarely are the names of women found in the Biblical lists of ancestors or in official state documents. Refer again to the discussion on the subject of traveling women disciples in the notes for pp. 128 and 140.

6.　　　John Crossan cites the historian Josephus saying that Pilate, as a clever and ruthless governor, did indeed intersperse among the crowds soldiers armed with cudgels but disguised in civilian dress. They were to spring into action if a riot began and incite the crowd to violent action or cause a mass flight. In this way Pilate could justify the use of armed force against the mob. See Crossan, *Jesus, A Revolutionary Biography*. p. 138.

p. 277

7.　　　Eggs and fish have been added to the bread Eucharist of Emmaus by the author of Gabriel. The egg was added both because it was a common food and because this was an Easter Eucharist. Today eggs are an important part of Easter folk celebrations and have an ancient and global sacred history. The egg is a sign of the repository of new life hidden dormant inside us, and the chick breaking out of the shell has been for Christians a symbol of Christ coming out of the tomb. Eggs were once buried with the dead to nourish them on their journey to the next world. See Biedemann, *Dictionary of Symbolism*, p. 112.

　　　The Emmaus meal is much like the gift of a filled Easter egg waiting to be opened. Perhaps the third millennium will see all the rich implications of this meal fully comprehended and lived out by disciples. The first mysterious grace-filled gift of that roadside event is that an Emmaus Eucharist table holding the mystery of Christ's presence lies hidden and waiting in the folds of every tablecloth. The second is the sacrament of affirmation, or Emmaus encouragement, given to the two hopeless disciples by the Risen Christ. This Gospel sacrament is in great need today.

　　　The radical church, the church of social, liturgical and religious reform, has been called the fastest dying church in the world, says Ched Myers. It is rare to see the enthusiasm and hope of the early years of the second half of the twentieth century, which abounded with zestful renewal in the life of the church and a desire for ecumenical unity. Weariness and sadness burden many servants, as well as members, of the church. This weariness is not just due to overwork, but is more a measure of what afflicted the two disciples on the road to Emmaus, the loss of hope. Myers says, "The radical discipleship movement today is beleaguered and weary. So many of our communities...(that have tried) to integrate the pastoral and prophetic, resistance and contemplation...are disintegrating.... The gravity exerted by imperial culture's seductions, deadly mediocrities, and deadly codes of conformity pull our aspirations plummeting down. The ability of metropolis to either crush or coopt movements of dissent seems inexhaustible." See Myers, *Binding the Strong Man*, p. 455. The twin Emmaus sacraments of the breaking of the bread and holy encouragement need to be celebrated together frequently by disciples so that Jesus' work of making all things new can continue.

p. 278

8.   Ched Myers speaks of the last days in Jerusalem and paints the image of a community that was living underground, symbolized by the disciples hiding in the upper room. He suggests that "safe houses" must have been necessary for a clandestine movement like the community of Jesus after his death. The role of Judas mirrors how easily, then and today, small radical groups can be infiltrated by the authorities, threatening both the intimacy of the group and its integrity. See Myers, *Binding the Strong Man*, p. 407.

In some ways Easter night is as important as Easter morning and holds out much for our reflection. The darkness and fear of Easter night has lasted for centuries and looms into the third millennium. It is present each time we hide in fear from being publicly known as Jesus' passionate and prayerful disciples, lest we be seen as fanatics or subversives. Underground or closet Christians are not restricted to ancient Jerusalem or the catacombs of Rome. Yet, Easter night's good news is intended just for those fearful disciples hiding behind a million locked doors, those sitting silently in public gatherings where racial, sexual or religious discrimination or social injustice is promoted. The Easter news is that regardless of how tightly locked are the doors, an Easter visitation is possible, a visitation that can free us from our fears and open us to new life.

9.   In the Gospel of Gabriel, the upper room is directly below the roof on which they built the Sukkot booth to celebrate the Passover meal (see chapter 17 on the Last Supper). The booth that had been constructed of palm and olive branches six days earlier is now dry and flimsy. For background on the Sukkot booth, see the note for p. 206.

p. 281

10.   In John's Gospel Jesus says to his disciples, "I have more new things to tell you, but now you are unable to hear them. When the Spirit comes, however, you will be taught the truth" (John 16: 12-13). After his death, that promise is unfolded in this assignment for them to take the good news across the frontiers of Israel and out into the entire world. The Holy Spirit — God's and Jesus' — nourishes and cultivates the many seeds of the Gospel, more numerous than those in a watermelon. The third millennium C.E. will hopefully see many new flowers of glorious beauty springing up from the rich old soil of Christianity. Issues today that are the sources of heated conflict and disagreement within the Christian churches are only the heads of a few such beautiful flowers poking through traditional Christianity's hard crusty soil. The Spirit of the Holy is watering them in a sacred springtime shower and constantly caressing their tender sprouts with the warm wind of heaven.

p. 283

11.   "Open the doors!" This command of a fearless Peter was echoed in the beginning of the second half of the twentieth century, not only for Roman Catholics, but for all disciples of Jesus the Christ. In calling the Second Vatican Council, Pope John XXIII opened the doors of the church, closed for so many centuries, to allow the modern world to come in. Not many years afterwards, fear quickly closed and locked the doors again. Historically, all revolutions, reformations and renewals have term limits. Reformers, once the reform is underway, often quickly find change to be dangerous and so shut the doors tight. "Open the doors," is the primal Petrine command which is a God-given, inspired challenge for the church to allow the rapidly changing, technological and artistic world to come inside. Opening the doors also means that the church must go outside its four safe walls and enter the life of the world. Unlike John the Baptist, whom people had to go to meet at the Jordan, Jesus went out to meet the people. Likewise, the church must take to the road and to the marketplace, instead of waiting for the world to come to it.

That apostolic command of "open the doors" will be heard again in the third millennium. Blessed are those who long to hear it, for its voice will be the voice of the Spirit calling us to open all the doors closed by
   the fear of the sacrifices required for real ecumenism,
   the fear of democracy and freedom of conscience,
   the fear of women and their right to full ministry in the church,
   the fear of sexuality in all its God-given forms,

the fear of a married clergy and bishops,
the fear of making mistakes and of martyrdom,
the fear of living mystics, saints and prophets,
the fear of the God-inspired gifts in non-Christian religions,
the fear of the Holy Spirit coming again and again and again,
    and the great fear of what might happen to the church
    if the Way of Jesus were embraced fully and followed.
        In the face of all these fears and others,
            "Open the doors!"

THE EPILOGUE

p. 285

1.   Historical dates listed here are from John Crossan. See Crossan, *Jesus, Revolutionary Biography*, pp. 126, 136, 139, 180. Dates for Peter and Paul are from John Laux, *Church History*, (Rockford, Ill.: Tan Books & Pulishers, 1989) p. 30.

There is evidence that the arrest of Peter and Paul, which led to their brutal executions, was a betrayal at the hands of a group of ultraconservatives among the early Christian community. The two apostles were handed over to the Roman authorities in an attempt to halt their efforts to reform the early apostolic church. Peter and Paul were trying to adapt to the needs of the growing church by removing the obligations of the Mosaic law for gentiles who wished to be baptized, including such requirements as Jewish dietary laws and circumcision. (This fact was noted by Archbishop John Quinn in his call for reform in papal authority. See the *National Catholic Reporter*, July 12, 1996 issue, in an article on Archbishop Quinn's address at Oxford University on June 29, 1996.)

p. 286

2.   The origin of the legend of the Holy Grail being taken to England by Joseph of Arimathea comes from the apocryphal gospel, *Evangelium Nicodemi*. This was expanded by a series of other apocryphal writings and was finally woven into Malory's book on the death of King Arthur, *Morte d'Arthur*. See *Brewer's Dictionary of Phrase & Fable* by Ivor Evans, p. 617.

BIBLIOGRAPHY OF FREQUENTLY QUOTED AUTHORS

BECKER, ERNEST, *The Denial of Death*. The Free Press, MacMillan Publishing Co., New York, 1973.

BERGANT, DIANNE AND KARRIS, ROBERT, eds. *The Collegeville Bible Commentary*. The Liturgical Press, Collegeville, Minn. 1989.

BIEDEMANN, HANS, *The Dictionary of Symbolism, Cultural Icons and the Meanings Behind Them*. James Hulbert, trans., Facts on File, Inc., New York, 1992.

BOORSTIN, DANIEL, *The Creators, A History of Heroes of the Imagination*. Vintage Books, Random House Inc., New York, 1992.

BORG, MARCUS J., *Meeting Jesus Again for the First Time*. HarperCollins Publishers, New York, 1994.

BRUEGGEMANN, WALTER, *The Prophetic Imagination*. Fortress Press, Philadephia, 1978.

BRUEGGEMANN, WALTER, *Hopeful Imagination, Prophetic Voices in Exile*. Fortress Press, Philadephia, 1986.

BRUEGGEMANN, WALTER, *Israel's Praise, Doxology Against Idolatry and Ideology*. Fortress Press, Philadephia, 1988.

CROSSAN, JOHN DOMINIC, *Jesus, Revolutionary Biography*. HarperCollins, San Francisco, 1994.

CROSSAN, JOHN DOMINIC, *The Historical Jesus, The Life of a Mediterranean Jewish Peasant*. HarperCollins, San Francisco, 1992.

DOWD, MICHAEL, *Earthspirit, A Handbook for Nuturing an Ecological Christianity*. Twenty-Third Publications, Mystic, Conn. 1991.

FRAZER, SIR JAMES G., *The Golden Bough*. MacMillan Publishing Co., New York, 1922.

HAMILTON, EDITH, *Mythology, Timeless Tales of Gods and Heroes*. Little, Brown & Co., Boston, 1942.

MALINA, BRUCE J. & ROHRBAUGH, RICHARD L., *Social-Science Commentary on the Synoptic Gospels*. Augsburg Fortress Press, Minneapolis, 1992.

MCKENZIE, JOHN L., *Dictionary of the Bible*. Bruce Publishing Co., Milwaukee, 1965.

MCKENZIE, JOHN L., *The Civilization of Christianity*. Thomas More Association, Chicago, 1986.

MCKENZIE, JOHN L., *Source, What the Bible Says About Contemporary Life*. Thomas More Association, Chicago, 1984.

MYERS, CHED, *Binding the Strong Man*. Orbis Books, Maryknoll, N.Y., 1988.

PANATI, CHARLES, *Extraordinary Origins of Everyday Things*. Harper & Row Publishers Inc., New York, 1987.

PILCH, JOHN J., *The Cultural World of Jesus*. (Cycle A), The Liturgical Press, Collegeville, Minn., 1995.

PILCH, JOHN J., "The Cultural World of Jesus, Cross-Cultural Reflections" (Columbus, Ohio: Initiatives Publications, 1995 [a series of periodicals on cycles B and C in pre-book form]).

PILCH, JOHN J., & MALINA, BRUCE J., eds., *Biblical Social Values and Their Meaning*. Hendrickson Publishers, Inc., Peabody, Mass., 1993.

PILCH, JOHN J., *Introducing the Cultural Context of the New Testament*. Paulist Press, Mahwah, N.J., 1991.

SANDERS, E.P., *The Historical Figure of Jesus*. Penguin Books Ltd., London, 1993.

WALKER, BARBARA G., *The Woman's Dictionary of Symbols & Sacred Objects*. Harper & Row Publishers, Inc., New York, 1988.

ADDITIONAL REFERENCES

CLAVELL, JAMES, *Gai-jin*, Delecorte Press, Bantam Doubleday Dell Publishing, New York, 1993.

COLLINS, RAPHAEL, trans., *The Roman Martyrology*. Newman Press, Westminister, Md., 1946.

EVANS, IVOR H., ed., *Brewer's Dictionary of Phrase & Fable*, Harper & Row, New York, 1981.

FREDRIKSEN, PAULA, *From Jesus to Christ*. Yale University Press, New Haven, 1988.

GRANT, MICHAEL, *Jesus, An Historian's Review of the Gospels*. Charles Scribner's & Sons. New York, 1977.

JOSIPOVICI, GABRIEL, *The Book of God*. Yale University Press, New Haven, Conn., 1988.

KELLER, WERNER, *The Bible as History*. William Keil, trans., William Morrow and Company, Inc., New York, 1980.

LEON-DUFOUR, XAVIER, *Dictionary of Biblical Theology*. Joseph Cahill, trans., Desclee and Co., New York, 1967.

MAY, ROLLO, *Love and Will*. W.W. Norton & Co., New York, 1969.

MERTON, THOMAS, *The Way of Chuang Tsu*. New Directions Publishing, New York, 1965.

New American Bible. Catholic Book Publishing Co., New York, 1992.

PELIKAN, JAROSLAV, *Jesus Through the Centuries*. Yale University Press, New Haven, Conn., 1985.

SHEEHAN, THOMAS, *The First Coming*. Random House, Inc., New York, 1986.

STEELE, THOMAS, *Santos and Saints*. Ancient City Press, Santa Fe, N.M., 1994.

WALKER, BRIAN, *Hua Hu Ching*. HarperCollins Publishers, New York, 1994.

ZINDEL, PAUL, *The Effects of Gamma Rays on Man-in-the-Moon Marigolds*. Bantam Books by Harper & Row Publishers, New York, 1970.